HOW TO
MAKE MONEY
IN ONE DAY
AT THE TRACK

by

Charles S. Romanelli

A Fireside Book
Published by Simon & Schuster Inc.
New York   London   Toronto   Sydney   Tokyo

Fireside
Simon & Schuster Building
Rockefeller Center
1230 Avenue of the Americas
New York, New York 10020

Manufactured in the United States of America

10 9 8 7 6 5 4 3 2 1 Pbk.

Library of Congress Cataloging in Publication Data

Romanelli, Charles.
    How to make money in one day at the track / by Charles S. Romanelli.
        p.   cm.
    "A Fireside book."
    1. Horse race betting.   I. Title.
SF331.R8   1989   89-31403
798.401—dc20   CIP

ISBN 0-671-66652-5 Pbk.

Published in association with Darnay Hoffman Books.

To Tom Ainslie, for his enthusiasm many years ago and his on-the-money suggestions more recently.

To Darnay Hoffman, for spotting a live one and getting his money down.

To my wife, the "Mary" of Chapter XX, who continues to be the Best Bet any man could have made.

Contents

FOREWORD

by Tom Ainslie

Although this uniquely helpful book will be brand new to almost everyone, it actually is a freshly updated and expanded version of a work published in 1965. It was an excellent book then. It should have made a whopping impression on the racegoing public. But scarcely anyone knew it existed.

During that year I was writing my own first book about handicapping Thoroughbreds. I was keenly alert to happenings in that particular market. But many years passed before I learned (quite by accident) that a New York City schoolteacher named Charles Romanelli had written some astute advice for recreational racegoers.

The book's obscure birth and quick death were a crying shame. In a field of sporting literature overcrowded with mediocrity and worse, it really should not have taken all this time to get Romanelli's truly deserving project a second chance. But this long overdue second chance is for real.

As all that implies, I have been enthusiastic about *How to Make Money in One Day at the Track* ever since I finally saw it for the first time, back in the 1970s. I approve of what this author has to say, and I like his style. He comes directly at you and shows in the frankest and friendliest way that you can make a buck at the races without becoming a professional horseplayer. To achieve this modest enjoyment demands no excesses. You need not engage in years of obsessive study. You can go on about your business just like a normal human being. When the spirit moves you and your schedule permits, you go to the track to have a good time, knowing full well that winning supplies more pleasure than losing. And your chances of winning will increase substantially if you follow the prescriptions in these pages.

Charlie Romanelli's message is not for folks hoping to learn the secrets of instant and unlimited riches. Charlie loves racing and winning but has a sound sense of proportion about both. Hunters for miracles will have to take their trade elsewhere. This book offers the rest of you a stimulating recreation, not a matter of life and death. It shows that anyone with sufficient interest in the game can enjoy it immensely as an occasional racegoer.

Another strength of the book is that Romanelli occupies territory on which others (including me) have never been able to achieve a firm footing. He gives the beginner a specific way to survive at the track and on occasion to prosper there, and that's that. He does not find it necessary to supply the voluminously detailed background with which most of us evangelists of handicapping try to equip our readers, hoping as we do to convert every wayfarer into an expert.

Which is not to say that Romanelli merely prescribes a few arbitrary rules—in the manner of the swindlers who sell miracle systems through the mails. No, the procedure in these pages is quite comprehensive. It pays due heed to the fundamental factors with which all good handicappers operate. It simply reduces the scale on which the recreational racegoer need deal with such factors before making a selection and placing a bet. For example, it offers a most resourceful way to make productive use of running times without getting into the dire complications that befall most amateurs (and many professionals) who try to do their own speed figures. For another example, it helps players to develop betting styles attuned to their individual temperaments.

The instruction is not at all complicated. Romanelli guides his reader with great care and consideration from one step to the next. Persons who have never dared to seek their own winners by analyzing the past-performance records in the *Daily Racing Form* can now graduate to that special excitement with just a bit of practice and absolutely no laborious study. They will find that brave approach infinitely more fun than playing horses chosen by others.

I take special pleasure in helping launch Charlie Romanelli on his second attempt to reach the public with his estimable book. So will the reader, after seeing what Charlie has to say.

PART ONE

THE HARD FACTS OF RACING

Why This Book?

Racetrack fans have been provided with two kinds of books to help them make a profit on the horses. Some books give details of *systems* of betting which are based on the fact that many winning horses show common factors in their past-performance records. If, in any given race, a horse shows these factors, it is the selection.

Other books concern themselves with *handicapping*. These provide methods of rating horses in a particular race against each other, or of spotting factors which may be crucial in forecasting the winner of a particular race.

Although system players and handicappers have long had an honorable and undecided war over the merits of their methods, one thing seems evident. None of the books that promote these methods are suitable for the bettor who doesn't wager every day.

The reason is simple. The systems and the handicapping methods found in most books are designed to give the reader a winning *season*. But the occasional bettor wants a winning *day*.

Now, the key to a winning season is restraint. In order to show a profit using a system, you must pass up any race that doesn't fall under the conditions of the system. Systems are profitable simply because they exclude so many doubtful races. Unfortunately, occasional bettors discover, more often than not, that on the day they go to the track their system applies to none of the races being run.

The same goes for handicapping. The sentence one reads most often in handicapping books is, "If you can't decide between two horses, pass up the race."

But this is just what occasional bettors don't want to do. They are there for a full day at the track, and if nine races are offered, by golly, they are going to bet them all. And this includes hurdle races, two-year-old races, maiden races, and turf races for young horses that have never raced on grass before—all the races that everyday bettors are urged to avoid as being very risky prospects.

Unlike other books, which certainly are useful to daily bettors, this book is designed for people who go to the track on holidays, on the days of big races, or on an occasional outing. Its aim is to help them go to the track on *any* day and come home with a profit.

It will do this by:

1. Presenting a logical approach to horse race selecting that will enable the beginner to avoid costly pitfalls and get the experienced (but losing) bettor on profitable paths.
2. Providing methods of playing those races that most handicappers say to avoid.
3. Suggesting methods of betting (as distinguished from methods of picking winners) that will make a winning day more probable.

A special feature of this book is the opportunity it provides to have two days at the races without risking a penny. The result charts and worksheets at the back of the book are taken from an actual day at Aqueduct, plus a day at Hollywood Park. Using these you can test your ability to select and to wager. Since the testing element of this feature will be lost if you know the winners, DO NOT LOOK AT PAGES 222–259 UNTIL YOU HAVE MASTERED THE METHODS OF BETTING AND SELECTING.

CHAPTER I

A Look at the Losers

Watch the crowds pour into a racetrack on a warm summer day.

They are of all ages. They are of all types. Young bankers and old bankrupts. Clergymen and sinners. Professional gamblers and novice bettors.

They form a vast throng of varied people united in an air of excitement. They all have hope. They all have confidence. They are all looking forward to a thrilling afternoon of fun and profit. The air crackles with voices raised in joyful expectation.

Now, watch a few hours later as the crowd files out the gates. The air of expectation is gone. A few hopes have been realized. Most have been dashed.

The crowd, wonderfully varied just a few hours before, now has but two types: winners and losers. The losers are in the vast majority.

Many are explaining in great detail to not particularly interested listeners how much they should have won if only it had not been for any of a hundred bad breaks. The opening word in most sentences is *if*. "If I had only done this . . ." "If only that horse hadn't . . ."

The closing statement in all of these laments is the same. Sometimes it is spit out in bitter anger. Sometimes it is said with the cheerful acceptance of a fact long known to everybody: "You can't beat the horses."

Yet, walking beside the losers are a few men and women who have done just that. Some were lucky. Nothing needs to be said here about the other winners, those who won using knowledge and judgment, since they are the subject of this book.

But what about the losers? Why did they lose? In general, the reasons are not many:

1. Some lost not because their judgment was poor, but because they had no judgment at all. They bet on "lucky" numbers, familiar names, jockeys, colors of silks, almost anything but a reasoned prediction as to which horse would win. If these losers had a day of excitement, their money was well spent. We wish them luck the next time they buy a pari-mutuel ticket, but we know that losers they always must be.

2. Many lost because they relied on the judgment of others. Tips from the barber (but why is he cutting hair if his information is so good?), selections of newspaper handicappers, picks on tip sheets, etc.

Some of the selectors who work for newspapers or tip sheets are excellent, but these handicappers are themselves handicapped since they must make their picks on the day before the races are actually run with no knowledge of late track conditions, of which horses are scratched, of how the horses behave in their prerace workouts, etc. This explains in part why even the very best selectors rarely average more than 30 percent winners and why even these experts will lose as many as 15 to 35 races in a row.

For those unlucky souls whose day at the track comes while their favorite handicapper is in the midst of a long losing streak, we have sympathy. Again, better luck next time.

3. Many bettors who made their own choices lost because their methods of selecting were poor. Others lost even though their predictions were solid. In the 1988 running of the Aqueduct Handicap the clearly best horse was a gallant old gelding named King's Swan. This eight-year-old veteran took the lead coming into the stretch, repulsed the efforts of two or three younger horses that tried to stay with him and won with the command and bearing of a horse with superior class.

Unfortunately for those who had bet on him, as King's Swan surged to the lead in tight quarters, he cut off Native Wizard, causing him to be momentarily checked by his jockey. Native Wizard probably had no chance to win (his jockey did not even put in a foul claim), but after reviewing films of the race the stewards correctly disqualified King's Swan for interference. Despite finishing easily in front, the "best" horse lost.

Luck in the running of a race, both good and bad, is one of the more spicy ingredients that make racing the tasty dish it is. Still, bad racing luck has caused even the most canny bettors to leave a large part of their investment at the track.

4. In addition to bad racing luck, two other factors occasionally cause even the expert selectors to leave the track mumbling. These are the truths that make handicapping an art rather than a science:

    a. Horses are not machines.
    b. A horse race is not the solution to a problem in mathematics.

The charts showing the past performances of horses are a mass of numbers. Predicting winners involves balancing and sifting these figures. But horses are living creatures, often temperamental, sometimes obstinate, and, simply because they sometimes don't feel like running, often unpredictable.

A horse race is a match between a number of these living, driving, excitable creatures that have mounted on their backs men with varying abilities, personalities, and motives and that have been saddled by trainers who have equally varied abilities and motives.

A selection picked with the wisdom of an angel will lose if the horse or its trainer isn't in the mood to win.

Even if horses were machines, if they could always be counted on to exert their top efforts, the problem of selecting would not be simple. What happens when, on the basis of their past performance, three or four of these "machines" are judged to be equal? Now, every day at every track there are two or three races in which it is almost impossible to decide among the top contenders. Occasionally a racing card will come up with all of its races like this. On such a day even our angel, with all her heavenly intuition, would have difficulty leaving the track with a few dollars under her wing.

5. On most days, fortunately, winners are not quite that difficult to come by. But despite having enough winners to make a profit, many bettors leave the track as losers because they manage their money, and themselves, poorly.

If they have a big hit, they put too much of their winnings on horses in races that are too difficult to predict. If they fall behind, they make emotional choices, betting desperately on horses that may (but rarely do) bring them even.

Hungering for a big score, they combine their winning selections with other horses in exactas or trifectas and never cash a ticket. (To collect on an exacta, you not only have to select the first horse, you have to name the second horse as well. A trifecta requires picking the first three horses in the correct order of finish.)

Most racetrack fans eventually gain some skill in selecting winners. Not many acquire the equally important skill of managing their money.

These, then, are the losers. They select either with no judgment or with poor judgment. They are victims of bad racing luck. They combat a racing card that can't be conquered. They select wisely but bet foolishly.

This book cannot miraculously change these losers into winners. No expert handicapper can pretend to counteract the "breaks" that form so great a part of racing. No system can come up with many winners in those races where three or more horses have an equal chance to cross the finish line first. And no words of mine can change an emotional plunger into a relaxed bettor who is aware of the risks and who knows when they should be taken.

What I can do is show you how a winning day *is* possible and, given a racing card with a reasonable number of playable races, how you can have an excellent chance to end your day at the track not saying, "If only I had done this, I wouldn't have lost," but, "If I had not set a goal and bet to reach it, I would not have had such an exciting, enjoyable, and profitable afternoon."

CHAPTER II

A Winning Day

"You can beat a race, but you can't beat the races."

Although I've read this statement a hundred times, I still smile whenever I come across it. Most people don't realize it contains a mammoth contradiction.

If you *can* beat a race, what's to prevent you from betting on this single race and quitting? You have beaten the races.

Presumably, you can beat one race because the winner is such an outstanding horse that it easily whips its competitors. Now, what is to prevent you from coming out of retirement when the same conditions exist and winning again. And again, and again.

If you can beat one race, you can beat another one like it. The secret, of course, is to wait until the conditions are just right. This is what all successful professional horseplayers do. They may have different methods of playing, different conditions to wait for, but all successful racetrack gamblers have one characteristic in common—patience.

Outside of blind hope, the characteristic most common to amateur horse-players is *im*patience. Amateurs, those who go to the track seeking a winning *day* rather than an annual profit, show a fantastic lack of restraint. If there are ten races, they'll bet on all ten and the daily double and the twin double, and they'll even take a chance on the car the racing association is raffling off.

For the man or woman who goes to the track only occasionally (less than a dozen times a year), there is something to be said for this lack of restraint. The occasional bettor goes to make a profit, but he or she also goes for thrills and excitement; and although a closely matched horse race is a thrilling spectacle— a sporting experience that is satisfaction in itself—there's nothing like having a wager on the back of one of those sweating, driving animals to give your excitement a keen edge.

And so, although I may preach restraint, although I may advise skipping those races that are extremely difficult to beat (on some days this may mean half the card), I know that most occasional bettors cannot pass up the opportunity to make a wager.

If "restraint" falls on deaf ears, then something must be substituted to make a winning day possible. If you intend to bet on every race, you must at least have a *goal,* an amount of money you would be satisfied to win.

Ask an average man entering the track what he'd consider a "good" day.

More than likely, he will not have a ready answer. "I'd love to make a big killing," he'll tell us. His dream is to hit a big daily double and cash a series of ever larger bets ending with a profit in the thousands.

He has only the vaguest estimate of how much he'd be *satisfied* to win. Whatever the figure, it's large.

This attitude almost always ends up in a loss. The reason is simple. After the first three races most bettors are behind. Their dreams of big winnings are beginning to sour. If they have no goal, if they have no method of accounting for early losses, they will usually begin to bet emotionally. They will start to pass up the best horse in favor of one that might get them even. Once they begin this, disaster is not long in coming.

Then, too, if you want to make a huge profit, you have to bet in a certain way. You have to be ready, for example, to parlay some of your winnings and even to reinvest some of your capital in the late races. In order to win big, you have to take big risks.

This is one of the most difficult lessons for the occasional bettor to learn. He sees the racetrack as a large bag of gold just waiting to be poured into outstretched hands. And he can't understand, at the end of his racing day, why so little of it has poured into his. He fails to realize that the mathematics of racing odds make a sensational profit possible only to those bettors with a lot of money and a lot of nerve.

The bettor dreaming of making thousands from a small investment forgets a truth of great importance. The payoffs, on the average, are simply not that large. One third of all races are won by horses paying less than 2–1. This is hardly the return on which dreams are made (unless the bettor has planned in advance to make a series of parlays). Only one out of ten races ends in a payoff of more than $20. To win a jackpot under these circumstances, without risking an equally large jackpot, is not easy.

Winning days (even huge ones) are possible, but only to the bettor who makes clear to himself how much he can realistically expect to win considering the particular racing card he has to beat and the amount of money he is *honestly* willing to risk.

Once this is done he will adjust the amounts he will bet according to the goal he has set. He will also vary the kind of bet (two horses to win, back up for place, selected exactas, show parlay, etc.) so that it will advance him toward his goal.

What is a realistic goal? This, of course, depends on the type of person you are: how much you can afford to expend in nervous strain. A win of $50 may be enormous to some bettors; it may be little better than breaking even to others. And so, I cannot set a goal for you.

I can, however, outline three general approaches to betting and suggest methods of achieving goals within these approaches.

Approach A is to attend the races expecting to pay all expenses (a minimum of $10; if you drink and dine in one of the swanky clubhouse rooms, it can set you back $50 or more) and make a small profit, perhaps enough for dinner in a modest restaurant.

Approach B, requiring a different style of betting, is to look for a moderate win. Success here will mean winning an amount of money equal to the amount you are honestly willing to lose. If you are willing to risk $50, your goal will be an end-of-day profit of $50.

Approach C is to aim for a spectacular win, five or more times the amount you are willing to lose. Thus, if you are willing to lose $50, your aim is to win over $250. Obviously, as you will see in Part Three, where these approaches are given in detail, your chance of losing your entire capital is great in Approach C, while your chance of losing it in Approach A is very small. The chances of success are equally reversed.

Which approach is best? A comparatively new bettor should probably begin with the first approach. He is more apt to make mistakes, to overlook factors which, though stressed in this book, he may forget under the pressure of having to make up his mind quickly. And he is more likely to bet emotionally. He will soon learn that racing provides plenty of thrills even when the bettor is looking for a small return.

The experienced bettor who gets to the track only a couple of times a year should certainly try the third approach. If he loses his stake, he at least has lost it looking for the pot of gold.

A bettor who expects to go to the track more than a few times during the season should consider Approach B. Here the chances for showing some profit each day are good and the chances for showing a sizable profit at the end of the season are also good.

The shrewd bettor does not wager foolishly. He does not play hunches. He does not bet on a horse simply because *if* it wins it will pay a big price. Above all, he makes careful preparations before putting his money down.

But the wise bettor does even more than this. Not only does he prepare for each race, he prepares for the *day*. Before he so much as consults a racing paper, he sets his goal. Once his goal is set he is ready to prepare for each race. This involves getting the answers to three questions:

1. Which horse seems likely to win?
2. In terms of my goal, how much should I bet?
3. How should I bet the horse (all to win, back up to place, begin a show parlay, etc.)?

A careful reading of Part Two should make you more able to decide which horse seems likely to win. Part Three is designed to increase your skill at wagering, as distinguished from selecting. Part Four gives you an opportunity to test what you have learned.

SELECTING THE HORSE

CHAPTER III

The Logic of Horse Selection

A friend of mine who teaches history at a New York university once visited me while I was struggling with the problem of devising a system that would apply to a particular type of race.

He smiled at the many hours I had spent on researching the problem, and he suggested the whole thing could easily have been worked out in a few minutes by one of the simpler electronic computers used so much these days in science and industry.

"How many factors are involved?" he asked, in a tone that indicated machines capable of sending rockets to the moon could easily predict the winner of a horse race.

I spent the next hour talking to him about some of the things involved during the minute or two in which the average horse race is run.

He was impressed. He hadn't realized that such a large number of factors could affect the outcome of a race. When I started talking about the changing importance of the factors from race to race and the many clues to the ability of a horse (some of which seemed contradictory), he threw up his hands and declared that the information was so unmathematical, it couldn't even be *fed* to a computer.

I had to agree with him. Things are vitally important in some races, unimportant in others. Predicting winners cannot be reduced to a simple, or even complex, mathematical formula.

The whole art (not the science) of estimating a horse's chances in any particular race is a matter of judging the varying importance of the following factors:

1. The horse—its past performance and present condition.
2. The horse's human connections—its trainer and jockey.
3. The conditions affecting the entry of horses and the running of the race.

Let us look at each of these in some detail.

THE HORSE

Despite the fact that horses are not machines, the most important prediction a selector can make in any race is which horse has the most *speed*.

The vast majority of races, including those races for two-year-olds in which many horses are running for the first time, are won by horses that have demonstrated a high speed *at the distance* sometime in the past. In fact, about half of all short races (six furlongs or less) are won by horses that have run the best or the second-best time at the distance within the past thirty days.

The distance must be emphasized. Just as with human runners, horses seem to divide themselves into sprinters and long-distance runners. A horse that is an excellent sprinter may fail at distances over a mile. It will be entered in a long race primarily as part of its training. Similarly, few horses with the endurance to win races of longer than one and one-eighth miles have the lightning speed needed to win races at six furlongs (three quarters of a mile). These horses also seem to be entered in races at unsuitable distances for the purpose of conditioning.

Although speed at the distance in the past thirty days is an excellent indication of a horse's condition, there are many reasons why the horse with the greatest speed may not win the race. The following factors must also be considered before simply betting the horse with the best recent time:

1. *The pace that develops in the race may be unsuitable for the fastest horse.* Some horses run well only if they lead. If they are allowed to set their own pace, they will run in fast time and win. If, however, another horse challenges them during the early stages of the race, they will run the first part of the race in sizzling time but will have nothing left at the end. Their time may be far poorer than usual.

Similarly, there are horses that plod during the first part of a race and then make one tremendous run toward the end. If the early pace is too slow, they make their usual run in the last couple of furlongs, but their time will be slower than usual. These races are frequently won by front-runners that have conserved their energy.

One-run horses can also suffer from a torrid early pace. They may run their usual waiting-type race and get so far outdistanced that they actually give up and don't produce their usual stretch speed.

2. *The competition is another factor that often prevents the fastest horse from winning.* Horses run against each other rather than against the clock. Some horses are better fighters than others. These fainthearted ones may run extremely fast races in weak company, but when placed against fierce competitors they seem to run much slower. This frequently happens when female horses run against males. Against fillies or mares they seem to have sparkling records, but when racing against male horses they often seem to lose their will to win and run in times far slower than usual.

3. *Poor racing luck may also decrease a horse's time.* In addition to chance happenings such as stepping awkwardly into a hole in the track or being actually interfered with by another horse, there are other more common things which might happen. The one-run horse may find himself blocked by a wall of horses, and be forced to take up before going far to the outside to pass. The front-runner may be primed to win but may have its feet set awkwardly when the gates open and not get its usual lightning start.

4. *The horse may get a poor ride.* An inexperienced rider may misjudge the pace or get caught behind horses. A careless rider may let his mount get tricked into a tiring early pace. A mediocre jockey may not be able to hold his horse together in the last stages of the race, thus decreasing its time from when it was handled by a top-notch rider.

5. *The odds may not be right.* Racing is undoubtedly well protected against chicanery. Nevertheless, there are stables that can operate at a profit only by betting and winning on their horses. If the price is too low, the jockey may be instructed to run the horse in such a way that its best time may not be possible. Perhaps the easiest (lawful) way to have a horse run slower than usual is to have it run unusually fast in the early part of the race. It will apparently be trying hard, but it will have nothing left at the end. Such horses frequently win the next time out at more attractive odds.

Since all of these factors may prevent the fastest horse from winning, the experienced bettor attempts to foresee them. He does not simply pick the fastest horse. He asks:

1. Will the pace be right? This can often be told from the early speed of other horses entered.

2. Does the horse have a good jockey? Will he avoid the mistakes that can lose the race? Is he able to avoid the situations that create poor racing luck?

3. Are the odds right for this horse? While a knowledge of racing stables is invaluable here, the occasional bettor can at least note the odds at which the horse has won in the past. If your selection frequently loses at short odds, and it is being bet down, think twice before you make your bet.

Many of the races lost by the horse that seemed fastest according to the charts are won by the horse that has the most *class*.

What do I mean by the horse with the most "class"? Essentially, class means the ability to beat a high grade of horses. The horse in the race that has beaten the highest grade of horses would be considered the horse with the most class.

Since high-grade horses usually run in fast times, the final arbiter of class is usually speed. However, there are some horses that have the ability to win by overpowering their opposition. Quite often they beat lower-class speed horses in times that are slower than the speed horses' average.

At some point in the race the classier horse will challenge the "faster" horse. The strong-striding class horse will cause the weaker horse to shorten stride and give up. The class horse wins not because it is the fastest (against a clock the other would be), but because it is the best competitor.

Consequently, you must not simply look for the horse that has shown the greatest speed; you must also determine whether the race contains a horse with fighting heart, the kind that may have the gameness to whip the speed horse. Some means of estimating class are given in Chapter V.

THE TRAINER

The key to a race lies in the answer to the question, "Which is the best horse?" But this key can be turned only when the bettor has answered an even more difficult question: "Is the horse intended to win?" The answer to this question lies in the mind and the ability of the horse's trainer.

Judging the ability of horses is relatively easy compared with judging the ability of trainers. We can at least see how many races and how much money the horse has won. But with trainers it is far more difficult.

The racing program each day lists the five or ten trainers who have saddled the most winners at a meeting, but this is often misleading, because the listing is usually done according to the number of wins the trainers have had. Trainers with large, active stables will naturally have the highest number of wins. Excellent trainers with smaller stables and only a few wins will not make the list.

Even if we took the trainers who had the highest percentage of wins, this would still not be decisive, since trainers enter many horses in races without expecting them to win. Sometimes this is intentional, since the stable would like to establish a few losing races in order to build up the odds on a horse. There need not be any trickery here, since a horse can be entered against competition it will almost certainly not beat.

Then, too, some of the very best trainers believe that the only way to get a horse into condition to win is to race it in events it will probably lose. They believe a race is a far better "tightener" than a workout, and they would be surprised indeed if their horses won. This confuses things for the handicapper, since the sure losers lower the trainer's percentage of winners.

Finally, the best horses usually go to the most well-known (but not necessarily the best) trainers. The best trainer in the world will have difficulty in establishing an imposing record if he has a poor class of horses.

Any person who goes to the track daily is almost certainly going to end up losing if he doesn't quickly educate himself in the manner in which trainers place their horses. With this information he can then make an approximate judgment on the ability of trainers, since he will figure not how many winners a trainer has, but how often a trainer wins when he's apparently trying.

The occasional bettor is in no position to do this. Consequently, he must consider all trainers as having equal ability. Under no circumstances should he bet a horse simply because it is entered by a leading trainer.

What you, as an occasional bettor, must determine is whether the trainer is racing the horse with some expectation of winning. This can be known to some extent from the past-performance charts. Chapter VI, Spotting the "Hot" Horse, is intended to help you do this.

What can be said now is that the past performance of any horse has to be examined with at least one eye on its trainer. For example, if the horse has had a few bad races, was he really expected to win? Was he placed with horses of higher class? Was he placed with older horses? Was he placed at a "wrong" distance?

The motives of the trainer, therefore, are important to consider in any evaluation of a horse's record. This, incidentally, brings to light an interesting contradiction in racing statistics. That is, they contain within themselves a factor that may ruin their usefulness.

It is well known, for example, that female horses do poorly against male horses. The statistics "prove" it: Not too many female horses tackle males, but those that do win only half as many races as they statistically should based on the percentage of times they are entered.

The question to ask with a general statistic like this is how many of those female horses were entered by their trainers knowing they had very little chance of winning. All of the other general statistics connected with age, class, and pace may be questioned in the same way.

What the occasional bettor must do is be mindful of the percentages but examine the race before him in a way that will expose the trainer's intentions. Perhaps, for example, a bet on a filly may be worthwhile if we have some reason to believe that the horse is well-meant.

THE JOCKEY

I have said that speed at the distance is a key factor in picking winners. And yet in most short races the winning horse beats the fifth horse by *less than two seconds!* Horses may run for three-fourths of a mile and the horse that finishes fifth will be beaten on the average by less time than it takes to read this sentence!

When races are won and lost in such split seconds, it is obvious that the jockey is a highly important factor in the making of a bet.

Think of the times during a race when a jockey must show his skill. At the start he must be able to get his horse quickly out of the gate. Almost immediately after, he must determine the pace. If it's too slow for his horse, he must try to take the lead. If it's too fast he must drop his horse back at a speed that won't be tiring but at which it won't be outdistanced.

If he's behind at the head of the stretch he must determine whether to go outside of the horses in front of him, whether to pray for a hole opening up between horses, or whether to try to find room on the rail. All the time he must be careful not to interfere with any of the other horses. In the stretch drive he must get the most out of his horse, and sometimes, in the close races, he must try to get his horse's head up at the precise instant it crosses the finish line.

In some races a horse may be so superior it could win carrying the jockey's mother on its back. With a very inferior mount, the most capable jockey in the country will win only when the other horses plunge into the infield lake. One of the oldest and truest axioms of racing is, "A good jockey, a poor horse, a poor bet." Poverty is the ultimate goal of those bettors who think they can come out ahead betting jockeys.

During the course of an afternoon you may come across only one race in which there is a single outstanding horse. In most races you will have to decide between two or more horses capable of hitting the finish line first. In making your choice, the jockey must be given some consideration.

It is not always easy to tell the best jockey. Of course, the program lists the leading riders along with the number of firsts, seconds, thirds, and unplaceds they have had; but just as with the leading trainers, this too may be misleading. The best-known jockeys get the best horses. Many competent jockeys rarely get more than average mounts.

The best jockey, therefore, is not necessarily the one with the most wins. He is the one who can give your horse its best ride. This will vary with the kind of horse you're considering. There are some excellent jockeys who seem to be better with front-runners. Others excel with horses that stay off the pace. If you have an experienced jockey who fits the horse, he is "best." It doesn't matter if he isn't one of the leading riders.

How are you, as a bettor who doesn't study the charts daily, to know if your horse has a jockey that suits? If the jockey is a leading rider and he has never ridden the horse before, it's a safe assumption the trainer has gotten his services because he can do the job.

On the other hand, if he is a leading rider and he has lost with the horse before when it was apparently in good condition, he may not be best for this type of horse. It may seem unlikely that a trainer will do this, but jockeys' agents are persuasive and they seek out the best horses even when their boys are in a rut or not particularly suited to the horse's running style. Trainers will go along for a couple of races before they make a switch.

If the rider on a horse you like is not a leading rider, do not automatically rule out the horse. Riders who are not in the top ten at the average racetrack win about 30 percent of the races. This means that from two to four races will be won each day by jocks who are not in the top ten. The thing to investigate is not the jockey's standing, but how he has performed on the horse in the past. If he has given him good efforts, the horse certainly qualifies for a bet.

If the rider is an apprentice (one who either has never won or has won less than a certain number), he presents special problems. The question to answer is, "Why did the trainer choose *this* apprentice?" Sometimes the apprentice is a leading rider at the meeting and he has been chosen for his ability. Sometimes the trainer will gamble on the boy's inexperience in order to get the weight allowance that will help his horse win. Sometimes he chooses an apprentice simply to give him experience in a losing cause. How to decide is discussed in Chapter VI, Spotting the "Hot" Horse.

THE CONDITIONS

The fastest horse with the best jockey may be a very poor bet in some races because the conditions are not right. On the other hand, the conditions may be perfect for a less able horse. How to use the conditions that affect the entry of horses and the running of the race will be fully discussed in further chapters, but it is important that they be introduced now.

First and foremost are the conditions under which horses may *enter* races and the conditions that prescribe what *weight* they will carry if they run.

I am amazed at the number of experienced bettors who fail to read the conditions for each race. They are readily available, being printed as part of the programs for most tracks, and also printed at the beginning of the past-performance charts of each race. The entry conditions are designed to bring together horses of approximately equal ability, and the weight conditions are designed to handicap horses that have done better than the rest in the past. Very often your final choice should be made by asking which horse suits the conditions.

Even the experienced bettor needs to be reminded about the kinds of races created by certain *entry* conditions:

1. *Claiming races:* To enter a horse in a claiming race an owner must agree that his horse can be purchased (or claimed) for a specific amount. This prevents high-class horses from winning race after race in cheap company. The highest claiming price a horse has won at, and the lowest claiming price he's run for, are some indications of its class.

2. *Nonclaiming races:* Horses may not be claimed from certain kinds of races— allowance races (so called because horses of poorer past performance are "allowed" a weight advantage), handicap races (in which the better horses are "handicapped" by weights determined by the racing secretary), and stakes races (allowance and handicap races in which the owner pays a fee for entering which is added to the purse put up by the racing association and divided among the

first four finishers). Races for maiden horses (those that have never won) may be either claiming or nonclaiming.

3. *Races based on past-performance conditions:* Horses may enter many races only if their past records permit them. For example, there are races for horses that have never won, for horses that have won only once, for horses that have not won in a specified period of time, for horses that have not won at a specified distance, for horses that have never won an allowance race, and for horses that have never won a certain amount of money.

4. *Races based on age and sex conditions:* Many entry conditions require horses to be of a certain age or sex or both. For example, there are races for three-year-old fillies, two-year-old colts and geldings, etc.

Within each of the races set up by initial conditions, there are conditions for assigning weight. There are general weight allowances for age and sex. A three-year-old competing against older horses will receive a weight advantage according to the month (the advantage lessens as the colt gets closer to four years of age). Similarly, a female horse receives a weight advantage whenever it runs against males.

Weight is assigned according to past performance. For example, the weight conditions may specify that all horses will carry 124 pounds, except that a horse that hasn't won in the past thirty days will get a three-pound advantage, in sixty days a five-pound advantage, and maidens will get an eight-pound pull.

In some claiming races a horse will get a weight advantage if its owner will agree to allow it to be claimed for a smaller claiming price. For example, in a $12,000 claiming race horses may receive two-pound advantages for each $500 they drop from this price down to $10,000.

Finally, horses receive an apprentice jockey allowance of from three to ten pounds depending on whether, and how long since, the rider has won his first race.

The *post position* of the horse (its place in the starting gate) is also a condition which must be given some consideration. There is not much doubt that in a sprint at five furlongs an outside post position is a disadvantage to a horse with early speed. Even in longer races, when the start is close to a turn, the outside is a handicap. At Aqueduct, for example, the start of the one-and-an-eighth-mile races is very close to the first turn. A speed horse on the outside must expend considerable energy going to the front since it has to go wide around the first turn. Far more often than not, these horses die in the stretch because they have been used up in getting the lead.

The *track condition* is also a key factor in selecting a horse. Most races are run on fast tracks and present little problem. Occasionally, a track will be scraped more sharply near the rail, giving the inside horse an advantage over horses running on the deeper outside. Unfortunately, the occasional bettor can have no knowledge of this.

However, it is wise to note where the experienced jockeys are trying to place their horses during stretch drives in the first few races. If they seem to be avoiding the outside, and if horses making moves on the outside seem to be floundering, the track advantage on the inside must be considered.

Of course, if it rains before or during a racing afternoon and the track is declared good, muddy, or sloppy, the track condition becomes a major factor in selecting. Chapter XII, In Case of Rain, gives some tips on how to select when the track is "off."

Most races are run on dirt, but one or two races in an afternoon might be run on an inner grass course called a turf course. Just as some horses improve considerably on an off track, others do much better on the turf. Whether this is because they get better striding action on grass, or whether they run better when no other horses are kicking dirt in their faces, is a question difficult to answer. At any rate, turf races require special judgments.

The final condition you must consider is the *type of pace* that will probably be set. You must ask if there are horses in the race whose style of running interferes with the chances of the horse you are thinking of backing.

If you choose a front-runner, for example, is there another front-runner in the race that will run your horse into the ground? If you select a come-from-behind horse, will the pace be slow, leaving the front-runners too fresh for your horse to overtake? These and other questions must be asked in an effort to imagine how the race will be run, and how this running will affect your horse.

In this chapter some of the factors that must be considered in making a selection have been briefly mentioned. Now, how can you use these factors to make a logical selection?

In each race you begin by noting the horses that have a chance. They have demonstrated their ability to win, either by having run the distance at high speed in the recent past, or by having beaten horses of the same class in previous races, or by being well prepared for the race in question.

You decide among these horses by determining which is especially well-meant by having a good jockey and/or by being well placed according to the conditions.

The logical selection will not always win, but it does in a percentage of cases so high that it will surprise the skeptic who is convinced that the "horses can't be beaten." Fewer than one out of fifty races are won by horses that have not forecast their ability to win by their past speed, or class, or workouts, or suitability to conditions.

The difficulty is that in many races five or six horses show something in their past performances which will indicate them as possible winners. The experienced and frequent bettor deals with these races in the best of all possible ways—he skips them.

But you, as an occasional bettor, must make a choice. If not impossible, you find it difficult to pass a race. The remainder of this book is designed to help you make the best choice—the one that research and experience have shown to be most successful—in races that are difficult to handle.

CHAPTER IV

Picking the Fastest Horse

The first task of the bettor, as we have seen, is to determine which horses can be expected to run the distance in the fastest time. Especially in sprint races, we disregard for the moment factors such as class and race conditions and concentrate on sheer speed. Our assumption is that horses which have run fast in the past will again do so in the race in question.

Determining which horses have the best chance of running the distance in the best time is made easy by the information available to bettors in the racing papers. In the past-performance section of these papers the selector can find when and where the horse has run in the past, under what conditions, his position at various times in the race, and his final time and position.

Throughout this book, statistics from the *Daily Racing Form* are used. Many bettors hesitate to use these charts because the vast array of figures and symbols seems impossible to fathom. Yet, by spending a few minutes on the detailed section called "Explanation of Past Performances," which is printed in the *Racing Form,* you can make available to yourself an amazing amount of information on the history of each horse in the race.

To make it easier for you to use speed in making your judgments, the *Form* computes "speed ratings" for each of the horse's past races. The time shown for the race is the time it took the *winner* to cover the distance. The speed rating is a numerical system for telling you how fast the horse you are considering covered the distance.

It is computed as follows: The record time for the distance at the track is given a rating of 100. For each fifth of a second slower than the track record, one point is deducted. Thus, if the horse runs the distance four seconds slower than the track record, it will receive a rating of 80.

Next to the speed rating, and separated from it by a dash, is a number which gives the "track variant." This gives some indication of the condition of the track on the day the horse ran.

It is computed in this manner: With allowances made for certain very short and very long distances, and for changes in the weather during the afternoon (for example, a change from fast to sloppy caused by rain), the average speed rating for all the races except turf races run during the afternoon is computed. The difference between this average and 100 is the track variant. The figure "100" is used because that would be the average speed rating if every race was run in record-equaling time.

Suppose that on an eight-race card four races were run in speed ratings of 81 and four in speed ratings of 79. The average speed rating would be 80. The track variant would be 20. The higher the track variant, the more the track is supposed to be "off." A very low number, such as an 8 or a 9, would usually (but not always) indicate a lightning fast track.

Except in certain cases which will be explained later, you are advised to ignore the track variant because it can be misleading. For example, at some tracks the records for certain distances have been set by outstanding horses running under the fastest of track conditions. Since these records are used to compute the ratings, the average horse will receive a rather low speed rating. If a number of races are run at the distance during the day, the average speed rating will be low and the track variant will be high, which would mistakenly indicate that the running surface was slower than usual.

In addition, there are certain days on which the card is filled with cheap horses. The average speed rating will be low, and the track variant will again indicate a slower than usual track. For these reasons, the track variant is ignored except in a few cases explained below where it must be used to compare past performances.

The horse that has the highest speed rating at the distance in any of its past races is by no means to be considered the fastest horse in the race. Obviously, a horse must be in condition in order to duplicate its best race.

It has been estimated that most horses racing regularly stay in peak form for about thirty days. Frequent racing builds up a horse so that it can produce its best effort, but it can sustain this best effort for a only a short time. Then the fatigue of racing begins to take its toll, and the horse must be rested or eased up in its training.

For this reason, your first selecting operation is to find the two horses with the best speed ratings *in their last two races at the distance at any time in the past thirty days.*

If, in a six-furlong race, five horses have raced at six furlongs in the past thirty days, their speed ratings, with the most recent race on top, might look like this:

Horse A	Horse B	Horse C	Horse D	Horse E
67	81	84	79	79
75		82	88	80
86		75	75	79

The horses which are selected first, simply on the basis of recent speed, would be Horse D (an 88 in its next to last race) and Horse C (an 84 in its last race). Horse A is eliminated for the moment. It has run a good race within the past thirty days, but its last two races were poor. Sometimes these horses bound back, but if we have no way of explaining its last two poor races, its recent form must be considered suspect.

The fact that Horse D ran a poor race last time out does not necessarily mean i is going out of condition. There are many reasons why horses run in times slower than usual: bad racing luck, poor ride, tough competition, adverse conditions, etc. Horses C and D, which we'll call the "top two" from now on, have shown speed in the past month and may still be in condition to win, but what about horses that may be rounding into form? How can we spot them as being potentially the fastest in the race?

The key point to remember is that very few horses suddenly increase their speed ratings from those they have set at some time during the past month. A horse may show a large increase in speed rating from its previous race because for some reason it ran in abnormally slow time, but very few horses win in times that are greater than one second (or five speed-rating points) better than their best time in the preceding thirty days.

Of the horses that do show an increase greater than five points, most are either young, rapidly improving horses or older horses that have had only one race after a rest period.

As a matter of fact, many races are won in times that are *slower* than the best of the horse's previous efforts in the past month. The *average* winning speed at six furlongs for older horses is only one fifth of a second better than the winning horse's previous high for the month. For three-year-olds the average is two fifths of a second. (Since these are *average* winning times, then obviously many races are won in times that are slower than the winners have run in the past thirty days.)

Furthermore, the vast majority of older horses that do win in faster times than they have run in the past thirty days have run at least as well at *some* time in the past.

Consequently, the second thing you must look for is horses that have had speed ratings as high as the top two. If there are such horses, and if they have run within five points of the top two within the past month, they must be considered as potential winners.

The less than five-point difference between these horses and the top two in the past month indicates that these horses may be ready to run their best, and their best would be good enough to win. For example, if Horse E had done an 84 for six furlongs at any time in the past, it would have to be considered as a contender.

Many horses need a race or two to reach top condition after they have been rested. Therefore, you must look carefully at any horse that has raced only once in the past thirty days. If before that race it had rested for one month or more, *and* if it had equaled or bettered the speed rating of the top two at any time in the past, it must also be considered.

For example, if the 81 turned in by Horse B had followed a layoff of two months, and if it had earned an 84 or better for six furlongs at some time in the past, it must be considered.

Thus, the basic method for selecting the speed horses is fairly simple. First, we find the two horses with the highest speed ratings at the distance in the past thirty days. Then we look for horses that have run faster than this at any time. If there are any, and if they have run well in the past month (within five points of the top two) or if they returned to racing after a layoff, they are considered speed horses as well.

Some further steps must be taken since the speed ratings do not always reveal the fastest horses. A few reasons why low speed ratings may conceal the fastest horse are as follows:

1. Horses are *erratic,* some much more so than others. Occasionally, a horse that has been sulking suddenly "gets on its feed," wakes up, and runs its best race in months.

2. Horses may have been *intended* to run slowly. Because racing is well policed, we sometimes learn of trainers and riders being penalized by stewards for "inconsistent handling." These are the flagrant violations of racing law which sometimes happen. More often, a horse can be made to run a poor race by pitting it against tough competition or by forcing it to run in a style to which it is unsuited: setting a fast pace if it is a come-from-behind horse, laying back if it is a front-runner, etc.

3. Horses may have been *prevented* from running fast because of poor racing luck, a poor ride, an unusually fast pace, stiff competition, etc.

4. The horse may have been running in races at different distances, and therefore it has no speed rating for the *distance* in question.

5. The horse may have run under different *conditions* in its races in the past thirty days. It may have carried an excessive amount of weight. It may have run on an off track or on the turf. It may have raced at a different racetrack, where the speed ratings are not comparable.

All of these may conceal horses in top condition ready to win. How can you uncover these potential winners?

Horses that have been running very poorly and then suddenly wake up win about one race in fifty. There is no way of telling when one of these erratic ones is in the mood. It is, of course, senseless to bet on a horse hoping that it repeats a good race it may have had some time ago.

Excuses for bad races in the past thirty days can sometimes be seen in the charts in the *Daily Racing Form.*

So far, we have mentioned the *Racing Form* as if it were a single paper. Actually, it comes out in two formats, one printed in the East, in the style of the now defunct paper *The Morning Telegraph,* and one printed for the rest of the country.

Both editions give basically the same information, but the "Eastern" *Form* includes a one- or two-word comment on how the horse ran each of its races. Sometimes, the chart caller will indicate the manner in which the horse ran with terms such as "gamely" or "tired." If the horse had trouble during the race, the caller will have comments such as "blocked," "poor start," "wide," or "close quarters."

The "Western" *Form,* which is published in a narrower format, has no room for comments on each race. However, in recent years this edition has added a "trouble line" underneath any past performance in which the horse has encountered some difficulty during the race. The comment or the trouble line may indicate poor racing luck or a poor ride or both. If such a horse has ever raced as well as the top two, it must be listed with the speed horses.

If you are charting a sprint race and a horse has run its last race at a distance of one mile or more, you must compute for yourself the speed rating for the sprint distance it covered. This can be done by making use of fractional times and position calls for the race.

For example, the fractional times for a mile race may look like this: :47 1:12 1:39. They are the times recorded after a half mile, three quarters of a mile, and the full mile by the horse *in the lead* at each position. To estimate what the horse in question did, look at its "position" calls. They may appear like this in the "Eastern" *Form:*

$$6 \quad 4 \quad 4^2 \quad 4^1 \quad 4^{1/2} \quad 7^5$$

Reading from left to right, these figures indicate the horse had post position six, was fourth after the first quarter-mile, was fourth and two lengths behind the lead horse after a half mile, was fourth and one length behind the leader after three fourths of a mile (at the "quarter pole," which is one-quarter mile from the finish), was fourth and one-half length behind the leader at the so-called stretch call (about one eighth of a mile from the finish), and faded to seventh, five lengths behind when the winner crossed the finish line.

One length in racing is considered the equivalent of one fifth of a second. Since the horse was one length behind the leader at the quarter pole, his time for six furlongs was one-fifth second slower than the leader's. If the track record for six furlongs is 1:10, the leader's time of 1:12 would constitute a 90 speed rating. Since the horse we are considering was one length behind at this point, his speed rating for six furlongs would be 89.

This method of estimating the speed rating must be used with one important caution. The six-furlong distance run in a longer race is not the same six furlongs run in a race at the six-furlong distance. Mile races at some tracks, for example, are begun from a chute on the far side of the track. The horses may run for a half mile before they come to a turn. At the six-furlong distance they may come to a turn after only a quarter mile.

Since horses slow up somewhat as they navigate turns, the times for the six furlongs of those longer races starting from chutes are usually a bit faster than those run at the six-furlong distance.

Consequently, if you are estimating the speed rating, note if the race began from a chute. (The start and finish of races are printed in the track program and in the *Racing Form*.) If it did, the horse should be considered only if its speed rating is greater than the speed rating of the *top* horse (rather than the top two).

So far, we haven't considered the track and weather conditions that prevailed on the days these figures were earned. Fortunately, in many races we can simply presume the conditions were not sufficiently different to force us to adjust the figures. In many other races, however, we must make some adjustments. We will be making our final choices on differences of only fifths of a second. Obviously, the wind conditions, the condition of the track surface, the temperature, and the presence of rain or snow will all play some part in affecting the time of the race. A 78 rating performed while running in a sea of mud against a wind full of driving rain is not the same as a 78 done on a crisp autumn afternoon.

The professional player who uses speed ratings has a way of interpreting these numbers. He knows the times that horses should produce in each type of race. By comparing these times with the times they actually ran on a particular day, he can come up with a figure that shows just how fast or slow the track was.

The *Racing Form* gives us some help by noting tracks that are "good," "sloppy," or "muddy." But even these notations can be misleading. Some tracks judged to be "sloppy" are really "wet-fast." Horses dig through the sandy slop into a harder subsurface and actually run times faster than usual. On other days the track condition may change over the course of the day. Horses may hit the stretch on a track labeled "fast," only to be greeted by an unforecasted driving, pelting rain which will slow them considerably.

How can you, as an occasional racegoer, find the fastest horses without having a pro's knowledge of track conditions? You can't do it precisely, but you can make a reasonable approximation by using track variants.

Track variants are figures that have to be used with care because, as we have said before, they measure two things: the conditions at the track and the quality of the horses running that day.

On some days, the racing secretary is forced to put together a card that is simply awful. It may contain four or five maiden events, a route race for the cheapest claimers, and a feature for mediocre allowance horses. The track may be perfect, but these races will be run in slow times, producing a high track variant. Conversely, especially on weekends, the card may be loaded with the kinds of races that bring out the fastest horses in the barns, and the very same track will have a very low track variant.

That is why it is foolish to do what some fans do. They simply add together the speed rating and track variant for all the horses being considered and use this total as the speed figure. They will eliminate Horse X with an 89-10 figure because its total (99) is so much less than that of Horse Y, which has an 81-25 (106).

The problem is that both speed ratings may be honest. Horse X is downgraded although he may have run on a day when the races were filled with quality horses. Horse Y is upgraded although the races on his day may have been slow.

Rather than ignore the variants or simply add them to the speed rating, there is a method in between that is not as good as a professional's, but it will usually keep the contenders in consideration without needlessly eliminating them at an early stage. This will take you about twenty minutes, but it will be well worth your while. Prior to handicapping, figure the *median* track variant for the past thirty days at the track you are considering. Begin by listing the dates for the past month on which racing occurred. (Remember that, with very few exceptions, the track variant is the same for all races run on the dirt for any date that you find, so you need not be concerned with the horse's finish or speed rating.) Then skim through the *Racing Form* and find races run on these days. In most cases, you will find at least one mention of every day's variant for the past month.

Do not take an average, but find the median (the figure that is halfway between the highest and the lowest track variants). For example, if you have twenty-five racing days, find the figure that is thirteenth from the highest or the lowest figure.

Once you find the median, allow two points on either side for some consideration of the quality of the horses that produced the figures. For example, if the median is 15, then we will take any variants from 13 to 17 as being normal for that track for that month. We will leave most speed ratings alone, but some speed ratings will have points added or subtracted because of high or low track variants.

Supposing the normal track variant for the horses we listed on page 38 was 13 to 17. To simplify things, we will look at only three horses:

Horse B	Horse C	Horse D
81-21	84-17	79-16
	82-15	88-11

Horse B's track variant of 21 is 4 points higher than our normal of 13 to 17. We add four points to the speed rating (write it next to the number on your *Form*) giving it a rating of 85. Horse C has variants within our range. Horse D's next-to-last race has a variant that is two points less than normal. Give that race an 86 rating.

By using the track variants we have done two things. We have lowered the best time for the last month to an 86, so when looking for horses that have run as fast in the past we will use that figure. We have also put Horse B into the group of fastest horses. Its first race after a layoff was quite good, only one point below the top for the month. Presuming it had run well in the past, and expecting a little improvement, Horse B may indeed turn out to be our top choice.

Suppose you don't have the time to figure the normal track variant. Or suppose your day at the races comes early in a racing meeting, when horses have been running for less than a month. What about horses shipping in from other tracks? What about those variants?

Adjustments have to be made for very high or very low variants. You can get a general guide from knowing the normal variants at very fast tracks and very slow tracks.

Hollywood Park in California almost always has excellent weather. Track variants for its races tend to be low. In the 25-day meeting in November and December of 1987, the track variants ranged from 8 to 22. The median was 14, and on half the days the variant was from 12 to 16.

The inner dirt track at Aqueduct was constructed for winter racing. The times run on this surface are comparatively slow and the track variants correspondingly high. In the January 1988 meeting, the variants ranged from 13 (undoubtedly on a track that was hard and frozen) to 32. The median was 21 and the normal range was 19 to 23.

With these facts in mind, you will probably be safe in making adjustments for speed ratings if the track variants are lower than 15 and higher than 20 at any track.

And so, if you did not know the normal track variant for the horses listed on page 44, and you used the general range of 15 to 20, the horses would now be rated as follows:

$$\text{Horse D} \quad 88\text{-}11 = 84$$
$$\text{Horse C} \quad 84\text{-}17 = 84$$
$$\text{Horse B} \quad 81\text{-}21 = 82$$

Horse B would not be in the "top two," but with a race so close, coming after a layoff, it would certainly be one of the contenders.

Although this method of selecting speed horses may seem laborious and confusing to you, if you perform the steps in order you will find that the job can be done quickly and simply:

1. Find the horses with the best and second-best speed ratings at the distance in the last two races run in the past thirty days. (If only one race was run in the past month, use that race only.)
2. Add any horse which has equaled or bettered that speed rating at any time in the past if it meets one of the following conditions:
    a. a speed rating within the past thirty days which is within five points of the top two;
    b. only one race after a layoff of thirty days or more;
    c. an excuse in its last race (poor ride, poor luck, poor pace, etc.).
3. In sprint races (six or seven furlongs), calculate the six-furlong speed ratings of those horses that have run at longer distances in the past thirty days. Consider them as contenders if their speed ratings are equal to the top two, if the race was not run out of a chute. If the race was run out of a chute, the speed ratings must be greater than that of the top horse.
4. If there is considerable difference in track variants, adjust the rating according to the "median" track variant you have calculated or use the general range of 15–20.

When this is done, you will have two or more horses that can be considered to have the speed necessary to win the race.

You will choose among these horses on the basis of class and conditions, the subject of the next two chapters.

CHAPTER V

Picking the Horse of Highest Class

Whether we refer to humans or horses, "class" is a judgment of quality not necessarily disclosed by appearances. Some people can get by for years simply by looking classy, but horses never can. They must prove their quality by beating other horses.

Since high-priced claiming horses run faster than low-priced, and since stakes horses run faster than both, in one sense class and speed are the same. A fast horse is obviously "classier" than a slow one and, as a potential winner of more purse money, is obviously more valuable to its owner.

An owner is not likely to deliberately lose a horse of quality. Some horses are, therefore, never entered in claiming races. Others are not normally entered in claiming races at prices lower than their worth. Consequently, the kind of races in which a horse has been entered (stakes, allowances, or claimers) gives some indication of its class.

But class is more than speed or an owner's estimate of value. There are other more direct ways in which a horse shows its quality. Sometimes class shines out when it means making up an enormous, seemingly impossible amount of ground. Sometimes class is shown by giving an extra burst of effort when, apparently beaten in the stretch, a horse comes on again to whip one that had driven past it. Sometimes class shows when the horse wins despite all kinds of mistakes made by its jockey.

All these exhibitions of class can be summed up in the word *fight*. A horse with class is a horse that will outgame its competition. It will wear down horses that have better times, causing them to break stride and falter. Eager to win, it will conquer the horses whose only quality is sheer speed. Therefore, in addition to selecting horses on the basis of speed ratings, you must also determine if there are any horses of superior class in the race.

How can the charts be used to tell if a horse has class? Just as a person's class may be revealed by the company he or she keeps, the company a horse has competed against tells us much about its class. In general, the highest quality race a horse has won and the lowest quality it has lost give a good idea of its class.

If, for example, in a $20,000 claiming race you note that no horse except one has won a race for a higher claiming price, and this horse has won a $30,000 claiming race at some time in the past, you may conclude that it is superior in class. If it has never raced before for less than a $25,000 claiming tag, this is further evidence of superior class.

Similarly, in allowance races, a horse that has competed in stakes races is probably of superior class to those that have competed in allowance races only.

Using the kinds of races a horse has been entered in and won to indicate class presents some problems, however.

The horses running at any particular claiming price vary widely. A horse winning a $20,000 claiming race may have beaten a weak field of horses that are generally moving up in claiming price or coming off layoffs or losing their condition. So the highest price a horse has won at is a good, but like everything else in racing, not an absolutely firm indicator of class. A number of in-the-money finishes at or near its highest claiming price will confirm that the horse's back class is solid.

What kind of difference in claiming price is significant? A horse that has won at a claiming price of $11,500 can hardly be considered superior in class to one that was never victorious for more than $10,000. Remember, we are looking for *superior* class, not a meaningless edge. Consequently, there must be a difference of at least 50 percent in claiming price wins to indicate a superior class horse.

In a race for $10,000 claimers, for example, a horse with a win of $15,000 is (or was) a classier horse. In a $20,000 race, we look for a $30,000 winner.

Young horses present another difficulty in using claiming price as an indication of class. Quite often a three-year-old will develop late or will be handled by a different trainer who may get more out of it. Such a horse will move up in the claiming ranks, and may actually be far superior to a horse which, having won at a higher claiming price in the past, now has started to decline.

The big question with improving three-year-olds, therefore, is not how much was the claiming tag they have won for in the past, but how good are they someday going to be. This is not an easy question to answer from the charts.

With two-year-olds, claiming price tags are nearly meaningless. A trainer will normally enter a two-year-old in a high-priced claiming race until it proves it doesn't have the ability. He will drop the horse down gradually until it seeks its own level. On the way down it may be entered in and win a race at a $20,000 claiming price. In that race may have been other horses also seeking their own levels. The win may have been over a comparatively cheap band, all destined to run in the lowest-price claiming ranks. Yet, as a three-year-old early in the season our lucky horse will still be sporting that $20,000 win in its record. This should be given no credit at all in an estimation of class.

When a horse can clearly be seen as a higher-class horse, your problems are not over. You must ask yourself why a trainer will take the chance of losing a horse for less than its worth.

There are roughly three reasons why a horse may be dropping in claiming price:

The horse may no longer be worth as much money to the owner. He may realize his horse can no longer win the higher-priced claiming races and he brings it down to a more sensible level. Or the horse may have broken down, and the owner hopes someone will put in a claim so he can "sell" the horse at a good price.

The latter is unfortunately fairly common. Everyone is looking for bargains at the racetrack. Knowing this, trainers may sharply reduce the claiming price on horses that will probably never win again, hoping that someone will claim. The stewards will, of course, refuse to permit an unfit horse to run, but quite often the horse's infirmities will not be readily apparent.

If, therefore, a horse has won recently in a higher-priced claiming race in good time, the bettor must be wary. If the horse's legs are heavily bandaged, if it has had no recent workouts, you must be even more cautious before considering it a class horse.

If, on the other hand, an older horse has lost a number of races at the higher claiming price in reasonably good times, you may be putting your money on a sound animal. This is especially true if it has been claimed during the season at a higher price and has not won for its new owner. No owner likes to lose money. If the horse is sound, the stable may be all out to win.

A horse may also be dropped sharply in claiming price because the stable simply no longer wants to own it. Owners have many reasons, apart from the condition of the animal, for wanting to dispose of a horse. They may be getting out of racing, or they may need cash to buy another horse they've been following. Quite often the stable stands a chance of making more money by having the horse claimed in a race cheaper than its normal class, *if* it wins the purse.

Such a horse makes an excellent bet, since the most important thing you can have going for you is a stable vitally interested in winning. If the horse has a top jockey, if it is entered at a suitable distance, if it has been training well for the race, you have some evidence that the stable intends to win.

Some horses are gradually dropped in claiming price to affect the odds. This is done especially by the kind of trainer who races his horses into condition. He will use a series of races at claiming prices decreasing race by race until his horse is racing at a claiming price that is lower than the price at which the horse had won prior to its break in training.

Then, the trainer will raise the horse slightly in claiming price. The horse will seem to be rising in class, although it has actually won at a higher claiming price. If the horse is in shape, the stable wins at good odds.

Since the conditions for allowance races vary so greatly, it is very difficult to evaluate the class of allowance horses by the kinds of races they have won. Of course, a proven stakes winner running in an allowance race can be seen by everyone to be the class of the field. (Such horses, incidentally, do not make good bets when they are entered in a race simply to prep for a stakes race in the coming days. They are usually made low-priced favorites, and they frequently lose to cheaper horses in top condition.)

One rough method of estimating the value of allowance horses is to note the amount of money earned in the past two years. This information is contained in the *Racing Form,* along with a record of in-the-money finishes, to the right of the large figure which gives the weight carried by the horse.

Horses that run more often have a greater chance of collecting purses and usually win more money. Consequently, by itself the total amount of money a horse has won is not a sure indication of its class. You can get a better idea by dividing the total amount of money won during the season (or during the last season, if it is early in the year) by the number of races run. The horse with the highest ratio of earnings to starts is often the highest-class horse in the race.

.   .   .

Earnings and past competition give a rough idea of class, but what you really want to know is which is the horse with spirit, the horse that will give its all to win. It has been mentioned that extremely fast speed is not necessarily a mark of class, although the ability to run fast is an essential factor in making a horse more valuable than others.

What we are looking for is the fighting ability some horses have, enabling them to overpower and beat horses in times that are slower than the beaten horses are usually capable of running.

One way of detecting the horse that seems to have the conquering instinct is to look at the pattern of its past races. If the horse is a front-runner, does it stay close when challenged, or does it quit completely and fall many lengths behind? If, in its past few races, it has hooked up in a front-running duel for the largest part of the race (three post-position calls) and still managed to finish in the money, it is a horse that has shown gameness.

Does the horse ever make up ground in the stretch? Does it ever pass horses who are also making stretch moves? In any of its races has it ever given up the lead and then come on again to win?

If the horse has shown such examples of fight, it must be considered as a potential winner unless the times in the races in which it has shown gameness are more than ten points below the top speed horse in the race. (If its times are bad, it will be outrun for all its gameness.)

These "fighters" are not too common. They can sometimes be found dropping slightly in claiming price. Because of their mediocre times, they are often overlooked and pay off at dandy odds.

This chapter has given you a few ideas on what class means and the problems of determining it from the charts. These, then, are the things to look for in judging the class of all horses entered in the race:

1. Check the highest claiming price a horse has won at; check the lowest claiming price it has run at. If both are higher than the claiming price of the race being handicapped, the horse is certainly dropping in class. If the horse is dropping sharply, attempt to determine by workouts and conditions if the horse is sound.
2. Estimate the quality of allowance horses by the number of stakes the horse has won, or even been entered in. Sometimes horses are entered in stakes to satisfy the pride of their owners, but most often they are given some

chance of getting at least part of the purse. A horse that has run in stakes races (even one) must be given a class edge over a horse that has not.

3. Estimate roughly the quality of allowance horses by dividing the amount of money each has won by the number of starts each has made.

4. Check the pattern a horse runs in most of its races. Look for a horse that:
   a. fights to get and keep the lead.
   b. runs close to the pace and then makes up ground.

CHAPTER VI

Spotting the "Hot" Horse

Consider the costs of owning a stable of racehorses. Unless the stable has its own breeding farm (an enormous expense if done on a scale large enough to produce a number of winning horses), the horses must be purchased or claimed. Yearlings (unbroken horses less than two years old) may be purchased at auctions at prices ranging from $500 to amounts ranging in seven figures. The prices are usually high, despite the fact that a very great number of these babies will never even get to the races, much less take a share of winnings.

Claiming prices of horses that have already been trained range from less than $3,000 at small tracks to more than $100,000 at the major ovals. Many horses have been sold outright for higher amounts.

Very few horses, unless they are trained and owned by the same person, can be maintained and prepared for races at the big tracks at a cost of less than $10,000 per year. Public trainers charge $60 a day for training and stabling a horse. Add vet charges, insurance, shoeing and vanning costs, and you can see that an owner will have to put out more than $20,000 a year to run a horse.

Check the amount of money horses have won in your *Racing Form*. Note how many don't earn their keep. Even those total winnings figures are deceptive. Every time a horse wins, the standard take for trainer and jockey is 10 percent each.

Because of the high costs of purchase and training, most horses do not show a net profit for the stable. Of course, the racing fan is most aware of the bargains in racing, the Stymies that are claimed for $3,500 and then go on to win hundreds of thousands. The racing fan rarely reflects on the vast number of horses that never win a race, that never even collect a share of a purse.

In only a few stables do the moneymaking horses earn enough to balance out the horses that produce little or no income. Of the other stables, a small number are owned by people who for the love of the sport or for the advantage of the tax losses are prepared to lose money (and lots of it) each year.

The majority of stables, however, are not operated on the assumption that they will end up in the black from purse income. How do these stables survive? Very simple. They collect winning bets on their horses.

It is for this reason that the most important thing a bettor can decide is whether or not a horse is well-meant. Is the horse expected to win?

Trainers, and the owners who listen to their advice, can be, and are, often wrong. And yet, if a trainer has a horse capable of winning, and if the stable must survive on winning bets in addition to purses, it is logical to expect the trainer to place his horse in the spot where he will get the highest and/or safest return.

Fortunately, the bettor who reads the charts carefully is often in a position to know which of the horses are well-meant.

First of all, the horse must qualify either through speed (either recently or some time in the past, as explained in Chapter IV) or class (as explained in Chapter V).

Years ago, it was not unusual for stables to hold back a horse for six months until the chance for a mammoth killing presented itself. In this era of extremely high racing costs few stables can afford such luxuries. Hence, very few longshots win *completely* as a surprise. Somewhere in the charts available to the bettor will be an indication of speed or class.

In the vast majority of cases the indication will be in the past thirty days. How, after all, can a trainer know a horse is ready to win unless it demonstrates something to him during a race or during a workout? Most of the things that tip off a trainer during a race are available to the chart reader: speed, lengths gained, ability to hold pace, etc.

Workouts present a special problem because of the chance of their being inaccurate or incomplete. But, although the early morning watchers who report to the racing papers may occasionally miss a morning workout or report it incorrectly, the fact that a horse *has* worked out is almost always known. This fact alone is of great importance, as you will see.

To repeat, then, the chart reader is capable of discovering most of the horses that are well-meant. You must first determine, through examinations of speed and class, which horses are capable of winning. Next, you look for certain changes that may show the trainer's hand, and by examining other factors, you attempt to determine which horse is best suited to the various conditions of the race.

Any of these changes may point out a well-meant horse:

1. Jockey change. Unless it is examined in conjunction with other factors, a change in jockeys means nothing. Jockeys get their mounts mainly through the efforts of their agents (unless they are under contract to a particular stable). Very often, a horse will have a different rider because the jockey who has been riding it is unavailable owing to prior commitments, or because the agent of another jockey has been more persuasive.

A jockey's agent is a professional race selector. His livelihood depends on getting his "boy" on the best mounts. That is why a change to one of the top three jocks in the standings (see your program for the listing) may be significant. The jockey's agent has chosen what he considers to be the best horse in the race for his rider.

There may, however, be other reasons for the change. For example, the agent may have agreed to take this mount as a favor in exchange for getting a ride on a top horse in a forthcoming feature. Nevertheless, a change from a mediocre to a top jockey must always be given consideration and, in some cases, may be the reason for making your final choice.

In general, the changes to look for are:

a. From a mediocre jockey to a top jockey.
b. From any jockey to an apprentice jockey (the horse gets a weight allowance, which the trainer may feel is necessary.
c. From any jockey to one who has done well with the mount in the past.

Other changes may be significant, but you may not have the experience to be aware of them. For example, some jockeys are better with front-running horses; others are better with horses that make a late rush. Some jockeys excel in turf races; others are masters at handling fractious two-year-olds.

Until you get some experience at the track, there will be no way for you to know these things. There is no reason, however, for anyone to miss one of the three changes just mentioned.

And you should also note when the jockey change seems to be for the worse. It may tell you that the stable may not be interested in winning on that day. (Some betting stables get a horse in such shape that virtually anyone could steer it home; in that case, knowing that many fans bet on jockeys rather than horses, they choose a mediocre jockey for a better price. This happens, but not often.)

2. Distance. A change in distance, like a change in jockey, in and of itself may not be significant. It can, however, be the crucial tip-off indicating a horse ready to win. This occurs most often when horses are dropped from longer distances to sprints. If a horse led or was close to the pace for the first six furlongs of a longer race, and the pace was fast, the horse may be ready to win at a distance of six furlongs. (To estimate the pace run for the first six furlongs of a longer race see page 41.)

Many trainers, knowing their horses are not distance horses, race them into shape in this manner and then have them win sprint races at good prices. Note that it is not important whether the horse was leading at the six-furlong mark. The jockey may have been told not to extend it early. What is important is that the horse closely followed a fast pace, one that would probably be good enough to win today's race.

A horse moving up in distance must be played more carefully. Most distance races are won by horses that have won at or near a route distance. Sprint winners rarely have the stamina to last more than a mile.

One indication that a sprinter has achieved stamina is its running at or close to an extremely fast pace for most of the sprint distance in its last time out. For example, if a horse leads or presses a leader for the whole race and finishes within a few lengths of the leader, it indicates that it may be able to make the same kind of run during the latter part of a longer race. If, on the other hand, the horse leads all the way and is not really pressed at the end, there is simply no telling how it might do at a longer distance. Such horses win long races occasionally, but most often lead and tire.

What about a horse that has made a big late gain in its last race, picking up five to ten lengths, but failing to catch the winner? Most fans, seeing such a race in the charts, can't wait to get to the windows to bet this type. But a late gain in a short race is no sure indication of the stamina needed to win a long race.

Here, it is the *kind* of gain that must be examined. If the rally is made only in the stretch, there is every reason to believe that it will not do well in races more than one furlong longer.

Such a horse is a "one-run" horse with only a relatively short kick. Such a short kick may be good enough to win at six furlongs when the front-runners have been going at top speed and the horse had to make up a relatively short amount of ground, but over the longer routes, it probably will not be able to muster the strength for this lightning burst. (See Chapter IX, "The Final Choice in Long Races.")

On the other hand, a horse that runs leisurely during the first quarter mile of a sprint, and then makes a determined bid during the entire last half mile, is a horse that may have the stamina to last. If there are other indications that the horse is well-meant, such a horse may make a good bet in a long race.

3. Weight. One of the most debatable aspects of racing is the importance of weight. Some handicappers insist that weight is of crucial importance. They point out that enough weight can stop any horse—very few horses win carrying more than 124 pounds at a mile or more—and that trainers, who should know their business, will enter their horses at lower claiming prices simply to have a few pounds taken off.

On the other hand, if you consider only those races where there are significant differences in weight, a surprisingly large percentage are won by the horse carrying the *highest* weight. This indicates that weight can be overrated as a handicapping factor.

Also in dispute is whether high weight is more of a handicap in the torrid pace of sprint races or during the fatiguing lengths of route races. Since high-weighted horses win a large percentage of both kinds of races, this argument also cannot be definitely settled.

The important thing is not whether weight is a crucial aspect of handicapping—normally, it isn't. The important thing is that *trainers* consider weight important. If the trainer has made some move to get weight off his horse (choosing a hot apprentice or entering it for a lower claiming price), he may be thinking that he will get just enough edge to win. A weight drop, in conjunction with other factors, may be the tip to the hot horse.

One thing worth mentioning now which will be repeated later is: *Never get off a horse only because it carries high weight.* "Too much weight" may be a typical trainer's excuse, but the horses with the highest weights, even those giving away more pounds to those they recently competed with, win an extraordinary number of races.

4. Type of race. Many trainers race their horses under conditions in which they are not likely to win. Either they are racing them into condition, or they are giving them a couple of poor races to get a decent price at the mutuels. The following are changes of importance which should be circled in your *Form:*

a. From a race versus colts to a race for fillies only. Some top handicap fillies beat top handicap colts. Very Subtle beat the boys in the 1987 Breeders' Cup Sprint; Genuine Risk handled them a few years back in the Kentucky

Derby; and, years ago, Shuvee used to routinely shame the males in long races.

However, in cheaper races very few fillies beat colts even with a weight allowance (another knock on the importance of weight). Probably more of them could, but there are so many races for fillies and mares only that it is foolish for a trainer to tackle the boys. When one does, it is almost always to get a competitive but losing race into the filly so that she will be ready for her next race against her own kind.

b. *From a race on the turf to a race on the dirt.* Horses are specialists. Some are excellent on the turf but only mediocre on the dirt. And some perform beautifully on the dirt but woefully on the grass. A trainer may think his horse might like the turf, so he tries him on the grass. Or he may run him on the turf for conditioning and/or better odds next time out on the dirt. Whichever, when a confirmed dirt horse is returning to the dirt after a race on the grass, the change is important.

c. *From a race against older horses to a race for three-year-olds only.* Three-year-olds are not fully developed. When a younger horse takes on an older, it's like a high school track star trying to beat a college track star. The younger athlete is not very likely to come home a winner. It is rare for a three-year-old to beat older claiming horses or older handicap horses before August in the racing season. (Restricted allowance races are another story. Most of the horses entered in three-and-up races are three-year-olds and the four-year-olds still eligible under the conditions usually end up in claiming races.)

For years there was no way of knowing when a three-year-old had been entered against older horses. The professional kept a record of this and was able to spot three-year-olds when they returned to races they could win. Now, however, the Eastern *Form* uses a "3" and an "up" arrow to indicate that the race was for three-year-olds and up. Users of the Western *Form* should check the selector giving graded handicaps and comments. Occasionally, he will note "back with three-year-olds." Unless you are familiar with the horses, this will be the only way you can be aware of this significant change.

d. *From open company to state-bred.* In the past decade many states have tried to build their breeding industries. As an encouragement to breeders, they run races restricted to horses bred only in that state. Such races are indicated by an S in a square before the claiming or allowance designation.

Many state-breds are capable of winning in open company, but a change from open to state-bred almost always indicates a race against easier competition.

e. *A drop in claiming price.* A horse that has won a race in the past for 50 percent more than today's claiming price has back class. Do not confuse this estimate of class with a drop in claiming price from the last race. A drop of even $1,000 may be significant for a horse with a speed figure. Remember, every time a stable runs a claimer it risks losing it to a trainer on the alert for sharp horses. By itself, a drop in class is no reason to bet a horse, but when combined with other factors, the class drop may make the horse your final choice

Special attention should be given to a horse which has run two, three, or four races at a claiming price higher than the figure for today and is now returning to the claiming price of its last *win*. It may very well be back at a level it can handle.

5. Claimed in its last race. Whenever possible we should follow the moves of the professionals. By claiming a horse, a trainer and his owner have risked a lot more money than we are likely to bet. Most owners want a quick return on their investments. Because they must run at a higher claiming price for at least thirty days, most horses that have been claimed do not win their next time out. However, those horses that show one of the top two speed ratings *and* a claim last time out win 40 percent of the time when there are no other horses showing trainer moves, and 25 percent overall.

The reason for this is simple. The condition books for races are printed two to three weeks in advance. While some trainers claim horses that once were capable in the hopes of bringing them back to their former glory, others look for horses at their peak hoping to place them quickly in a race they can win. Often the horse is claimed with a future race already in mind. A horse claimed in its last race with good time makes a powerful bet.

6. Six days or less since its last race. Except at the lowest claiming levels, most horses do not run more than a couple of times a month. A horse expends enormous amounts of energy in a race, and most horses need time to recover. No competent trainer will risk injuring a horse or even possibly ending its career by bringing it back to the races too quickly. Most commonly, horses get from seven to fifteen days off between races. It is unusual for a horse to be raced again in six days or less. When a trainer does this, we must believe there's a reason.

7. Thirty days or more since its last race. Racing and training. Training and racing. Most horses, like most humans, simply need a break now and then. This, along with the almost inevitable leg injuries, is the reason horses are kept away from the races for a month or two. A serious injury may sideline a horse for six months or more. Trainers know that every race is simply another chance for a horse to break down, so quality horses may race fewer than a dozen times a year with rests of two or more months between racing sessions.

Some bettors hesitate putting their money down on a horse that hasn't raced for more than a month, especially if it is not one of the top horses in the country. Indeed, many horses do come up short in their first race off a rest period. But the bettor who refuses to play a horse *only* because it has been idle for a while is in for more than his share of disappointments, since a lot of races are won by horses that have been freshened.

Here again, the reason is simple. Not only may the rested horse be eager to get back into competition—the true Thoroughbred loves to run; it is his reason for being—but the owner and trainer are eager for a payday. The costs of keeping a horse are almost the same whether the animal has been racing or not. Some trainers race their horses back into condition. Other trainers get them in condition and try to win at the first pop (frequently at a nice price). The stable knows the horse is ready, but the only way we can know is by public workouts.

8. Workouts. Not only horses coming back after layoffs but also horses that have been racing show their readiness to win by one or more good workouts.

Until a few years ago, the average fan had only a vague estimate of what constitutes a fast workout, unless he made a study of the workouts at the track he favored. Now the *Daily Racing Form* provides some help by indicating with a bold-faced dot (the "bullet") the best workout at each distance each morning.

This is a major help, but it is not the whole story. Some truly excellent workouts do not receive bullets because they were not the best that morning. If a superb sprinter like Groovy worked out, he would almost always work in 34 "and change." Another horse working the same morning might have done a very creditable 35 and got no bullet. The bullet will almost always go to a horse working "handily" (ridden with some urging), while a horse working almost as well but only "breezing," or working from a starting gate, will not receive the morning's prize.

You should, therefore, check the workout page in your *Form* to get some idea of what constitutes a "bullet" work. If the works were done over a fast track, you can use the bullets to help you recognize excellent workouts that did not earn bullets.

The speed of the work is important, but the number of works is equally important. The major horses will almost always have three workouts in two weeks or less prior to a big race. If a minor horse shows multiple works in a short period (14 to 17 days), it is some indication that the trainer is working the horse into shape.

On the other hand, few horses win with only one work after a layoff. Some do, and the experienced racegoer knows which trainers get their horses ready this way. Almost all horses are galloped each day, and sometimes these gallops, along with one public-work tightener for speed, are enough to get a horse ready.

For the most part, we will abandon a horse that has not had at least three workouts in the past three weeks after a layoff. On the other hand, a horse with a couple of bullets and some other indicators, such as good back time, must always be considered a prime contender.

9. Peak condition. A simple (but not always sure) indicator of peak condition is a win in the horse's last race or a finish within a half-length of the winner. Most horses stay in top form only a very short while. Consequently, the trainer with a horse that can get two wins in a row or a horse that is ready to win after a close-up effort will try to get it in another race as soon as possible.

A horse coming back to the races in six days or less after a win or a near-win must be considered especially well-meant.

Sometimes a trainer will not be able to find a suitable spot for his horse after it has demonstrated that it's ready to romp. One way he can keep it in shape is by entering it in competition where it is unlikely to win. In this case, when the horse returns to competition it can handle, we spot it by noting the drop in class or conditions. A win in its *next-to-last* race (especially if it won as a favorite) is a very strong trainer move, since it may show that he is angling for a win today at better odds.

But the trainer may not want to race the horse at all until he can win with it. A good, but losing effort against better horses will certainly lower the odds when it is well placed. Or a tough race may take its toll, and the horse may no longer be in the peak of condition.

Yet, the trainer has to keep the horse in shape. The only way he can do it is by giving it morning workouts. Hence, consecutive workouts between races are significant. The speed of the workouts is not overly important, but if they are fairly long (five furlongs or over), the horse is being kept in peak shape.

10. Odds. The major tracks attract some major bettors. In 1987 the New York Racing Association made a study of wagers of $100 or more for a fourteen-day period. They discovered that 183 persons each wagered almost $1,000 a race. These bettors, who totaled less than 2 percent of the attendance, accounted for 42 percent of the handle (the entire mutuel pool). Even more amazing, *four of the big bettors accounted for more than one percent of the total take!*

The study did not reveal how often these major bettors agreed on a selection, but there is no doubt that these power bettors had to have a lot of winners or they wouldn't be operating for long.

Bets of that magnitude are difficult to keep hidden. Either word will get out or a few massive bets on the same horse will be noted instantly on the tote board. A swift drop in odds may very well indicate the "hot horse."

The horses picked first or second in the consensus box of the *Racing Form* experts usually wind up as the favorite and second-favorite in the betting. If some other horse, especially one that isn't picked at all by any of the experts, is suddenly made the favorite or a near-favorite, then obviously some major bettors must have started a tidal wave of interest.

Should you be swept along, too, and put your money down on this "hot horse"? Perhaps.

On your day at the track you may see people with clipboards feverishly jotting down information from TV screens giving information on exacta payoffs or total amounts bet. They are known as chartists, and they are trying to find some abnormal amounts bet on certain horses, assuming the big bettors will try to hide their bets in exotic wagers. Over the years I have seen many chartists, but I don't remember seeing any for two seasons in a row.

Some hot horses win. A lot of them don't (and because we have mutuel betting, when these heavily bet horses lose, the winners frequently pay nice prices).

Prudent advice from many years of watching the bet-down horses is this: If the horse is your selection, stay with it (except possibly as noted below). If the horse is not your selection, don't bet it, except as a saver or as an exacta possibility.

Forget the "hot horse" for a moment and consider the odds on the horse you have selected. If it is a huge longshot (30–1 in a claiming race, 12–1 in an allowance race), proceed with caution. The fact that so little money is bet on a horse that has some positive factors (otherwise you wouldn't have chosen it) may show that the stable itself isn't interested in cashing a bet that day. It's also possible they have been extremely close-mouthed.

If the horse is not a huge longshot, take a look at the odds at which the horse went off in its best races in the past, those which it won or finished within one length of the winner. Compare those odds with the odds it is being bet at in the race under consideration. If the horse is a favorite, or bet down to odds of less than 3–1, and it usually wins at higher odds than these, you are advised to be cautious. Some trainers have notoriously bad records with horses that are bet down. You may still bet the horse, but only if there are other factors indicating it is well-meant.

On the other hand, if the horse has won in the past at odds comparable with those it is going off at in the race being considered, the bettor has added reason to believe the horse is well placed. To get a further line on the trainer's strategy, check any other horses he is running on the day's card. If the trainer rarely wins unless his horse is a favorite, or if he frequently loses with low-priced horses, you should consider the *trainer's* past performance as important as the horse's and bet (or not bet) accordingly.

Sometimes you find that a horse usually wins or finishes close up at low odds, and it is today being overlooked in the betting. Two things are possible. Either the fans are blind to the horse's merits and are betting unwisely on one or two other horses, or the horse rarely wins unless it is clearly the best in its field.

When the first case is correct, an overlay situation presents itself (one in which the horse returns a far better price than it should), and the bettor, after he carefully ascertains his reasons for betting the horse, should make a larger than usual bet. Again, as much information as that day's racing paper provides on the trainer should be gathered. If, in reviewing the finishes of other horses on the program, you note that he occasionally does win with a middle-priced or long-priced horse, an overlay in the race under consideration is a definite possibility.

Some trainers, either because they do not run betting stables, or because they prefer safer bets, rarely win with horses other than favorites or near favorites. They get their horses into shape, usually by racing them, and then enter them in races where their chances are so good they are obvious to all. If the trainer is suspected of being this type, and his horse is at fairly high odds, you must carefully review the horse's chances before you make your bet.

The odds are also very useful in estimating whether a horse is meeting easier or tougher competition. If a horse did well in terms of finishing in the money or racing at high speed in its next-to-last race, one would expect that it would go off at lower odds next time out. Quite often, however, you will note that in its last race it went off at higher odds. This means it must have been meeting better horses at the same claiming price. If the horse is still in form, as indicated by a workout or a fair effort in its race against the tougher competition, it usually makes an especially good bet when it meets horses closer to it in ability.

When is a horse well-meant? When is it suitably placed? How can we spot the hot horse? Let us summarize the points to look for.

Among those horses that can win because of speed or class, look for the following *changes:*

 1. A better jockey.
 2. A return to its best distance or racing surface (turf or dirt).
 3. A drop in weight.
 4. A change in type of race, e.g., from open company to state-bred.
 5. Claimed in its last race.
 6. A return to the races in six days or less.
 7. Freshened for thirty days or more and returning with good workouts.
 8. Bullet works or three workouts in fourteen days or less.
 9. A win or finish within a half-length of the winner in its last race.
10. Appropriate odds.

This may seem like far too many things to look for. Actually, if you are methodical in the way you handle the past performance charts, the contenders in each race will be clear after only a few minutes of examination. (An economical way to mark up your *Racing Form* and locate the contenders will be given in Chapter VIII.)

Making your final choice among the contenders will take a bit longer. Part of that process is imagining how the race will be run. That is the subject of the next chapter.

CHAPTER VII

How Will the Race Be Run?

There are some good handicappers who do not use speed ratings, class changes, or trainer moves as the primary tools to make their selections. They use these methods, but only to eliminate horses that have little chance of winning.

With a knowledge of the way most of the horses in the race usually run combined with a knowledge of how the track on a particular day favors a certain type of runner, these handicappers make a prediction on how the race will be run and which horse has the best chance of hitting the wire first.

They may bet only one or two races a day. On some days they will bet none. Their aim is to wait for a race in which pace, post position, and track condition give one contender a major advantage over the others.

The occasional racegoer cannot wait for a race where pace, post position, and track bias clearly favor one horse, but he should have some knowledge of the importance of each of these in making a final selection.

1. Pace. It has already been mentioned that some horses have confirmed styles of running. Some always try to get near the front, seemingly unwilling to have any horses near them. Others, slow to start, make one great, ground-gaining move at the end. Still others rarely lead, but stay close to the pace and press the leaders.

Among the horses that have a chance to win, you should distinguish any confirmed front-runners, pressers, or closers. You then ask if the race is suitable to the style of the particular horse.

Front-runners often make the safest bets. In front, the horse cannot get into trouble. It need not go wide to pass other horses, nor does its rider have to hope for an opening hole. As the leader, it can get to the rail and save valuable ground all the way around the course.

Almost a third of all races are won by horses that have led from wire to wire. The main question you must ask before you bet a front-runner is, "Will it tire?" One of the most frustrating things at the track is to watch your horse lead all the way to the last sixteenth of a mile and then flounder in the final yards.

To avoid such bets, note how the horse runs. Does it usually take a long early lead and tire badly? Does it quit when pressed by other horses? Or is it the type that can be pressed all the way and still win?

To get further insight into the horse's chances, examine the pace of the races it has won. If it is the type of front-runner that takes a rather long early lead, notice if it wins only when it can set a leisurely pace. Look at the results of the previous day's races in the front of the *Racing Form* to get some idea of what the usual fractions are. Scan other races in the past-performance charts until you get some average figure for the first quarter and first half mile.

If there is another front-runner in the race, one that may not even be a contender, notice what its early fractions usually are. If they are usually fast, this front-runner will probably finish off the contender in a punishing pace. A tiring front-runner, even though it is a contender on the basis of speed or class, should not be bet in a situation like this.

On the other hand, a front-runner that has demonstrated its ability to hold a lead under pressure makes a good bet. You can spot this kind of horse by its position calls. If it holds a head or neck lead for three calls and tires only slightly in the stretch, it is a horse that can stand pressure.

Check its winning fractions and compare them with what can be expected from the other front-runners. If there is no horse with early fractions as fast as the front-runner in question, you may have an excellent bet.

For example, suppose *when it wins* a horse usually runs the first quarter in :22 and the half in :45. If no other horse runs better than this, the chances are the front-runner in question will be able to withstand early pressure and win with speed in reserve.

If there is another horse in the race that consistently runs the first quarter in better than :22, see if that horse is a quitter. If it, too, can stay on the pace, neither horse is a good bet. If it *is* a quitter, the front-runner with guts may make a good bet *if* there is no closing horse that is dangerous at that pace.

Horses that press (those that do not take the lead but are among the first three horses after the first half mile) win about two out of every five races. The winning fractional times of a presser should be compared with those of any front-runners in the race. If the best front-runner usually goes the *half mile* in slower time than the presser, the presser has a great advantage. If the front-runner does the half in faster time than the presser, your best bet may still be the presser, if the front-runner is one of the long-lead-then-quit variety.

Closers (horses that run poorly for the first half mile) win less than one out of four races. Any horse that has to wait until it gets its best stride always has three obstacles to overcome: a pace so slow that front-runners are left with fight at the end; a pace so fast that even the best late rush cannot make up the distance; and a wall of horses to get through or around. In large fields at tracks with short stretches this last obstacle is not easily overcome.

A closer has an advantage, however, when most of the horses are confirmed front-runners or pressers. The early-speed horses tend to kill each other off as first one and then another tries to get and hold the lead. A relaxed pace cannot be set and most of the horses will be struggling as they hit the stretch. If the track oval has enough room for a horse to make up late ground, the race then becomes a setup for a good closer.

The type of professional horseplayer who believes "pace makes the race" waits for one of these two situations:

a. The race contains a single front-runner who will probably be able to set an unpressed early lead and have enough energy left in the stretch to win by a comfortable margin.
b. The race contains two or more front-runners (it is "loaded with early speed") and only one really solid presser or closer who should win going away after the leaders die in a suicidal pace.

As an occasional racegoer, you cannot wait for one of these ideal betting situations. But as part of your selecting process, you should predict how each of the prominent horses will run if it runs a winning race. In your *Form* write the letters "F," "P," or "C" in the margin next to horses that are confirmed front-runners, pressers, and closers. Prior to making your final choice, ask: "If each runs at its most suitable pace, which horse will have the greatest advantage?"

2. Post position. Each post position takes up more than three feet of space in the gate. The horse in post position twelve is more than thirty-five feet farther from the rail than the horse in the first post position. How much of an advantage or disadvantage is post position?

In races where there is a long run to the first turn, an outside post position is not a real disadvantage, even to a front-runner. A horse with early speed can stay on the outside until it is clear of horses and then gradually move over to the rail, losing an insignificant amount of ground in the process.

But an outside post position is a great disadvantage to a confirmed front-runner in a race where the first turn is close. In order to get the lead it will be forced to run around horses on the turn and add extra lengths to its race. The struggle to get to the lead around the first turn is more than usually tiring, and after it wins the lead, the horse has little left at the finish.

The poorest post position for a presser is in the middle of the pack. Other horses running close to the pace may force it to run wide most of the way. If it has an outside post, the jockey can usually drop the presser back slightly and then take it to the rail, where it can save ground. Of course, the greatest danger for a presser is to be blocked behind the front-runners, unable to get out because the closers are moving on the outside.

Sometimes this is the result of a poor ride; other times, it's just poor racing luck. But one of the most frustrating track experiences is to watch your horse, full of fight and vigor in the stretch, with no place to go. Occasionally, a presser in this situation can sneak through on the rail if the front-runner goes wide (horses tend to go wide when they are tiring), but more often than not it has to wait for a chance to get to the outside. Almost always, this costs it any chance of winning the race.

Post positions are usually of little advantage or disadvantage for closing horses. Occasionally, a pace will be so slow that a closer on the rail will be blocked, but more often than not the closer will start slowly and be taken directly over to the rail, where it can save ground.

Once you have established the running style of each contender, you should ask of each horse whether its post position gives it a significant advantage or puts it at a disadvantage.

3. Track conditions. Obviously, some horses are at a great advantage on an off track. This is a special situation which is treated in Chapter XII, "In Case of Rain."

Even on fast tracks, however, some horses have a distinct edge. Some tracks are constructed with sharp, tight turns and with comparatively short stretch runs that clearly favor front-runners. As an occasional bettor, you will probably be unaware of this. You may get some help in determining which type of horse has an advantage by surveying the winning styles in the past-performance and result charts.

Apart from the way they are laid out, most tracks on most days will seem to favor a particular type of runner. Handicappers call this a "track bias." Sometimes the bias is the result of wind—front-runners bucking a strong wind are at a decided disadvantage. At other times it is caused by the depth of the track surface. Because these "biases" exist, on certain days almost all of the races will be won by front-runners; on other days, closers will be kings.

Tracks are scraped often and sometimes this gives an advantage to horses on the part of the strip (usually the inside) where the track cushion is shallowest. Here again, few bettors can be aware of this, but you can get some information on which "alley" is fastest by watching the jockeys during the early races. If, in the stretch, a jockey in the lead takes his horse to the middle of the track, this may indicate that the rail is "deep."

At the same time, if a strong front-runner with an inside post had difficulty in lasting on the rail, this would be further evidence that the horses on the inside are running at a disadvantage.

This may seem slight, but in an evenly matched race the advantage gained by running over the fastest part of the racing strip may be decisive.

One of the joys of horse race handicapping is that nothing is certain. How dull it would be (and how unrewarding in a system of mutuel betting) if every race ran according to the way everyone predicted it would!

What actually happens in a race simply wouldn't happen if horses were machines. The front-runner who always quits badly will sometimes last to the wire. The closer, in clear striking position, might have no punch at all. In the early races the inside may have been a disaster, but in the last race, against all odds, as the other horses go wide for better footing, one jock will move his horse to the rail and somehow eke out a victory!

And so, all of our predictions on how a race will be run, all of our calculations on the importance of post position and track bias, will sometimes lead us astray. Nevertheless, along with speed, class, and placement by the trainer in a suitable race, our final decision may be based on how we think the race will be run.

CHAPTER VIII

The Final Choice in Sprints

WORKING OUT THE FINAL FIGURES

You have been given over twenty factors to check out in terms of speed, class, and suitability to conditions. How, you are probably asking, can anything but a computer digest and make use of these assorted factors?

To help you manage this new information so you can "make money in one day at the track," here are some useful hints. First, note these factors in your racing paper and, then, as the more significant items appear, some can be transferred to a worksheet where a balancing and judging operation can be performed.

If you attack the past-performance charts in an orderly manner, you can save a considerable amount of time and effort.

Here are the steps to follow to most quickly glean the important factors from the chart:

READ THE CONDITIONS OF THE RACE

Note especially the age, sex, and past-performance limitations, the claiming price or allowance entry conditions, and the manner in which weight is assigned. All of these will be important in determining if a horse is well placed.

You are now ready to mark up the *Racing Form* to find the horses with a chance to win. The quickest way to do this is not to examine each horse in turn—that will come later when you have isolated the contenders—but, instead, to run down the columns, vertically marking the factors shown by most winners.

FIND THE HORSES WITH THE BEST RECENT TIMES

1. Indicate any horse that has not run in the past thirty days by drawing a line on top of the date column across to the top of the speed rating column.

2. Look at the last-race speed ratings of the horses that have run *sprints* (six or seven furlongs) in the past thirty days. Circle the top rating and any rating within one point of the top.

3. Look at the speed ratings of the next-to-last races. Circle any that are higher than the "top last" and any within one point of this.

4. Look at the horses that did not run at sprint distances the last time out. If they were close up at the six-furlong marker, compute their ratings as explained on page 41. If this rating is equal to the top figure so far (last or next-to-last race), write it underneath a "tent" symbol in the speed rating column (for example, /86\ ).
   Cautions:
   a. Do not forget to adjust for track variants. Use the method described on page 45, or use 15–20 as an average range.
   b. If you are charting a major track and the race was run at a minor track, ignore the horse for now.

5. For all horses, including those that have run in the past thirty days, put a square around any sprint speed rating that is equal to the highest marked so far. These are horses with better "back times."

FIND THE CLASS HORSES

1. Use a down arrow to indicate horses dropping in claiming price, or going from stakes to allowance races, from open company to state-bred, etc.

2. Look at the last time the horse ran at today's claiming price. If it won or finished within a half-length of the winner, circle the win and circle the claiming price.

3. If a horse won a claiming race that is 50 percent higher than today's claiming price, circle the claiming price and the win.

FIND THE TRAINER MOVES

For all horses, including those marked so far, circle the following:

1. The date if the last race was run within the past six days.

2. Any bullet workout within the last thirty days.

3. The third workout, if the horse had three works in fourteen days or less.

4. A win or a finish within a half-length of the winner at a sprint distance in its last or next-to-last race.

5. A win at *any distance* in its last race.

6. The odds, if the horse went off as a favorite in its last or next-to-last race. For our purposes, a favorite is a horse that went off at odds of 3.4 or less. (In a California *Form*, 3¼ or less.)

7. The claiming price, if the horse was claimed in its last race (indicated by a small "c").

8. A win at any time in the past if the horse has been running distance races and the last time it won was the last time it ran in a sprint.

All of this may seem to take a lot of time, with just about every horse receiving some positive marking. There are indeed some sprint races where almost every horse has a chance to win, but in most races you will find only two to four horses that must be considered. There may be only a couple of horses with good recent times, perhaps one horse coming off a layoff with good back time, or only one or two horses that seem to be placed specifically in this particular race by their trainers.

NEGATIVE FACTORS

After you have identified the horses with a good chance to win, you should then eliminate from these contenders those that show negative factors.

However, sometimes this step will lead you astray. One of the most joyless races to watch is one that is won wire-to-wire by a contender you have eliminated because of some negative factor. This will happen, and if the mutuel is high enough, it may produce one of your "I should have, I could have, I would have" stories.

However, your successful days at the track will occur most often if you follow the probabilities and avoid risky wagers on horses that rarely overcome their negative factors. Here are some reasons to exclude horses:

1. Poor consistency. The *Racing Form* prints each horse's record of in-the-money finishes for the past two years and also for its lifetime. A horse that rarely wins (1 for 15, 2 for 30) either lacks the will to win or is being trained by a man who still hasn't figured out how to place his horses. In either case, it would be foolish to expect the horse to wake up or the trainer to suddenly get smarter.

2. Seeking three wins in a row. Many horses are able to win two in a row but few go on to three or more victories (although one or two horses at a meeting may produce a long winning streak). The reasons for this are simple. Racing is fatiguing. Winning is even more grueling. Most horses simply cannot muster the energy to win three races in a row. More important, winning usually means a rise in claiming price or an advance in allowance conditions, so that the competition becomes keener. Eliminate the horse seeking multiple victories unless it has somehow been placed in a race where it has little to beat.

3. Last race a win in a maiden claiming race. Maiden winners have the lowest percentage of repeat victories. Even with a drop in claiming price, they are usually running against horses that are much more competitive than the nonwinners they have recently trounced.

4. A horse chosen because of some "trainer move," whose last three races were very poor (never close to the pace, finishing ten or more lengths behind the winner). The trainer may be making desperate moves—there is no reason why you should.

5. Three-year-old claimers running against older claiming horses before the fall season. Here we have the boys running against the men. Sometimes they win, but most often these horses are entered with a future victory in mind.

6. Horses coming off layoffs with insufficient workouts. This is the most problematic reason to exclude a horse and should be used only when there are a lot of contenders. Remember, horses are usually exercised every day. A trainer may know his horse has been brought to excellent shape on the farm. He may give it one public workout because track rules require it or he thinks it needs a little tightener. He knows his horse is ready, but, with only one or two mediocre workouts, we can't be sure.

Consequently, in a race with two or three other contenders, you should reluctantly eliminate the horse that hasn't raced in the past thirty days and hasn't had three works in three weeks.

FOUR MARKED CHARTS

When the process for rating each horse had been completed, your racing paper will be a mass of lines and circles like the sample past performance charts on pages 74–77.

To show the importance of speed, class, and trainer moves in all types of races, I have included a handicap race on the turf and a claiming race at a long distance. As you can see, the paper has been marked in the same fashion for these races as it is for sprints, except that in the handicap race, earnings per start have been written in next to the yearly races won and earnings section. (This is a major indication of class for this type of race.) In a turf race, only the turf speed ratings are circled.

The Aqueduct charts are from the "Eastern" *Racing Form*. The Santa Anita charts are from the edition published on the West Coast.

Often, after you have marked up your paper, you can immediately make a judgment since only one horse stands out. However, most of the time, you will need the help of a worksheet to compare the essentials of the leading contenders.

The aim of the worksheet is to isolate the most important factors from the

4 AQUEDUCT

START
6½ FURLONGS
AQUEDUCT
FINISH

6½ FURLONGS. (1.15) CLAIMING. Purse $15,000. 4-year-olds and upward, weight, 122 lbs. Non-winners of two races since April 15 allowed 3 lbs. Of a race since then, 5 lbs. Claiming Price $14,000; for each $1,000 to $12,000, 2 lbs. (Races when entered to be claimed for $10,000 or less not considered.)

Tim Collins

Dk. b. or br. g. 8, by Sonny Collins—Tried, by Tim Tam — $14,000 — Br.—Franks John (La) — Tr.—Papaycik Edward — 117
Own.—Windham Farm
Lifetime 83 14 14 16 $181,064 — 1988 8 0 4 2 $12,030 — 1987 9 3 0 1 $19,970 — Turf 2 0 0 0 $540

30Apr88- 9Aqu	fst	6f	:22⅗	:46	1:10⅕	Clm 14000	5	10	3¹	41¾	42	32¾	Migliore R	b 117	*3.10	86-13	Empathetic 113² Weebok 113¾ TimCollins117¹	L'ckd closing resp	12
23Apr88- 7GS	fst	6f	:22⅕	:45⅘	1:11⅗	3↑ Clm 18000	10	7	73¼	61¾	41¼	41¼	Verge M E	b 116	*2.10	83-19	MichaelN'Henry116ⁿᵒTht'sDistinct116¹Alltime119ⁿᵏ	Jostled start	12
1Apr88- 7GS	fst	6f	:22⅗	:45⅘	1:11⅕	Clm 18000	1	4	8³	54¼	3⁴	31½	Verge M E	b 116	6.40	84-21	Raising Seven 1161½ [D]Allatime 116ⁿᵒ Tim Collins 116¹	Bumped	10

1Apr88-Placed second through disqualification

21Mar88- 8GS	fst	6f	:22⅗	:46⅕	1:11⅗	Clm 20000	5	7	63¼	43½	3³	5⁵	Verge M E	b 113	3.50	79-26	Dandy Danny 116¹ T. V. Outake 116¹ Aprils Son 1112½	Weakened	8
8Mar88- 8GS	fst	6f	:21⅘	:45⅖	1:11	Clm 20000	8	6	77¾	6⁶	4¹	22½	Verge M E	b 112	4.90	84-23	One Bon Bon 1162½ TimCollins112²BrigintineKid116¹	Closed well	8
22Feb88- 2GS	fst	6f	:22⅖	:45⅘	1:11⅗	Clm 18000	2	4	4⁴	41½	3ⁿᵏ	2ⁿᵒ	Verge M E	b 116	2.80	84-22	Capo Cane 112ⁿᵒ Tim Collins 116¾ Razzle 109ⁿᵒ	Just missed	6
9Feb88- 8GS	fst	6f	:22⅕	:45	1:10	Clm 18000	1	4	52¾	42½	35½	2½	Verge M E	b 116	*1.60	91-15	Capo Cane 109½ Tim Collins 116ʰᵈ Chocolate Dancer119⁶	Gamely	6
9Jan88- 2Pha	fst	6f	:22⅖	:45⅗	1:11	Clm 18000	4	4	64¼	3⁵	3²	1ⁿᵏ	Verge M E	b 119	4.60[D]	86-20	[D]Tim Collins 119ⁿᵏ Kona Way 112² Main Stem 116⁴	Bore out	9

9Jan88-Disqualified and placed third

27Nov87- 5Pha	fst	6½f	:23⅖	:46⅖	1:17⅕	3↑ Clm 18000	6	5	53½	4³	5⁵	57¼	Verge M E	b 119	6.80	80-22	Alaskan Gambler 116¾ Aprils Son119³FuddyDud1161½	No menace	8
17Nov87- 5Pha	fst	5½f	:22⅖	:45⅘	1:05⅕	3↑ Clm 16000	3	6	74¾	52½	4¹	1ʰᵈ	Verge M E	b 114	4.70	94-25	Tim Collins 114ʰᵈ C. R.'s Siesta 116ⁿᵏ Reliable Jeff 116½	Driving	7

LATEST WORKOUTS Apr 21 GS 4f fst :48⅘ b — Mar 30 GS 4f fst :50 b — Mar 17 GS 4f fst :49 b

Volt

B. g. 5, by Lines Of Power—Case History, by Nearco Blue — $14,000 — Br.—Cline M H (Ky) — Tr.—Odintz Jeff — 112⁵
Own.—Demarco N
Lifetime 49 7 6 5 $86,407 — 1988 10 0 0 1 $2,000 — 1987 15 3 1 1 $27,822 — Turf 3 0 1 0 $3,000

27Apr88- 2Aqu	fst	1	:45⅘	1:10⅘	1:37⅘	Clm 12000	8	1	12½	1²	22½	75¼	Belmonte J F	b 113	39.30	74-18	HotAmber112½VisibleForce117¹WickedWik117¹	Speed to stretch	9
21Apr88- 9Aqu	fst	7f	:23⅕	:47⅕	1:25⅗	Clm 12000	3	11	83¾	86½	11¹³	10¹³	Samyn J L	b 113	18.70	60-26	One's Castle 113ⁿᵒ Hot Amber 1173¾ Luna Lula 108ⁿᵒ	In tight	12
7Apr88- 2Aqu	sly	1⅛	:48⅕	1:14	1:54⅕	Clm 12000	2	11	11¹¹	10¹¹	7¹³	612¾	Santagata N	b 113	7.00	51-26	Happy Agent 113¾ Wine Merchant 114¹ Flip ForJ.K.113ⁿᵒ	Outrun	11
28Mar88- 9Aqu	fst	1⅛	:48⅕	1:14⅕	1:55⅘	Clm 12000	9	11	10¹⁰	85½	4²	3²	Correa C J⁵	b 108	10.10	56-30	Absolute Authority 1151¾ Ryna's Rajah 117ⁿᵏ Volt 1082¼	Rallied	12
20Mar88- 3Aqu	fst	1	:47⅕	1:13⅖	1:39⅗	Clm 14000	10	5	42½	42½	65½	67¼	Correa C J⁵	b 112	16.30	61-27	Hot Amber 117² Mr. J. V. 1152½ Reprocessed 1171½	Wide	12
7Mar88- 9Aqu	fst	1¹⁄₁₆ [•]	:48⅘	1:14⅘	1:48⅗	Clm 12000	11	11	11⁷	106¾	7¹⁰	68¼	Santagata N	b 113	13.30	58-25	Macho 112² Ambassadorship108ⁿᵏProverbialII117¾	Wide 1st turn	12
2Mar88- 2Aqu	fst	1¹⁄₁₆ [•]	:48⅘	1:14	1:48	Clm 17500	10	1	11½	1ʰᵈ	9⁹	10⁹	Davis R G	b 117	13.60	60-21	Quindcillion117¾DrbyJunior117ⁿᵒFrdomsEdg113ⁿᵏ	Set pace, tired	12
21Feb88- 9Aqu	fst	6f [•]	:22⅘	:47	1:12⅖	Clm 17500	2	6	41¾	5⁴	56½	57½	Davis R G	b 117	17.30	74-21	RockyKnave1124¾Askrano1172¾TooToughtoBeat117ʰᵈ	Bumped st.	12
30Jan88- 2Aqu	fst	6f [•]	:22⅘	:46	1:11⅖	Clm 25000	3	7	74¼	74¾	99¾	87¼	Lovato F Jr	b 117	23.50	80-17	Truth Be Told112ⁿᵏDarrellWaltrip1171½RoyalSlander1131¾	Outrun	12
15Jan88- 3Aqu	fst	1¹⁄₁₆ [•]	:48⅕	1:12⅘	1:47	Clm c-17500	9	2	2¹	2⁴	10¹²	1011¾	Migliore R	b 117	7.90	62-19	Print Money 113ⁿᵒ Royal Slander 1171¾ Lauren M. 113ⁿᵒ	Stopped	12

Squire Percival

Gr. g. 4, by Iron Ruler (Ire)—Knight's Damsel, by Knight Counter — $14,000 — Br.—Franks John (La) — Tr.—Tropia Anthony — 112⁵
Own.—Old Glory Stable
Lifetime 27 5 5 5 $72,222 — 1988 6 1 1 3 $20,130 — 1987 13 1 3 1 $24,826 — Turf 6 1 1 0 $10,720

29Mar88- 4Aqu	fst	6f	:22	:45⅘	1:11⅖	Clm c-17500	8	9	7¹⁰	66½	4⁴	32¾	Romero R P	b 119	4.60	80-28	TiltThePocket117¹StraightDancer1221¾SquirePercivl119ⁿᵏ	Rallied	11
19Mar88- 9Aqu	fst	7f	:23⅕	:46⅘	1:24⅘	Clm 16500	2	7	41¾	51¼	2ʰᵈ	1ʰᵈ	Romero R P	b 115	4.40	77-23	Squire Percival 115ʰᵈ Galaxy Island 1152¾ Centurian1171¾	Driving	12
9Mar88- 2Aqu	fst	6f [•]	:23	:46⅘	1:12⅕	Clm 16500	10	9	53½	42½	23½	2⁴	Romero R P	b 115	3.50	79-26	EqualTerms117⁴SquirePercival115³Dusty'sDynmite1171½	2nd best	11
26Feb88- 6Aqu	fst	6f [•]	:22⅕	:45⅕	1:11⅕	Clm 30000	10	5	5³	64¾	10¹⁴	1013¾	Santagata N	b 113	17.20	74-22	Never Waiver 117ⁿᵏ Truth BeTold108ⁿᵏTiltThePocket115²	Outrun	10
17Feb88- 2Aqu	fst	6f [•]	:22⅕	:45⅖	1:11	Clm 30000	8	7	3¹	3²	3ⁿᵏ	31½	Peck B D⁵	b 108	25.30	88-21	Rexson's Quill 117½ NeverWaiver117¾SquirePercival108¾	Even try	12
1Feb88- 2Aqu	fst	6f [•]	:22⅖	:45⅘	1:11⅗	Clm c-17500	3	6	4⁴	31½	2¹	3¾	Kaenel J L	b 117	9.40	85-23	Killer Joe 117½ Shine Diulus 119ⁿᵏSquirePercival117ⁿᵏ	Weakeend	10
5Dec87- 9FG	fst	6f	:21⅘	:45⅗	1:11⅕	3↑ Clm 25000	7	3	3⁴	31½	33½	5⁷	Torres M R	b 114	6.20	82-19	Aerial Display 115ʰᵈ Tetou 1151½ Tan Jade 115³		8
31Oct87- 9LaD	fst	1¹⁄₁₆	:48⅗	1:12⅗	1:45⅖	3↑ Clm 25000	2	5	67¼	67¼	5⁸	37¼	Whited D E	114	10.20	78-18	Tarver 1161¾ Bold Bob's Dusty 1135½ Squire Percival 114ⁿᵏ		7
18Oct87- 5LaD	fm	1¹⁄₁₆ (T)	:47	1:11⅗	1:43⅖	3↑ Clm 25000	11	8	56½	7²	63¾	86¾	Whited D E	114	10.50	77-13	Tarver 116½ Jamboree 1091½ Spruce Spirit 113½		12
27Sep87- 8LaD	fm	1¹⁄₁₆ (T)	:47	1:11⅕	1:42	Temp Hill H	4	7	85¾	85¼	7¹¹	59½	McCauley W H	113	54.20	81-08	Caros Love 114³ Good Sam 109² Sovereign Dignity 1153½		9

LATEST WORKOUTS Apr 30 Aqu 5f fst 1:02⅗ b — Apr 23 Aqu 4f fst :47⅗ h

Luna Lula

Dk. b. or br. c. 4, by Lawmaker—Aula, by An Eldorado — $12,000 — Br.—DiLibero Celestino (Fla) — Tr.—LaBoccetta Frank — 113
Own.—Laboccetta F
Lifetime 21 2 2 5 $25,580 — 1988 7 0 0 2 $3,600 — 1987 5 1 0 0 $10,200

21Apr88- 9Aqu	fst	7f	:23⅕	:47⅕	1:25⅗	Clm 12000	9	4	72¾	7⁶	3⁴	33¾	Bermudez J E⁵	b 108	9.30	69-26	One's Castle 113ⁿᵒ Hot Amber 1173¾ Luna Lula 108ⁿᵒ	Checked	12
11Apr88- 2Aqu	fst	6f	:22⅘	:47	1:12	Clm 13000	8	6	21½	2²	3¹	65½	Migliore R	b 115	4.40	74-23	FlyingSkipper108²RockyKnve1081½SecretConclve117ⁿᵏ	Bothered	10
1Apr88- 2Aqu	fst	7f	:23	:46	1:24⅖	Clm 13000	8	4	2½	11½	21½	5⁶	Migliore R	b 115	6.80	73-24	Ideal Solution 113⁴ Weebok 113ⁿᵏ Artimon 103ⁿᵒ	Tired	13
23Mar88- 9Aqu	fst	6f	:22⅕	:45⅘	1:12	Clm 12000	5	3	3¹	1ʰᵈ	1ʰᵈ	3¹	Santagata N	b 113	31.70	79-24	Soleri 112½ Visible Force 117½ Luna Lula 113²	Weakened	12
13Mar88- 9Aqu	fst	6f [•]	:22⅗	:46⅗	1:12⅕	Clm 12000	6	5	64¾	64½	99½	1211¼	Santagata N	113	24.90	72-18	Spectacular Cat 1172¼ Soleri 112ʰᵈ Reprocessed 117¹	Outrun	12
24Feb88- 3Aqu	fst	6f [•]	:23⅗	:47⅖	1:13⅗	Clm 12000	11	1	31½	3³	109¼	12¹⁰	Santagata N	113	52.40	66-21	Flippant 117ⁿᵏ Mc Michael 108¹ Saskatchwan 117ʰᵈ	Stopped	12
21Feb88- 9Aqu	fst	6f [•]	:22⅘	:47	1:12⅖	Clm 15500	10	10	85¾	106¾	12²⁴	1227½	Santagata N	113	54.80	54-21	Rocky Knave 1124¾ Askrano1172¾TooToughtoBeat117ʰᵈ	Fell back	12
1Nov87- 9Aqu	fst	6f	:22⅖	:45⅘	1:11⅗	Clm 16500	11	2	86¾	12¹⁶	12¹⁹	1217¼	Venezia M	115	15.60	66-24	Alert Paster 117ⁿᵏRoyalPerformer1171¾PershingPach114²	Outrun	12
5Mar87- 1Aqu	fst	6f [•]	:22⅗	:47	1:13	Clm 25000	8	4	4³	4³	34½	56½	Santagata N	117	*1.00	72-20	Grotonberg 1083¼ Class Gift 1172¾ T. V.TonyD.117½	Flattened out	12
15Feb87- 4Aqu	fst	6f [•]	:23	:48	1:13⅖	Clm 20000	6	2	42¾	1ʰᵈ	1⁶	18¼	Santagata N	113	3.30e	77-30	Luna Lula 1138¼ Pass the Cup 108¾ Cadman Plaza 1145¼	Handily	8

LATEST WORKOUTS ●May 5 Aqu 4f fst :47⅕ h — ●Mar 21 Aqu 3f fst :36⅘ h — ●Mar 9 Aqu [•] 5f fst 1:01 h

Dangerous Talk

Ch. h. 5, by Tanthem—Bara Babe, by Barachois — $14,000 — Br.—Shields Jr & Miller (Fla) — Tr.—Galluscio Dominick — 112⁵
Own.—Shields Joseph V Jr
Lifetime 1 1 0 0 $7,200 — 1987 1 1 0 0 $7,200 — 1986 0 M 0 0

29May87- 2Bel	fst	6f	:22⅗	:46	1:10⅘	3↑ Md 30000	5	5	32½	2½	1³	16½	Vasquez J	120	3.60	88-13	DangerousTalk1206½SweetEnding110½SaintAsaph120²	Ridden out	14

LATEST WORKOUTS Apr 24 Aqu 4f fst :49⅗ bg — Apr 14 Aqu 5f fst 1:03 bg — Apr 9 Aqu 5f gd 1:01⅖ h — Apr 4 Aqu 5f fst 1:03 b

DAILY RACING FORM, FRIDAY, APRIL 8, 1988

7 AQUEDUCT

START
6 FURLONGS
AQUEDUCT
FINISH

6 FURLONGS. (1.08) ALLOWANCE. PUrse $30,000. Fillies and Mares, 3-year-olds and upward foaled in New York State and approved by the New York State-Bred Registry which have never won a race other than Maiden, Claiming or Starter. Weights, 3-year-olds, 115 lbs. Older, 124 lbs. Non-winnrs of a race other than claiming since March 15, allowed, 3 lbs.

Talc Two

Dk. b. or br. f. 3, by Talc—Ruckus, by King's Company
Br.—Edwards James F (NY)
Tr.—Ferriola Peter
Own.—Zimmerman Justine

115

Lifetime 11 1 2 3 $45,440 | **1988 4 1 1 1 $25,740** | **1987 7 M 1 2 $19,700**

12Mar88- 7Aqu	fst	6f	⊡:22⅗	:46⅕	1:13	ⒻⓈAlw 30000	8	3	3nk	11½	11	3¾	Correa C J5		111	7.60	78-22	Unsanctioned 116no Victoria Creek116¾TalcTwo1116½	Outfinished	9
25Feb88- 7Aqu	fst	1 1/16	⊡:47⅗	1:13⅗	1:49⅘	ⒻⓈAlw 31000	1	1	11½	1½	32	59¼	Correa C J5		111	18.90	51-25	Elegant Moment 1212¼ Family Fraud 113no Int'lGuest116no	Tired	9
10Feb88- 9Aqu	fst	6f	⊡:23⅖	:48⅗	1:15⅗	ⒻⓈMd Sp Wt	2	1	1hd	11½	12½	12	Correa C J5		116	*1.50	66-29	Talc Two 1162 Squawter 1212½ Devious Angel 121½	Driving	12
31Jan88- 9Aqu	fst	6f	⊡:22⅗	:46⅖	1:12⅗	ⒻⓈMd Sp Wt	3	3	1hd	11½	12½	23¼	Correa C J5		116	*1.90	78-17	Unsanctioned 1213¼ Talc Two 1163 Noble Pat 121½	No match	12
13Dec87- 4Aqu	fst	6f	⊡:23	:46⅖	1:13⅕	ⒻMd 45000	8	10	85½	76¼	56½	24¾	Davis R G		113	*1.60	73-16	Natural Elegance 1084¾ Talc Two 113½ Feverish 113½	Fin. well	12
26Nov87- 3Aqu	fst	6f	:22⅘	:46⅘	1:12⅘	ⒻMd 70000	4	2	11½	11	23	46	Davis R G		113	18.40	71-33	Glencaple 1172¾ Miss Embassy 1131¼ Outshine 1132	Weakened	9
11Nov87- 6Aqu	sly	7f	:23⅘	:48⅗	1:30	ⒻⓈMd Sp Wt	10	3	34½	35	36	710¼	Davis R G		117	3.60	41-36	Lovely Moments 117hd AnthenianGirl1174LovelyCharis1172	Tired	11
19Oct87- 7Bel	fst	6f	:23	:47⅕	1:13⅕	ⒻⓇN YStallion	6	3	1½	2hd	34	38½	Davis R G		112	11.60	64-28	Mithrandir 1126½ Cool Embrace 1122 Talc Two 112no	Weakened	9
19Oct87-Run in divisions																				
7Oct87- 6Bel	my	1	:46⅕	1:12	1:38⅗	ⒻMd Sp Wt	5	1	3½	710	726	741¾	Pezua J M	b	117	9.20	30-22	TopPincher1172¼Topicount1179MissEmbassy11711	Speed for half	7
3Sep87- 8Bel	fst	6f	:22	:44⅗	1:11⅕	ⒻⓈMohawk	6	4	36	36½	410	512¾	Romero R P		112	4.80e	70-17	StrawberryBurrh1142½EmpressTigere1144¼Tiger'sBurn1125½	Tired	7

LATEST WORKOUTS **Mar 10 Aqu ⊡ 3f fst :37 b**

Action Dancer

B. f. 3, by Nostrum—Surasa, by Raise a Native
Br.—Santagelo George (N.Y.)
Tr.—Pascuma James J Jr
Own.—Santancelo G L

112

Lifetime 3 1 1 0 $22,140 | **1987 3 1 1 0 $22,140**

2Oct87- 7Bel	fst	7f	:22⅖	:46⅕	1:25⅕	ⒻAlw 28000	8	1	2hd	3½	814	926½	Martens G	121	12.10	49-24	CloseIn1211½HighlandPenny11610StaunchFlame111nk	Tired badly	10
24Sep87- 6Bel	fst	6f	:23	:46⅗	1:11⅕	ⒻⓈMd Sp Wt	12	2	2hd	11½	16	18¼	Antley C W	117	*2.20	83-20	ActionDancer1178¼OatsToGo1173½HarvrdMistress1171	Ridden out	13
13Sep87- 6Bel	sly	6f	:22⅕	:46⅘	1:12⅖	ⒻⓈMd Sp Wt	1	3	12	2hd	22½	23½	Martens G	117	17.20	73-23	L'Eclat 1173½ Action Dancer 1173¾ OatsToGo1171¼	Best of others	10

LATEST WORKOUTS **Apr 5 Aqu 4f fst :48⅗ h** **Mar 30 Aqu 5f fst 1:01⅗ h** **Mar 24 Aqu 4f fst :49⅖ b** **Mar 18 Aqu 4f fst :48⅕ h**

What a Femme

Dk. b. or br. f. 4, by What Luck—Willful Femme, by Intentionally
Br.—Abis Corp & Fox J P & A S (NY)
Tr.—DiMauro Stephen L
Own.—DiMauro S

116[5]

Lifetime 4 1 1 1 $25,380 | **1988 4 1 1 1 $25,380** | **1986 0 M 0 0**

29Mar88- 7Aqu	fst	1	:46⅕	1:11⅖	1:38⅘	ⒻⓈAlw 31000	7	5	65	67	710	89¾	Migliore R	117	3.40	62-28	Shinnecock Lassie117hdNoblePreview1122¾Maidwell1172½	Outrun	13
26Feb88- 4Aqu	fst	6f	⊡:23⅕	[illegible]	1:13⅕	ⒻⓈMd Sp Wt	12	1	11	11	11½	12	Migliore R	122	*.60	78-22	What a Femme 1222 Aljadam 1222 Battle Song 1221¾	Driving	12
10Feb88- 4Aqu	fst	6f	⊡:22⅗	:47	1:13⅗	ⒻMd Sp Wt	2	8	36	26	26	36¾	Migliore R	122	*.80	69-29	NobleWish1225PreciousTiffini1221¾WhatFemme1221¾	Bumped st.	8
30Jan88- 3Aqu	fst	6f	⊡:23	:46⅗	1:12	ⒻMd Sp Wt	6	3	11	1hd	1½	12¼	Melendez J D	122	10.50Ⓓ	84-17	ⒹWhtFemme1222¼EdgeofMorning117nkLwn1221¾	Bore in midstr	7
30Jan88-Disqualified and placed second																			

Squawter

Ch. f. 3, by Noble Nashua—Apalachee's Squaw, by Apalachee
Br.—Flying Zee Stables (N.Y.)
Tr.—Martin Jose
Own.—Tri Noble Stable

112

Lifetime 2 1 1 0 $22,140 | **1988 2 1 1 0 $22,140** | **1987 0 M 0 0**

6Mar88- 9Aqu	fst	6f	⊡:22⅖	:46⅗	1:13⅖	ⒻⓈMd Sp Wt	9	1	21	2hd	13	13¾	Krone J A	121	2.80	77-20	Squawter 1213¾Producer'sCouch1212¾Planchette121½	Ridden out	12
10Feb88- 9Aqu	fst	6f	⊡:23⅖	:48⅗	1:15⅗	ⒻⓈMd Sp Wt	11	4	2hd	21½	22½	22	Krone J A	121	*1.50	64-29	Talc Two 1162 Squawter 1212½ Devious Angel 121½	2nd best	12

LATEST WORKOUTS **Apr 6 Bel tr.t 3f fst :36⅕ h** **Mar 25 Bel tr.t 4f fst :49⅕ h** **Mar 19 Bel tr.t 4f fst :50 b** **Feb 29 Bel tr.t 4f fst :49 h**

8th Santa Anita

TURF COURSE
1 MILE
SANTA ANITA
Start • • Finish

1 MILE. (Turf). (1.35) 1st Running of the BUENA VISTA HANDICAP. $75,000 added (plus $25,000 Breeders' Cup Premium Awards). Fillies and mares. 4-year-olds and upward. By subscription of $50 each to accompany the nomination and $750 additional to start, with $75,000 added, of which $15,000 to second, $11,250 to third, $5,625 to fourth and $1,875 to fifth. Weights, Tuesday, March 1. High weights preferred. Starters to be named through the entry box by the closing time of entries. A trophy will be presented to the owner of the winner. Closed Wednesday, February 24, 1988 with 31 nominations.

Sly Charmer

B. f. 4, by Valdez—Miss Pele, by Sea Hawk II
PEDROZA M A **114**
Br.—Jones A U (Ky)
Tr.—Barrera Lazaro S
Own.—Jones A U

1988	2 2 0 0	$45,100
1987	9 2 0 2	$38,450
Turf	8 4 0 2	$80,700

Lifetime 11 4 0 2 $83,550

10Feb88-7SA 1 ⓣ:4621:1121:373fm 10 118 33½ 21½ 1hd 11¼ DlhoussyE3 ⓕAw44000 87-13 SlyChrmer,GoldenGlxy,Rose'sRcord 9
9Jan88-7SA 1⅛ⓣ:4721:1211:512fm 9½ 116 72½ 53½ 21½ 1no VlenzulPA6 ⓕAw38000 70-24 SlyChrmr,NirobiExprss,TimForHrt 10
30Dec87-3SA 1 1/16 :472 1:123 1:453m 6½ 116 3½ 31 42½ 48¾ VlenzulPA4 ⓕAw38000 65-23 Behind TheScenes,Akron,Imagining 5
14Nov87-5SA 1⅛ⓣ:4841:1441:523fm*8-5 115 2½ 1½ 11 1½ VlenzulPA1 ⓕAw30000 64-25 Sly Charmer, Maidee, Mush 10
14Nov87—Drifted out, bumped start
16Oct87-5SA 1⅛ⓣ:46 1:1121:491fm 5¼ 114 55½ 52½ 52 3½ StevensGL3 ⓕAw30000 80-19 TimeForHart,JustMine,SlyChrmer 10
16Oct87—Wide into stretch
11Sep87-7Dmr 1 ⓣ:4731:1221:381fm 5½ 120 77 66 34½ 3½ DlhoussyE6 ⓕAw24000 79-20 DerMorgn,TimeForHrt,SlyChrmer 10
11Sep87—Bumped start
15Aug87-3Dmr 1 1/16 ⓣ:4811:1221:433fm 3½ 1155 74½ 96¼ 87 88½ Gryder AT5 ⓕAw23000 73-13 SlctASong,TmForHrt,BggrsWldRd 10
3Aug87-5Dmr 1 1/16 ⓣ:47 1:1131:431fm 16 120 53½ 31½ 42½ 65¼ VlenzulPA7 ⓕAw23000 79-14 Davie'sLamb,Develop,GoldenGalxy 10
3Aug87—Poor start; bumped 1/8
25Jly87-4Hol 1 1/16 ⓣ:4721:1131:43 fm 9¼ 115 1hd 11½ 12½ 11¼ Valenzuela PA1 ⓕMdn 79-19 SlyCharmer,OueeeBebe,CatfishLdy 8
19Jly87-4Hol 6f :22 :452 1:10 ft 77 1115 86½ 85¾ 66¼ 68¼ Patton D B8 ⓕMdn 85-07 MissWillie,LdyAnnbelle,BoldlyDrivn 9
Mar 3 SA 4f ft :473 h Feb 20 SA 5f ft 1:002 h Feb 8 SA 4f ft :493 h Jan 30 SA 5f ft 1:003 h

*Pen Bal Lady

Ch. f. 4, by Mummy's Game—Northern Queen, by Northfields
DELAHOUSSAYE E **119**
Br.—Highfield Stud Ltd (Eng)
Tr.—Palma Hector O
Own.—DeCarlo-LaTorre-Rbnstn Etl

1988	1 0 1 0	$15,000
1987	4 2 0 1	$164,150
Turf	11 5 2 2	$168,787

Lifetime 12 5 2 3 $191,287

17Feb88-8SA a6½f ⓣ:213 :4421:143fm 17 118 53 41½ 42 23 VelsquezJ2 ⓕMnrva H 83-14 Aberuschka,PenBalLady,Aromcor 10
9Aug87-8Dmr 1 1/16 ⓣ:4721:1111:421fm 10 115 73¾ 84½ 99¼ 99½ Solis A7 La Jolla H 79-12 ThMdic,SomthingLucky,SvonTowr 11
9Aug87—Grade III; Lugged out
12Jly87-8Hol 1⅛ :461 1:101 1:483ft 3½ 121 66 65 44 35½ DlhssE5 ⓕHol Oaks 88-09 PerchnceToDrem,Schuist,PenBlLdy 6
12Jly87—Grade I
17May87-8Hol 1 1/16 ⓣ:4621:1031:411fm*2-3 119 94¾ 2hd 1½ 11¾ DlssE8 ⓕHnymn H 88-09 PenBlLdy,SomeSenstion,Dvi'sLmb 9
17May87—Grade III; Wide 3/8 turn
25Apr87-8Hol 1 ⓣ:47 1:1111:352fm 5 117 66½ 53½ 41 11½ DlhoussyE5 ⓕSenorita 90-14 PenBalLady,Sweettuc,Davie'sLamb 6
20Sep86♦4Ayr(Scot) 6f 1:104fm 16 120 ⓣ 64½ WldronP ⓕFrth of Clyd LindasMagic,Attempting,KyVerde 13
30Aug86♦3Chester(Eng) 7f 1:313sf *3 126 ⓣ 37 RchrdsA Mtchls Nsy H BrewinTime,ShadeofPle,PenB'Ldy 10
19Aug86♦1York(Eng) 7f 1:264gd 12 120 ⓣ 3½ RichrdsA Eglntn Nsy H Gulf King,JaysSpecial,PenBall.ady 14
1Aug86♦4Thirsk(Eng) 7f 1:28 gd *3 121 ⓣ 12 RichrdsA Sessay Auctn PenBalLady,BothyBallad,GrecinJos 6
2Jly86♦3Warwick(Eng) 7f 1:26 gd 2¼ 123 ⓣ 12½ CauthenS ⓕStrt & Prkr PenBlLdy,FreshThoughts,BsicBliss 6
Mar 2 SA 5f m 1:003 h Feb 25 SA ⓣ 4f fm :512 b (d) Feb 10 SA 6f ft 1:15 h Feb 4 SA 5f ft 1:00 h

Davie's Lamb

B. f. 4, by Unpredictable—Davie Lady, by Bold and Brave
TORO F **117**
Br.—Meadowbrook Farms Inc (Fla)
Tr.—Canani Julio C
Own.—Deals On Stable

1988	3 1 0 1	$38,190
1987	15 4 1 4	$142,250
Turf	11 4 1 3	$161,640

Lifetime 24 6 1 8 $180,440

7Feb88-11TuP 1 1/16 ⓣ:4831:13 1:44 fm*6-5 121 41½ 51¼ 2hd 12 OlivrsF6 ⓕTwlgt Tr H 92-08 Davie'sLamb,TurnAndDance,Willh 11
22Jan88-8SA 1 ⓣ:4721:1131:373fm 9½ 120 53 55 44 32 Toro F5 ⓕAw60000 85-13 MyVirginiaReel,Mausie,Davie'sLmb 9
22Jan88—Broke slowly; rank 7/8 turn, backstretch, steadied near 3/8
6Jan88-3SA 1⅛ⓣ:4821:1311:50 gd 4¼ 117 43 42½ 31½ 44¾ VlenzulPA5 ⓕAw60000 72-23 MyVirginiReel,MissAlto,HcllyDonn 9
31Oct87-9BM 1 1/16 ⓣ:4711:1311:45 yl *3 121 37 31½ 31 44 Toro F7 ⓕB M Oaks 77-22 Soft Copy, Fraulein Lieber,Abrojo 10
11Oct87-8BM 1 ⓣ:4721:1211:371fm 3 116 74¼ 54 1hd 11¼ DizAL10 ⓕSan Jose H 87-16 Dvie'sLmb,WildMnor,RtherHomly 12
11Oct87—Bumped start
30Aug87-8Dmr 1⅛ⓣ:47 1:1211:502fm 3 117 85¾ 52¾ 94¾ 63 TorF12 ⓕDmr Oaks 78-21 LizzyHre,ChpelOfDrems,DcwnAgin 13
30Aug87—Grade II; 5 wide into drive
14Aug87-5Dmr 1 1/16 ⓣ:4721:12 1:424fm*3-2 115 22½ 2½ 1½ 13½ Toro F7 ⓕⓇSn Clmnt 96-18 Davie's Lamb, Develop, WildManor 7
14Aug87—Run in divisions
3Aug87-5Dmr 1 1/16 ⓣ:47 1:1131:431fm 2½ 117 43½ 42 31½ 11¾ Toro F4 ⓕAw23000 84-14 Davie'sLamb,Develop,GoldenGalxy 10
10Jun87-8Hol 1 1/16 :464 1:114 1:44 ft 6½ 115 63¼ 75½ 78 714¼ Toro F3 ⓕⓇItsn T Ar 75-16 HelloSweetThing,KeyBid,LdyyNskr 7
17May87-8Hol 1 1/16 ⓣ:4621:1031:411fm 5½ 115 72¾ 73¾ 53 32½ ToroF5 ⓕHnymn H 85-09 PenBlLdy,SomeSenstion,Dvi'sLmb 10
17May87—Grade III
Mar 1 SA 4f m :514 h (d) Feb 24 SA 4f ft :483 h Feb 18 SA 4f ft :491 h Jan 30 SA 4f ft :471 h

10th Santa Anita

1 1-16 MILES
SANTA ANITA
START FINISH

1 1/16 MILES. (1.40⅕) CLAIMING. Purse $25,000. 4-year-olds and upward. Weight, 122 lbs. Non-winners of two races at one mile or over since December 25, allowed 3 lbs.; of such a race since February 1, 5 lbs.; since December 25, 7 lbs. Claiming price $25,000; if for $22,500, 2 lbs.(Claiming and starter races for $20,000 or less not considered).

High Regards
DELAHOUSSAYE E 115
Own.—Elliott & Rutherford

Gr. c. 4, by Johnlee n' Harold—Double Security, by Double Lea
Br.—Rutherford J D (Cal) 1988 6 1 0 2 $22,150
Tr.—Williams George L $25,000 1987 5 0 1 0 $4,945
Lifetime 17 2 2 3 $42,495

13Mar88-9SA 1 1/16 :464 1:112 1:432ft 4½ 115 43½ 43 46 38½ Black C A 5 32000 75-15 L. A. Fire, Savor Faire,HighRegards 6
13Mar88—Bumped start
3Mar88-5SA 1 1/16 :452 1:101 1:432ft 14 116 67½ 44½ 3nk 12¼ DelahoussyeE 11 20000 84-19 HighRegrds,SilvrSurfr,TrusT.Dnus 12
17Feb88-9SA 1 1/16 :462 1:114 1:444ft 22 116 66½ 43 34 35 DelahoussyeE 11 20000 74-23 MischivousMtt,SbrnHro,HghRgrds 11
6Feb88-9SA 1 1/16 :464 1:12 1:45 ft 50 115 63 3½ 31 42¼ Black C A 6 20000 74-18 BrgndyBons,Hrrson'sTrn,BronzTdr 12
6Feb88—Broke out, bumped
13Jan88-9SA 1 1/16 :461 1:103 1:441ft 8 116 67 36 44 47 DelahoussayeE4 20000 73-20 J. B. R.'sDream,NomadBoi,Amatar 10
3Jan88-2SA 6f :212 :442 1:11 ft 12 1115 108¾ 68½ 67½ 54½ Banderas A L8 25000 78-17 Cliff'sPlc,SundncSqur,SuprmStnd 12
3Jan88—Broke slowly; wide into stretch
23Dec87-9Hol 1 1/16 :463 1:114 1:441ft 10 115 55½ 65 66 910½ Shoemaker W8 25000 71-19 Dncllthdncs,P.T.Hustlr,StllitExprss 9
28Nov87-2Hol 6½f :214 :444 1:17 ft 5 116 89 98 76¾ 64¾ ShoemakerW2 [S] 32000 88-12 DelVolnte,GretNegotitor,HdlinNws 9
28Nov87—Wide into stretch
14Nov87-2SA 6f :212 :443 1:112ft 12 116 65¼ 57½ 47½ 22¾ Shoemaker W10 25000 78-22 SwtwtrSprings,HighRgrds,Shrwdy 11
14Nov87—Wide into stretch
14Oct87-1SA 6f :214 :444 1:102ft 8½ 116 41¾ 54½ 43½ 45 DelahoussayeE4 32000 81-16 Cleverg,HoustonBrgg,GrtNqotitor 11
Mar 25 SA 3f ft :364 h Feb 15 SA 4f ft :512 h Feb 4 SA 4f ft :472 h Jan 29 SA 6f ft 1:152 h

High Touch
WD
OLIVARES F 115
Own.—Jandy Stud Farm

Dk. b. or br. g. 6, by Rising Market—Libya, by Sir Gaylord
Br.—Westerly Stud Farms (Cal) 1988 1 0 0 0
Tr.—Luby Donn $25,000 1987 3 0 0 0 $2,450
Lifetime 16 2 2 0 $35,650 Turf 1 0 0 0

12Mar88-2SA 6f :213 :442 1:092ft 4 116 75 65½ 57½ 67¾ Stevens G L 11 20000 83-19 Bizeboy, Alitak, Bold And Greene 12
1Mar87-1SA 6½f :214 :442 1:162ft 6½ 116 77 65 54 43¾ DelahoussayeE 2 32000 84-15 SprbMomnt,DshonorblGst,Dnsprt 12
1Mar87—Broke out, bumped; steadied near 1/2
17Jan87-3SA 1 :462 1:111 1:373ft 5 116 54 62¾ 75¾ 78 Baze G 7 62500 72-18 Pettrx,SilverHero,NorthernProvidr 8
3Jan87-3SA 6f :214 :441 1:094ft 10 117 66 45½ 54¾ 57 Baze G 3 Aw29000 82-16 Zabaleta, SaltDome,NorthernPolicy 7
3Jan87—Wide into stretch
18Oct86-7SA 6f :22 :444 1:092ft 14 117 86¾ 86¾ 45 23½ DelhoussyeE 8 Aw28000 87-20 Quip Star, High Touch, High Hook 8
8Sep86-7Dmr 1 1/16 :454 1:10 1:41 ft 8½ 119 21 55 35½ 67½ DelhoussyeE 1 Aw25000 87-14 Ack AckHeir,GoSwiftly,JackNCoke 7
8Sep86—Bumped start; lugged out early
9Aug86-9Dmr 1 1/16 :452 1:094 1:424ft 8½ 118 3nk 12½ 13½ 1¾ DelhoussyeE 6 Aw20000 86-14 HighTouch,AngleArc,Hrrison'sTurn 7
9Aug86—Lugged in 1/16
23Jly86-7Dmr 6f :214 :452 1:093ft 6¼ 119 73½ 53½ 43½ 52¼ StevensGL 5 [S] Aw19000 88-12 AnothrBloom,Bugrin,FlyingLssons 10
23Jly86—Bumped start
20Jun86-7Hol 7f :212 :442 1:214ft 3 116 55 42½ 41½ 56½ McHrgueDG 2 Aw19000 88-10 Slyly Gifted, In Toto, Noticiero 8
Jun86-3Hol 6f :22 :453 1:103ft 5¼ 117 97½ 97¼ 67½ 21 Pincay L Jr 7 Aw18000 90-11 BoldTopsidr,HghTouch,PowrfulEys 9
Mar 23 SA 4f ft :472 h Mar 5 Hol 5f ft 1:003 h ● Feb 22 Hol 6f ft 1:124 h Feb 15 Hol 5f ft 1:00 h

Siberian Hero
STEVENS G L 115
Own.—Sofro D I

B. h. 6, by Nasty and Bold—Tundra Queen, by Le Fabuleux
Br.—Tartan Farm Corp (Fla) 1988 4 0 1 1 $10,275
Tr.—Canani Julio C $25,000 1987 12 4 3 1 $82,700
Lifetime 43 7 12 8 $174,084 Turf 21 1 5 6 $48,247

28Feb88-9SA 1 1/16 :463 1:11 1:434gd 3¾ 115 64¼ 42½ 54½ 45½ Cordero A Jr 8 28000 76-18 Bananas, Claramount, Jazz Player 8
28Feb88—Wide final 3/8
17Feb88-9SA 1 1/16 :462 1:114 1:444ft 4½ 116 44 3½ 1½ 2nk Toro F 3 c20000 77-23 MischivousMtt,SbrnHro,HghRgrds 11
17Feb88—Broke in, bumped
24Jan88-10SA 1 1/16 :471 1:114 1:434ft 4½ 1115 32 42 32½ 34 Gryder A T 2 32000 78-18 ExoticMotion,L.A.Fire,SiberinHro 10
24Jan88—Broke out, bumped
6Jan88-7SA 1 :461 1:104 1:353ft 4¾ 1135 42 32½ 55½ 610¾ Gryder A T 2 50000 79-19 GoodTste,LstCommnd,HisHighness 8
13Dec87-9Hol 1 1/16 Ⓣ:471 1:111 1:422fm 7½ 116 11 1hd 2½ 99 Santos J A 5 62500 73-16 Pinstripe II, Kensof, Centenary 12
8Nov87-3SA 1 :473 1:114 1:391gd 4½ 1095 33 32½ 31 11¼ Gryder A T 3 45000 72-25 SiberinHero,Centenry,SpdyShnnon 7
10Oct87-10SA 1 1/16 :48 1:121 1:44 ft *2½ 118 31 31 2hd 1hd Meza R Q 6 25000 81-17 SiberianHero,L.A.Fire,MightyBuck 11
7Sep87-9Dmr 1 :444 1:093 1:35 ft 4½ 117 45 22 33½ 47 Pincay L Jr 9 62500 86-14 He'sASaros,IdelQulity,LstCommnd 9
7Sep87—Bumped start
26Aug87-5Dmr 1 1/16 :452 1:101 1:421ft 3½ 117 57 43½ 33 24 Pincay L Jr 9 62500 85-15 ForignLgion,SibrinHro,BngBngBng 9
2Aug87-9Dmr 1 :451 1:103 1:363ft *2¾ 117 45½ 31½ 2hd 1nk Pincay L Jr 6 50000 85-12 SbrnHro,ForgnLgon,GodThghtWlly 8
Mar 20 SA 4f ft :483 h Mar 14 SA 5f ft 1:04 h ● Mar 8 SA 4f ft :47 h

jumble of marks you have made on the *Racing Form*. A simplifying worksheet, like the one that follows, would have these headings:

Horse's Name	Speed Ratings		Class	Positive Factors	Negative Factors
	Last 30 Days	Best Ever			

If the horse has not run in the last thirty days, put the number of days since its last race under "Last 30 Days." If it has been running at a different distance, put down WD (for wrong distance), unless you can compute its sprint ratings from its six-furlong time. This will be put under the symbol $\wedge$.

Under "Class" indicate whether the horse has been claimed or is moving significantly up or down in class. Also, if it has won or finished well in a much higher class, this should be shown.

Positive factors would include all the trainer moves you have marked on the *Form*.

Negative factors should include indications of poor consistency, very poor last race, insufficient workouts, etc.

How are the horses listed? First, put down on the worksheet the horses with the top-two speed ratings (plus any ties, and don't forget the ratings made from fractional times). Add any horse that has run a speed rating equal to or better than the top two at any time in the past, if it has a speed rating not less than five below the top two in the past thirty days. These "best evers" were put in squares when you marked up your paper.

Any horse that has not run in the past thirty days but has run a speed rating at the distance that is equal to or better than the top rating must also be listed.

Put down any horse that must be considered because of class—either a significant drop from its last race or a win (or close finish) at any time that is at 50 percent higher than today's claiming price. For allowance horses, note any stakes activity.

Finally, put down the horses that show indications of having been placed in this race to score.

A worksheet for the Aqueduct and Santa Anita races on pages 74–77 is printed on the next page. If you do not understand the abbreviations or symbols, see page 80.

	HORSE	SPEED RATINGS		CLASS	POSITIVE FACTORS	NEGATIVE FACTORS
		Last 30 days	Best ever			
④ Aq.	Tim Collins	86-13	91-15			0/8 CON, but 6/8 in the $
6½f	Volt	⌃86	80-17	↑2G		0/10 CON
14G Cl.	Squire Percival	41 days	88-21	3 in 30G		Claimed last; ↓3½G; Fitness? Only 2 works since layoff
	Luna Lula	74-23	79-24	Won 20G	4fB	0/7 CON
	Dangerous Talk	11 mos	88-13	↓Md. 30G		Only three works/ 30 days after year layoff
⑦ Aq.	Talc Two	78-22				
6f	Action Dancer	5mos.	83-20		Three works/ 15	
Non-win	What a Femme	⌃76	78-22			
One Allow (fil.)	Squawter	33 days	77-20			Three works/ 20 mediocre
⑧ SA	Davies L.	(92,1¹⁄₁₆Tup)	87	10G (15GTC)* Won 3TC stakes	Three works/16	Has lost to Pen Bal
Mile TC	Sly Charmer	87-13;	←	7½G (10GTC)↑		No stakes
Stakes 4+	Pen Bal Ldy	WD	90	35G (15GTC) Won 2 stakes	Second race after layoff	
⑩ SA	High Regards	75↓;	84(W.14-1)←		Won 20G↑ 2yrs. CON 1/11	
1¹⁄₁₆	High Touch	WD	86		{Best race in Aug. 1986 {0/4 two years	
25G Cl.	Siberian Hero	76↓	85	↓;Cld.(2); W*50G	4fB	

*Lifetime TC earnings/start in parentheses

I have given you only some of the horses in each race, but in all of the races I have included the winner.

After you have understood how the information from the *Racing Form* has been condensed on the worksheet, decide on who you think the winner of each race will be. The results will be given later on in the chapter.

Abbreviations and Symbols Used on Worksheets

B	Bullet workout after last race.
BP	Bullet workout prior to last race.
Cld	Claimed. Cld(2) means it was claimed on its second-to-last race.
Con	Win consistency. 3/23 Con = the horse won 3 of 23 races.
Days	The number of days since the horse's last race. (This is given instead of a speed rating for horses that have not run in the past 30 days.)
Exc	An excellent workout. It did not receive a "bullet" in the charts.
G	Money in thousands of dollars. With an arrow, it indicates a change in claiming price. $\downarrow$ 10G = a drop in claiming price of $10,000. Without an arrow, it indicates earnings per start. $12\frac{1}{2}$G = the horse's earnings divided by the number of races it has run in the current year = $12,500. (If the horse has run fewer than five races in 1988, the figure is for the past two years.)
GTC	Lifetime earnings per start on the turf.
ND	No distance. The horse shows no race at the distance in the charts.
TC	Turf course.
TCB	Bullet work on the turf course.
W	Won the race. The horse won the race referred to.
WD	Wrong distance. The race referred to was at a distance different from the race being handicapped.
WKS	Workouts. 3WKS/22 = three workouts in twenty-two days.
*	Favorite. The horse went off at odds of less than 3.4–1.
$\wedge$	The computed speed rating for six furlongs done in a race of a mile or more.
$\square$	The number in the square is the best speed rating the horse has ever earned.
$\downarrow$ or $\uparrow$	A drop or rise in claiming price.
	The horse's finish and lengths behind are indicated this way: 5^{12} = the horse finished fifth, twelve lengths behind.

At this point it would be convenient for me to say that all you have to do is select the horse with the most positive factors and fewest negative factors on the worksheet and you'll come up with a winner.

Unfortunately, this would ignore the very large truth that most system players overlook: a horse race is not simply the working out of a mathematical problem. The factors we have used to isolate the contending horses are not all equal, and they cannot be given numerical weights or "points" because their importance varies from race to race.

In some races a horse will have nothing but superior class going for it, and it will beat a horse that scores points on all sorts of other factors. In other races, a horse may be at the peak of its condition, qualifying as a contender only because of its speed rating, and beat a horse that has shown much more class.

In general, what you have to look for are the answers to vital questions about the horses that qualify. If a horse has class, is there anything to indicate that its physical condition is good enough to beat the speed horses? If a horse qualifies because of its speed, is there anything to indicate it hasn't reached its peak? If a horse seems well suited to the conditions of the race, is there anything to indicate it has the speed or class to whip its competition?

Even though some sprint races are won by horses that show only speed, class, or trainer placement, most are won by horses that show a combination of factors. As a general rule, a horse will show itself as a winner by rating highly on either class or speed, and then have at least one indication that it is well placed.

The easiest races to decide are those in which one horse has a number of "keys." This was clearly the case in the races listed on the worksheet.

In Race 4, at Aqueduct, Tim Collins had the best recent time and the best back time. All the other horses had serious negative factors. Tim Collins went off as third choice, and won, paying $9.40.

In Race 7, Action Dancer clearly had the best back time, had shown some class by racing forwardly against open company, and was certainly being pointed to the race as indicated by its steady workouts (three in fifteen days). It won and paid $7.00.

Davie's Lamb may have been more difficult for you to pick, but its last good race plus its tie in top earnings per start on the turf made it a strong contender. It won and paid $16.40.

Finally, Siberian Hero was dropping in class with a bullet workout. It had the best time at the distance and had been claimed in its next-to-last race. Paying $7.20, it was made a well-deserved favorite.

In the Aqueduct sprint races there was little doubt as to which horse to play. In most races, however, you will have the interesting problem of trying to decide among a few horses that seem to be potential winners.

When a few horses qualify as strong contenders, you should first try to separate them according to pace. Do the track conditions seem to favor a certain type of runner? Is the race likely to be won by a confirmed front-runner or by the only horse with a good closing kick?

If the winner is still not clear, then make your choice according to the preferences given in our "final choice in sprints."

THE FINAL CHOICE IN SPRINTS

1. First Preference—Horse that has one of the top speed ratings in the past thirty days *plus* some indication that the trainer is spotting it for this race. (For example, a return to the races after a win within the past six days, claimed in its last race, a bullet work, etc.)
2. Second Preference—Horse that has been rested or running at the wrong distance, with a bullet work *and* a drop in class.
3. Third Preference—Horse with the top recent time *and* the best back time.

Quite often, a horse will rate well in all three categories of speed, class, and conditions. As explained in the chapters on betting, this horse will become one of your solid plays of the day. The horse will not necessarily go off as a heavy favorite, since often it will be overlooked by the fans who play a horse that shows nothing except a flashy last race.

Occasionally, none of the contenders will hold a definite advantage in the final choice factors. The race must be classed as extremely risky, and the question of which horse to bet and how becomes a problem of money management rather than selection. This is discussed in Part Three, Betting to Make a Profit.

In races other than sprints for older horses your selection of contenders and your final choice will depend on a few other factors. These will be discussed in the chapters that follow.

CHAPTER IX

The Final Choice in Long Races

The experienced racing analyst looking over the selection methods given so far would undoubtedly agree that following them will produce many winners in sprint races. Since they emphasize speed and class, and since they attempt to discover which horses may be especially well placed in a given race, the methods have to be successful. There simply is no other logical way to estimate which horses can and will win.

"But," the racing analyst would object, "although speed ratings are fine for six-furlong races, what about the distance events? In a typical race at a mile and an eighth, more than half the horses will have been running at different distances during the past thirty days. How can you figure comparative speed ratings for them? And besides, the longer races are tests of stamina *and* speed rather than speed alone. How can your methods account for stamina?"

These are good objections. Nevertheless, in handling distance races it must be remembered that speed is still of crucial importance. Fast recent times of route races will indicate many potential winners.

Consequently, in those races where almost all the horses have been racing at the long distance of today's race, your first step is to isolate the contenders by listing the horses with the top-two speed ratings in the past thirty days, adding those horses that have run as well in the past at the distance and are now within five speed-rating points of the top two, adding the class horses, and finding any other horses that may have been especially pointed for the race.

In other words, in those races where all the horses have been running at the distance, the methods for finding contenders in distance races are the same as the methods used for sprint races.

But there are two problems with distance races, neither of which is obvious to new (and some old) students of the *Form*. The first has to do with the speed ratings themselves and the second arises from the fact that at some tracks there are two radically different types of distance races.

The track you are visiting may offer races at a mile, at a mile and seventy yards, at a mile and one sixteenth, and at a mile and one eighth. A distance race may start near the finish line in front of the stands and proceed around two turns back to the finish line. Other distance races may start from a chute on the far side of the racetrack, proceed up the backstretch, and run around one turn to the finish line, much like a sprint race.

It would seem as if we should be able to lump all these speed ratings together and determine the fastest horses just as we do in sprints. Speed ratings are, after all, indications of how close a horse came to the track record, and an 80 figure for a mile should be comparable with an 80 figure for a mile and one eighth.

The problem is that while the ratings may be the same, the records that determine the ratings may differ considerably. Let me give an example. In 1968, the great Dr. Fager, one of the fastest thoroughbreds ever, shattered the seven-furlong record at Aqueduct in a time of $1:20^1/_5$. Few horses since have come close to this time, which determines the speed ratings for seven furlongs.

Until fairly recently, when the Aqueduct six-furlong record was broken, the average high-priced claiming horse ran the six furlongs in an 86 speed rating, while the same type horse ran the seven-furlong distance in an average of only 79.

Seven points is an enormous difference! Even with the more recent six-furlong record, the difference is still a substantial five points. You can see that in sprint races, where we consider a difference of two points enough to eliminate a horse, how mistaken our judgment will be if we simply consider six- and seven-furlong ratings to be the same.

Even today, many horses with seemingly mediocre seven-furlong speed ratings are overlooked by bettors who simply lump all ratings together. These speed-rating sleepers pay some dandy prices.

Some track records were set by super horses like Dr. Fager. Other track records were set on days when the track surface was so fast that these records are out of kilter with records set on a normally fast day.

Some distances are rarely run and only infrequently carded for the best horses. These track records are slower than others, so the speed ratings will be inordinately high. For example, the three major New York tracks run few important races at six and one-half furlongs. The track records are comparatively slow. Speed ratings for the six-and-one-half distance in New York are about five points higher when compared with six-furlong ratings.

The steady racegoer who makes selections according to speed ratings can compile average ratings for the various distances at a particular track and come up with figures to raise or lower the ratings if there are significant differences. But what can you, as an occasional bettor, do about this?

If you have the time, you can make a rough estimate of speed-rating averages by using races listed in the *Form* you are using for the day.

Suppose you are handicapping a race at one mile and one eighth and in the past thirty days the horses have been running at that distance and also at a mile and at a mile and seventy yards. Look in the past-performance charts for races run at the distance by horses of the same class. Since the speed ratings given are for the particular horse and not the winner, to get the speed rating of the winner add one point for each length the horse finished behind the winner.

For example, if a horse finished fourth, three lengths behind the winner, and had a speed rating of 81, the winning speed rating was 84.

If ten different races over a fast track for the same class of horse can be found, a rough average of winning speed ratings can be estimated. If the averages for the various distances are about the same, then the ratings for the distances can probably be safely lumped together. If, however, you find that one distance has an average that is three or more points different from another, then you should add these points to the ratings that are lower. For example, if you find that the average mile rating is 80, and the average for one mile and seventy yards is 84, add four points to the mile ratings of the contenders.

Another hedge the occasional bettor must take is to use a *five*-point difference to include the speed horses. If the top number for a mile race is a horse who ran an 80, for example, you should include with the speed horses any horse who ran a 75 at any route distance in the past thirty days. Similarly, the best back times would be 75 or above. It is better in the preliminary stages of selecting contenders to include a potential loser than to exclude a potential winner.

What about horses that have been running at sprint distances during the past thirty days? First of all, in a long race for horses older than three where most of the horses are distance horses, a *confirmed* sprinter should probably be eliminated. Sprinters win longer races occasionally, but not often enough to make satisfactory wagering propositions.

However, in races where there are only a few distance horses, sprinters may be selected as contenders, if there are indications that they have acquired the stamina needed for distance races. Significant things to look for are a long late gain capping a drive of at least half a mile, or a race in which the horse was pressed or was pressing a leader most of the way. If neither of these things appears in a horse's last two races, do not bet the horse. It is probably being run at a longer distance for training purposes.

Another problem facing the unwary occasional bettor is that races run out of chutes around one turn are not at all the same as races run around two turns at the same distance. Two-turn races are most often won by front-running horses from inside posts who sprint to an early lead, cruise around the first turn, take a breather on the backstretch, extend a bit on the second turn, and have enough left to hold off horses in the stretch.

One-turn chute races from a mile to a mile and one eighth (Belmont Park has a very unusual chute distance of a mile and one quarter) are most frequently won by closers. The front-runners usually cannot get a sufficient lead to take a breather down the long chute and are usually caught by the pressers going around the far turn. At that point the closers usually start looping horses and get to the lead some place in midstretch. It is not at all uncommon in these races for the last horse on the backstretch to be the first at the wire.

In some two-turn races in which there are a lot of front-running horses, a closer may get over to the rail, save ground all the way, make one big run on the turn and catch the tiring speed horses. So closers should never be eliminated in two-turn races. On the other hand, front-runners make risky bets in distance races coming out of long chutes.

Special mention must be made of races run at the mile distance out of a chute. These are undoubtedly the most difficult to handicap, since they are not really distance races, and yet they are too long to be won by horses that set torrid fractions throughout.

Jockeys have as much difficulty with these races as handicappers. Should a jockey ride his horse as a speed horse and try to win wire to wire? Should he stay close to the pace, hoping the front-runner falters? Should he drop way back and then come with a long, hard stretch drive?

These are the things he must decide in the seconds after the race has begun. Only the very best jockeys can rate horses properly in mile races. Consequently, in the final selection, more than usual weight should be given to the jockey, since his quick thinking and skill will count heavily.

Races at seven furlongs should be considered sprint races. If the average win speed ratings for six and seven furlongs are not widely different (although they may be at some tracks such as Aqueduct), all the speed ratings can be lumped together and the speed selection made from the top two, as in any sprint race. In most cases the nod should go to the horse that has been competing at seven furlongs if its speed rating puts it in, or close to, the top two. This is because the seven-furlong distance is not as common, and if a trainer is running his horse back at that distance after it showed relatively good speed, he probably thinks the distance is suitable.

In sprint races, you selected as contenders any horses within two speed-rating points of the top horse. In distance races, you take any horse within five points of the top. In the first stages of the selection process you will usually have more horses among which to choose. You select the final contenders according to what the charts tell you about stamina. Which horse has the staying power to go a long, tiring distance?

In general, the deciding factor in judging stamina is *how* the horse finished its last race at the distance. For this, the horse's position and time at the six-furlong mark can be used.

For example, let us say the fractional times in the charts for the horse's last mile-and-an-eighth race look like this:

$$:47 \qquad 1:12 \qquad 1:52$$

The second mark indicates the horse in the lead in that race ran six furlongs in one minute and twelve seconds. The time that elapsed between this point and the winner crossing the finish line was forty seconds.

Supposing the horse we are rating had position calls like this:

$$7 \qquad 8 \qquad 8^9 \qquad 6^7 \qquad 5^5 \qquad 4^2$$

This would indicate that it has post position seven, that after a quarter of a mile it was the eighth horse in the race, that at the half mile it was still eighth, nine lengths in back of the leader, that after six furlongs it was sixth, seven lengths in back, that at the stretch call it had come up to fifth, five lengths back, and that it finished fourth, two lengths behind the winner.

Notice that the horse made up five lengths on the leaders from the six-furlong mark (6^7) to the finish (4^2) (one and one-eighth miles, or nine furlongs). Consequently, it ran the last three furlongs in one second less time than the fractional time listed for the race (each length being calculated as one fifth of a second), or thirty-nine seconds in all.

In a similar manner, the fractional times for the other contenders would be calculated. The horse running the last three furlongs in the best time, whether as a closer or as a front-runner, should be considered the one to beat, *if* the pace of the race is suitable for it.

Actually, when all the horses have had races at the distance within the past thirty days, the horse with speed and stamina usually can be spotted rather easily. The real problem is to pick a winner when most of the horses have been racing at different distances during the past month.

Since the late fractions will be for distances from an eighth of a mile to five sixteenths of a mile, they cannot be compared easily. You will have to use other methods to determine stamina. These include (1) a good late gain in the last race (five lengths or more); (2) a race in which the horse set the pace most of the way, not failing until the final call, which would indicate it as in good shape but a bit "short"; and (3) a strong workout of seven furlongs or more after a long race.

In those long races where there are many three-year-olds that have never competed at the distance before, the bettor must choose the horse which apparently can sustain a drive the longest. Again, fractional time and points of call indicating late gains are the deciding factors, rather than high speed ratings for six furlongs.

How, then, shall you handle long races?

1. For those horses that have been running at the distance in the past thirty days, select the contenders according to the speed rating, class, and suitability, following the procedures outlined for sprint races.
2. For those horses that have *not* been running at the distance, determine if there is a substantial difference in the relative worth of the speed ratings by examining past winning races in the charts. If you do not have the time for this, all horses within five points of the top horse would be considered contenders.
3. From the list of contenders select the horses that show the greatest stamina as indicated by:
   a. A good late gain in its last race.
   b. A long, grueling pace-setting or pace-pressing race (provided the horse is not a confirmed quitter).
   c. One or two long workouts (seven furlongs or more) after a recent race.
   d. Fast time for the last part of its last race.

4. Of those horses with proven stamina, choose the one best suited to the pace that is likely to develop. In general, in a two-turn race, favor the front-runner. In a distance race out of a chute, favor the closer.
5. Two reminders:
   a. Never choose a confirmed sprinter unless it has shown stamina by having been on a fast pace for all or almost all of the distance in its last race.
   b. In mile races more emphasis than usual should be placed on the jockey as a means of choosing among qualified horses.

THE FINAL CHOICE IN DISTANCE RACES

1. First Preference—Top time horse with the best stamina *plus* a trainer move.
2. Second Preference—Horse dropping in class with a win at the distance and a trainer move.
3. Third Preference—Horse with a sprint race in the past thirty days with a back time at a long distance that is equal to or better than the best time run by any horse in the last thirty days ("top last").

CHAPTER X

The Final Choice in Two-Year-Old Races

Many experienced racegoers never bet on two-year-old races. To them it makes no sense to bet on a race in which few horses have run well enough to establish form. They have also seen too many races where a potential winner is left in the gate, or bolts, or goes very wide in the stretch, or commits some other costly mistake because of its lack of experience and schooling.

It also makes no sense to these track regulars to place a bet on a race which includes horses that have never raced before and on which, therefore, no definite prediction can be made.

The bettor who goes to the track daily can afford to pass up most two-year-old races since the older horses provide enough action. But the bettor out for an occasional day's fun cannot, especially if the card calls for two or three such races.

Since you, as an occasional bettor, *will* play the two-year-old races, what is the best choice you can make?

You should begin by remembering how two-year-olds are brought to the races.

For racing purposes, all horses have the same birthday. On January 1 all horses born during the preceding year are considered one year old. Generally, as yearlings they are broken and made used to some of the ways of racing.

Most of the horses born in the Northern Hemisphere are born during the same three-month period, so that difference in size as yearlings is due more to different rates of development than to being born earlier or later, although the month of birth is still a factor early in the year.

Some horses have grown large enough and have trained well enough to be raced in the warmer climates shortly after they become two-year-olds. The standard distance is three furlongs along a straight course.

In March the distance is increased to five furlongs, and the horses race around a turn for the first time. In June and July the standard distance for two-year-olds is five and one-half furlongs, and in August most tracks schedule two-year-olds for the standard sprint distance of six furlongs.

The type of races arranged for two-year-olds also varies as the season grows older. In the beginning of the year most of the three-furlong races are for maidens that cannot be claimed, and all horses carry the same weight. The majority of five-furlong races are also restricted to horses that have never won, although in many of these races, horses may be entered to be claimed. Some claiming and allowance races are carded for horses that are ineligible for maiden races, having already won a race.

By July the two-year-old season is in full bloom. Still, the majority of races are carded for maidens in order to give as many horses as possible the chance to win at least once. Many more maiden claiming races are scheduled in order to give the horses of less quality a chance to visit the winner's circle.

Because of the great variety of types and distances of two-year-old races, it is clear that not all of these make poor betting propositions. Of course, the early three-furlong dashes are hazardous. Most of the horses entered have never run before, and those that have improve rapidly and erratically. And at such a short distance, even a slight mistake can lose a race.

But, toward the end of the year most two-year-olds have had a sufficient number of races to establish their form; their improvement from race to race is far less rapid, and definite class lines can be established. Some of these races present excellent betting situations and can be profitably handicapped according to the methods given in the preceding chapters.

The main problems occur earlier in the year when many of the races are loaded with first-time starters, and many of those that have run will show races at different sprint distances. The following questions must be considered:

1. When should you bet a first-time starter?
2. How can you contend with the manner in which two-year-olds greatly improve from race to race?
3. How can you handle speed ratings at five, five and one half, and six furlongs?

Some general statistics give hints as to how to handle these problems. First of all, they show that many occasional bettors foolishly ignore horses that have never raced before. It is true that the percentage of races won by first-outers may not seem to be high in races where only one or two horses have never been to the post before, but it is only slightly less than the percentage of first-starters entered. In races where half the entrants are racing for the first time, slightly less than half of those races are won by these horses. So first-time starters win their share of races.

A daily bettor can pass up a race with some nicely bred first-starters with good workouts, but the occasional bettor has to take his chance, either with them or against them.

Another general statistic that is useful concerns current form. Other than races won by first-starters, close to four out of five races at five and one-half furlongs are won by horses that have finished fourth or better in their last race, although they comprise fewer than two out of five horses entered.

This statistic becomes even more informative and amazing if we examine only those races with ten or more entries where there are three horses or fewer that have finished fourth or better. In these races, one of the horses that has finished well wins about four out of five races!

(This compares well with the figure for *all* horses, two years old and older. There, the proportion of races won by horses having garnered a bit of the purse money in their last outing is only three out of five, and this includes many races where most of the horses have done well in their last outing.)

What other factors, besides winning a share of the purse in previous races, point out a horse likely to win? As with all sprint races, speed is of the greatest importance. Five-furlong races are over in less than a minute. The fastest horse usually wins.

This can be seen in the statistics, which show that 50 percent of all five-and-one-half-furlong races are won by horses that have one of the top-two speed ratings at that distance. (In the early part of June when all the horses are competing at five and one-half furlongs for the first time, the same percentage holds when you take the top-two speed ratings for five furlongs, the longest distance these horse have run yet.)

Almost all the other winners, including the first-time starters, signify their readiness to win by having good, multiple workouts within ten to twelve days prior to the race.

As we have already noted, the occasional bettor has been given a tremendous help by the "bullets" that signify the best morning work at the distance. But workouts that have not been given bullets may be excellent and may point out a horse that is ready to win.

The experienced bettor can spot these workouts. No definite figures can be given to help the occasional bettor since the time varies from track to track, but you can get some idea by checking the list of workouts for the previous day printed in the *Racing Form*. The best workout at each distance is printed in boldface type. Usually, the best workouts are done by older horses, so any two-year-old that has worked within a second of these times must be considered speedy and fit.

It takes judgment, however, to determine which workouts are best. A good workout at five furlongs is probably more indicative of good condition than a brilliant workout at three furlongs. Furthermore, it is difficult to tell how hard the horse was urged. The letter "h" (for handily) indicates some urging, while "b" (for breezing) indicates only mild urging. These give some indication of how vigorously the horse was worked, but they are, of course, the judgment of the workout clocker. There is a gray area between handily and breezing where it is difficult to say just how much the horse was exerted.

Everyone can spot the really fast workouts, and any horse with a speedy work must be considered as a contender. Most bettors overlook the slower, breezing workouts since all they compare is time. But most of the sleepers that pay big prices can be tabbed from breezing workouts. In a race where the top four-furlong workout is :48, a breezing workout as high as :49 may indicate a far superior horse, since there is no telling how fast it might have worked if it had been handily urged.

Similarly, workouts from the gate (indicated with a "g", as "hg" or "bg") should be given special emphasis, since a horse loses a fraction from a standing start.

Perhaps even more important than the times of workouts are their number and distance. If a horse has had two or three workouts at four or five furlongs since a recent race (or three workouts in two weeks if it has never raced), its trainer is probably pointing it for a win, since no trainer wants to needlessly break down a promising two-year-old.

The occasional bettor who picks a horse with a close finish last out and a speedy workout may be onto a good thing, but simply picking the horse with the highest speed rating probably leads to more torn-up tickets than any other method of selecting two-year-olds. The problem arises when the horses have been running at different distances. Virtually all five-furlong track records and most five-and-one-half-furlong records have been set by two-year-olds. Many two-year-olds can come close to these records, and so the speed ratings are quite high.

On the other hand, all of the six-furlong records in the country have been set by older horses, some of them the top sprinters of their day. Few of the developing two-year-olds can come close to equaling these marks. Consequently, when a two-year-old moves from five and a half to six furlongs, there is a considerable drop in speed rating.

Each track is different, but a general rule of thumb is that a six-furlong rating is five points better than one at five and one half, and a five-and-one-half rating is five points better than one at only five furlongs.

For example, if one horse has a six-furlong rating of 82, another has a five-and-one-half rating of 86, and a third has a five-furlong rating of 90, the fastest horse is probably the one with the 82 rating.

Speed ratings are a definite key to two-year-old races, but you should always prefer the good six-furlong rating to the somewhat higher five- or five-and-one-half-furlong rating.

To select the contenders in two-year-old races, therefore, you must concentrate on last finish, speed ratings, and workouts. Can class also be used to point out possible winners?

In general, the answer is no. It must be remembered that most two-year-olds are unknown quantities. Because of this, most of them are started in races in which they cannot be claimed. They may, as chance has it, be running against what turns out to be the top two-year-old of the year, also out for its first start. They may also be running against a very cheap grade of horses.

Therefore, having raced in or even won a maiden special-weight race is not necessarily an indication of class. What is more important in judging class is the times in which the races (whether maiden special-weight or maiden claiming) were *won*.

Quite often a horse with a good but not sensational speed rating will finish eight or nine lengths behind a classy winner. (Its winning time shows that it's classy.) The jockey, knowing his horse had no chance to win, did not punish it. A horse such as this, which can be spotted by the speed rating of the winner, is the kind that shows the greatest "improvement" and often pays excellent prices.

The class of two-year-olds is therefore indicated less by the designation of the races it has competed in (maiden special-weight) or by a claiming price than by the time of the winner in its last race.

You have been told how two-year-olds get to the races and the things that are in the past-performance charts of most two-year-old winners. How can you systematically select a potential winner in a two-year-old race if such a race is being run on the day you go to the track?

1. The two horses with the highest speed ratings at the distance in the past thirty days are considered the ones to beat, since either one of these horses will be the winner almost half the time. (Reminder; add five points to six-furlong times if some of the horses have been running at this distance.)
2. To this list of contenders add any horse with a speed rating within five points of the top two *if* it meets one of these conditions:
   a. Its last race was run against horses of a higher class than the top two, as judged by the speed rating of the winner.
   b. It finished fourth or better in its last race.
3. Add any horse, including first-starters, that seems ready to win because of its workouts. They must be good, frequent (three within two weeks), and long (four or five furlongs). Remember that a breezing workout in average time indicates a very sharp horse.
4. Consider any horse that is returning to the races in six days or less. This happens rarely, since few trainers will risk overracing a young horse.
5. Also consider any horse that was claimed in its last race. Very few two-year-olds are claimed, especially maiden claimers. When it happens, someone must know something.

THE FINAL CHOICE IN TWO-YEAR-OLD RACES

1. First Preference—If a horse has one of the top-two speed ratings *and* it posted this rating in a race where the *winning* speed rating was higher than the *winning* speed rating in any of the races run by the contenders, this horse is the choice.
2. Second Preference—A first-starter with a bullet work. (Watch the board. A first-starter that is not a consensus pick and takes late money must be bet, at least as a "saver"—a bet made in conjunction with a major bet so you avoid losing money on a race.)
3. Third Preference—A horse that has raced within five points of the top-time horse and had an in-the-money finish in its last race, which was called "gamely" by the chart writer. A five-point improvement in speed rating is not at all unusual for young horses.
4. Fourth Preference—Any horse that was claimed in its last race or raced within the past six days must be bet, regardless of speed rating, at least as a saver.

If you follow this procedure, you will not win every two-year-old race, but you will have the percentages working in your favor. And, as in any gambling venture, this is what you should look for.

CHAPTER XI

The Final Choice in Special Situations

A. MAIDEN RACES FOR OLDER HORSES

Most racetrack enthusiasts disparage races for horses three years old and older that have never won. They feel that because the horses running in these races are inconsistent or cheap or both, anything can happen. Since most bettors know that to bet on a maiden horse when it is running against horses that have already won is a most unprofitable venture, they feel that handicapping a race chock-full of winless horses is fruitless.

Yet, in maiden races for older horses a higher than average percentage of favorites win. This indicates that some sort of form applies and that after many of these races the wise bettor can cash a winning ticket.

These races are actually easier to pick than two-year-old maiden races because they frequently contain no first-starters. The bettor can get a history of *all* the horses' races and therefore make a decent choice.

In the early part of the year the average race card will contain at least one and sometimes two or three maiden races for older horses. As the months go by fewer of these races are scheduled since there are fewer maidens around. Many have been retired without winning; some have won their first race and are competing against better horses.

The typical midseason maiden race will have ten three-year-olds and two four-year-olds competing. At least half of the three-year-olds can be dismissed from consideration immediately since they have run so poorly.

While maiden races do a little better than all races in terms of percentage of winning favorites, the opposite end of the scale is also true. Maiden races have more than their share of huge longshots than other races. Sometimes these longshots show something somewhere in their back races, but more often they are in the group of horses that handicappers dismiss immediately because of their very poor recent races.

Nevertheless, *most* of the three-year-old maidens that win exhibit one or more of these:

1. Relatively high speed rating in the past thirty days; either the best or second best of all horses running.
2. The highest speed rating at the distance at any time.
3. A "rally" in its last race (or next-to-last, if it had an excuse in its last).
4. Three workouts in two weeks or less, or a bullet work before or after its last race.

It has been stressed that horses with the highest speed ratings in the past month win a large percentage of the time in all races, including maiden races.

The other three points are especially relevant to maiden races. As horses win maiden races there is a constant decrease in the quality of the fields. A horse that ran a fast race once may not even have to duplicate that race to win against a cheaper field. Consequently, the horse that has the best time ever is frequently the winner in a time that is less than its best.

A rally in one of its last races is an indication that at last the horse is both in condition to run and in with horses it can beat.

Horses that do not win are too expensive to keep. If a trainer works out a maiden three times in two weeks, it generally indicates that in his opinion the caliber of the maidens on the track grounds is within winning range of his horse. Such a horse may win only one race in its career, and the trainer will prefer sharpening the horse through works rather than taking the chance of a near miss that will surely lower its odds the next time out.

This may be the only chance the horse will get. A surprisingly large number of maidens finish in the money a couple of times in their racing lives but never win. The purses they receive for these finishes are not nearly enough to pay their keep. Hence, the trainer will always prefer a single victory (with its prospect of a cashed bet for stables that must wager) to quite a few in-the-money placings.

The horse that narrowly missed in its last race because it tired is sometimes made the favorite in its next outing. If the pace is right, this horse may become your bet, but in general, preference should be given to the horse that has indicated increased stamina by rallying in its last race, or to the horse that seems to be pointed for a win by having had shortly spaced workouts.

Longshot lovers should pay special attention to any horse that has not raced in the past thirty days or more, having been given a layoff after a few dismal races. Whatever the reason for its poor showing in the past, a bullet work may indicate that the trainer at last has his horse ready. Since most fans quickly eliminate those horses that have always finished far back, when these horses win (and enough do to make them always bettable, at least as savers), they usually pay off in figures that really light up the tote board.

Early in the year, most tracks will have separate races for maiden three-year-olds and maiden four-year-olds. On January 1, all the two-year-olds become a year older, but they are still not capable of competing against older horses.

Later in the season, if there are still four-year-old maidens around, and they are entered in the maiden special-weight race you are handicapping, they should be examined with great care. If they show even one of the factors mentioned on page 98, they should be preferred. They often will win at upset prices.

The reason for this is not hard to find. A stable has maintained a horse for two racing seasons at great expense without ever having won a purse (or cashed a win bet). The owner and trainer are banking on at least one victory for the horse to pay its way. If the horse had no better than an average chance of winning, the stable would certainly have retired it at the end of its first unsuccessful season. After still another unsuccessful season, they would not hold on to it if it could not win. Hence, four-year-old maidens that show anything at all are prime betting prospects.

(This, of course, does not apply to those horses owned by good souls whose stable consists of but one horse; either through misplaced but blind confidence, or through a desire to stay in racing in some fashion, these people run their horses until they eventually break down.)

There is no way to use the class of races a horse has been running in to make a selection in maiden races. A drop in the maiden claiming price does not always mean much, since most horses running at the higher maiden-claiming tags are overvalued. Of course, if horses are about equal in speed ratings and workouts, the edge should be given to the one dropping in claiming price.

This is especially true with horses which have been running in maiden special-weight races (nonclaiming) and are running for the first time in a claiming race. A trainer who has not risked having his horse claimed during a whole season will be wary of losing it when it finally looks as if it might win (as indicated by speed ratings or workouts). If it is claimed, he will want to collect the purse and, possibly, a bet.

Another change that improves the chances of a contender is a drop from a race open to horses that have won to a race restricted to maidens. ("Clm 7500" indicates a race for winners and nonwinners; "Md 7500" indicates a claiming race for maidens only; in both cases a horse could be claimed for $7500 but the caliber of the horses in the maiden race is usually much lower.)

This drop from *open* claiming races to *maiden* claiming races is especially important in the case of four-year-olds. Frequently, it may be the crucial reason for choosing a four-year-old. Against weaker competition, the older horse can often overcome the weight it has to carry because of its age and even improve its time.

Another indication of weaker competition comes when a female horse moves from maiden races for both sexes to a maiden race restricted to fillies only (indicated by an "f" before MdSpWt or Md 3500). A filly should not be selected for this reason only, but if she qualifies on other grounds, she may be in the winner's circle at last.

The thing to look for in maiden races for older horses is a horse that has at least *two* of these factors:

1. Four years old.
2. The highest speed rating at the distance at any time.
3. One of the two top speed ratings at the distance in the past thirty days.
4. A rally in its last race.
5. Three workouts in two weeks or less or a bullet work, especially after a layoff.
6. A drop in the quality of horses it has been competing against:
   a. From maiden special-weight races to maiden claiming races.
   b. From open claiming races to maiden claiming races.
   c. From races for both sexes to races for fillies and mares only.

Many times a horse will have a number of these factors in its favor. It will usually be bet down to become the public choice. Do *not* get off this horse, since it is a solid favorite, one that wins more often than the average for favorites in general.

B. STAKES RACES FOR OLDER HORSES

Stakes races are sometimes the easiest and sometimes the hardest races to handicap.

One of the biggest problems in selecting is eliminated—because of the large purse you know that *all* of the horses are trying—and, therefore, the problem of spotting a horse intended to win does not come up.

In addition, in some of these races you have expert help. For all *handicap* races, the racing secretary assigns weight. His aim is to have all horses finish in a dead heat for first. He gives most weight to the best horse and lets the poorest horse in with the smallest load. If the stakes is a handicap, you can get the racing secretary's opinion by seeing which horse has high weight.

You sometimes get a break in those stakes races run under *allowance* conditions. Frequently, a great horse entered in such a race will not have to tote nearly as much weight as it would if the race were run under handicap conditions. In some races, those in which all horses of the same age carry the same weight, this advantage may be overwhelming.

On the other hand, stakes races frequently contain a number of factors which make the selection of a winner difficult according to the methods given so far.

Stakes races attract horses from all over the country, which makes speed ratings rather cumbersome and complicated. In addition, since stakes horses run at varying distances, many of the horses may not have a speed rating at the distance. Then, too, since stakes horses do not run as often as cheaper horses, more than the usual number of horses entered may not have had any kind of a race in the past thirty days.

To overcome these difficulties, your first step is to rate the horses according to their quality. This can be done by examining the kind of races each horse has won and the total money earned during the past two years.

In an important race there will usually be four kinds of horses:

1. The superstars—these horses have won stakes races at the big tracks. Although big tracks have some minor stakes, you know these were important races because of the earnings listed for the horse.
2. Good stakes racers—these are the horses that run in major stakes but rarely, if ever, win. Occasionally they come in the money, but most of their victories have been in allowance races.
3. Good allowance horses—these horses run in stakes races occasionally, but

their main efforts have been in allowance races where they have a good, but not outstanding record.

4. Mediocre allowance horses—these are the horses that really do not belong in a race with superstars. Often they are entered simply to get their owners' colors on the track. They may occasionally win an allowance race, but in general their records are poor. Sometimes they have claiming-race losses in their background.

It is helpful to pencil in next to a horse's name a number from one to four which rates its quality according to the kinds of races it has won. In many of the smaller-pursed stakes races there will be no superstars.

In a little over half of all stakes races, no more than two horses will be given a top rating (either a "1" or, if there is no superstar, a "2"). Because a good horse frequently scares the main contention into other stakes around the country, in slightly less than one out of three stakes at major tracks, there is only a single horse that will earn a top rating.

In those races where there is only a single horse rated a "1" or "2," this horse wins almost 75 percent of the time. In those races where there is more than one top-rated horse, one of the top-rated horses wins almost 90 percent of the time! (Of course, here the problem is choosing between the two, three, and occasionally more top-rated horses.)

Since the top-rated horse occasionally loses, the next judgment you must make is whether one of the factors that causes such a loss is present. These factors are:

1. Too long a time between races. Even the greatest horse needs racing to sharpen its ability to compete well against horses that are nearly as good. If a good horse has not run in over a month, and it has not had three or four workouts, it often will be short for the big race.

2. An unsuitable distance. Some horses excel at sprints, some at long distances. When one of these quality horses is placed in a race of unsuitable distance, it is often not good enough to beat those of the next grade. This applies especially to sprinters that are placed in races of more than a mile.

3. Too much weight. The star horses are given the most weight. Sometimes the racing secretaries overdo it. The important thing is not the number of pounds, but the number of pounds given away to the horses in the next grade.

Any time a horse is carrying more than 125 pounds and is giving away more than seven pounds to a horse with the next rating, you have some research to do. You must first determine if the horse has ever won at that weight. If not, you must determine the highest weight at which it has won, and the number of pounds it *gave away* in that race (at least as shown by the other two horses finishing in the money).

Weight can be given too much consideration, of course, but if an excellent horse has lost before at the weight it is expected to carry, and if the second-line horses are getting a big advantage in weight, the top horse becomes a risky bet.

4. Facing improving competitors. The "best" horse may be beaten by a rapidly improving horse, winning a stake for the first time. This occurs especially in the stakes for younger horses.

Nevertheless, if a superstar loses, it is almost always beaten by another superstar (if there are any in the race) or by a good stakes racer (class 2). Only rarely will a good allowance horse beat both a good stakes horse *and* a superstar, and then only with a good helping of racing luck. Hence, if for some reason (weight, distance, too long idle) the top-rated horse cannot be played, you make your selection from the horses in the next grade.

What kind of horses beat horses in the next higher rank? Quite often, they are top-grade horses that have done fairly well in stakes in the past. They usually show their readiness to upset the favorite by a fast allowance win or by a series of long, brilliant workouts.

Even more often, when a top-rated horse is upset it is beaten by a horse at the peak of its condition. This happens most often in races where the top-rated horse has not raced in some time but is nevertheless given an enormous weight package. If the race contains a horse that has just won at the track over the distance of the race in question, in a time that is close to the top horse's best time at the distance, you may have an excellent bet, since it usually returns a nice price.

Finally, even the best horses lose because of the pace that develops in the race. The superstars show their class by being able to produce more than one burst of speed during a race. They can wear down a couple of front-runners and pressers, and then give another effort to hold off a closer.

Nevertheless, they occasionally lose to a second-ranked horse that is favored by the pace. This happens most often in races where the main contention comes from closers. The jockey on the superstar, knowing he has to save his horse to make a late challenge, may let a front-runner steal away to a lead that becomes insurmountable.

Consequently, even in races where the top-rated horse is outstanding, you must determine if a pace may develop that will aid another horse.

The procedure, then, for selecting a stakes race winner is as follows:

1. Rate the quality of the horses using this scale:

"1"—horses that have won major stakes races.
"2"—horses that have done well in, but have not won, major stakes races.
"3"—horses that have won allowance races.
"4"—horses that have won only a few races, have lost many allowance races, and may have been entered in claiming races.

2. If the race contains only one horse in the highest rating, bet this horse unless:

a. It has been away from racing for more than a month and its workouts have been neither frequent nor long.
b. It is running at a distance not suited to its talents.
c. It is giving away more weight than it has ever done in the past.
d. The race contains another horse that has shown great improvement in its last few races.
e. The pace of the race is unsuitable.

3. If the race contains more than one top-rated horse, use the above factors as a means of eliminating all but one, making your final choice on the basis of best recent form at the distance.

4. If the top-rated horse is risky because of one of the factors in item 2, bet the horse in the next grouping that has had a winning race at or near the distance over the track in its last outing. If there is no such horse, bet the horse in the grouping with a winning race at or near the distance at *any* track in its last outing. (If a horse has shown enough to warrant shipping in, it merits the choice over horses that have been losing at the track.) If no horse in this grouping has won its last time out, choose the horse with the highest speed rating at the distance in the past thirty days.

C. STAKES RACES FOR THREE-YEAR-OLDS

Three-year-old stakes races often have horses that have proven themselves in past stakes and thus qualify as stars. But these same races also often have horses that are still developing and may now be ready to beat the best. They must be considered contenders along with the horses of proven quality.

Consequently, your approach to stakes limited to three-year-olds has to be slightly different from that for stakes for older horses. You should still rate the horses according to quality, but you should give equal consideration to speed ratings, to workouts, and to the best indication of developing class—fast late fractions.

The 1988 Florida Derby at Gulfstream Park is a good example of a race that had a surprising winner that shouldn't have been all that much a surprise. Entered in this mile-and-one-eighth test was Forty Niner, the two-year-old champ, trained by the revered Woody Stephens. Forty Niner had the best time for the distance at the track, earned in a hard-fought victory by a nose in a lesser stake a few weeks earlier.

Opposing him were Ruhlmann, a California speedball with incredibly fast workouts; Notebook, the horse that almost nipped Forty Niner after pressing him nearly all the way; and three other horses coming out of the same minor stakes, including a late-closing horse named Brian's Time, which had won only two of five races.

Forty Niner, a winner of six of eight races, including five stakes, was clearly the horse to beat, although Ruhlmann, who had a blistering 95 speed rating in its last race at Bay Meadows, was made the favorite.

Forty Niner had won his last race wire to wire, with a last fraction of $32^2/_5$, barely outlasting Notebook. In that same race, Brian's Time, three points less in the speed rating, had closed from eighth, ten lengths behind, to fourth only three lengths out at the finish, in a very fast 30 seconds flat. He also had three works in eleven days including an excellent seven-furlong breeze.

The bettor had to decide whether Ruhlmann had the kind of blazing speed to go wire to wire at a mile and one eighth, or whether Forty Niner had the class to again outgame his opponents, including Notebook, who had barely missed, and Brian's Time, with his great ability to close.

Those who decided that good late fractions are an indication of class and stamina were richly rewarded with a $60 payoff when Brian's Time came from far back to beat Forty Niner by a head.

Not all, or even a majority, of three-year-old stakes races are won by closers, but most are won by horses that show, among other things, a superior late fraction, a high speed rating, and a good long workout.

Much has been written in the past few years about a numerical method rating the breeding of horses entered in the Kentucky Derby called the dosage index. No horse, including many beaten favorites, that has exceeded this index has won the Derby in the past forty years.

Actually, this index may be coincidental. A little research shows that almost all of the winners of the Derby during the past two decades have *demonstrated* their stamina for a mile-and-one-quarter race by having one of the top speed ratings at a mile and one eighth (when adjusted for different tracks) and either the best or second-best final three-eighths fraction.

For three-year-old stakes (sprints and distance races), the following method is used:

1. Rate the horses for quality as you would if they were older stakes horses.
2. Include among the contenders any horse that shows:
   a. One of the top speed ratings at the distance.
   b. An excellent workout, preferably at seven furlongs or more for a distance race.
   c. One of the top-two closing fractions.

D. ALLOWANCE RACES

There are basically two types of allowance races. One type restricts the horses that may be entered according to the number of wins. The conditions may read: "Allowance. Three-year-olds and up which have never won a race other than a maiden or claiming."

The other type of allowance race is open only to those horses that have failed to win an allowance race in a certain period of time, or an allowance race with a certain purse, or both. These allowance races have conditions that might read: "Allowance. Four-year-olds and upward which have not won two races of $21,500 in 1987–88." They are technically referred to as "classified allowance" races, but we will refer to them as "money" allowance races because of the importance of the money won by each horse in determining whether it is a contender.

Normally, a horse will race in win-restricted allowance races until it "runs out of conditions." The larger tracks offer allowance races for nonwinners of four allowance races.

The "money" allowance races at the major tracks attract horses of a wide range of class. There may be a superstar, coming off a layoff, looking forward to a major stakes race. The trainer is using this race as a tune-up. There may be a number of good quality stakes and allowance horses and even a couple of horses eligible to run in win-restricted races. When a race comes up like this, the best method is to treat it as if it were a stakes race. Go for the top-quality horses.

Quite often, those entered in "money" allowance races will not be of star quality. All of the horses may have won only allowance races. The class and consistency of these horses can be evaluated by dividing the number of races run in the current year by the total earnings for the year. (Take the past two years if the horse has run fewer than five races in the current year.)

The two horses with the top money figures are considered the horses to beat. Find these and then include as contenders those horses with the top speed ratings at the distance within the past thirty days.

Quite often, the two top money horses will also have the top speed ratings. One of these horses will win two thirds of the time. Naturally, horses with speed and class stand out, so the payoffs are low, but these solid favorites make good bets as long as the odds do not become so low that the race becomes one to watch.

To choose among the contenders, use your knowledge of pace. And since these races are almost always late in the program, you can also use what you have learned about track bias from the early races.

In many ways, these races are the most fun to handicap, since they usually include top-quality older horses which run gamely and in predictable manners. Following is my recommended method for money allowance races:

1. Rate the horses according to quality as if it were a stakes race. If all the horses seem to be in the same class, find the two horses with the best earnings-per-start ratio.
2. Include horses with the top speed ratings at the distance as you would for any other race.
3. Make your final selection on the basis of pace, jockey, and other positive factors.

Win-restricted allowance races are more like stakes races for three-year-olds. In the better races, there will be many horses that have been raced sparingly. There will usually be a few horses returning from layoffs, and there will probably not be a class standout. Since the horses have not won enough times, their class and consistency cannot be determined by an earnings-per-start ratio.

Workouts are more important in these races than in any other type of race, since these higher-quality horses are frequently brought to peak condition through morning exercises.

Sometimes a trainer has to put his horse through workouts because there are no races that fit his horse's entry conditions. At other times, the trainer will be aware that the horses his horse can't beat have recently won. Since they can no longer compete against his horse in a win-restricted allowance race, he will prime his horse for a top effort. The bullet work or a few works in two weeks are the signal that now the horse is well-meant. More allowance races are won by horses with good workouts than with any other single factor.

Therefore, choose the contenders in restricted allowance races if they show *two* of these factors:

1. One of the top-two speed ratings in the past thirty days.
2. A bullet workout or three works in two weeks.
3. A stakes race last time out—this may indicate a drop in class—with good back time.
4. A race within five points of the top speed rating with good back time.

E. TURF RACES

Races in the United States, unlike those in Europe, are run primarily over dirt tracks. In recent years, however, many of the major racetracks in the country have installed turf courses, and more and more horses are being trained to run on grass. If the occasional bettor is attending a large track, there is a good chance a selection will have to be made on at least one turf race.

This presents a special problem, since some horses run far better on grass than on dirt. Some trainers believe that it is the shape of a horse's hoofs that causes improvement on grass. Others believe certain horses have the kind of action that makes them dig in better on turf than on dirt. Still others feel that many horses dislike having dirt kicked into their faces; this doesn't happen on grass, and they do much better. Whatever the cause, there is no question that some horses improve on the grass.

If all the horses in the race have been running on the turf during the past month, you have no problem. You simply use the turf speed ratings and the class and condition factors presented in previous chapters.

However, you may well have to handicap a race where some or all of the horses have not been turf racing. This happens most often at the northern tracks where turf racing is abandoned during the winter and spring until the grass is ready to handle competition. At the beginning of the turf season there will be many races where you will have to compare the speed ratings of horses that have run recently on the turf with the ratings of horses that have been running on the dirt. Turf and dirt speed ratings, like ratings for different distances, cannot simply be measured against each other.

Many of the records set on turf courses have been set by horses that are not of the very highest caliber. Consequently, turf speed ratings are generally higher than dirt speed ratings for the same distance. (Remember that the speed rating is computed by subtracting one point from 100 for each one-fifth second a horse runs slower than the track record. A relatively slow track record will mean a high speed rating for most horses.)

To solve this problem you should operate as follows:

First, disregard any horse that has *never* run on the turf. Very few horses win their first turf outing against established competition. (The only exception to this rule is in some turf races for three-year-olds where most or all of the horses have never run on the turf. Obviously, most of the horses can't be eliminated, so all of the horses must be considered, using the method to be given.)

You will then be left with horses showing races on the turf at some time in the past, but not necessarily in the past thirty days. From these, select the horses with the top-two speed ratings made on the *dirt* at the distance in the past thirty days. Then, select the horses with the top-two speed ratings made on the *turf* at the distance in the past thirty days.

If the horse with the best speed rating at the distance on the turf at any time has not been included, it should be added to the list of contenders.

You then determine whether the horses with the top-two speed ratings on the dirt are capable of winning the turf race. If their best times for the distance on the turf are not as good as the best times the other contenders have run on the turf in the past thirty days, they should be eliminated. You are always safe in figuring a horse will not suddenly run better on the turf than it has ever done before.

If, however, a horse with one of the top-two speed ratings on the dirt has in fact run better on the turf than the horse with the best turf speed rating in the past thirty days, it may make a good bet if it is in condition. If it won its dirt race, or finished within two lengths of the winner, or showed any of the other things that indicate a horse in good shape (kept close to a fast pace, rallied, etc.), it must be considered ready to run a good race on the turf.

It is then grouped with the horses with the top-two speed ratings on the turf and the horse with the "best ever" on the turf, and a final choice is made on the basis of class, pace, and suitability as explained in previous chapters.

As I mentioned before, in a race for three-year-olds where few horses have shown turf experience, you will have to consider horses with top dirt times and no turf ratings as contenders. Either the trainer is throwing in a race to mask his horse's form, or he feels he has a horse in peak condition that is versatile enough to score on any surface.

If a horse with no turf experience shows a trainer move—such as a bullet workout, a race within six days or less, or claimed in its last race—it may well turn out to be your primary bet. A move like this indicates the trainer thinks his horse has a shot, and whenever we can, we should be guided by the moves of the professionals. Even a mediocre turf workout may be significant. If the horse showed little in the workout, why is the trainer still running him on the turf? The workout may have been better than it seems.

Briefly, these are the methods for selecting potential winners of turf races:

A. For races in which most horses have run on the turf:

1. Eliminate any horse that has never raced before on the turf unless it has a very strong trainer move such as returning to the races in six days or less. Then it should be played as a saver.

2. Make two groups of horses according to speed ratings run during the past thirty days. In the first group place the top-two horses with marks at the distance on turf, plus the horse with the best time ever on turf at the distance. In the second group place the horses with the top-two marks on dirt at the distance.

3. Eliminate the horses with the top-two dirt marks unless they show a turf race in the past with a speed rating for the distance as high as the top-two turf contenders.

4. Mark your final choice according to class, weight, pace, and other factors mentioned in previous chapters.

B. For races in which few horses have run on the turf:

1. Rate the horses as you would for any long race on the dirt.

2. Pay special attention to horses showing a trainer move (a race within six days or less, a bullet work, or any workout on the turf) indicating that he thinks he might have a grass winner.

F. JUMP RACES

Most gamblers refuse to even consider betting on hurdle and steeplechase races. They feel overcoming the normal obstacles in a race is hard enough without having their bets ride on horses that must make ten or more difficult jumps. Not only can a bad jump cause a horse to fall, spilling its rider and losing all chance, but a bobble on one of the jumps may be enough to cause a horse to lose the race since it takes valuable seconds to get it back in stride.

You probably do not have the caution of your professional racetrack colleagues. If you go to the track on one of the days a hurdle race is scheduled (some major tracks such as Monmouth Park schedule as many as two a week), you are not apt to pass up one of your chances to get some money down.

In your favor is a fact often overlooked by the pros: hurdle races show an amazing consistency, as evidenced by the fact that they have the highest percentage of winning favorites of all types of races.

If you choose to bet a hurdle race, therefore, one of the simplest and wisest bets is the favorite. Your chances of cashing a small winning ticket will be about one in two.

Favorites lose either because of a bad jump or because the public, swayed by a good last race, picked a horse of poor class. The bad breaks cannot be foreseen; the quality of the horse can. For this reason (and also because it's more fun), you should make some attempt to handicap hurdle races.

These long races are tests of endurance rather than speed. The simplest way to see if a horse has the endurance to win a long jump race is to see how it has finished in the past year in such races.

If a horse has never raced in a hurdle or steeplechase event before, ignore it. Very few horses win a jump race the first time out.

For each of the other horses, note how many jump races it has won and how many it has finished within ten lengths of the winner. You will have to find this information in the charts, since the *Form* doesn't give a summary of jump-race wins. Normally, the horse with the greatest number of jump-race wins should be the selection, since it has shown the greatest consistency in endurance and jumping ability.

However, the *class* of wins must be considered—a few close-up races against higher-class company are obviously more indicative of a quality horse than a few wins against cheaper company.

Two other indications of class should be used. One is the amount of money won during the previous and current years. If a large amount of money was won during the previous year, it can be safely assumed that this was won in jump races, since few trainers will risk a moneymaking horse over treacherous hurdles and obstacles.

Frequently, another indication of class can be seen in the weight the horse has been asked to carry in allowance and handicap races. The latter are especially indicative, since they give an expert racing handicapper's opinion of the horse. If a horse has been given high weights in previous handicaps and is now getting in lighter because of the conditions of the allowance race it is entered in, it frequently makes a good bet.

Comparative times are not very useful in judging the merits of jump horses. Quite often their previous races in jumping events have been at a different distance over different tracks. Even if two horses have covered the same distance, the time is not necessarily indicative of anything, since over such long distances a slightly slower or faster pace could mean the difference of seven or eight seconds.

More important than time is the manner in which a horse finished. Like a horse in a distance race on the flat, if a jumper gained ground in relation to the eventual winner, there is every reason to believe it is getting into winning form.

To sum up, then, the bettor selects a winner in a jump race by concentrating on endurance. You do this by finding which horse qualifies according to the following standards:

1. Most wins in jump races this year.
2. Most close-up finishes (within ten lengths) in jump races this year.
3. Highest weight assignments in previous allowance and handicap jump races.
4. Highest total money won in the past two years.
5. Best late gain in its last race.

If a horse qualifies on three of these five tests, it is likely to be the favorite. It is also likely to be the winner.

CHAPTER XII

In Case of Rain

When it starts to rain at a racetrack, many of the regular bettors fold up their form charts, put their pencils back in their pockets, and head for home. There are so many variables to consider in a horse race that adding one more, a track surface that may or may not be to a horse's liking, is simply too much.

The occasional bettor, out for a full day's racing enjoyment, is not likely to follow the lead of the more experienced racegoer. If he has planned to go to the races, he will endure the elements, and he will bet a full card whether it rains, snow, or blows up a hurricane!

Many professional gamblers will not bet if the track is even slightly "off." (Track ratings are fast, good, sloppy, and muddy. Occasionally, a track may be called slow or heavy.) There are too many horses that run either poorly or erratically on anything but a fast track.

And further complicating the matter, there are too many horses that improve in the mud. Some horses have hoofs which seem to be shaped to dig into off surfaces without slipping or sliding. On the other hand, some horses do poorly on rainy days even when shod with special mudshoes (mud caulks). These horses probably sulk when hit in the face with flying chunks of wet dirt and will not do their best in sloppy conditions.

One final reason for being cautious about betting when the track is not fast is that the track itself may not be as "off" in one part as it is in another. Some tracks dry out better and faster on the outside; others, for one reason or another, seem to be faster on the inside. Thus, the post position of a horse and the ability of its jockey to find the best route are two more factors which must be added to a list of problems that is already quite long.

Although many regular bettors do not bet when the track is off, there are a few system players who have evolved methods of betting on horses *only* on off tracks. These are not particularly useful for the occasional bettor, however, since they work well only in specific races, and quite often an entire race card must be passed because the conditions are not right for any horse to qualify for a bet.

What the occasional bettor needs on an off day is not a system but a reminder to use all the help the racing papers give him.

He can look at the horse's past performances and see how it has run when the track has been off. (Abbreviations for track conditions, such as "fst" for fast and "gd" for good, are placed just in front of the numbers indicating the distance.) The things to look for in these races, besides wins, are finishes within three lengths of a winner.

Another help given by the *Racing Form* is the ratings on the ability of horses to handle off tracks. After the horse's name may appear the symbols ∗, ×, or ⊗ indicating a fair, good, or superior mud runner, respectively. A horse with no symbol has not shown a particular preference for an off track. The classification is made largely on the basis of past performances, so most younger horses, which have not run often enough in the mud, do not have such ratings.

The kind of pace a horse usually runs is extremely important in estimating how the horse will finish on an off track.

A front-runner, for example, has a definite advantage. It has no mud lashing into its face, its jockey can choose whatever part of the track seems fastest, and its jockey may be able to pace the horse so that its opponents are unable to gain sufficiently in the stretch.

The come-from-behind horse is at a big disadvantage. If it lags too far behind on a very sloppy track, it will never be able to make the driving surge needed to come up on top.

But racing has no absolutes. I have been at the track on rare days when the mud seemed to be especially tiring for front-runners. In most, if not all of the races, the front-runners staggered in midstretch and the closers plodded by them.

The day after a heavy rain presents the most difficult of all track surfaces to "read." The track is neither muddy nor dry but is getting back to normal. It is almost impossible to predict which type of runner will have an advantage. In general, however, unless the early races show something unusual is going on, you should favor a front-runner over a closer on an off track.

A horse's workouts and its date of last race may also give you a tip as to the horse's real ability on an off track. At the large racetracks a trainer is not likely to bring a horse back to the races in less than seven days if he does not think it has a chance to win. Similarly, a horse that has obviously been sharpened to give a good effort by being worked three times in less than two weeks must be considered as a horse that is trying, since the trainer, aware of the track conditions, did not scratch it.

Finally, class is important in races over poor tracks. It seems to take more stamina and more heart to run in foul weather over a wet, mud-clinging surface. A horse with good performances in higher-class races may have a good chance, *if* it is in shape.

With this information noted in your *Racing Form*, the method for picking horses on tracks rated sloppy or worse is as follows:

1. Select the contenders in the same fashion as usual on the basis of speed ratings, class, and suitability.

2. Ask of each contender these qualifying questions:

   a. Does it have a good record in the mud?
   b. Does it have at least a fair mud mark?
   c. Is it a front-runner or presser?

3. If a horse gets a "yes" on one of the above, it continues to qualify as a contender.

A horse that has one or two poor off-track races in the past might stay as a contender if it shows the kind of trainer move that indicates the horse has definitely been aiming at this particular race. Since the trainer hasn't scratched his horse, he may think he still has a chance for the top prize. (He may also be keeping him in as a favor to the racing secretary—small fields are bad for business.)

The indications that the trainer may think he has found his spot despite the weather are:

   a. A return to the races in less than seven days.
   b. Three workouts in two weeks or less.
   c. A workout on an off track since the horse's last race.

4. Among the contenders, make your final choice on the basis of these criteria:

    a. Which horse has an advantage in pace?
    b. Which horse has an advantage in post position because the track favors the inside or outside?
    c. Which horse has been shod with mud caulks?

The answer to *a* can be found in the *Racing Form,* but how can you find the answers to *b* and *c?* To take the last first, most of the large tracks have a board indicating the kind of shoes a horse is wearing. The board is frequently located over the odds board, and the color designations it uses are explained in the program.

If you are alert during the first couple of races, you can learn whether the inside or outside of the track gives an advantage. Notice where the winning jockeys place their horses in the stretch. If they were on the rail, did they come out to the middle? If they were outside, did they go for the rail? Even more important, were there any horses on the rail or on the outside that did not run good races despite the fact they were proven mudders in shape? Answers to these questions are likely to tell you whether a bet on the rail or on the outside may be more risky.

A note on a track that changes during the course of an afternoon: because of rain during the races, tracks may worsen from fast all the way to muddy. Because the rain-soaked track from the previous day may drain and dry rapidly under a bright sun, a track may change during the afternoon from sloppy, slow, and good, to fast.

When the track is changing, how should you make your selection? In general, I have always felt that stewards are slow in changing their track ratings. Hence, if a heavy rain falls during the race, make your selections using the "off track" criteria outlined in this chapter, even if the track is officially listed as fast.

On the other hand, if you go to the track on a day following an afternoon of heavy rains, and the track is still listed as sloppy for the first race, despite the fact that excess water has drained off and the sun is shining, it is usually wise to ignore the official rating and make your selections on the basis of a fast track.

The same suggestion holds true when a track is listed as "good." If a track is officially "good" and the weather is clearing, make your selections for a fast track. If a track is officially "good" and the weather is getting worse, make your selections for a sloppy track, using the methods of this chapter.

PART THREE

BETTING TO MAKE A PROFIT

CHAPTER XIII

Profit or Loss

Having a profitable day at the track is not only a matter of selecting winners. The difference between a profit or a loss, once the elements of handicapping are mastered, lies in *how* you bet your money—how much you bet on a particular horse; whether you bet it to win, place, or show; whether you make "exotic" bets; and if you win, how much of your money you bet on the races that follow.

This can easily be seen if we imagine three horse players who begin with the same capital ($36) and who have the same three winners in nine races: a favorite that pays $5 to win, a fairly well-played horse that returns $10, and a longshot that comes in at $20. (Mutuel payoffs are always quoted in terms of $2 bets.)

At this stage, we will keep it simple. Our imaginary players will bet to *win* only, no exactas, no trifectas, no doubles.

Player *A* is the systematic sort who decides to bet the same amount ($4) on each race. His three winning wagers are therefore worth twice the amount listed on the pari-mutuel board: $10, $20, and $40 for a total of $70 gross. Since he bet a total of $36 on nine races, his profit is $34.

Player *B* knows that she will bet every race, but before she places her first bet, she attempts to decide which horses will make her *Best Bets* in terms of either their likelihood to win or their chances of paying a good price. She finds three horses she likes, and she decides to bet more of her capital on these. She proportions her money so that on six horses she bets only $2, but on her three Best Bets she wagers $8.

If Player *B* is lucky enough to guess right on all three of her winners, she will cash tickets worth $20, $40, and $80, which will give her a total profit of $104 when the $36 spent on tickets is subtracted.

If Player *B* guesses dreadfully wrong and her three Best Bets fail, while her three winners come up with only $2 on them, she will get returns of $5, $10, and $20 but end up *losing* $1 since her bets cost her $36 in all.

Player *C* also knows he will bet on every race, so he divides his money equally on all races. But he is out for a huge profit. He also selects three horses as Best Bets and decides to parlay them. If his first Best Bet wins he intends to put the whole wager and profit on the second Best Bet, and then bet this wager and profit on the third.

Let us suppose that Player *C* used his very best handicapping methods and came up with three winning Best Bets, the same horses players *A* and *B* won on. His $4 bet on the favorite returns $10. A couple of races later he bets this $10 on the longshot, his second Best Bet, and this 9–1 shot returns him $100. He then waits until his final parlay horse runs, bets $100 on it, and collects $500 at the window. His total profit is $472. (He bet only $28 of his capital, since he did not use the money he had planned for the second and third horses in his parlay.)

Let us give Player *C* just slightly less luck. We will still give him three winners, but unfortunately one of them was not among his Best Bets. Let us say his parlay on the favorite and longshot work, but then he loses the $100 on a poor choice. His 4–1 shot wins but he has only $4 on it, giving him a return of $20 and a *loss* of $8. (He bet $24 on six non-Best Bets and collected $20. He bet $4 to start his parlay, but lost that when his third race didn't click.)

Thus, with the same capital and the same winners, it is possible to show a profit of $34, a profit of $104, a loss of $1, a profit of $472, and a loss of $8. These are but five of the innumerable variations.

As many bettors have discovered, it is possible to have a losing day with five winners and a winning day with but one. If you consider the further variations of betting to place and show, it is clear that the chances for showing a profit or loss depend heavily on *how* you bet your selections, even if you ignore the much chancier exotic bets.

To know how to bet, you must understand the mathematics of betting. The next few chapters discuss the odds in special situations. You must know these in order to master the methods of betting needed to reach your goal.

CHAPTER XIV

The Mathematics of Betting

At most tracks it is possible to make eight different kinds of bets. You can bet that your horse wins, that it places (finishes first or second), or that it shows (finishes first, second, or third). You can also bet that you will be able to pick the winners of the first and second races (the daily double). A few tracks have added a "late double" in which you try to pick winners in two consecutive later races.

Over the past fifteen years, all tracks have offered "exotic" wagers on some or all of the races. These include exactas (or perfectas), in which you attempt to name in order the first and second horses to cross the finish line; quinellas, in which you call the first two finishers without regard to the order in which they finish; and trifectas, in which you try to predict the horses finishing one, two, and three.

In order to get huge payoffs (possibly to compete with the incredibly popular lotteries!), some tracks offer Pick Six (or Pick Nine!) betting in which the bettor attempts to select the winners of six (or nine) straight races. Assuming each race has eight horses, the mathematical odds of picking six straight are over 250,000 to 1. Consequently, on many days, no one "hits the six" and the pool is carried over to the next day. Sometimes these pools reach a million dollars or more.

The money bet in these various ways is placed in separate betting pools. The money bet on a horse to win, therefore, has no connection at all with the money bet on it to place. It is not unusual for one horse to be a favorite in the win pool and another horse to be a favorite in the place pool.

Before any money is given back to the lucky winners, a certain percentage is removed from the pool as profit for the track and taxes for the various levels of government. At most tracks this money, known as the "take," is at least 15 percent and sometimes as high as 25 percent. If, for example, $100,000 is wagered, $15,000 will be the take, and the amount forming the Net Pool (the money divided among the winners) will be $85,000.

The payoff in the win pool is calculated by dividing the total amount bet on the winning horse, say $10,000, into the Net Pool ($85,000). The result gives the return on each dollar bet, including the dollar wager, or $8.50 for each dollar. Now, since the smallest amount you can bet is $2, the mutuel board shows payoffs for $2 bets, which in this case would be $17. (Some tracks take $1 bets but the payoffs continue to be shown in the traditional amounts.)

The place pool is calculated in a different manner. The amount bet to place on the horses finishing first and second is subtracted from the Net Pool. What remains is the profit earned by the bettors of these horses. The profit is then split equally between the two groups of bettors. The profit for each group is then divided by the amount bet on it to determine the profit on each dollar. To this is added the dollar bet, and the result is the profit and wager in terms of dollar bets.

The show pool is calculated in the same manner as the place pool except the amounts bet on the *three* winning horses are subtracted from the Net Pool and the profit is divided into thirds before the profit on each horse is calculated.

In betting for place or show it makes no difference, as many new bettors mistakenly believe, where a horse finishes. It will pay the same price for show whether it finishes first, second, or third. A show bet is simply a bet that your horse will finish in one of the first three spots.

Exotic bets are paid off like win bets except the "take" is usually higher. In California, the take is 20 percent on all exotic bets, including doubles. In New York, the take is 17 percent for all bets except for trifectas, where 25 percent is removed before the winners divide the profits.

Once the take is out of an exacta bet, the amount bet on the horses finishing in the 1-2 order is removed and the payoff is calculated like a win bet. So in a California exacta pool of $100,000, if only $1,000 is bet on the winning exacta, the payoff would be about 80–1, or $160 for a $2 bet. (Seems low? You forgot to "take" that 20 percent off the top.)

BETTING TO PLACE

The man who goes to the track frequently and makes one or two solid bets each time will always profit more at the end of the season if he bets to win *only*.

If he bets to place he will make a few more trips to the cashier's window, but his annual profit will be less than if he ignored place betting and bet twice as much to win.

I say this even though I know of many bettors who play *only* to place and who, year in and year out, show a substantial annual profit. But their bets are carefully chosen and almost always involve heavy favorites where the difference in payoff between win and place is not worth the risk of betting to win.

For most bettors, the mathematics of pari-mutuel betting makes wagering to place inadvisable except at certain odds.

On a *win* bet, the pari-mutuel system allows those bettors who backed the *winner* to divide the amount bet on all of the losers.

This is not the case with place betting. Those backing horses finishing first or second divide the amount wagered on all horses not finishing first and second. At first glance this may seem reasonable, but as far as profit margins go, it overlooks two things.

First of all, the profit to place is almost always less than half and frequently about one third of the profit on a win bet. This is because the amount bet to place on the other horse finishing in the one or two spot must be removed before the profit is figured. The pie gets smaller before it can be cut up.

But even when this difference is a negligible amount, place betting is unprofitable over the long haul for a much stronger reason. Although the net payoff to place is almost always less than half of the net payoff to win, the mathematical odds of finishing second are not cut in half. In a twelve-horse race the winner must beat eleven horses. Mathematically, it has an 11–1 chance. To finish first or second, it must beat ten horses. Mathematically it has a 10–1 chance. Yet, it will pay off as if it had to beat only five horses.

In brief, then, the payoff for place is only as much as if your horse had to beat half the horses but one. For this reason, the long-term bettor is wise to avoid place betting except in special situations.

The occasional bettor, on the other hand, must bet to place more often. His season lasts only one day (despite the fact that he may be out again in a week), and his profit must be shown at the end of the day. There is nothing worse than reviewing a losing day in which a profit might have been made if one had "backed-up" a horse or two that had paid fair place prices.

Once the bettor has decided on a horse, he can make a judgment on whether it is worthwhile to bet it to win *and* to place. This can be done accurately if the track has a totalisator board, which lists the amount bet on each horse to place. The amount of profit will depend on which horse also finishes in the one-two spot. If the other horse has been lightly bet to place, the profit will be greater than if it had been heavily bet to place.

In order to make a reasonable decision, you should always assume that the horse with the most money on it for place according to the totalisator board will finish in the one-two spot with your horse. In that way, you will be calculating your minimum payoff.

If you use the method I have given on pages 121–122, you can actually calculate the minimum payoff price you will receive if your horse and any other horse finish in the first two places. This, of course, would be cumbersome and your estimates would be off somewhat because you would be calculating before the windows closed.

In the hectic minutes before a race goes off you will have far more important things to do than calculate place odds. A simple rule of thumb to follow is this: For horses going off between 4–1 and 10–1, the $2 payoff for place will be the same as the number on the board. For example, a horse going off at 5–1 to win will pay about $5 to place. A 9–1 shot would pay about $9 to place for a $2 bet.

The actual payoff will depend on the odds of the other horse finishing first or second and on the size of the field, but this rule of thumb will be sufficient for determining whether to put some money on your selection to place.

Place betting should be used in most cases as insurance. You want your place bet, in most cases, to cover the cost of your wager. Consequently, if you are betting a horse at 6–1 (or even 5–1 in a field with ten or more betting interests), you can usually expect a $6 place payoff, so *one third* of your wager should be made to place.

For example, if you are betting $12 on a race, and your horse is going off at 7–1, you should bet $8 to win and $4 to place. If it wins, you will get a good payoff ($64 to win and about $14 to place). If it loses but finishes second, you will recoup your bet.

If you are backing a horse at 10–1 or more, the prudent bet is to wager *half* of your bet to place (or as you will see later, to put it "underneath" horses in exacta bets).

BETTING TO SHOW

Betting only to show, especially on higher-odds horses, almost always ends up in a loss for the day. Many track newcomers think that if they bet conservatively they may not win much, but at least they will win. This is certainly true, but betting to show is not always betting conservatively; frequently, it is betting stupidly.

Remember that before the show pie gets sliced, the amounts bet to show on the horses finishing first, second, and third are removed. Since the favorite finishes in the money on the average of two out of every three races, the amount of profit left to be divided into three parts is usually small. Consequently, about one third of all show payoffs are less than $3, and almost 60 percent of show prices are less than $4.

In a twelve-horse race the simple mathematical odds against a horse finishing in the first three spots are 9–1. To work against these mathematical odds in an effort to get payoffs of less then even money is foolish.

Many people buy win-place-show combination tickets on all their horses on the theory that if their horse finishes second or third they will at least "get their money back."

This is not often true if the horse finishes third, and it is frequently false even if the horse places and its win odds are less than 6–1.

It is true that some of the money bet is refunded, but what about the extra losses when the horse runs out of the money? In the long run (and usually in the run of a day too), you will come out far ahead if you use the $6 for win tickets only. One winner at 5–1, with the extra $4 being multiplied on the win end, makes up for and probably surpasses all the place and show returns you would get during the course of an afternoon with your combination tickets.

It should go without saying that if you are betting a huge longshot (20–1 or more), a small insurance bet should be made to show. Mammoth payoffs light up the tote on occasion, but only on occasion. The chances are that on any single day *no* horse will win at odds of 20–1 or more. For example, if you went to Hollywood Park every Saturday and Sunday in June 1987, you would have seen win mutuels of $42 or more in only three of the 72 races (and two of these came on one day!).

However, on any single day the chances are that at least one 10–1 shot will finish in the money. It may very well be the one longshot you are playing that day, so a token bet to show (enough to get your money back) is worthwhile.

At 20–1 or more, therefore, if you are betting $12 on a race, bet $5 to win, $5 to place, and $2 to show. If you finish third, you will get most of your money back. If the favorite finishes out of the money, as it will about one third of the time, you will probably make a bit of a profit.

Although strictly betting to show will usually lead to a loss for the day, it is possible to have an exciting—and a *winning*—day at the track by betting show parlays. (More on this in Chapter XVII, Betting Horses in Combinations.)

CHAPTER XV

When to Bet Favorites

The races *can* be beaten. Year in and year out a small group of professional bettors make their living at the racetrack. Although a small part of this group consists of men who make their money by backing horses at extremely low odds, most successful bettors claim they finish in the black each year by waiting for the right horse *at the right price.* These men think nothing of waiting days for the right situation. Quite often they find the right horse, but they pass it by if the price is less than 4–1.

Most of these men could come up with a fairly high percentage of winners below these odds, but their profits would disappear as the inevitable losers ate up the smaller returns.

They know that no horse is ever certain to win. They know that if they bet every race they are bound to lose *most* of their bets. They conclude quite correctly that the way to profit is to severely restrict the number of bets, and then bet only above certain odds (usually 4–1, although some pros with high-percentage methods will bet heavily on lower-priced horses in certain situations).

The math is simple. By not betting any horse below 4–1, the minimum return on a hundred-dollar bet is $500 (including the money wagered). If a man wins but one of every four bets, his profit is a handsome 25 percent ($100 profit for each $400 wagered).

The occasional bettor is not, of course, in a position to practice such a waiting game. No one forces you to bet every race, but few can resist making some sort of wager on each race if they know their times at the track are few in number each season.

This means the occasional bettor cannot wait for the most profitable odds.

He must, if he attempts to get a winner in each race, be prepared to bet on a number of short-priced horses, since they win a large number of races.

If a racing card of nine races were to run as close to the average as possible, three of the races would be won by favorites. One of the favorites would be an odds-on choice, one would be a little better than even money, and the third winning favorite might pay a shade more than 2–1.

Three of the other races would be won by either the second or third choices in the betting, with prices of less than ten dollars. One race might be won by a longshot paying more than $20, and the final two races would have payoffs between $10 and $15.

Most days vary from the average. You are just as apt to find a day in which no favorites win (strings of ten or more losing favorites usually happen *twice* during every long racing season), as a day in which six out of nine races are won by favorites.

Since your day may be any kind of day, you must be prepared to bet the horse you think will win regardless of the price. The surest way to have a losing day, a way that is extremely common among occasional bettors, is to abandon your first choice in a race only because that horse is made the betting favorite.

The question is not whether you should bet favorites (you have to if you're betting every race and the favorite is your choice), but what makes a *solid* favorite. On the other hand, what kind of favorite makes a risky bet in view of the small rate of return?

The answers to these questions are in individual races, but general percentages are helpful as overall guides.

THE ODDS

Slightly more than one out of three races are won by favorites. This proportion includes the odds-on favorites (horses that return a profit of less than $1 for every $1 bet), which form about 40 percent of all winning favorites. Horses bet down to less than even money win roughly 60 percent of their races. (They finish in the money in about 90 percent of their races.)

A rule of thumb for you to remember is in the following table:

Favorite's Odds	Wins
Less than even money	2 out of 3 races
Even money to 2–1	1 out of 3 races
More than 2–1	1 out of 4 races

Incidentally, one of the spots not to overlook the favorite is in the last race. These favorites do not win more times than in other races, but they do pay slightly better prices (usually more than 2–1). The reason, as everyone who has ever been "behind" knows, is that the occasional bettor, in an effort to end the day with a profit, shuns the favorite for higher-priced horses. When these favorites are solid, they make good bets for those who are fortunate enough to be able to bet on them.

WEIGHT

Quite often a bettor will back off a favorite because he feels it's carrying too much weight in relation to the rest of the field. "Why should I risk two dollars to win three," he thinks, "when the horse is high weight? If the horse were going off at good odds, then the weight would be a risk worth taking, but not when the chance for profit is so low."

It has already been mentioned that weight is one of the most difficult factors to assess. In general, high weight is a negative factor, but it should never be the sole reason for getting off a favorite.

In claiming and allowance races, weight is usually assigned on the basis of wins during the past one to twelve months. In handicap races, the track secretary gives the highest weight to the horse with the most likely chance to win on the basis of past races. Consequently, the high-weighted horse is usually the horse with the best recent form and with high earnings.

Since good recent form is a factor in selecting a winner, it is not surprising that in those races where the high-weighted horse has at least two pounds more than any other horse, the high-weighted horse wins about 25 percent of the time. And if the high-weighted horse is a *favorite*, it wins almost 40 percent of the time, a percentage somewhat higher than for all favorites in general.

A study of the distances at which these high-weight favorites win reveals no particular pattern. Hence, another rule of thumb is: do not get off a favorite simply because it is high weight at any particular distance, sprint or route. These favorites win more than their share of races.

SIZE OF FIELD

Obviously, the chances of every horse in the race are increased when the field is small. Besides having fewer horses to beat, there is less chance of being blocked or having some other accident happen. It is not surprising that the percentage of winning favorites increases in small fields.

In races among seven horses or less, the favorite wins more than 40 percent of the time. In races with fields of ten horses or more, the favorite wins slightly less than 30 percent of the time.

You can be slightly more confident if you are backing a favorite in a small field. On the other hand, since a large number of favorites do win in big fields, you should not let the size of the field alone be the factor that gets you off the favorite.

Much more important than the number of horses running against the favorite is their quality. It is not how many are in the race, but how many seem to have a predictable chance to beat the favorite that you must consider.

COMING OFF A WIN

In addition to getting his horse into conditioin, the trainer is responsible for placing it in the best possible spot. Sometimes, this means racing it with better horses until it is ready to win. After it wins, the best possible spot is usually determined by the conditions set down for various races. As a winner of its last, the horse frequently stands out and is made a favorite. How often do these horses win?

In "money" allowance races specifically for horses that have not won *two purses* of a certain amount in the past month or two, a recent winner is often made the favorite. These horses also win at a rate somewhat better than usual for favorites, hitting the winner's circle about 55 percent of the time.

Allowance races that restrict horses according to the number of races won also show a better-than-average number of repeat winning favorites. About 42 percent of horses that have won their last race *and* have been made the favorite in the next higher set of conditions reach the winner's circle.

When horses break their maidens in claiming races, they are sometimes made favorites in open claiming company. As favorites, they do poorly, winning only 22 percent of the time. On the other hand, experienced claimers going for two in a row do fairly well as favorites, winning about 40 percent of the times they become the choice of the public.

Only about 16 percent of all horses win after having won their last race. Yet, when a horse going for a repeat win is made a favorite, it wins somewhat over 40 percent of the time. Except in those races where a horse has just captured its maiden win, you should not get off a favorite looking for two in a row simply because the percentage of repeaters in general is low.

TYPE OF RACE

There is only an insignificant variation in the percentage of winning favorites for stakes races, allowance races, and claiming races. Some of the races for better horses may seem to have more favorites winning, since many of these races have comparatively low payoffs. In these races, a comparatively higher percentage of well-bet second and third choices win, giving the impression of a higher percentage of winning favorites, but actually the overall percentage is no higher than in races for cheaper horses.

What about races in which there seems to be a large number of big payoffs—two-year-old races and maiden claiming races?

Two-year-old favorites frequently lose because they are beaten by rapidly improving horses or first-starters. In all classes of races for two-year-olds, the percentage of winning favorites is less than for older horses. The most secure type of two-year-old favorite runs in the better class of races: maiden special weights and allowances, where they win about 30 percent of the time, or only a little less than the average for all horses. On the other hand, favorites in two-year-old maiden-claiming races win only 20 percent of the time. These horses account for the poor showing of two-year-old favorites in general.

Three-year-old maiden races show a better-than-average winning percentage for favorites. The caliber of horses that have been winless as two-year-olds and have still failed to win at three is generally low. Frequently, however, one of these horses stands out as better than the rest. As favorites, they win better than 40 percent of the time. You should never get off the favorite in these races simply because most of these winless horses are unreliable.

SPEED RATINGS

Speed ratings at the distance have been stressed as a primary tool of the bettor who wins. More than any other device, speed ratings can tell you if you are backing a solid favorite.

In those races where the favorite has either the top speed rating or the second highest, the favorite wins about 44 percent of the time. This compares very favorably with the 34 percent for all winning favorites.

Now, horses are made favorites for many reasons other than speed ratings.

Sometimes it is the horse's good showing in its last race. Sometimes a horse of superior class will be made the favorite. At other times the action of the odds board itself determines the "chalk" horse. When a horse takes a big drop in odds there is usually a scurrying for the windows as thousands of fans try to "get on the hot horse."

But when a horse is made a favorite and it is *not* in the top-two speed ratings at the distance in the past thirty days, it wins only 22 percent of the time. Or putting it another way, favorites that are either first or second in the speed ratings win about twice as often as those that are not.

Even more significant, in *sprint* races where a favorite is *not* among the top two in the speed ratings, it is beaten by one of the horses with either of the two highest speed ratings at the distance in the past thirty days about 45 percent of the time!

Quite often so much attention is given the favorite that the speed horses are overlooked completely and pay excellent prices. This happens especially in allowance races when a class horse is returning to the races after a rest. The public almost invariably bets these horses down. And yet, as every trainer knows, only the very best horses can win their first time out after a break in training, unless the caliber of the field is quite low.

When a class horse that hasn't raced in a while becomes the favorite, you are in a position to cash a good-sized ticket by placing your money on one (and, if the odds are right, both) of the horses with the highest speed rating at the distance in the past thirty days.

By avoiding the favorite that does not have one of the top-two speed ratings, you can save money four out of five times. But how can you avoid the losing favorites that *are* among the top two in speed ratings? How can you tell if a high speed-rating horse is a solid favorite?

One way is to compare its speed rating in the past month with the best time it has ever run the distance. Very few horses consistently run a distance in the same time. Their ratings vary considerably as they attain and lose sharpness. You should always look for the horse that is *going* to run its top race; you should avoid the horse that has turned in its high rating and is now going to descend the form cycle.

If a horse has run the distance at a higher speed rating in the past and it is currently in the top-two horses for the past thirty days, you have every reason to believe the horse has not peaked. Such horses make excellent bets. Very often they are made favorites, and they should be, because as favorites they win almost 60 percent of the time.

On the other hand, those horses that are in the top two in speed ratings for the past thirty days and are then bet down to favorites but have *never* raced in faster time win only 35 percent of the time, or only a little better than the average for all favorites.

Another kind of horse that is bet down is one that shows a large difference in speed rating from the next highest horse. By a large difference I mean three points or more. Three points may seem rather small, but when you think that one point is equivalent to a length, three points is considerable. If the horses run a race equivalent to their very best during the month, the top speed-rating horse would win by three full lengths. Most races are not won by that wide a margin.

The horse with a speed rating more than three points higher than its nearest competitor makes a good bet, and since its speed rating is so prominent, it is usually made the favorite. As favorites, these horses have a good record, winning somewhat more than 60 percent of the time.

They make risky bets as favorites, however, when they are moving up in class or, even more significant, when they are advancing from maiden races to races for horses that have won at least one race.

In a maiden race or a race of lower class, a horse may be able to set a high speed because no other horse effectively challenges it during the running of the race. When it is moved up in class, it very often is not allowed to run its best race because of the increased staying power of higher-class horses.

In such a situation, you can often cash a good-sized ticket on one of the horses in the next two speed-rating spots if they have been running in higher-class races than the favorite.

In general, however, in *sprint* races speed ratings are good indications of a winning favorite as shown in this table:

If the Favorite Is the Horse with	It Wins
One of the top-two speed ratings but *never* faster	35%
One of the top two, but with a higher "best ever"	60%
The highest speed rating, which is at least three points higher than the next highest	60%

Since speed ratings are so important in sprint races, what kind of horses beat the favorites when the favorites have the top speed ratings?

I have said that a favorite that has one of the top-two speed ratings at the distance in the past thirty days will be beaten about eleven times in twenty. (The figure is only eight in twenty if the horse has run faster in the past. I am concerned now with *all* favorites that have one of the top-two speed ratings.)

Of these eleven races, the *other* horse that has one of the top-two ratings will win about four times. A horse that is not in the top-two speed ratings but distinguished mainly because it is a horse of superior class, according to the methods of Chapter V, will beat the favorite in three of these eleven races.

A horse not in the top-two speed ratings during the month but with a speed rating at the distance some time in the past equal to one of the top-two ratings, *and* a speed rating in the past month that is not less than four points below the top-two ratings, will win another three races out of the eleven in which the favorite is beaten.

These figures are more easily seen in a table:

WINNERS OF EVERY TWENTY SPRINT RACES IN WHICH FAVORITES ARE EITHER FIRST OR SECOND IN SPEED RATINGS

Won by favorites	9	(45%)
Won by other horse in top two	4	(20%)
Won by class horse	3	(15%)
Won by horse not more than four points below top two that has run as fast as either in past	3	(15%)
Won by some other horse	1	(5%)

Now, in every race there is a horse that shows some class and a horse or two that have run faster in the past than the top-two speed horses. If your horse is bet down to be favorite, and you are betting it because it has one of the top-two speed ratings, should you get off it and back one of the other horses?

In general, the answer is no, *unless* the horse that may beat the favorite qualifies for other reasons. Horses that beat favorites because of their class or past speed usually show themselves in other ways. Sometimes it is by combining both of the factors mentioned—that is, they not only are dropping in class from a last race or a win, but also have run faster than the speed horse favorite in the past.

Quite often, they show something that will indicate a good race coming up: closely spaced workouts, races in much better class to get in shape, or a good rally last time out. They show so much, in fact, that if you have handicapped correctly you will have chosen them instead of the favorite that happens to be one of the top-two speed horses.

SUMMARY—WHEN TO PLAY FAVORITES

Favorites should never be played simply because they are favorites. On the other hand, if your selection is bet down to the role of favorite, do not greedily switch to another horse on the outside chance that it may beat the favorite and pay more money. This is usually folly, since on the day you go to the track you can expect about three favorites to win.

The solid favorite, one that should never be bet *against,* is one that shows a number of positive factors such as:

1. It has a substantially better speed rating at the distance in the past thirty days than any other horse.
2. It is the class horse in the race.
3. It has raced even faster in the past.
4. It is meeting horses that have never run as fast as it has in the past thirty days.

Most favorites do not show all four factors. A good favorite, one that is worth a bet, will have one of the top-two speed ratings for the month and at least one other factor.

If for reasons of speed, class, and conditions you have singled out a horse and it has been made the favorite, one of the following is *not* a good reason for switching your bet:

1. It is the high weight of the field.
2. It is in a very large field.
3. It is looking for two wins in a row.
4. It is in a cheap race.

The risky favorites are the ones that show one of these factors:

1. It is not one of the horses that has one of the top-two speed ratings for the month at the distance. (Remember, these favorites lose almost 80 percent of the time.)
2. It has one of the top-two speed ratings, but one or more horses have run faster than this rating in the past, and the selected horse has never done better. The bet is especially risky when, in the past thirty days, one of the horses that has done better in the past has run within four speed-rating points of the top-two horses.
3. It has one of the top-two speed ratings, but a horse of superior class is competing against it and the class horse has factors such as good workouts showing it is ready.
4. It has one of the top-two speed ratings for the month, but the race in which it showed its speed was against inferior horses in terms of class or racing conditions.
5. It is coming off a maiden victory meeting horses that have won more than once or that have been trying for two victories for some time.
6. It is bucking the percentages in age and sex: a three-year-old against older horses; a female against male horses.

In almost all cases you will come out in better financial shape for the day if you get off favorites that exhibit one of these six points. Although favorites win three races a day on the average, they lose the rest, and it is the favorites that exhibit one of the six points above that account for most of the losses by favorites.

If you have no strong second choice, it may be time to hunt for a longshot.

CHAPTER XVI

When to Bet Longshots

There are many ways to assure yourself of leaving a racetrack broke. One of these is to play longshots simply because they will pay more than 10–1. On any day you might go to the races, the chances are that only *one* horse will pay more than $20. To bet longshots in each race against a percentage like that is to court disaster.

Of course, longshots *do* come in. And as I have said, very few longshots are complete surprises. Some regular bettors can make money playing longshots, but they can do it only if they pass up race after race waiting for the right spot. Even then, they have to ride out strings of losers.

The occasional bettor cannot do this. Still, during an afternoon it is often necessary, and always thrilling, to make a bet on a horse that will pay off in large figures. This should be done only in those races where picking a winner is difficult because the logical choices all have knocks against them, or because the horse you gave a slight edge to has been bet down to become a risky favorite according to the factors on page 135, and you have no clear second choice.

In choosing a longshot you will have to risk a bet on a horse that also has some knocks against it. If it had none, it would be the favorite. Generally, the knocks against a horse revolve around poor recent form or poor class relative to the other horses. If a horse suffers from both of these, forget it. These are the longshots that almost never win.

But if a horse with poor recent form has shown some speed and class in the past, it may make a good bet. Similarly, if a horse with good form is making what seems to be a rise in class, it may be the kind of sleeper that pays off at lip-smacking odds.

Good recent form means, among other things, winning or finishing close up in one of its last two races. I mention this because it is surprising how many longshots have won their next-to-last race! The fans evidently discount such winning efforts as being against poor company or simply the result of good luck. And this judgment seems to be confirmed by a poor race last time out. Once in a while, you should throw out the miserable last race and play the longshot who won two-back.

Good recent form also includes, for the front-runner, a longer stay in the lead before tiring, and for the come-from-behind horse, a good late surge. Quite often these are overlooked by fans who interest themselves only in where a horse finished and by how many lengths it was beaten.

Another indication of sharpness is in workouts. It cannot be stressed too often that if a trainer works out a horse three times in two weeks, and the horse has been in competition, the trainer is usually going to try to win with the horse as soon after these works as possible. If, prior to the workouts, the horse gave some indication of improved form either by longer staying power on the front end or by a good late close, there is a good chance the trainer has been saving the horse for a spot where he can get a longshot price.

Thus, the first thing to look for in a possible longshot winner is a combination of good (but deceiving) form and workouts to increase or hold sharpness.

Many longshot winners are overlooked by the bettors because they have been competing on smaller tracks and are running for the first time on larger ovals. If a horse has *won* at a smaller track and is not running against a strong field, it may be well-meant at a long price.

Many bettors spot the horse that turns out to be the winning longshot but do not bet it because it has been soundly beaten by the favorite.

Picking horses, or discarding them, strictly on the basis of how they have done against other horses in the race is a poor method of selecting. It is to forget a fundamental fact that has been continually stressed: horses are not machines. They cannot always be expected to run their best. They go through cycles of improvement and cycles of decline. When a horse is at its worst, it can be whipped by all kinds of inferior animals. Furthermore, horses are not always asked to run their best.

Consequently, a horse that is worthy enough to bet on the basis of other factors should never be passed over because one or another of the horses in the race under consideration has beaten it.

This is especially true for two- and three-year-old horses where improvement is often rapid. With younger horses the wise bettor constantly looks for the horse showing the greatest chance for an improved race. Sometimes this will mean betting a horse that is made a longshot because it was beaten badly its last time out by a few of the horses it is competing against.

Many of these young horses, and also first-starters, show their ability to win at high prices by their workouts. It should be remembered that to be good a workout does not have to be extremely fast. What to spot is a horse that seems to be working out in average time but with the indication "b" for breezing after it. This means the horse has worked well without being urged. Under exertion there is no telling how fast it might run.

Quite often a horse becomes a longshot simply because its *last* race was poor. Last races are significant, but they must be looked at carefully. The horse may have lost because it moved up slightly in class, it may have met better horses within the same class bracket, or it may have had some excuse that did not appear in the charts.

These horses can often be spotted by their odds and finishes in their last *two* races. If a horse ran well in its next-to-last outing, you would expect its odds to drop in its next race. But if its odds went *up* in that race, it indicates it was meeting better horses. Quite often after a poor finish in its last, such a horse will be completely overlooked by the bettors and will win at fancy odds if it is meeting its own kind.

You should never begin your handicapping of a race by looking for a longshot. You should never let the odds board convince you that a longshot has a chance. *After* handicapping, you bet a horse to win either because of its odds or despite its odds.

To take the second case first, you bet a longshot because you disagree with the majority of fans who are overlooking your horse in their eagerness to play a flashy but risky favorite. Your selection just happens to be a longshot, and if it has enough going for it, you may even think of making it your key bet of the day.

In other races, you bet a longshot because you may not be able to make a choice among many evenly matched horses. In this kind of race anything can happen. This doesn't mean you automatically choose the contender that will pay the highest price. Instead, you examine the contenders for the factors shown by most longshots.

There are two kinds of factors to look for. You search first for the horse that shows the kind of improved *form* that is overlooked by many of the fans:

1. If a horse is a front-runner that quit badly in its last race, did it run a very hot pace before it tired?
2. If a horse is a closer, did it make the kind of late gain that saw it make up many lengths but still be outrun badly? This kind of horse frequently wins at high odds because the jockey will get it in stride earlier.
3. Did the horse have a win, or a near miss, in its next-to-last race and then go off at higher odds in its last race? This indicates it ran poorly because it was running against better horses.
4. If the horse is a two-year-old, whether first-time starter or not, did it post a good *breezing* workout of four furlongs or more in the past ten days?

You should also look for a horse that has shown some glimmer of *class* in the past as indicated by one of these:

1. A speed rating at the distance close to that of the top rating in the race.
2. A finish within five lengths of the winner at a considerably higher-class claiming price or an allowance race against good horses.
3. A win at a higher-class claiming price.

If an "improving-form" longshot and a "higher-class" longshot are both in the race, choose the "improving-form" one. You are betting the class horse on the hope that it wakes up. The other, more solid bet is on a horse that has already awakened.

Remember that a horse going off at odds of 10–1 or more should always be backed up for place. After having shrewdly picked a huge longshot, there is nothing worse than watching it get nipped at the wire and pay double figures for second, knowing that you don't have even a single place ticket in your pocket.

CHAPTER XVII

Betting Horses in Combinations

Only those who lead extremely holy lives can expect to make a decent profit in their day at the track if they bet the same amount on each horse. A person who expects to play $2 a race, for example, needs a longshot at whopping odds (20–1) or six winners at low odds in order to make $20 to $25. Both of these things are possible; neither is likely.

Considering all the reasons why a well-selected horse can lose, you should realistically hope for not more than three winners on any particular day. The straight bettor, with three winners at moderate odds, probably does little more than break even. In order to make a decent profit, you must bet your horses in some kind of combination, or you will not reach your goal for the day.

You can also try to increase your profits by making exotic bets (exactas, quinellas, etc.), but that risky business requires a separate chapter. For the moment, let us concentrate on how to combine the profits made from *win* bets.

Although there are many methods of combination play, essentially they fall into three categories: Best Bets, parlays, and profit-spreading methods.

BEST BETS

Prior to the beginning of the day's program you select two or three horses as your Best Bets of the day. You not only plan to bet more on these horses than on the others, but plan to "if" some or all of the profits you have at any one point on them.

This may seem obvious, but few occasional bettors make such plans. They begin by betting what for them is a standard amount, say $5. If they win, they almost inevitably increase their bets on the next couple of races without considering whether their selections deserve an increased bet.

They are "hot," they think, but their money is usually quickly gobbled up by the cool betting machines. It cannot be stressed enough that a winning day is normally the product of *planning*. Part of this planning involves the selection of Best Bets on which more money (either capital or prior winnings) is to be bet.

How much more should you bet? This depends entirely on your goal. Let us say you are willing to lose $30 on a nine-race card in an effort to make a profit of $100. You plan to bet $6 each on three key horses and $2 each ($12 total) on the other six races. Although you are always ready to be surprised, you assume this $12 is a loss.

Since you are risking $30, your Best Bets have to gross $130 in order to make a $100 profit. Let us say your first key horse comes in at 4–1 odds. Your $6 investment returns a profit of $24. How much should you bet when your next key horse comes up? The answer is, enough to reach your goal, but not more than half of your Best Bet pool.

You began with $18 in your Best Bet pool. It is now up to $42. Your maximum bet should be $21, the other $21 to be saved for your next key bet. If your second Best Bet wins at odds of 3–1, your $21 bet will bring back a profit of $63 and your Best Bet pool will be up to $105.

On your last bet, you wager only enough to bring your gross up to the required $130. If it goes off at 2–1, for example, your bet would be $12.

If one of your $2 bets happens to come in while you are waiting to make a Best Bet, this naturally is added to your Best Bet pool, lowering the amount you will have to bet in order to make your $130 gross.

The Best Bet method is perhaps the most efficient of all the combination methods. It forces you to select races worthy of larger bets, and it keeps your mind on your goal, preventing a big loss in profits on horses that don't deserve more than token bets.

PARLAYS

Win parlays also require you to pick a number of Best Bets before the races begin, but here you plan to collect your first bet and bet the entire return on another race and then, possibly, on a third, etc. Win parlays pay off at astronomical odds (a three-horse parlay, beginning with $2, on horses averaging $12 payoffs, will result in a profit of $430. But win parlays are extremely risky.

The mathematical odds of randomly picking three straight winners in three races that have eight-horse fields are 343–1.

Parlays can, of course, be made from place and show bets. We have already noted that betting every race to show will almost always result in a loss for the day. But for a bettor who is really out for a day of fun and who would be unhappy losing more than a small amount of money, *show parlays* can be an excellent way to have an enjoyable day at the track with little risk and with a chance to pay all expenses and make a small profit.

The manner in which a show parlay can build up capital can be seen if we compare a straight show-betting day with a day in which a show parlay was planned.

Player A bets $8 to show on each of the nine races offered that day. He collects on six races with an average mutuel show price of $3 (a $12 return for the $8 bet). On his six winning races he collects $72, but he has bet $72 for the day so he breaks even and still has to pay expenses. If he cashes seven tickets (a total of $84), he will profit $12. Eight out of nine winning bets will net $24, and if he sweeps the card, he will make a $36 profit (bet $72, collected $108).

Player B knows that the chances of going nine for nine even when playing for third are slim indeed. It can, however, happen—once or twice a month the *Racing Form* Consensus or a newspaper handicapper will have every first choice finish no worse than third. But in the unlikely event that all of Player B's horses run well on the day he ventures to the track, he would like to be rewarded with a little more than a 50 percent profit on his potential investment ($72 for nine races).

A show parlay beginning with $8 and winning nine races where the payoff is $3 will result in a profit of almost $300. If two $4 payoffs are placed anywhere in the string, the profit will be a whopping $500 for the $8 investment.

But player B is aware of two things. There is an enormous probability that his string will be broken. In fact, even if he bets the favorite, there is one chance in three that he will lose the very first race! He also knows that he is betting a show parlay because he isn't the type to risk large sums on any one race. But if he gets hot, after the fifth race his bet will be $60. To complete the parlay in the ninth race he will have to bet $202.

He knows he will not be smiling if he goes that far and loses. So he decides to be riskier than Player A, but he will not recklessly run all of his profits through the machines. Instead he will try for only three in a row. He will plan on using a beginning capital of $32. This will allow him to start the parlay a total of four times, if he fails to win three in a row. If his horses run very poorly—let us say he loses the first four races—he will use the other $40 he brought to the track, only now his initial bet will be $10. If he loses four more consecutive races—eight races in a row without even one of his choices finishing third!—it's time to go home.

Let us give Player B a day more in line with his good selecting skills. He starts off well by hitting the first three races. His $8 bet has grown to $27 (at a $3 mutuel price, his first $8 becomes $12, that $12 bet returns $18, and the final $18 bet returns $27).

This $19 profit raises his capital to $51. All of his succeeding bets will be one-third of whatever his capital is at the time.

His fourth-race bet will be $17 (one third of $51). If he wins, the $3 payoff will give him a return of $25.50 and his capital will be just shy of $60. His next bet will be $20.

If he loses the fourth race, his capital will be down to $34 and his bet will only be $12 (approximately one third of $34). His bets decrease because he doesn't want to be wiped out by four losers in a row.

Player B gets very lucky. He hits nine-for-nine. Using his conservative method, his capital will have grown to $127, for a profit of $95 when the $32 he planned to risk is removed—and he's also had an afternoon of fun.

The straight show bettor who goes only five-for-nine wagering $8 a race and getting back $3 mutuels will lose $12. The modified parlay bettor will lose about the same, depending on which races he loses. With six winners, he will probably do a little better than the straight wagerer, and he will be far ahead if he has seven or eight winners.

Show parlays are fun, and they can be profitable. A good spot to begin a parlay is the last three or four races. If you are out for the day with three friends, and each of you contributes $5, and you play a horse that finishes in the money in each of the last four races, your original $20 investment will grow to almost $100 if the show payoffs are a moderate $3. That should at least handle the bar bill no matter what restaurant you go to after your day at the track.

A last word on betting to show—remember that you are picking your *best* horse. You never pick a horse because it *might* show; you pick it to win and bet it to show under the assumption that two horses you ruled out might get lucky or be in better condition than the charts indicate.

If the selection principles in the previous sections of this book are followed, strings of four to seven show bets will not be unusual.

ROUND ROBINS

A parlay is a method of betting in which the profit and wager from one bet are placed on another horse. A *round robin* is a series of parlays. In a three-horse parlay all three must win or you lose your money. In a three-horse round robin you make a profit if two out of three win.

It works this way. If you are a $2 bettor, you begin by betting $4 on Horse A—half of this is for a parlay with Horse B, and half for a parlay with Horse C in a later race.

If Horse A wins, you bet half the profit and wager on Horse B. You also add $2 so that you can parlay Horse B and Horse C. If Horse B wins, you pocket the amount won on the A–B parlay. You then bet that half of the money you had saved from your first winning bet on Horse A to form the A–C parlay. You also bet the profit and wager from the $2 added to the Horse B bet to form your B–C parlay.

Your three-horse round robin is therefore a series of three $2 parlays: Horse A and Horse B, Horse A and Horse C, and Horse B and Horse C.

It is also possible to make round robins out of more than three horses. The investment rises sharply as the number of horses in the round robin increases. The table below shows the cost of a six-horse round robin:

Horse	$2 Parlays with Horses	Cost
A	B, C, D, E, F	$10
B	C, D, E, F	8
C	D, E, F	6
D	E, F	4
E	F	2
		$30

To figure out the amount any particular $2 round robin would cost, simply multiply the number of horses in the round robin by one less than that number. A seven-horse round robin costs $42 (7 × 6), for example.

To figure out how much your initial bet should be, multiply $2 by one less than the number of horses in the round robin. To begin a seven-horse round robin, you would bet $12 ($2 × 6) on the first horse.

Round robins can be bet for any amount. Figure out how much a $2 round robin would cost. Then multiply this by $2 units. For example, a five-horse $2 round robin costs $20. If you are a $10 bettor, it will cost you five times as much, or $100.

Except in Las Vegas casinos (and with those bookmakers who still take turf wagering), where people bet a few horses in combination because they will not be present for the actual running of the races, round robin betting is not common. But the concept of making a series of two-horse parlays is worth knowing.

If, prior to the first race, you have selected three or four Best Bets, you should plan on betting more on these races. One way of doing this is to bet even more on the first of these Best Bets so that a parlay (or some fraction of your winnings) can be wagered on your other Best Bets.

An example of an actual day at the track will show you the amounts that can be won betting round robins.

Let us say you were at Aqueduct on Saturday, March 19, 1988, and you thought highly of the chances of Well Proven in the second race, Hayes Hope in the third, and Afleet in the feature.

These horses were chosen as examples for two reasons. First, their payoffs were fairly low. Even with low returns on each bet, round robins can produce a healthy overall profit. Higher-priced horses will naturally result in much higher profits. Second, they were all clear Best Bets. The first two combined top recent times with far superior back times. Afleet had earnings per start that were almost triple its nearest competitor and was returning to the races with three bullet works.

To play a $2 round robin on these horses you first bet $4 on Well Proven. It wins at $8.60 and you collect $17.20.

You then parlay half your return (say $9) on Hayes Hope, saving the other $8 for a parlay with Afleet. You also bet another $2 so that you can have a parlay on Hayes Hope and Afleet.

Hayes Hope wins by four lengths and pays $8.60, the same price as your previous winner. You collect $47.30 for your $11 bet. Of this amount, $39 is removed as the proceeds from your first parlay.

The other $8 plus the $8 saved from your first bet is placed on Afleet, which wins at $5, giving a return of $40.

The gross return is $79. The profit on this $6 investment is $73. A $10 round robin ($30 investment) would result in a profit of $365.

How does the round robin compare with the other ways of betting these horses? A $2 straight bet on each horse would net a profit of only $16.20. A $2 win parlay would return $95.

Very few people have the stomach to bet three-horse win parlays. It takes considerable nerve to place your whole profit from a successful two-horse parlay on a third horse. For this reason, many people prefer three-horse round robins, although the investment is greater ($6 instead of $2) and the return is less. But the risk is less, too, since if one horse loses you still make a profit.

In the above example, if either Well Proven or Hayes Hope had lost, the profit would have been $14 (about double the $7.60 you would have profited with straight win bets on your two winners). If Afleet had lost, the profit would have been $33 (the $39 you removed minus the $6 investment).

Again, these are comparatively low-priced horses. If Kiawatha, a chancier Best Bet but still the *only* horse in the seventh race with a bullet, is substituted for Afleet, its $19.40 payoff would result in a $188 profit for this $2 round robin. If Kiawatha and only one of the other two horses had won, the profit still would have been $70.

Round robin bettors know that if they win only one of their parlayed races they will lose their entire investment. Still, if you develop a knack for spotting the type of horse that has a high win percentage (even if at low odds), round robin betting may be just the thing for your day at the track.

PROFIT SPREADING

Many people find that their heavily parlayed Best Bets have a way of running into bad luck, while those horses on which they have only a token bet seem to come in. Although they win three races, they still leave the track losing money.

Of course, a nine-horse round robin would prevent this, but its high cost ($72 for the $2 bettor) usually makes this unpalatable. Besides, if you begin with a few losers, you *seem* to be very far behind. With a nine-horse round robin, for example, if you lose the first three races you have spent $42. Knowing you have to win three out of the next six races in order to make a profit, it is difficult not to begin betting emotionally.

Rather than starting with large bets, many people are more comfortable waiting until they have a winner before they increase the size of their bets. Once they have a hit, they rely on a mechanical system to spread the profit instead of saving it for a Best Bet.

In the long run, the Best Bet method is superior, but I am including a mechanical method for those bettors who have difficulty discerning Best Bets, and also for use on those days when nothing on the card stands out.

Before I describe the mechanical method I have found to be most productive, I must explain what's wrong with mechanical systems in general. They must be compared with the simplest mechanical system of all, betting the same amount on each race whether you win or lose.

Obviously, if you make the same bet on each race and have only one winner, you will end the day in a better situation than if you wasted the profits on this race on your other losers.

What is not so clear is that if you have two winners you almost always come out better making straight bets than if you followed a mechanical profit-spreading system. Sometimes even three winners when bet straight are more productive than when some of your profits are mechanically spread.

If this seems strange, remember that you not only win more by having more money on your winners, you *lose* more by wasting profits on your losing bets.

It is not so much the number of winners but how they are spread that counts.

For example, let us say you bet $4 on each of the nine races, and you pick the winners of the first, fourth, and seventh races at the good prices of $12 each (for each $2 wager). You collect $24 on each of these races for a total gross of $72. When your nine-race investment of $36 is removed, your profit is $36. You have doubled your money making flat bets.

Now, let us say you use one of the popular mechanical methods which involves making the same flat bet on each race until you get a winner. Then you spread the entire return over the remaining races. When you get a second winner, you spread *half* the return over your remaining bets.

Using this system your first bet would be $4. You win the first race and you happily divide your return of $24 over each of the remaining eight bets, so that $3 is added to your standard $4 bet. When you click in the fourth race your return for $7 is $42. You take half this return (say $20) and divide it among the remaining five races so that your remaining bets will be $11. You hit the seventh race all right, but the money lost on the eighth and ninth races so reduces your profits that you make less than you would by straight betting. The following betting chart makes this clear.

STRAIGHT $4 FLAT BETS

Bet	Return	Profit
$36	$72	$36

SPREAD ALL, THEN HALF

Race	Bet	Return	Amount Added to Each Race
1	$ 4	$ 24	$ 3
2	7	—	—
3	7	—	—
4	7	42	4
5	11	—	—
6	11	—	—
7	11	66	16
8	27	—	—
9	27	—	—
	$112	$132	Total Profits: $20

This chart shows what is wrong with most mechanical systems. Immediately after a win the system is usually ahead of the straight betting method. For example, after the seventh race, straight $4 bets would show a profit of $44 (you collected $72 and wagered $28).

Using the profit-spreading method, at the end of the seventh race you would have bet $58 and collected $132 for a profit of $74.

But the next bet following your win takes a far bigger bite from your profits than a normal flat bet. A short string of losers using a machanical system is usually enough to put you behind.

Furthermore, a mechanical system shows its greatest profit when you win the last race. If you had won the ninth race instead of the seventh (at the same odds), your profits would have been $42 instead of $20. The last race becomes far more important than it should.

To repeat, if you have four or more winners, any mechanical or percentage method of spreading profits is better than simple flat betting. If you have only one or two winners, no mechanical system can show more profits than straight flat betting. The problem is to discover a method that will provide more profit having three winners than a straight flat-betting method.

There is such a method, but it cannot be used without a price. The price is agreeing ahead of time to two conditions:

1. Your aim is to have three winners to win a specific amount of money. If you have fewer than three winners, you accept the fact that you will do worse than you would have done making straight flat bets.
2. If you get three winners and you have not reached your goal, your succeeding bets should be no larger than needed to reach your goal at the odds at which the horse goes off. For example, if you have had three winners and you are $20 short of your goal, your next bet would be $5 if the horse you like is going off at 4–1.

You do this to prevent your profits from being eaten away by having three successive losers in the last three races.

The method is fairly simple:

1. Estimate the amount of money you are *genuinely* prepared to lose if you have the worst of possible days. Take one third of this amount and hold it in reserve. The use of this reserve fund will be explained later. Divide the larger amount into *five* equal bets. This is your working capital.
2. If you get a hit in your first five races, add the entire amount to your remaining working capital and divide it over the next *five* races, or whatever races remain. If fewer than six races remain, include your reserve in the working capital before you divide.
3. After your third hit, if you have not reached your goal, bet only enough on the remaining races to reach your goal at whatever odds your horse goes off.

For example, let us say that you are willing to risk the same amount as our flat bettor in the previous example, $36, and you have the same winners. (See page 147.) Your goal is to make a profit that is three times your betting money; you want to leave the track with $144. You would divide your money into a working capital of $24 and a reserve of $12.

Dividing your working capital by five, your beginning bets are $4 (with $4 left over). Your score in the first race brings your working capital to $44. Dividing this by five, your bets on the second through sixth races will be $8.

Your bets in the second, third, and fourth deplete your working capital to $20, but at the end of the fourth you have tickets to cash worth $48. Your working capital is back up to $68. Since there are only five races left, you can afford to include your reserve of $12, bring your capital up to $80, and your bets on these races will be $16 each.

You spend $48 on the next three races, bringing your capital down to $32. But when the seventh race is over your tickets are worth $96, bringing your capital to $128.

At this point your profit is $96. Your bets on the eighth and ninth races are only as much as needed to hit your goal. Since your aim was to make a profit of $108, you are only $12 shy of your goal. Your bet on the eighth race will be only $6 if your horse is going off at 2–1 in the eighth.

If it wins, you've reached your goal; if it loses, you bet enough on the ninth to make a profit of $18. If it wins, again you've reached your goal. If it loses, you still have lost far less than you would have if you had continued a mechanical system over the last two races.

Now, why pick a five-race spread, and what about the reserve pool?

First of all, a five-race spread is picked because if you have three winners it is impossible to have *two* losing strings of more than five. For example, if Providence has destined you to win three races, and you win the first, then lose the next five, there aren't enough races left to lose five. You will win two out of the last three.

Actually, if you are destined to win three races, you can't have two losing streaks of more than three in a row. But you could have one losing streak of six, so that is why the percentage is to spread your money over five races.

But what if you win one and then lose five? Your working capital is gone. But there is always your reserve. You use it to set up a round robin or parlay, depending on where your losing streak has brought you.

For example, if you lose the first five races, your working capital is gone. With the $12 left you set up a four-horse round robin. If you win the first and lose the second through sixth, you set up a three-horse round robin. If your working capital ends at the seventh race you bet a $12 parlay on the last two races. And if you lose the first two, then win the third, and lose the next five, your bet on the last race will be your entire reserve of $12.

Remember, the system is based on the condition that you are willing to lose all in an effort to have *three* winners.

Why three? There is nothing mystical, nothing "lucky" about the number three. You try for three winners because you need three winners to make any money with the moderate prices that come up in almost any race. Of course, one good longshot can put you in the profit column for the day, but our concept of having a goal in mind will take care of this. Let us say that the combination of a favorite and a longshot puts you over your goal. You can either revise your goal (sometimes this is courting disaster) or make token bets for the remaining races.

With two winners at moderate prices you make only enough to break even (whether you attempt a mechanical system or not). With three short-priced horses, making the same flat bet, you may not even break even.

And so, you aim at three winners because three is what you need.

CHAPTER XVIII

Playing the Daily Double

Most racetracks have expanded the opportunity to bet the daily double. In addition to the traditional double on the first two races, they now offer a double on two later races. In New York the "late double" involves the last two races. Other states take this wager on two late races such as the seventh and eighth. California doesn't have a late double at all, although it can be expected that this popular bet will not be kept out of the West for long.

The daily double is a completely separate betting pool not connected at all with the win betting on the first two races. Once the track and tax "take" is removed, the daily double pool is divided among all those who have selected the winners of both the first and the second races.

Sometimes the double returns are very high, sometimes they are very low, but about half of all doubles pay less than $50, and about one tenth pay less than $20.

Almost always the double pays considerably higher than a win parlay on the first two races. The exceptions occur when factors other than the merits of the two winners are involved. For example, since many people like to pick things in pairs, combinations involving the same number (7 and 7) or the same jockey frequently pay slightly more as parlays than as doubles.

One reason why doubles pay more than parlays is that in a parlay you are taxed twice. When you make your first bet, the 15–20 percent take is removed. When you put your winnings on the second horse, the big hands of state and track scoop out their cut once more. On a daily double, the freight is charged only once.

Doubles used to be the only form of blind betting at the track. Prior to the computer age, there was no way of flashing the payoffs for all possible combinations. If there are twelve horses in the first race and twelve in the second, there are 144 possible combinations. Until computers and TV monitors were put into use, the only information you had were the "win" odds on your horse in the first.

Today, except at the smallest tracks, you can learn prior to the race what the possible payoffs will be and how they are changing. This is an invaluable tool for the regular bettor. It is one that should be put to greater use by the occasional bettor.

Because computerized betting now makes it possible to bet large amounts with the push of only a couple of buttons (instead of the time-consuming punching out of separate tickets as in the past), it is still possible for stables to use the daily double for betting coups even though the betting is no longer blind.

If they have a "hot" horse, they know that betting heavily on it will almost certainly kill the odds as the fans become aware of the large bet and rush to get some money on it. Instead, they "wheel" the horse in the double (bet it with every horse in the other race), and no matter what horse wins the other race, they collect more money than they would have if the public had been aware of the stable's large bet.

Because the double usually pays more than a parlay, many people buy a number of different combinations thinking the price is worth it in order to come up with the right one. Sometimes this pays off, but to attack the double by figuring on buying a set number of combinations, say three horses in the first with three in the second, is not particularly wise.

First of all, the rate of return on these combinations is not often very high. More than half of all doubles pay less than $50. If you *do* win at that price, you have spent $18 on what amounts to a return of less than 2–1. If your combinations include two favorites, and they win, quite often you discover you have gambled $18 to do little more than break even or actually lose money. This is just not smart money management.

Secondly, the mathematical odds against hitting two races in a row are very high. If each race has ten horses, the odds are 100–1. Of course, in many races quite a few horses can be excluded. I should say "can *usually* be excluded." Occasionally, a longshot will come in, accounting for an "Uncle Sam" double (one that pays more than $600; to collect you must register with the U.S. Internal Revenue Service for tax purposes).

But even though you can usually exclude horses as sure losers in each race, you rarely can afford to buy enough combinations in each race to adequately cover the horses that can *possibly* win. If you can afford it, the chances are that you will lose money on the deal because of the relatively low odds paid by most doubles.

On the other hand, if you limit your combinations to perhaps two horses in each race, your rate of return goes up when you hit, but you don't hit nearly as often.

If the difference between the odds and the rate of return is so poor, is the double a sucker bet? Should you just bet a couple of "lucky" numbers, perhaps your mother-in-law's age, and forget handicapping? Or should the double be skipped entirely?

The answer, as with most things, is it depends—on the particular races that make up the double, on your goal for the day, and on the methods you are using to reach it.

Aside from these variables, for most bettors the daily double is the *best* of all possible bets. We have seen that a winning day almost always requires betting horses in combinations. The daily double is a beautiful combination bet.

Not only does it usually pay better than a parlay, but when both or even one of the favorites is knocked out, the payoffs are extraordinary. The early double at Aqueduct on March 18, 1988, is hardly unusual. The first race was won by the second choice in the betting. It paid $9.80. The second race was taken by a horse bet down to 7–5 favoritism. It paid $4.80. A $2 parlay on these horses would have returned $23.50 ($9.80 × $4.80 = $47.04 ÷ $2 units = $23.52). The double payoff was a whopping $41.40, almost 80 percent more than a parlay!

Exacta payoffs are often high also. But there is a major difference between exacta and double betting that makes the double much more attractive. *Winners* are fairly predictable among the handful of contenders in each race, and we can bet a relatively small number of combinations to try to catch the double. But horses that finish *second* are often mysteries. As we shall see when we discuss exacta betting, many horses that get the second prize would hardly be considered contenders to win.

So, in almost all strategies for a successful day at the track, a separate amount of money should be set aside for the daily double and, where it is offered, for the late double.

How much should be set aside? This depends on what you expect from your day at the track. Since there is a special thrill in "being alive" after the first race, especially for a hefty payoff in the double, even the bettor who is out for a good time without risking too much money should figure on betting at least a couple of combinations.

Those aiming at a more ambitious (if more risky) goal should allocate up to 20 percent of their capital for the first two races, especially if these include Best Bets. If they are using the profit-spreading method outlined on page 149, part of the one-third capital put into reserve should handle the late double.

How many combinations should be made? The answer lies in the types of races that are offered, the goal you are seeking for the day, and the method you are going to use to reach this goal.

You should consider the early double as an extra race on the card. Only here, instead of betting only one horse to win, you can back up your bet with "savers" in each race and still make a good profit.

If you have two horses in each race that you think can win, bet the two in the first into the two in the second for a total of four combinations. If you have more than two contenders in each race, it will probably not pay off to bet more than six combinations.

Remember, the mathematical odds against hitting the double are high and the payoffs are frequently low. If the double pays only $30, and you have bet $12 in combinations, you are getting less than 2–1 for having picked the winners of two races!

In those races where there are a large number of contenders, your best return will come from using the "key" horse method. Narrow the field in each race down to the one horse that you think will win on the basis of speed, class, and trainer placement. Make this your key horse. If you are betting $2 units, bet a $4 double on your two key horses. Bet $2 doubles on two savers in the first race into the key in the second to make sure that you are "alive" when the first race is over. Bet a $2 double on your key in the first into *only one saver* in the second race, for a total investment of $10. If the odds are right, you should also bet enough to win on your key horse in the first to at least get back the money you are investing in doubles.

If you have the money, why not make more combinations and increase your chances of winning? It is all a matter of possible payoffs. Whether you are a $2 bettor or a $200 bettor, you should approach the double in the same way.

If you use the methods of speed, class, and suitability described earlier, and you identify three contenders in a race, one of these three will win about 50 percent of the time. Your chances of winning two races in a row with three contenders in each are therefore only one in four. If you bet nine combinations (three horses into three, for an investment of $18), over the long haul your winning doubles must pay an average of $72 for you to break even, since you will win only one out of every four doubles. But the average double does not pay that much, so you must bet fewer contenders, concentrating on the horses most likely to win—your "key" horses.

Sometimes a race will turn up in which there will be two contenders, virtually impossible to separate, with the rest of the field looking pretty weak. In these races, make both of the horses "keys" but still limit the number of horses you put with them. Look at the possible payoffs on a TV monitor that gives prices for the double. If the lowest possible payoff on any combination is not at least 3–1 for your total investment in doubles, you are making a bad bet, since we should not expect to win more than one double in four. If this combination includes a horse that cannot be eliminated, you must increase the amount you are betting on this combination. You are hoping for one of the bigger doubles to come in, but if a small one hits, a slight increase in the amount bet on it will bring the payoff close to the 3–1 return we are looking for.

A successful single day at the track will sometimes come about because of one big hit—the big double or the big exacta that puts you well above your goal for the day. Far more often, your winning day will be the result of a number of horses bet to win in combination. How should you integrate the double into your overall strategy for coming away from the track a winner?

Prior to entering the track, you should probably have decided on one of two basic strategies:

1. You have selected three or four races that you have considered Best Bet possibilities. You expect to bet more on these horses and to bet them in combination.
2. Or you have selected one horse in each race and are going to use a mechanical profit-spreading method.

If you are using the Best Bet method, the first two races may contain:

1. None of your Best Bets.
2. Two of your Best Bets.
3. One of your Best Bets.

If none of your Best Bets are in the first two races, then, with one exception to be explained later, you should never buy more than four double tickets (combinations of the two horses you think might win the first couple of races, but don't think highly enough of to consider Best Bets). If one horse in the first is a longshot, it should also be backed to win. It is not a good situation to have a 20–1 shot come in without your collecting a penny. It is particularly bad when the realization hits you that you are betting the equivalent of $42 in the second on horses that you consider risky.

If two of your Best Bets are running in the first and second races, bet three fourths of the amount of money on these two combinations in the double that you would have if you were betting your first Best Bet alone. Bet the other fourth on your Best Bet to win. For example, if you had decided to risk $12 on each of three Best Bets and two of them were in the first couple of races, begin by buying an $8 double on the Best Bets in the first two races and bet $4 to win on your Best Best in the first race.

The Best Bets are your "keys." You are hoping both horses win, but you should also take out some insurance. Consequently, you should bet one or two $2 savers in the first race into your second race Best Bet. You should also play your first race Best Bet into a couple of savers in the second. Your investment in doubles will be $12 to $16.

If a saver wins the first race, you will probably not have to make a win bet in the second. Bet it only if the double will pay less than the $12 win bet you would have made.

If your Best Bet wins the first, make no additional bet in the second. You have an $8 double going and you are also alive with a couple of savers, a nice position to be in. You have also collected a $4 win bet on the first race.

Suppose your second Best Bet and your savers fail to make it in the second race. How bad off are you? You have missed a chance for a big payoff, but your situation isn't desperate. You have the return from your $4 in the first, and you also have saved the $12 you would have bet in the second. This money can be applied to your third Best Bet.

What if only one of your Best Bets is running in the first or second races? Should you invest in a wheel, that is, combine your key horse with every horse in the other race so that you must collect on the double as long as your key wins?

The strategy behind a wheel is the hope that one of the horses hooked with your Best Bet will be long-priced, giving a better return on your money spread out on every horse in the other race than on your Best Bet alone. So, the question is, how often is a wheel worth more than the same amount bet on the horse to win?

A wheel was certainly worth it on February 20, 1988, at Aqueduct. If you, like almost everyone else, thought that Precious Tiffini was a "lock" in the first race (it was bet down to 3–5) and wheeled it with everything in the second, you would have been delighted when Robbin Native crossed the finish to complete a $142.60 double.

Since there were twelve horses in the second race, a wheel on Precious Tiffini would have cost $24 plus an extra ticket on the favorite in the second race (this is a customary bet with wheels in order to avoid a loss if the favorite comes in with the wheeled horse), making a total outlay of $26. The profit on the double would have been $116 ($142 − $26).

If, on the other hand, the $26 had been placed on Precious Tiffini to win, the profit would have only been $16, since the $26 win bet would have returned only $42 for a horse that paid $3.20 for every $2 wagered.

This huge difference between wheel and win bet is a rare, rare exception. Four out of five times the straight bet on your key horse (whether it is a favorite or not) will pay more than a wheel because well-bet horses will win the other race, and about one time in ten you will lose money by betting a wheel when the second or third choice completes the double.

If you are tempted to wheel your horse, make sure you check out the double possibilities and buy extra tickets on those combinations that will return less than if you put all your money on your horse to win. For example, $20 to win on a 3–1 shot will pay $80. If you are making a ten-horse wheel, you must get an extra ticket on any horse that will pay less than this.

Of course, everything depends on the kind of race you are considering wheeling into. If it is a truly bad race where almost anything can happen (a two-year-old maiden race on the turf, for example), then a wheel with extra tickets on the lower-paying doubles might be in order.

But if the race you are considering wheeling has a number of legitimate contenders difficult to choose among (which is why that race can't be considered a Best Bet race), then a generally more rewarding strategy is this: bet your Best Bet horse in doubles with three or four of the contenders in the other race; figure out what a wheel would cost and bet the difference between what you have bet on doubles and the cost of the wheel to win on your Best Bet. This way, you have a chance to collect both your win bet and your bet on the double.

If you are using the Best Bet method and neither the first nor the second race has a standout horse, you should bet only one or two combinations that would equal what your token bets on these races would be. A fairly heavy bet in doubles might be made, however, when you have a situation in which the first and second races *both* have horses that can be expected to be made favorites despite their having knocks against them that make them risky.

If this happens and *if* you can narrow the contenders down to two or three in each race (excluding the favorites), you have a good chance of hitting a double at a price that makes the money spent on the combinations worth the risk.

Because so many people wheel one or both of the favorites or hook them with other horses, the double turns out to be large, even if the two winning horses are moderately priced. This is what causes a double of over $100 when both horses pay only about $12.

If you hit the double, do not become one of those unfortunate bettors who are far ahead early in the day but end up leaving the track with pockets that contain little more than lint and carfare. The stories are plentiful and are not restricted to occasional bettors: "I was ahead ____ dollars, but I gave it all back." (You can fill in the amount.)

You have won two races. A good day at the track can usually be had by winning three. Don't presume that because you have hit the double, the rest of the day will be an endless round of joyfully cashing tickets. It may happen, but the percentages say you will probably win only a couple of more races.

If you have hit a big double, one that has already put you ahead of your goal, set a new objective, but be reasonable. Set a goal that can be reached by using no more than *half* your profits.

If you have not reached your goal and you are using a spread method, spread your profits and working capital over the remaining seven races. Bet no more on any one race than what it takes to reach your goal.

Those using the Best Bet method should proportionally increase their wagers on the remaining Best Bets but should continue making token bets on the races that do not contain standout betting propositions. Simply having more money to bet a race that would be skipped by a regular bettor does not make the race any easier to beat. Keep your profits for those races that really count.

If the track you are at offers a late double, use the same strategy you used in the early double. At many tracks, the late double will include the feature race. This often provides an excellent opportunity to bet a favorite or second choice into two or three horses and receive a payoff that will greatly surpass a win bet on the low-odds horse.

If you have had a particularly bad day, the late double often offers the opportunity for a big comeback, especially if one of the races has a Best Bet.

Two things should be avoided when playing the late double. First, avoid playing a large number of combinations when only two or three of these will pay enough to make your day a winning one. If you are behind, bet more on those combinations that will have you surpass your goal and pray that you don't need any savers.

The second pitfall to avoid is giving in to the temptation to bet horses you don't really like but which are the only ones that will get you out ahead. Strange horses win almost every day at the track but *never* when you need them. Trust the handicapping skills you have learned and bet the horses that you have selected to win. If the payoffs aren't worth the risk, go home early and save your money to partially finance another day at the track.

Here are the basic points to remember about betting the daily double:

1. Fit the double into your strategy for a winning day. Never be lured into making extra combinations because of high payoffs on horses that have only a slight chance to win.
2. If each half of the double contains no Best Bets, bet no more than four combinations, two horses in the first race into two horses in the second.
3. In races where there are many contenders, select a key horse in each race and bet it with two or three savers.
4. If each half of the double contains a Best Bet, bet three fourths of whatever you would have bet to win on the first race in a double combination with your Best Bet in the second. Bet the remaining one fourth on the Best Bet in the first to win. Also bet smaller amounts in saver doubles in each race in combinations involving the two Best Bets.
5. If you are using a profit-spreading method and you expect to bet every race, consider the early double to be an extra race. On a nine-race card, therefore, you plan on making ten bets. Under no circumstances should your bets on the early double and the first two races exceed 30 percent of your capital.
6. Bet a horse in a wheel only when one of the races is very poor. Make extra combinations on the lower-paying possibilities.

CHAPTER XIX

Playing Exactas and Other Exotic Bets

An exacta (or perfecta, at some tracks) will pay off if you pick the winner *and* the horse finishing second.

I know horseplayers who go to the track regularly and who play nothing but exactas. The most successful use different methods according to the number and type of contenders. Sometimes they will "box" three or four horses. Sometimes they will "wheel" a horse with all the other horses in the race. At other times they will bet one horse "up and back" with three or more horses.

These exacta buffs know that in most races it is difficult to pick one horse to win—the top horse in the *Racing Form* Consensus wins only 30 percent of the time—and straight win betting on the horse most likely to win will show only a small profit. They bet exactas because they think they can make more for their investment, and many of them actually show a decent profit at the end of the year.

For the occasional bettor, however, exactas are the biggest money burners the racing associations provide. They seem so easy—bet three or four horses; surely two of them will win and place—and many of the payoffs are so good. The temptation to bet a few combinations can hardly be resisted . . . and so the money goes.

Because successful exacta betting is difficult, I am tempted to say exactas should be completely avoided by the occasional bettor. However, exactas do indeed have their uses, even for the person not betting regularly. And, for this reason, something should be said about how to bet them in such a way that profits will be maximized.

Like other exotic bets, the basic math of exactas is poor. In a 10-horse race, for example, there are 90 exacta possibilities (each of the 10 horses can have any of the 9 others finish second). Most exactas pay less than $40. The problem is not with the math but with the fact that the kind of horse that finishes second in any race is often one that cannot be predicted at all.

A study of racing at Hollywood Park for the month of July 1987 provides an example that can be duplicated at any racetrack in the country. I chose this month at this meeting because the public had great success in picking winners. Of the 170 races with at least 7 betting interests, favorites won 66 for a very formful 39 percent. Overall, 99 races (almost 60 percent) were won by horses that "figured" in some sense because they were either first or second in the choices made by the public.

With horses winning according to form for such a high percentage, one would figure that heavily bet horses would finish to place at about the same rate. Not so.

In the 66 races won by favorites, 25 percent of the horses finishing second were sixth or higher in the betting. Some of these races had 12 betting interests. The horse that finished second was at least sixth in the betting, but in some cases the place horse was the highest-odds horse in the race. Most of these horses showed little in their past performances, and few would have been selected by the occasional (or regular) bettor.

As indicated by the high percentage of favorites and second choices, the public had little difficulty in discerning the contenders for the win position. But these win contenders did poorly for place. For example, in the 104 races that the favorite failed to win, it finished second only 23 times (about 22 percent), far below the number we would expect from its win average.

Knowing how difficult it is to pick two horses and expect them to finish 1–2, many fans take three horses and bet them in an exacta "box" presuming it will give them a big edge. (A "box" is a series of win-place finishes. If you box three horses, you are betting six combinations. A $2 three-horse box costs $12. A four-horse box costs $24.)

Boxing three horses gives you a few more ways to win, but it is almost always a bad bet. If you score on one out of three, a very good percentage, you need $36 payoffs just to break even on the three $12 bets you have made.

To show why boxing often leads to very bad days at the track, let us see how the expect handicappers paid by the *Daily Racing Form* did at Aqueduct on the last five Saturdays plus one holiday in February and March 1988. The end of a racing season is usually quite formful, because most of the horses have run at least once over the surface, and this season was no different with favorites winning 35 percent of the time.

The selectors represented in the Consensus box of the *Racing Form* did quite well these days in terms of both winners and exactas. If you boxed their three selections on these days, you would have cashed 17 exacta tickets in 51 races. (There were no exactas in three races because of a New York law banning exactas in short fields.)

The prices ranged from $11 to $70. However, nine of the exactas paid $19 or less. Consequently, if you had gone to the track on these five Saturdays and on the day Washington's birthday was celebrated and had boxed the Consensus picks, you would have wagered $612 and gotten back $462, for a loss of $150.

On two of the six days you would have done fairly well, collecting on five out of nine exactas (a super percentage) but ending with profits of only $19 and $25. On the day the $70 exacta came in, you would have visited the cashier's window a total of three times (the other exactas were $43 and $16). At the end of the day you would have earned a profit of $21.

Seems pretty easy, but what about the other three days? They ranged from poor to abysmal. On the best of these bad days you would have won three exactas out of eight races, but the prices were so bad you would have lost $35. Had you used this method on February 27, you would have had only one exacta, for a skimpy $11, losing $97 for the day. And if you were unfortunate enough to attend on Washington's birthday, you would have bet eight boxes for $96 and collected not a penny.

The first lesson about boxing horses in exactas is clear: if you box three good selections in every race, half the time you may end up with a small profit, and half the time you will show losses, sometimes disastrous ones.

The second lesson is that low-paying exactas do not come in often enough to be profitable as part of a box. Eight of the seventeen winning exactas had the lowest possible payoffs. The slight profit on these was not enough to carry the weight of the other wagers in the box.

Boxing three horses is occasionally a good idea. But the fact is, if you had bet all of your money on *only* the lowest-paying combinations instead of the six combinations that formed the box, you would have made a slight profit. If you had bet *only* the highest-paying combination, you would have made a slightly larger profit. So, usually, there is a better way than boxing.

A person who bets three-horse exacta boxes in every race is really making this statement: "My handicapping is so inexact that in every race I have to choose three horses to come up with one winner."

This does not have to be the case. Obviously, you can't make a single pick in every race, but in the chapter on favorites we pointed out certain kinds of horses that win at least half the time, and there are many other types of horses that have very high win percentages. To put two horses ahead of these is to waste money almost half the time.

If you are determined to bet exactas in almost every race, you will show a far higher profit if you use the method we used for daily doubles. Rate the horses in order, making one horse your key.

Sometimes one horse will be a clear standout and exactas should be placed "underneath" this horse as a means of increasing profits.

Fairly often, it will be difficult to home in on one horse. For example, we may have a horse coming off a good win in six days or less with the best time for the past thirty days. Usually, we can't go beyond this horse in our search for a winner. But in this race there might be a horse that has been freshened for a couple of months, is now dropping in class, has had good workouts, and has the top back time at the distance. All other things being equal (jockey, pace, etc.), there is simply no way of choosing between these horses. Therefore, both horses should be reversed (Horse A over Horse B, *and* Horse B over Horse A) for larger exactas, and (since we know that the second-best horses don't always finish second) a third horse might be placed below each for smaller bets as savers.

In races where there are three contenders difficult to separate, and one of them is the betting favorite, the horses should be rated in this order: 1—the highest odds of the three; 2—the favorite; 3—the third horse. Three combinations should be made; 1–2, 2–1, 1–3. We make these bets in order to have a fairly high percentage (the favorite, when it has no knocks, will come in first or second at least half the time) and also to be eligible for some of the high exacta payoffs (the 1–3 combo).

At least once or twice each racing day, the public gets excited over a horse that really doesn't deserve to be the favorite. When the favorite finishes third or worse, the exactas are usually quite high. If you have three contenders that you really can't separate, this may be the time to box. If the minimum exacta on any of your combinations is at least $60, go for it, since this will provide a reasonable return of at least 4–1 for your $12 investment.

Many fans have had their wallets emptied by consecutive losing exactas, so they (perhaps wisely) are too cautious to play them. But there are two situations in which exactas should be used as a tool for increasing payoffs:

1. If your win selection (especially if it is a Best Bet) is a favorite, part of your wager on the race should be exactas combining the favorite with horses that

have a chance to come in second. Always include at least one longshot. Remember that about 25 percent of the time the horse that finishes second to the favorite will be the sixth choice or higher. In general, you should be looking for a return of at least 4–1 on your exacta bets. For example, if you bet $6 in exactas, you should not bet any combination that pays less than $30.

2. If your final choice is 6–1 or higher, and the favorite has no real knocks against it, between one fourth and one third of your bet should be used in exacta bets with the favorite. Most of your exacta bet should be put on your horse to finish second to the favorite. For example, if your selection is 8–1 and you've decided to bet $18, put $12 to win, make a $4 exacta with the favorite on top of your horse, and a $2 exacta with the favorite underneath your horse.

A word on exacta wheels: The problem is much the same as with wheeling a horse in the double. Too often an exacta wheel will pay less than an equivalent amount on the horse to win. You need a longshot to come in second, but this only happens 25 percent of the time. Almost half the time a shorter-priced horse places, causing you to lose money on a wheel.

If you are inclined to wheel a horse, bet extra tickets on the second- and third-priced horses so that your return will always come close to a win bet.

The occasional player should play the exactas the way the most successful regular bettors do. They have no single method (such as boxing), but they adjust their bets to the situation presented by each individual race.

A summary of exacta suggestions is in the table that follows:

SELECTION	EXACTA BET
1. A single horse that is a standout favorite.	1. Play the favorite on the top of two or three horses including one longshot.
2. A single horse that is 6–1 or higher with a bettable favorite in the race.	2. Play your horse underneath the favorite for two betting units ($4 if you bet in $2 units); play your horse over the favorite for one unit. Play six units ($12) on your horse to win.

3. Two evenly matched contenders.

3. Reverse the two horses for two units (costs $8, if you bet in $2 units). Put a third horse underneath each to place for one unit.

4. Three evenly matched contenders, including the favorite.

4. The longest-odds horse is choice number 1. The favorite is choice 2. The third horse is choice 3. Bet three combinations: 1–2, 2–1, 1–3.

5. Three evenly matched contenders that do not include the favorite.

5. Bet any combination that will pay $60 or more; in most cases, this will mean boxing all three.

6. Four or more evenly matched horses.

6. Skip the exacta (and possibly the race). If the payoff is too high to resist, reverse the longest-priced horse with the other three, providing the payoff is at least $60.

EXACTAS OR QUINELLAS?

A few tracks offer exactas and quinellas on the same races. Does it make any difference which you bet?

Obviously, quinellas are cheaper. For a single bet, the quinella will pay off when your two selections finish in the first two spots regardless of which horse finishes first. Generally, the payoffs are about half the exacta return.

In races where the first two finishers have fairly close odds, a $4 quinella will give you a little more or a little less return than the same $4 you would have invested in a $2 exacta reversed.

However, when the horses finishing one and two have a great disparity in odds, the payoffs can be dramatically different.

The mutuel machines calculate each quinella combination as a single bet. It makes no difference which horse finishes first. Not so with the exacta pool. If a heavy favorite wins, the exacta will be low, less than double the quinella if a longshot finishes second. If the longshot wins, the exacta will be high, often more than three times what the quinella pays.

Once in a while, the longshot's price to win will be even greater than what it pays as part of the quinella. In this instance you have managed to pull off the difficult trick of naming the first two finishers, but you get less than a win bet for your expertise. Remember, though, had your longshot placed, you would have gotten the same return.

In the same race where the longshot pays $42 to win and the quinella pays only $38, the exacta might pay $120. If the heavy favorite had won, the exacta might pay $60.

And so, for the same $4 investment you might get back $76 (a $4 quinella), $60, or $120.

Whether you play exactas or quinellas depends in part on the possible payoffs (watch the TV monitors giving these), but mainly on your aim in making exotic bets.

If you are playing a longshot to win, and you are playing a favorite over the longshot as a saver instead of a place bet, then by all means bet a quinella. You are hoping for the big win bet to come in. If it does, than you will collect on your insurance bet too. Should the favorite beat you out, you will collect less than on a one-way saver exacta, but this is not the order of finish you are hoping for. It is, after all, a saver bet.

In those races where you are playing a standout favorite over some longshots, never bet quinellas. Once in a while the longshot will outfinish you, and you will collect nothing. However, if your judgment is right, more often than not you'll fare better by taking a chance with the two-unit one-way exacta than with the two-unit quinella.

Quinellas provide a cheap way of betting some money on a race you should skip because there are too many contenders. If you can't pass up a race where four or five horses have a good shot to win, and three of them are longshots, you can make a four-horse $2 quinella box for only $12.

WHAT ABOUT TRIFECTAS?

DON'T play them!

I am strongly tempted to leave it at that, but you deserve to know why trifectas (also called triples, which pay off if you pick the first three horses in exact order) are poor investments for the person who goes to the track only a few times a year.

I know, also, that no matter how convinced you become that the triple is usually a sucker bet, the lure of hitting what usually is the biggest payoff of the day on any single race will be too great to resist, so you might as well get a few pointers on how to bet them with the best chance of winning for the smallest cash outlay.

In a twelve-horse race the odds on collecting a trifecta bet using three random numbers such as your anniversary date are over 1,300–1. The newspapers play up the occasional five-figure payoff, but very few trifectas return the $2,600 that would be the payback if there were no takeout (a gouging 25 percent at most tracks) and if all combinations had the same amount bet on them.

To avoid the temptation of collusion among the professionals involved, the racing secretary usually puts into the triple spot on the card the race that draws the largest number of horses. Most often, this means a cheap race such as a maiden claimer or the type of race that attracts a large number of untried horses like a two-year-old race on the grass.

In New York, for example, where there must be at least eight betting interests in order to offer triple betting, the triple race more often than not is a maiden or state-bred race.

So, in addition to having the math against you, you usually have a race that's hard to handicap.

The very best of professional handicappers rarely pick the exact order of the first three finishers even in races that are comparatively easy to handicap. In order to have a reasonable chance of hitting the triple, you will have to make some combinations, either "boxing" horses (so that the order of finish will not matter) or hooking them in some other way.

As you add possible horses to your combinations, the price goes up rather astoundingly. A three-horse $2 box costs $12 (six combinations). A four-horse box costs $48 (twenty-four combinations). Boxing five horses requires either a wealthy spouse or lots of throwaway money. It will cost you $120 (sixty combinations). In a twelve-horse race, you will have burned it all if even one of the seven other horses decides to wake up and finish in the money.

One method that some triple players use is to reverse two horses for the top two spots and wheel every other horse in the race for the show position. In a twelve-horse race this will cost $40.

Sounds good, but in almost all races the payoff on a $20 exacta far exceeds the payoff on a triple wheel. If the favorite finishes third, the difference can be enormous. In the ninth race at Aqueduct on March 18, 1988, the exacta returned $99.60 while the triple paid off at only $190.00. If instead of wheeling your top two choices with the eight others in this ten-horse race (cost: $16) you had bet the same amount on an exacta, you would have collected $796.80. That's hardly a negligible difference.

The only time a wheel pays off better than an exacta is when an extreme longshot finishes third and the favorite finishes first.

Why not do a part-wheel? Your 1–2 combinations with the three longest shots in the race? Suppose you have a chance for a good exacta payoff, one that will return $100. Are you willing to risk $300, the amount you could get for a $6 exacta, on horses that have nothing going for them except high odds?

The most common triple bet is a three-horse box. Even in a small field of eight horses, the mathematical odds of getting a return on six combinations are 50–1. Good handicapping and good luck might cut these odds in half. Considering that many triples pay less than $300—when two favorites come in, it is not unusual for the triple to pay less than $100—after 100 triple races (a $1,200 investment), there is a good chance that you will not even break even.

I hope you are convinced that there are a lot better ways to invest your money at the track.

Still, if you are out for a day of fun, you will probably be unable to resist betting the triple races. The most efficient way to handle the triple is to bet it as if it were an exacta (see the methods on page 165), and then add a horse or two for the third spot.

For example, if you like the standout favorite and you would play two long-shots underneath it for exactas, reverse the two longshots in the second and third spots ($4) and then play one to three horses underneath each longshot for the third spot ($4 to $12).

Put horses in for third that show good times but nothing extra. Or add some horses you have eliminated because of negative factors. Prefer high-odds horses. If you are going to go for a bet where the odds are so much against you, it makes sense to look for a payoff that is commensurate with the risk.

If you are behind, the triple is the worst possible place to look for a comeback. It is always much wiser to invest a larger amount on a straight win bet, or a lesser amount on exactas, than to try to find the elusive combinations that will form the triple.

PICK SIX—SHOULD YOU TAKE A CHANCE?

One more time: it is much easier to find the contenders for the win spot than to find the likely horses for the place and show positions.

That is why the Pick Six (a bet in which you try to pick the winners of six straight races, usually the third through the eighth) is a reasonable betting proposition on those days when you have a few Best Bets and not too many contenders in the other races. To figure out how much it will cost, multiply the number of combinations through each race and then multiply by $2.

On a day when you have three Best Bets, for example, and you have two contenders in two other races and three in another, you would figure the cost this way:

Race	3	4	5	6	7	8	
Number of horses you bet	2	×1	×3	×1	×2	×1	= 12 × $2 = $24

Most tracks pay out a percentage of the pool to those who select five out of six. If you lose an early race, your investment is not completely gone.

On days when no person has selected all six races, most of the pool is carried over to the next day. When this happens for more than a few days, especially over a weekend when the betting is higher, the pool can grow to over $300,000 at a major racetrack.

It would be interesting to know how many of the huge Pick Six payoffs are won by betting syndicates that invest thousands of dollars in this type of bet. They bet every horse in one or two difficult races that are likely to produce longshots and then combine all those horses with most of the probable contenders in the others. They may make combinations like this:

Race	3	4	5	6	7	8	
Horses Bet	4	×9	×3	×3	×3	×4	= 3,888 × $2 = $7,776

This may seem like an enormous investment, but when the pool is in the hundreds of thousands of dollars, it makes good betting sense. Every huge bet at the track lowers the odds appreciably, not only because it is mutuels betting but because of the attention and imitation a large bet gets. Since Pick Six betting is blind, and since the bulk of the pool is there from previous days, the syndicate is getting very favorable odds for its wager.

If you are going to the track with a few friends, you might want to form a little syndicate for Pick Six wagering (providing that your friendship will survive a bad pick here or there).

Suppose you and three friends agree on single horses in two of the races, two horses in two others, and three horses in the final two. Your group investment would be only $72 ($1 \times 1 \times 2 \times 2 \times 3 \times 3 = 36 \times \$2 = \$72$), and if you win the first few races, the increased excitement is certainly worth $18 per person.

The next problem you will face is deciding who will give his or her social security number for income taxes on the newly found riches!

The first part of this book taught you the basic methods of finding the contenders in different types of races. You have just learned the many different ways of betting these selections.

Now, let's put handicapping and money management together. We'll spend a day at the races with three very different people and see how they make out.

CHAPTER XX

A Day at the Track with Mary, Dan, and Bob

Three people went to the track one day. They were not professional gamblers. Neither were they betting novices. They all knew the importance of setting a goal before they entered the track, where hard thinking about money, while always difficult, is practically impossible under the panic of being behind or the euphoria of being ahead.

One bettor decided he'd have an exciting day and make his expenses plus enough to pay for the drinks on the way home. The second thought she'd like to make more of a profit, about equal to the betting money she carried in her purse. The third, as always, decided to aim for a big hit.

Although the three set their goals in terms of what they wanted to win, the final decision was actually made on the basis of what each was honestly willing to *lose*.

Their motto may very well have been the catchphrase that accompanies all the advertising for the New York City Off-Track Betting Corporation: "Bet with your head, not over it."

The first man, "Don't Lose" Dan, was really unwilling to lose any money. Obviously, he was prepared to take some risk, or else he would be home watching a ball game. Dan enjoyed the atmosphere of the track, got a kick out of collecting winnings fairly frequently, and occasionally parlayed his small payoffs into a considerable profit. Above all, he selected and bet his horses in such a way that losing was not likely.

Our second player, Moderate Mary, was prepared to lose more than Dan because she wanted to win more, but she too wanted to leave the track with some of her working capital. On a very good day, Mary might come home with quite a bulging purse, but her basic goal was modest—she wanted to double the amount she was willing to risk for the entire day.

Bonanza Bob went to the track only a few times a year. He put aside the money for these occasional jaunts, and if he lost all his stake in an effort to have a spectacular win, he would simply consider it the price he had to pay for an exciting afternoon.

What Bob liked best was the quickened pulse that came from the possibility of a big payoff. But he was no fool. Sometimes he got very far ahead very early in the day. Despite the fact that he was ready to lose all, he knew that only a sucker would bet everything on the last couple of races just because there was an opportunity to gamble. His goal was considerably higher than Dan's and Mary's, but when it was in sight, he adjusted his bets accordingly.

Because all three are aware of the selecting methods in this book, they find the same contenders in each race. But because they have different goals, they sometimes make different final choices from among the contenders. And they have very different ways of managing their money.

Take a look at their approaches to a day at the track, and see which one most comfortably fits your personality. Which goal is most reasonable for you?

HOW DOES DAN SELECT AND BET?

Dan has been going to the races long enough to know that you can have a good time at the track and not risk much money by betting show parlays. He knows that if he gets a string of winners going he will have the thrill of making (for him) large bets with the track's money. He will be content with a small profit most of the time as long as he doesn't leave the track a loser.

Consequently, he plays his show parlays even more conservatively than described on pages 142–143. Once he wins *two* in a row, his next bet is one third of his capital. Let us say his capital is $24 and he also has $24 in reserve. His initial bet is $8. If his horse pays a $3 mutuel, he will collect $12. He puts this on the second race, he clicks again for a $3 payoff, and he cashes his ticket for $18. His capital is now $34, so he will bet $10.

Thereafter, whenever he loses, he will bet one third of his remaining capital, but not less than his beginning bet.

Needing at least a $3 mutuel, Dan bets to place if his selection goes off at less than 2–1, and he plays to win if his choice is odds-on.

Because of the type of horses he selects, Dan can usually expect to cash a lot of tickets. But what happens when he falls behind? Show parlays are dandy when you are hitting, but because the rate of return is so low it is difficult to make a comeback.

Dan is well aware of that, so he keeps in reserve half of the money he is genuinely willing to lose on any one day. He will start his show parlay no more than three times. Then, reluctantly, he will shift to win betting, spreading his reserve over the remaining races. But he will do two things that will help him take home some money on even the worst of days:

1. Once he gets even, he returns to show betting.
2. He bets no more on any race than it will take to get him even.

Let's say Dan starts off in the worst of all possible ways. He loses the first three races. He's out $24, half of the amount he's willing to lose. He will bet $4 to win on the six races that are left. He loses the fourth and fifth, but wins Race 6 at 5–1. The $20 profit cuts his losses to $12.

If the horse he likes in the seventh is 4–1, Dan will bet no more than $4 to win. If he wins, he's a little ahead and he goes back to show parlaying for the last couple of races. Should he lose the eighth, he'll go back to win betting in the ninth.

Dan avoids exotic betting. He bets one small daily double for fun, but he never bets exactas.

Does this seem too cautious for a man who goes to the track a couple of times a month? Possibly, but then you are not Dan. His method fits his personality and his goal.

He goes to the track hoping his show parlay will give him a large percentage profit for a small investment. It often does. When it doesn't, he's quite content to break even.

How does Dan select his horses? Of our three players, Dan is closest to a straight system player. In money allowance races and stakes races for older horses, Dan picks the horse with the highest money per start for the current year unless it has some serious negative factor such as insufficient workouts after a layoff. If he eliminates the top horse, he goes to the horse with the second highest earnings per start.

He knows that these high-earning horses are saddled by trainers who place their horses well. If they don't win, they'll take part of the purse two times out of three.

On those fairly frequent occasions when there is a tie for top money (for those quality horses who have earned $20,000 per start, for example, a difference of $1,000 per start is really negligible), Dan looks for positive factors—a bullet workout, best time at the distance, etc. Unlike other players, he will always choose a shipper when there is a tie, reasoning that no stable would van (or plane) a horse a long distance unless they were sure they could pick up at least some of the purse money.

In stakes races for three-year-olds, Dan uses speed ratings rather than earnings to make his selection. He chooses the horse with the top rating in the past thirty days *and* with stakes experience. He has seen too many speedballs that have never run in a stakes fade badly when they tangle with the better horses in their age group. Sometimes they win, but since he is looking for horses that can at least show, he will bypass the inexperienced horse with the top figure, selecting the next in line with proven class.

In all other races, Dan picks the horse with the best speed rating *in the past thirty days,* unless it has some serious negative factor. In sprints, his choice will be the best speed rating at the *exact* distance, providing it is no more than five points below the rating of a horse that has run a different sprint distance. For example, in a seven-furlong race, he will pick the horse with a speed rating of 80 for seven furlongs over a horse with a speed rating of 83 for six furlongs.

Only in case of ties does he look for positive factors such as a drop in class or some of the trainer moves mentioned in Chapter VI. His first tie-breaker is always a horse with better back time at the distance. On off track days he will choose a horse with a mud mark to break a tie.

In route races, with many horses running at different long distances, he will first take horses within five points of each other. His first preference is always the horse with the best closing time. He reasons that even the lagger who may not get up in time to win will at least make a move that will get him into the show spot.

Many of Dan's horses win, but he only collects on his lower-paying show bets. This never bothers him. He knows that a far higher number take a minor award, and this is what he needs to make his show parlay work.

HOW MARY SELECTS AND BETS

Mary's worksheet will contain all the horses Dan has on his, since she knows that horses with the top speed ratings in the past thirty days account for a large number of winners on any given day. These horses tend to be bet down, however, and not enough of them win for Mary to be able to double her money on most days.

Her method of selecting is to rate the horses according to the preferences given in the chapters on sprints and distance races and then apply the positive and negative factors mentioned in the chapter on picking horses in special situations.

Getting the race down to one selection is Mary's aim. She looks for a horse that has at least *two* of the three major aspects of selecting—good speed, proven class, and a clear move indicating trainer placement.

Any race that contains a horse like this becomes a Best Bet, and she plans her day around making larger bets on these races and spreading her winnings on them. She will not bet them, however, if they go off at less than 3–1. When Mary gets ahead, she bets only enough on succeeding Best Bets to reach her goal.

Sometimes she will get a race in which two horses show speed, class, and trainer placement. If she can't choose one on the basis of pace or jockey, she will bet both of them, providing one of them is going off at 6–1 or better. She needs those odds in order to get the 3–1 return she is looking for. If neither horse is 6–1, she will make only a token bet on the race.

Mary bets exactas only in those races where she is betting two horses to win. She reverses both her horses, and if one of her horses is not the favorite, she will put the favorite over her longer-priced horse.

Daily doubles form an extra part of Mary's plans. Unless one of the races contains a Best Bet, she bets only three small combinations: a key horse in the first with two in the second, and a saver in the first with a key horse in the second. If one of the races contains a Best Bet, she might put three or four horses into it depending on the possible payoffs. If both races contain Best Bets, she bets two units on this combination and bets savers into both Best Bets.

Mary gets out to the track one or two times a month. She knows that in her lifetime she will see a lot of races. This gives her the discipline needed to make only token bets on races that do not contain Best Bets. If one of these token bets pays off, she puts the winnings into her Best Bet pool.

HOW DOES BOB SELECT AND BET?

Bob knows that he will have his banner day only by getting a few big payoffs. He uses all of the methods described in this book to select horses, but after applying a few negative factors, he doesn't attempt to pick a winner. He lets the odds board do this. Within the limits noted below, Bob will always play the longshot among the horses he has selected as having a chance to win.

He is almost constitutionally unable to bet favorites. He will use them in doubles and play them over longshots in exactas, but he never bets them to win.

On the other hand, he rarely bets horses that go off at odds of higher than 12–1. He knows that between the odds of 6–1 and 12–1 there is very little difference in the percentage of winners. More horses win at 6–1 than at 12–1, but not many more. However, at 13–1 the decline in the number of winners becomes much more rapid. Consequently, except in maiden races and cheap claimers, Bob bets huge longshots only as savers. Of course, he will always put these very high-odds horses underneath his key horse in exactas, since this is one way of getting the high payoffs he needs.

Because of their better-than-parlay returns, Bob loves doubles. He selects one or two high-priced horses in each race, and then uses them with savers.

When Bob can't get 6–1 on a race, he will either skip it or bet exactas. He will never bet an exacta, no matter how sure it may seem, if the exacta board shows it will pay less than $30.

Since Bob is ready to lose all in an effort to have a spectacular day, he divides his profits and capital by the number of races remaining and makes that figure his bet for the next race. He begins with 10 percent of his capital for the first race and 10 percent for doubles. However, if he is well ahead by the time he reaches the sixth race, when he would be betting 25 percent of his capital, he bets only enough to reach his goal.

What is his goal? Bob is willing to lose $120 to make $1,000.

SARATOGA.   AUGUST 22, 1987.   TRAVERS DAY.

The Travers Stakes does not have the popular reputation of the Kentucky Derby, but horsemen know that this "Derby of the North" has determined more three-year-old champions than its better-known Southern cousin.

The 1987 Travers shaped up as one of the most exciting in years. Offering a purse of more than one million dollars, the Travers had attracted from all parts of the land the best young horses in training.

One of the stars was Alysheba, who had come from behind to take the Kentucky Derby and the Preakness but who had lost his bid to don the Triple Crown when he could not catch Bet Twice in the Belmont Stakes. Proving his Belmont win was no fluke, Bet Twice then outlasted Alysheba in the Haskell Stakes at Monmouth Park.

But the Travers was no match race. Entered also were late-blooming horses like Java Gold, who had missed the Triple Crown races, but who had just beaten older horses in the Whitney (a major stakes at Saratoga). Temperate Sil, winner of the California Futurity and pride of the West, looked like he had returned to form with a brilliant win in the Swaps Stakes. And Polish Navy, who had demolished his field in a tune-up stakes for the Travers, had to be given an excellent chance.

All in all, it looked like a horse-lover's dream race.

Dan, Bob, and Mary were part of the crowd of over 45,000 fans who jammed the historic racecourse to watch the Travers and to bet the interesting card the racing secretary had assembled.

There were two allowance turf races, one for older horses (Race 1) and one for three-year-old fillies (Race 5).

In addition to the Travers (Race 8), there were three other stakes races—a distance race for older horses (Race 4), a sprint race for fillies (Race 6), and a seven-furlong race for three-year-olds (Race 7), which had attracted some of the fastest young horses in the country.

Rounding out the card were two claiming races (3 and 9) and a maiden special-weight race for two-year-olds (Race 2).

The variety and quality of the races posed an interesting challenge to our three fans who looked forward to a great afternoon of sport.

There was only one problem. On the night before the Travers, the Adirondack skies had opened up, and for twelve hours torrents of rain had poured on the racetrack. The rain stopped just before morning workout time, but those who took advantage of the opportunity to watch the thoroughbreds go through their morning trials saw a racetrack that looked like an oval canal.

It seemed as if the trainers of all but the most experienced mud horses would scratch their mounts, and the day would be ruined with a series of races having very small fields.

But as the morning hours passed, the sun made hesitant attempts to shine on the thousands who arrived early to spread their picnic blankets, and the track began to dry out a bit.

There were some late scratches but only the sixth race was severely reduced. With a field of only five, there would be no exacta wagering on that race. Surprisingly, the two turf races remained scheduled for the very soft grass.

Because the track was so muddy, our three friends had to make the ability to run on an off track or soft turf a primary consideration in their handicapping. They would not look for mud runners, but they would certainly prefer them among the contenders.

Getting their *Racing Form*s early, Mary, Dan, and Bob marked them like the samples on pages 74–77 and made worksheets. To avoid repetition, a composite of their worksheets is reproduced.

The top horse in each race is Dan's selection to show. Mary's selections as possible Best Bets are those horses over the line in each race. Bob has chosen these horses also, but he adds the horses below the line even though they have negative factors. He will consider using them as savers in combination bets. If all the horses have negative factors, he might make one of them his key if the odds are right.

These are experienced bettors so they do not put all of the information available about a horse on their sheets. Only the significant factors used to make a choice are listed.

The basic order of information on the worksheet is: conditions of the race, name of the horse, speed ratings past thirty days, best rating ever (in a square) for today's distance, class determination, positive factors (including trainer moves), and negative factors. In a race like the seventh, where pace may be a crucial factor, notations of how the horses usually run are on the right side. "F," "P," and "C" indicate front-runner, presser, or closer. The other abbreviations they use are the same as those listed on page 80.

DAN'S SELECTIONS FOR SHOW BETTING

Dan had the easiest job of making his selections. All but three of the horses listed as Dan's horses (the top one on the worksheet in each race) had either the top time at the distance in the past thirty days or the top earnings per start (the method he uses for money allowance and older horse stakes races) and had shown ability to run on off tracks.

He had to use a tie breaker in the first race, choosing Fieldy, the shipper, over Far East, who had an equal amount of earnings per start.

In the seventh race, Homebuilder had the second best speed rating but was Dan's choice because the top horse had no stakes experience.

Finally, in the closely matched Travers, Java Gold was tied with two other horses in speed rating and closing fractions, but Dan made him his clear choice because of his superior ability to handle a muddy course.

MARY'S BEST BETS

In order to qualify as a Best Bet, Mary's selection has to have more than just speed. It must show some indication that the trainer is very serious about this

		SPEED and\or CLASS	POSITIVE FACTORS	NEGATIVE FACTORS
① $A1 TC	Fieldy	$7G per start	shipper	
	Far East	$7G per start	Best back time	
	Lead Kindly Light	↑ class	2 TC B's	{ Won only three races, Hasn't raced in 50 days
② MdSp 2 y.o.'s 7f	Dangerous Type	top 7f time	5fB in slop	
	Candlestick	WD	4fBP, back in six days!	
	Bionaire	WD	5fB	poor last (4¹²)
	Sunny Roberta	↓ stakes		poor last (6¹⁹)
	Defined		4fB in slop	poor last (6¹⁶)
③ 100G Cl. 6f	Aswan High	85 [95]	4fBP; has won in slop	
	Crivitz	91-6½ [86]	Won last 2 in good form	No slop races
	Splendid Catch	88-6½ [87]	Placed in stakes; 5fBP	
	Tonka Pass	87-6½ [84]	Mud mark	
④ Stakes 1⅛	Creme Fraiche	$35G per start	{ 6fB; won stakes; Superior mud mark	Probably be odds-on
	Proud Debonair	$32G per start	7fB; won stakes	
	The Watcher	↑ class	Mud Mark	Only $7G per start
	Jack of Clubs	↑ class	4fb; 2 works in 6 days	Only $7G per start
⑤ Non-win One A1 fillies TC	Best of Strangers	84 — ↑MdSp	4fBP	
	Our Lil Margie	WD [3½ mile TC]	Mile B	
	Banque Privee	72-1³⁄₁₆ [82]	5fBP (27 days)	Poor last (7⁹)
	Rullah Runner	ND	5fTC-B + 5fB	First turf race

		SPEED and\or CLASS		POSITIVE FACTORS	NEGATIVE FACTORS
⑥ Stakes fillies 6f	Clemna's Rose	- 85 $20G per start		4fB	Out 3 months
	Funistrada	WD 88 $8G per start		5fB; Mud Mark	
	Silent Account	WD 85 $7G per start		Mud Mark	
	Dearly Bred	- 85 $19G no stakes			Out 2 mos.; poor work

		SPEED and\or CLASS		POSITIVE FACTORS	NEGATIVE FACTORS	PACE
⑦ Stakes 3 y.o.'s 7f	Homebuilder	89 -		Placed in stakes; 4fB		F - P
	Templar Hill	- 88		Won stakes 2-6fB's		C
	Mr. S.M.	- 89 6f		Won stakes 6fB from gate		P
	Steady Labor	92 -		5fB	Never in stakes F	
	High Brite	- 84		Won stakes	Mediocre works F	
	Stacked Pack	WD; 86 6f			Never in stakes F	

		SPEED and\or CLASS		POSITIVE FACTORS	NEGATIVE FACTORS
⑧ Travers 3 y.o.'s 1¼	Java Gold	91	CLOSE 35¹	Beat older stakes horses; 6f super work; Mud Mark	
	Alysheba	91	35	Won Kentucky Derby Mile Work	No mud form
	Bet Twice	91	35	Won Belmont Mile Work	No mud form
	Polish Navy	93	36⁴	Won stakes 6fb	Stamina?
	Temp. Sil	81-1¼	84	Won stakes Mile Work	Speed poor?

		SPEED and\or CLASS		POSITIVE FACTORS	NEGATIVE FACTORS
⑨ 25 Cl 7f 3 y.o.'s	Royal Slander	73	84 6f ↓20G	Good mud races	
	Magic Feet	WD	81 6f ↓20G	Back in six days! Won on "good" track	Poor on "sloppy"
	Alert Paster	77 6f	86 6f		Poor slop races
	Tell It Honestly	61	74 ↓22G	Won race in slop	Last very poor (15²¹)
	Well Honored	WD	78-26 ↓25G	Back in six days!	Tired, only mud races

race. Among other things, Mary looks for a big drop in class, sharp workouts, or a quick return to the races.

Moreover, if there are more than two horses in a race that show these key factors, Mary will not make this a Best Bet race. For this reason, the seventh race is out immediately. There are just too many horses that have an excellent chance of winning.

The Travers is also difficult, but Mary feels the only Grade I stakes winner in the field with extraordinary off-track ability is Java Gold.

In the second race, Dangerous Type is definitely a Best Bet with her good time and bullet work, but Candlestick also qualifies. She is coming back to the races in only six days with a bullet work prior to this race. This was her first start and she ran quite well. If Mary can get 6–1 on either of these, she will give that race Best Bet status.

Our Little Margie in the fifth race had only one turf race in her brief racing history but that was a fast-closing third, a good indication of stamina. In addition, trainer Leroy Jolley had given his horse an excellent mile workout. Very few horses work out at a mile or over, and those that work well almost always race creditably the next time out. So, Margie is a Best Bet.

Finally, Royal Slander in the ninth has many of the things Mary looks for— top time at the distance in the past thirty days, excellent back sprint time, and a huge class drop. Mary considers this horse the best of her Best Bets, and she is pleased that it is running in the last race in case she has misjudged some of her earlier selections.

Mary will make minimum bets in the other races, perhaps going on one of Bob's longshots or playing an exacta for fun. If she wins, she will put this money in her Best Bet pool.

BOB'S LONGSHOTS

Bob is delighted with the card. In seven races he has morning-line longshots which are either top contenders or savers for exactas and doubles.

The fact that there will be no exacta betting in the sixth causes Bob no disappointment. He prefers doubles, and the seventh race has been made the second half of an "instant" double (a betting opportunity established in New York when exacta betting is canceled because there are fewer than six betting interests). Since the seventh is chock-full of bettable horses, he looks forward to the possibility of being alive for some big numbers if he is lucky enough to win the sixth.

Some of the morning-line favorites look definitely beatable to Bob. The only one he will consider betting (together with a longshot from his saver list) is Java Gold. Because of his super six-furlong workout (faster than most horses actually run a race at that distance), his trouncing of older horses in the prestigious Whitney Stakes, and his renowned ability to run on an off track, Java Gold certainly would qualify as a formidable favorite. But Bob has no stomach for favorites. He will use Java Gold, but he will still play as another key horse the contender that goes off at the longest odds.

Our three fans are quite adept at the art of fashioning a winning day. Using the methods suggested in this book, they have isolated the main contenders. But because they have different objectives and very different methods of betting, they do not agree fully on which horses can be chosen as their chief selections.

Is it possible that all three of them can have a winning day at the track?
We shall see.

DAN'S SHOW PARLAY

Method: When show parlay hits on two races, bet no more than one third of capital on succeeding races.

Goal: Have a good time. Make expenses and dinner money. Above all, break even.

Capital: $24 to start parlay three times; $24 in reserve.

Horse	Win Odds	Bet	$2 Show* Mutuel	Return	Working Capital ($24)
1. Fieldy	2–1	$ 8 Show	$3.20	$12.80	$28.80
2. Dang. Type	5–1	12 Show	4.80	28.80	45.60

Dan has won two in a row; he now bets one third of his capital.

3. Aswan High	2–1	15 Show	3.00	22.50	53.10
4. Creme Fraiche	3–5	18 Win	Lost		35.10
5. Best of Strgs.	7–2	12 Show	4.60	27.60	50.70
6. Clmns Rose	3–2	17 Place	3.20 (Pl.)	27.20	60.90
7. Homebuilder	7–1	20 Show	4.20	42.00	82.90

Dan has tripled his capital; he takes out his original capital to be sure he breaks even. New capital: $58.90 (All profit)

8. Java Gold	3–1	20 Show	3.80	38.00	76.90
9. Royal Slander	4–1	25 Show	5.00	62.50	114.40

Show Parlay Profit $114.40

*Except in Race 6, where Dan had to bet to place because of the odds, and for the same reason, in Race 4, where he had to bet to win.

MARY'S BEST BETS

Method: Spread winnings over Best Bets until goal is reached.

Goal: $80 profit.

Capital: $80 ($48 for Best Bets; $32 for token bets and reserve).

Reminder: Mary's possible Best Bets are above the line in the composite work-sheet. Since she cannot have more than two contenders (if then, one has to be 6–1), she has no Best Bets in Races 1, 3, 4, 6, and 7.

Horse(s)	Odds	Type of Bets	$2 Mutuel	Return	Working Capital ($48)	Maximum Next Bet
2. Candlestick	6–1	$4 Win on each	(Placed)	—	$36.00	$12
Dang. Type	5–1	$4 Exacta in Reverse	(Showed)	—		
5. Our Lil Margie	3–1	12 Win	8.60	$51.60	75.60	37

At this point, Mary has to get her capital up to $160 to reach her goal. She will put only enough to win on the next race to do this.

Horse(s)	Odds	Type of Bets	$2 Mutuel	Return	Working Capital	Maximum Next Bet
8. Java Gold	3–1	30 Win 5 Late Double	8.40	126.00	166.60	Goal reached
9. Royal Slander	4–1	No bet; alive in the double	35.20 (Double)	88.00	254.60	

Best Bet Pool	$254.60
Capital	48.00
Best Bet Profits	$206.60
Token Bets	26.00
Profit for Day	$180.60

BOB'S LONGSHOTS

Method: Spread capital and winnings over remaining races until goal is in sight.

Goal: $1,000   *Capital:* $120

Reminder: Favorites and those horses with negative factors (which are listed below the line on the worksheet) become savers for Bob. He will bet to win if he gets 6–1 on an acceptable horse. If the odds are less, he will bet the race only if he can get a double or an exacta that will pay at least $30.

1. Far East	5–2	Because of the odds, Bob has no key horse. However, he does have keys in the second race. So, he combines all his first-race horses with them. Investment: $12.
Lead Kdly Lt.	5–2	
Fieldy	2–1	

2. Candlestick	6–1	Bob is alive with two doubles after Lead Kindly Light won the first. He makes no win bets. Since the exacta possibilities are large, he reverses his key horses and puts each of them over three horses which have chances to place. Investment: $16.
Dangerous T.	5–1	
Bionaire	12–1	
Sunny Rob	18–1	
Defined	20–1	

Until midstretch, Bob looked like a big winner. Then, Defined ($42.80) passed both his key horses which finished second and third.

| Races 1 and 2—Bet $28   Returned: 0   Capital: $92 |

3. Splendid Catch	5–1	The odds say no win-bet is possible. Bob reverses the top two horses in $4 exactas and puts both of them over the third horse for $2 exactas. His total investment of $12 is lost when Crivitz wins.
Tonka Pass	7–2	
Aswan High	2–1	
Crivitz	8–5	

4. Proud Debonair   2–1
   Creme Fraiche   3–5
   The Watcher   7–1
   Jack of Clubs   10–1

Thinking that even the best can be beaten sometimes, Bob bets Proud Debonair for $12 in exactas. He is right—and wrong. Jack of Clubs ($23.40) noses the favorite.

Races 3 and 4—Bet $24	Returned: 0	Capital: $68

5. Best of Strangers   7–2
   Our Lil Margie   3–1
   Rullah Runner   33–1
   Banquee Privee   35–1
   Twitch   5–2

Sticking with his methods, Bob reverses his top two for $4 exactas, puts both of them over the two longshots for $2 exactas, and also puts the favorite over the two longshots for $2 each. At last! Margie passed Rullah in deep stretch for a $232 exacta.

Race 5—Bet $20	Returned: $232	Capital: $280

6. Silent Account   3–1
   Funistrada   5–2
   Clemanna's Rose   3–2

Bob can bet $75 on this race, but there is no exacta betting, and he has no win-bets. The seventh race, second part of the instant double, has six horses that can win, but Bob has knocks against three of them. He bets his top two horses into the three without negatives for $6 doubles (cost: $36). He really cannot exclude the favorite in the sixth, so he adds $4 savers with his three choices in the seventh (cost: $12). Total investment: $48.

7. Templar Hill   8–1
   Homebuilder   7–1
   Mister S.M.   6–1

When Funistrada ($7.00) romps in the sixth, Bob is alive for some good doubles. He boxes his horses for $4 exactas and then saves with the favorite entry over his horses for another set of $4 exactas. Total investment: $36. Bob could have bet more, but he knows if he hits the double and the exacta he will be a long way toward his goal. This is just what happened when Templar Hill closed from last to first beating Mister S.M. by a neck. His $6 double ticket was worth $244 and his $4 exacta returned $218.

Races 6 and 7—Bet $84	Return: $462	Capital: $658

8.	Java Gold	3–1
	Polish Navy	9–1
	Alysheba	5–2
	Bet Twice	4–1
	Temper. Sil	5–1
9.	Royal Slander	4–1
	Magic Feet	3–1
	Tell It Honestly	17–1
	Alert Paster	11–1
	Well Honored	8–1

Over $500 ahead, Bob would seem to be sitting pretty. However, as soon as he checks out the late double possibilities, he realizes he has a problem. Probably because of their mud-running abilities, Bob's key horses in the ninth are the favorites in the doubles. They are bettable as doubles, but there is no chance he will get the kind of odds he will need to make a goal-achieving win bet in the ninth. The only way he will be able to reach his goal is to win one of the three remaining bets he can make: the late double, the eighth race exacta, or the ninth race exacta.

So, using the TV monitors which tell him the possible payoffs, he works out his bets. He can bet half his capital ($335), but he doesn't have to. If any one of these bets comes in, he will reach his goal:

1. $50 doubles—Java Gold into his two keys ($100)
2. $20 doubles—Polish Navy, his only longshot, into his two keys ($40)
3. $10 doubles—Java Gold into his savers ($30)
4. $20 exacta reversed—Java Gold/Polish Navy ($40)
5. $20 exacta—Alysheba over Polish Navy ($20)

Knowing that four out of the five dirt races had been won by closers coming from far off the pace, Bob was not too concerned when Java Gold was running last during the early stages of the Travers. But he began to get a bit concerned when his key horse was still last, twenty lengths behind, with more than half the race over.

Then, getting the kind of thrill made possible only in the experiencing of a horse race, Bob watched jockey Pat Day begin to pick up horses on the far turn. Absolutely thriving in his world of flying mud, Java Gold rocketed past the tiring horses at the end of the pack, and Bob began to think he had a chance after all.

At the head of the stretch, Java Gold was third, stalking Polish Navy who was running second. Exacta possibilities flashed through Bob's mind. Coming down the stretch, Pat Day hit his mount a couple of times and with one crushing swoop it was all over—Java Gold by a widening two lengths!

It was good. Bob had witnessed a superb race. It was even better. He had the winner.

Bob's joy was dimmed only slightly when he realized that Polish Navy had finished third. The big exacta that would have put him over his $1,000 goal was not to be. Still, alive with five horses in the ninth, he was in a commanding position.

The thought of betting exactas with his keys and longshots never entered Bob's mind. He was goal-oriented. A win was all he needed to have his big day.

He was not through betting, however. He had five horses going for him, but there were seven others who could prevent him from winning the big prize. Experience had taught him to protect himself if one of these turned out to be a "hot" horse.

Sure enough, once the odds board lit up for the ninth he realized that Master Gene, a horse he had not even put on his worksheet because it had repeatedly been beaten by the other contenders (Royal Slander had whipped it by almost ten lengths in the slop), was bet down to 4–1, the same odds as Royal Slander.

And so, for insurance, Bob bet two $30 exactas, putting Master Gene over both his key horses. As it turned out, what Bob needed was not an insurance bet but a tranquilizer as he sweated out the photo that would decide his day.

Royal Slander, stalking the pace throughout and moving easily past horses in midstretch, looked like a comfortable winner. And then, O.K. Buster, a Monmouth shipper with woeful form in the slop, somehow began to relish the Saratoga mud. With every stride he gained yards of ground and hit the wire together with Royal Slander.

Because Buster had moved so fast in the last hundred yards, everyone was calling him the winner.

As thousands of losers not involved in the outcome moved toward the exits, Bob paced back and forth waiting for the board to light up with the winning number. He had a keen edginess about him, but he was not really apprehensive. He would not be disappointed no matter what happened. He had seen a few extraordinary races, and he would walk out a few hundred dollars ahead regardless of who won the race.

The roar of the crowd announced the naming of a winner. Number 10! Royal Slander had won by a whisker! Bonanza Bob had his big day. The double was only $35.20, but Bob's $50 double meant he would collect that figure twenty-five times.

Races 8 and 9—Bet $290   Return: $880   Capital: $1,248

Net profit for the day: $1,128

A LAST LOOK AT THE WINNERS

Could our trio have done better?

Sure.

Dan could have done considerably better if he was not so conservative. If he had gone for a three-horse parlay and then spread his capital over the succeeding three races, he would have made a profit of $225, about double what he actually made. (Use the chart on page 184 to figure this out.)

Should we say that Dan managed his money poorly? Absolutely not. Remember that Dan had to make tie-breaking judgments in the first and seventh races. Suppose he had made the wrong decisions. Losing the first, fourth, and seventh races, Dan's parlay capital would have been gone by the time the Travers field was entering the paddock for the eighth race. With the conservative method he actually used, if he had lost three races instead of only one, rather than being $24 behind after the seventh, Dan would still have been $26 ahead.

Certainly Dan is aware he could have won more money, but collecting on eight out of nine races was quite a feat. Dan knows that on most days he can count on collecting about six show bets. He plans his day with this in mind. If he wins more, wonderful. If he wins less, he won't really get hurt.

Both Mary and Bob did not bet aggressively toward the end as they neared their goals. Instead of betting $30 to win on the eighth and a $5 late double, Mary could have bet a $35 double. If she had done this, she would have won over $500 for the day.

And certainly Bob, who was ready to lose all, could have doubled his bets in the eighth. Had he done this, he would have left the track with almost $2,000 in his wallet.

These are "if's," and Mary and Bob are wise enough to know the "if's" work both ways. Royal Slander won his race by a vanishing nose. If the race had been one stride longer, his number would not have lit up the board.

If he had lost, and if they had bet more aggressively, Mary would have done little more than break even for the day, and Bob would have been less than $100 ahead.

Winning the last race of the day always produces a fine feeling. Winning a photo in the ninth is especially pleasurable!

Mary and Bob both know the last race could have gone either way. After the fact, it is easy to say they should have bet more. But Mary and Bob don't say this. They bet with their head, with a goal in mind. Betting more on the last couple of races would have been betting foolishly, despite the fact that on this particular day they lucked out in their photo.

In the last part of the book you will be given the opportunity to test your handicapping skills. Before you look at the practice days, you should think a little bit about yourself. What do you want to get out of a day at the track? What is a reasonable goal for you?

You have looked over the shoulders of three experienced fans who took on the challenge of the track and, with different approaches, came away winners.

Which approach best fits your personality? Which one best fits the amount you are *genuinely* willing to risk?

PART FOUR

PRACTICE AND PREPARATION

Two Practice Sessions: Aqueduct and Hollywood Park (Kentucky Derby Day, May 7, 1988)

If you have read this book carefully you have learned how to select horses and how to make the kind of bets that will most likely lead to a profitable end to your day at the track.

In this chapter you will get a chance to test your knowledge. The most essential parts of the past performances for the nine races at Aqueduct and Hollywood Park on May 7, 1988, will be presented for your analysis. You will also have a chance to handicap the Kentucky Derby.

This day was chosen because the widespread simulcast of the Kentucky Derby draws large numbers of occasional bettors to racetracks all over the country.

No matter how well you do on these simulated days at the track, I urge you to prove to yourself that you have gained the ability to select with better judgment and that the handicapping principles described in Part Two did not work by coincidence.

Purchase copies of the *Racing Form,* make worksheets for one of the tracks, and, when the results come out, notice how many winners are covered by the principles of selection given in Part Two. Selecting winners is an art. Like all art, it takes practice. The more you practice without risking your money, the less money you will lose when you put it on the line.

MARKING THE CHARTS

Do not be overwhelmed by the massive amounts of information given for each horse in the past-performance records. If you review pages 69–73 and you mark the charts systematically in the fashion suggested, you will see that relatively few things need to be marked and the contenders can be quickly spotted.

To prevent the charts from being too cumbersome to use as a practice tool, not all the horses entered are listed. However, every horse that has shown any positive factor in terms of speed, class, or suitability has been included. The actual number of horses in each race is listed on the right side of each *Racing Form* chart.

Here are a few additional reminders:

1. Don't forget to read the conditions of the races.
2. Remember to look for the negative factors mentioned on pages 72–73.
3. In distance races, wherever possible compare the closing fractions as an indication of stamina.
4. In the handicap races for older horses and in the "money" allowance races, make sure you compute the earnings per start for 1988 (or for 1987 and 1988 if the horse has run fewer than five times in 1988).
5. Once the contenders have been selected, make some prediction as to how the race will be run (review Chapter VII). Mark the chart with an "F" for front-runner, a "P" for presser, and a "C" for closer. In some races, your estimate of the pace may be crucial to your finding the winner.

THE ODDS

To the right of each horse's past-performance lines in the *Racing Form* pages to be shown here are the horse's closing odds. These are the actual odds the horse closed at. They are not the "morning-line" odds, which are only someone's estimate of what odds the horse will finally go off at.

Naturally, when you analyze the races in a nonpractice situation, you will not have this information, but you should be well aware of the odds at the track.

They are given to you here so that you will know how the public backed the various contenders and also to help you determine the type of bet you will make and the amount you will wager.

You should pay special attention to the favorite, just as you would at the track. Is it a solid favorite, or is it one that you should bet against? (See Chapter XV.)

If a horse you have selected as a contender turns out to be a longshot, try to figure out why it is not getting public backing. If you are convinced the fans are wrong, you may want to elevate the horse to Best Bet status.

PRE-HANDICAPPING RESEARCH

We are going to presume that you purchased your *Form* early in the morning and that you resisted the temptation to go to work immediately on the past performances.

Instead, you took about a half hour, made a calendar for the past thirty or so racing days listed in the *Form,* and found the track variants for those days in order to get the median variant. See pages 42–45 for the importance of this.

You also went through the paper trying to find bullet works so you could get an idea of a work that was excellent but did not receive a bullet because some other horse turned in an even more spectacular work that day.

This is what you discovered:

TRACK VARIANT		
	Median	Range
Aqueduct	23	21–25
Santa Anita	18	16–20

Add or subtract points outside this range.

An 80-18 at Aqueduct, for example, would equal a 77 (21 minus 18 = 3 points to be subtracted). An 80-28 would equal an 83 (28 minus 25 = 3 points to be added).

Distance Addition: You recall from the discussion of speed ratings that the seven-furlong ratings at Aqueduct are about 5 points less on the average than the ratings for six furlongs. Consequently, you will *add* 5 points to a seven-furlong rating if you are comparing it with a six-furlong rating in a sprint.

WORKOUTS				
	3f	4f	5f	6f
Aqueduct (and Bel. Park)	:35	:47	$1:00^3/_5$	1:14
Santa Anita (and Hol. Park)	$:34^4/_5$	$:46^3/_5$	:59	$1:13^3/_5$

Any workout that is equal to or better than these would have to be considered excellent.

Track Abbreviations: The *Racing Form* does a valuable service by giving the average purse value per race for the preceding year (1987). That number, rounded to the nearest thousand, is given next to the name and the state in the list that follows.

A win at a small track, one with a low average purse value, should not be given the same importance as a win at a major track.

Aks—Ak-Sar-Ben, Neb–9
Aqu—Aqueduct, N.Y.–28
Bel—Belmont Park, N.Y.–35
BM—Bay Meadows, Cal.–13
CD—Churchill Downs, Ky.–7
Dmr—Del Mar, Cal.–23
GG—Golden Gate, Cal.–14
Hol—Hollywood Park, Cal.–39

Kee—Keeneland, Ky.–22
Lga—Longacres, Cal.–7
OP—Oaklawn Park, Ark.–14
Pha—Philadelphia Park, Pa.–9
SA—Santa Anita Park, Cal.–31
Sar—Saratoga, N.Y.–41
Suf—Suffolk Downs, Mass.–7
TuP—Turf Paradise, Ariz.–5

CONDITION OF THE TRACK AT AQUEDUCT

New York City experienced seven hours of heavy rain before midnight on May 6. In the morning, the clouds lifted and the day was clear.

The track, which was officially called "good" for the first six races, presented a major problem for the bettor. It was clearly drying out, making it difficult to determine whether the mud horses should be given an extra edge.

Nevertheless, when you are making your selections, give special attention to horses with mud marks. For horses that have not been given an off-track designation, note if they ran well or poorly on tracks that were not called "fast."

The wet weather also had a major effect on the card. Race 1 and Race 4 were originally scheduled for the turf course. Rather than damage the grass, the stewards changed those races to the dirt course. When this happened, all but three of the trainers of horses in the first race scratched their mounts.

BETTING THE RACES

These practice days will be of most value to you if you do more than simply attempt to pick winners. Act as if you were actually preparing for a day at the track.

This means not only selecting horses to bet but also setting a goal and deciding how much you will wager to reach this goal. It also means changing the amount you bet as the racing day goes on, just as you would if you were at the track.

Here is a good way to make these practice sessions like genuine afternoons at the races:

1. Select the possible winners in each race and make up a worksheet listing speed, class, positive factors, and negative factors. Make your final decision from the worksheet. Note those races where the horses seem evenly matched, and mark those in which a heavier than usual bet may be called for.
2. Imagine you are investing an amount of money equal to the amount you are genuinely willing to lose. Be realistic. If you are willing to risk no more than $40 in your day at the track, don't make mind bets totaling $400.
3. Once you have done these two things, decide your goal for the day and the best means of achieving that goal. For example, will you have a show parlay? Will you try for a big hit by parlaying a few Best Bets? Will you use a mechanical betting system? How many daily double combinations should you make? Which races lend themselves to exacta betting?
4. Indicate on the betting chart following the past-performance records (page 200) how you plan to bet on each race. Of course, if you have winners you will change your bet, but it is essential to have your money planned *before* you look at the results.
5. After you have made your selections and planned how much you expect to invest on each from your capital, read the analysis of the first race, which describes the factors you should have considered in making your

decision and suggests the kinds of bets you should have made. Then look at the results of the first race. If you have a winner, and this changes the amount you bet in the second race, make the change on your betting chart. Keep a running balance, just as you would at the track, so that you know after each race just how near or far you are from reaching your goal.

Good luck!

BETTING CHART FOR AQUEDUCT, MAY 7, 1988

Race	Planned Bet	Actual Bet	Return	Profit on Race	Total Profit
1					
Double (1 & 2)					
2					
3					
4					
5					
Double (5 & 6)					
6					
7					
8					
Double (8 & 9)					
9 (Derby)					
10					

(3 Horses)

1 AQUEDUCT

1⅛ MILES. (Turf). (1.47) ALLOWANCE. Purse $33,000. 3-year-olds and upward which have never won two races other than maiden, claiming or starter. Weight, 3-year-olds, 115 lbs. Older, 124 lbs. Non-winners of a race other than maiden or claiming at a mile or over since April 1 allowed 3 lbs.

Quindecillion

Ch. c. 4, by Graustark—Damascus Rose, by Damascus
Br.—International Thbrd Breeders Inc (Ont-C)
Tr.—Martin Jose
Own.—Garcia J I

124

Lifetime	1988	11	3	4	0	$60,480
23 3 6 3	1987	12	M	2	3	$13,520
$74,000	Turf	1	0	0	0	

25Apr88- 6Aqu	fst	1	:46⅕ 1:11⅖ 1:36⅗	3↑ Alw 31000	9	4	52¼	31	2½	1hd	Velasquez J	b 121	10.80	83-24	Quindecillion 121hd Kunjar 1152¼ I've Done MyTime1134½	Driving	9
17Apr88- 6Aqu	fst	1⅛	:47⅗ 1:12 1:51⅘	Clm 22500	4	5	58½	44	32	2no	Santagata N	b 115	4.60	76-25	SocillyInformed110noQuindcillion1151½It'sAboutSvn117nk	Gamely	9
7Apr88- 3Aqu	sly	1	:46 1:11⅖ 1:38	Clm 25000	11	3	32½	2½	2½	21¼	Pulido H D	b 117	18.70	75-26	Fast Jack 1171¼ Quindecillion 1171½ Easton 1174	Game try	11
28Mar88- 4Aqu	fst	1⅛	:48⅖ 1:13⅗ 1:53⅖	Clm 25000	6	5	44½	42½	32	42	Pezua J M	b 117	9.60	66-30	Easton 1151¾ Road To Ponder114nkFreedomsEdge115hd	Checked	12
13Mar88- 1Aqu	fst	1 1/16 ⊡	:49 1:13⅘ 1:46⅗	Alw 31000	5	6	53½	54½	64	64¼	Santagata N	b 117	19.90	72-18	Feldspar 110¾ Knockon 117nk Target X. 117hd	Outrun	8
2Mar88- 2Aqu	fst	1 1/16 ⊡	:48⅘ 1:14 1:48	Clm 17500	9	10	97¾	86¾	64	1¾	Santagata N	b 117	9.40	69-21	Quindcillion117¾DrbyJunior117noFrdomsEdg113nk	Up closing yds	12
27Feb88- 2Aqu	fst	6f ⊡	:23 :46⅖ 1:12	Clm 14000	3	6	52½	42¼	52	41¾	Santos J A	b 119	8.20	82-19	Equal Terms 1121¼ Bienestar 108nk StraightDancer119nk	Even try	6
10Feb88- 1Aqu	fst	1 1/16 ⊡	:49⅖ 1:16 1:49⅗	Md 45000	4	3	43	21½	1½	12	Santos J A	b 118	4.30	61-29	Quindecillion1182OfficerKrupke1182¼BackAlleyJack12211	Driving	7
24Jan88- 2Aqu	fst	1⅛ ⊡	:49⅘ 1:14⅘ 1:54	Md 30000	3	8	62½	32	2hd	2no	Migliore R	b 118	*2.30	72-17	Bye Dad 120no Quindecillion 1183 Leopold I 1187	Just missed	12
21Jan88- 1Aqu	my	6f ⊡	:21⅘ :45⅗ 1:11⅗	Md Sp Wt	11	1	1016	1015	913	810	Lovato F Jr	b 122	16.00	76-21	Knockon 1222¾ Just Great 1221¼ Where's Billy 122½	Outrun	11

LATEST WORKOUTS Apr 4 Bel tr.t 4f fst :49⅖ b · Mar 25 Bel tr.t 4f fst :48⅘ h · Mar 19 Bel tr.t 3f fst :37⅗ b · Mar 8 Bel tr.t 4f fst :49⅗ b

* 2–5

Paris Office

Ch. c. 4, by Secretariat—Oui, by Le Fabuleux
Br.—Vanderbilt A G (Md)
Tr.—Violette Richard A
Own.—Vanderbilt A G

121

Lifetime	1987	12	1	0	3	$37,996
17 2 2 3	1986	5	1	2	0	$25,480
$63,478	Turf	7	0	0	3	$11,580

21Nov87- 3Aqu	fst	1⅛	48⅘ 1:14⅖ 1:53⅘	3↑ Alw 33000	2	6	67½	89¼	619	619½	Davis R G	b 115	4.60	46-30	Classic Move 117¾ Heritance 1157 November Beans 117½	Outrun	9
23Oct87- 8Aqu	fm	1⅜ Ⓣ	:52⅕ 1:42 2:19	3↑ Alw 33000	2	9	97¾	1014	812	88½	Romero R P	114	9.60	67-19	I'mEnthused114hdSlopeMster114nkChristopher'sTim1141¼	Outrun	10
12Oct87-10Suf	my	1⅛	46⅗ 1:11⅖ 1:50⅕	Yankee H	3	8	99¼	99¼	46½	56¾	Lovato F Jr	115	7.50	80-21	Foxy Ziad 1161½ Mister S. M. 1231¾ C'est Bon 1142½	Rallied	9
13Sep87- 8Bel	sly	1½	47⅖ 2:04⅖ 2:30	Lawrn Real	6	7	718	66	54	45½	Santos J A	114	4.10	64-23	Tertiary Zone 1141¾ Major Beard 1143¼ Sport Royal 114½	Hung	9
13Sep87-Grade II																	
19Aug87- 7Sar	sf	1 3/16 Ⓣ	:49⅕ 1:15 2:01	3↑ Alw 28000	3	8	817	813	43	3¾	Santos J A	112	5.10	60-39	Computer Code 114½ Classic Move 117nkParisOffice112nk	Bore in	8
2Aug87- 7Bel	fm	1¼ [T]	:50⅖ 1:39 2:03⅖	3↑ Alw 28000	4	4	42½	52½	72¾	63¾	Pezua J M	114	6.30	73-19	Patlomat 113no Core A Apple 112hd I'm Enthused 1121¾	Tired	8
13Jly87- 7Bel	fm	1⅜ [T]	:48⅘ 2:03⅖ 2:16	3↑ Alw 28000	9	6	611	67	47	34¾	Pezua J M	116	3.50	72-19	Sure Dad 1173¾ I'm Enthused 1161 Paris Office 116¾	Late bid	9
2Jly87- 7Bel	sly	1⅜	49⅘ 1:39⅗ 2:20⅗	3↑ Alw 27000	2	5	54	32½	1hd	1½	Pezua J M	111	*1.30	77-27	Paris Office 111½ Gone Cat 1122¼ I'm No Yankee 11710	Drivng	6
18Jun87- 5Bel	fm	1¼ [T]	:48⅘ 1:37⅕ 2:01⅘	3↑ Alw 27000	3	9	96¼	85½	62¼	3nk	Santos J A	112	*3.60	85-10	I'm Enthused 114hd True Vigor 117nk Paris Office 112½	Rallied	12
6Jun87- 9Lrl	fm	1 1/16 Ⓣ	:46⅖ 1:11⅗ 1:43⅕	[S]H S Finney	4	8	814	87¾	58	53¼	DeCarlo C P	111	4.70	84-18	Ten Keys 119nk Green Book 1221 Prolinage 1192	Wide	8

LATEST WORKOUTS May 3 Bel 3f fst :35⅘ h · ●Apr 28 Bel 5f sly 1:00⅖ h · Apr 23 Bel 5f fst 1:03 b

5–2

Jig Time Dixie

Gr. g. 3, by Jig Time—I'm for Dixie, by I'm For More
Br.—Bussmann R F Mr-Mrs (Fla)
Tr.—Hertler John O
Own.—Meadow Hill

115

Lifetime	1988	6	2	1	0	$32,040
6 2 1 0	1987	0	M	0	0	
$32,040	Turf	1	1	0	0	$18,600

29Apr88- 7Aqu	sf	1 1/16 Ⓣ	:50⅖ 1:15⅘ 1:48⅘	3↑ Alw 31000	2	1	11	1½	14	1nk	Valiente D	b 113	20.20	61-39	Jig Time Dixie 113nk Impersonator 1121 Revivalist 1122¾	All out	9
20Apr88- 4Aqu	fst	1	:47⅕ 1:13⅗ 1:40⅕	3↑ Md 35000	12	4	3½	1½	11½	1no	Valiente D	b 115	*2.10	65-26	Jig TimeDixie115noHanoverBear1134¾TopoftheRidge1084¾	Driving	12
8Apr88- 4Aqu	my	7f	:23 :46⅘ 1:25⅖	3↑ Md 35000	3	8	63¼	42½	54	54¾	Lovato F Jr	b 115	4.10	69-17	Brookie Boy 115½ Yonkel Yonkel 115¾ Mega Silver1153	No factor	14
29Mar88- 5Aqu	fst	1⅛	:50⅖ 1:15⅕ 1:54⅘	Md 47500	1	1	1½	1½	3½	46¾	Lovato F Jr	b 120	3.70	54-28	BltchtonExprss1183½ArctcSrvy1222½ArctcCmmndr118¾	Weakened	10
14Mar88- 2Aqu	fst	1 1/16 ⊡	:49⅗ 1:15⅕ 1:48⅕	Md 35000	6	1	1hd	1½	2hd	2nk	Lovato F Jr	b 122	7.40	68-20	Spookem Forbes 122nk Jig TimeDixie1224MegaSilver1177	Gamely	11
7Mar88- 3Aqu	fst	6f ⊡	:23⅕ :47⅕ 1:14	Md 45000	7	8	89¾	912	811	66¾	Lovato F Jr	b 118	22.80	67-25	Dawns Early Light1181RusticAura122nkMultipleTrails1182	Outrun	11

LATEST WORKOUTS Mar 25 Bel tr.t 4f fst :48⅘ h

5–2

Taken off turf course. Run on dirt at same distance (two turns).
Win wagering only. No exactas.
First half of Daily Double.

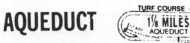

(8 Horses)

2 AQUEDUCT

6 FURLONGS. (1.08) CLAIMING. Purse $16,500. Fillies, 3-year-olds. Weight, 121 lbs. Non-winners of two races since April 1 allowed 3 lbs. Of a race since then, 5 lbs. Claiming price $17,500 for each $1,000 to $15,500 allowed 2 lbs. Races when entred to be claimed for $14,000 or less not considered.)

Clever But Costly

Own.—Malary Stable

$17,500 **Dk. b. or br. f. 3, by Clever Trick—Swoonlow, by Swoonen**
Br.—William Carl & James D. Conway (Ky)
Tr.—Lake Robert P

116

Lifetime 7 2 0 0 $22,710 — 1988 7 2 0 0 $22,710 — 1987 0 M 0 0

27Apr88-	1Aqu	fst	7f	:22⅖	:45⅕	1:25⅖	ⒻClm 17500	2	8	63¾	74½	44	42	Santos J A	b	116	13.90	72-18	PocketO'Swets116noPromistoYou112nkDncingSocks1181¾	Rallied	11
20Apr88-	3Aqu	fst	6f	:23	:47⅖	1:12⅘	ⒻClm 17500	6	7	64¾	66	56	58	Pezua J M	b	116	3.20	68-26	Man She's Sweet 1161¼ Int'l Guest1164DancingSocks1182	Outrun	8
29Mar88-	6Aqu	fst	7f	:21⅕	:45⅖	1:25⅗	ⒻClm 25000	7	3	44½	54½	56½	513	Romero R P		116	*1.80	60-28	Fini La Guerre 111½ Split Moment 1143 Bearly 1141½	Even try	9
11Mar88-	6Aqu	fst	6f	⊡:23	:46⅘	1:13	ⒻClm 35000	5	6	77¾	79	59	47	Romero R P		116	12.00	72-31	SucyVoyge116nkGoldenSweethert1113¾Nskr'sSong1163	No threat	8
29Feb88-	1Aqu	fst	6f	⊡:22	:45⅘	1:13	ⒻClm 45000	6	2	35	811	89¼	78½	Davis R G		112	2.50	70-25	Crafty Alexas 111¾ Dusty Donna 116½ Smartn'Irish116¾	Brief foot	8
22Feb88-	1Aqu	fst	6f	⊡:22⅕	:46⅕	1:13⅗	ⒻClm c-25000	4	6	3nk	41½	21	11¼	Santos J A		118	3.30	76-32	CleverButCostly1181¼CompltAccord1162½FirndFrosty1163	Driving	7
5Feb88-	4Aqu	fst	6f	⊡:22⅘	:47⅗	1:14⅖	ⒻMd 35000	11	3	2½	21½	1hd	1½	Santos J A		121	*1.60	72-32	ClvrButCostly121½RunForMyWif1192¾HonysucklQun1218	Driving	12

LATEST WORKOUTS Apr 11 Aqu 4f fst :49⅖ h ● Mar 24 Aqu 4f fst :48⅕ h

7–2

Miss Sherby

Own.—Gagliano S

$15,500 **Dk. b. or br. f. 3, by Cojak—Proudest Moment, by Proudest Roman**
Br.—Weinberg R (Ky)
Tr.—Barrera Oscar S

105^7

Lifetime 17 1 2 2 $23,270 — 1988 9 0 1 1 $5,610 — 1987 8 1 1 1 $17,660

4May88-	2Aqu	fst	6f	:22	:45⅖	1:11⅗	ⒻClm 22500	2	4	75½	98	95½	78¾	Walker E E7	b	107	46.10	73-19	Jessica Pie 111nk SplitMoment1165ChangeableQueen116½	Outrun	10
18Apr88-	5Aqu	fst	6f	:22	:45⅗	1:12⅖	ⒻClm 22500	10	6	98	68	88½	85¾	Romero R P		116	25.10	72-20	Split Moment1141¾CheekyToo114nkDiamondEvening116nk	Outrun	11
6Apr88-	4Aqu	fst	6f	:22⅖	:46⅖	1:12⅗	ⒻClm 30000	1	8	21½	41¾	63	67	Pezua J M		112	13.20	70-25	Kim Cat 116nk Jessica Pie 1121½ Provelvet 1181½	Taken up	8
2Apr88-	2Aqu	fst	6f	:22⅖	:46⅖	1:13⅘	ⒻClm c-17500	8	10	67½	69	65½	75½	Ortega P Jr5	b	111	8.20	65-22	DncingSocks1161Mymothrwrndm1131¾DGSis116nk	Pinched bk.st.	12
21Mar88-	3Aqu	fst	6f	:23⅕	:48⅖	1:15	ⒻClm 15500	5	4	4¾	21½	23	22¼	Ortega P Jr5	b	107	6.60	63-28	Lulu Dancer 1082¼ Miss Sherby1071½CharmingIrish1122½	2nd best	8
9Mar88-	4Aqu	fst	6f	⊡:23	:47⅕	1:14⅖	ⒻClm 20000	6	6	52¼	85¾	86¼	84¾	Correa C J5	b	108	28.60	67-26	Roleplay 1141¼ Mine 111no Mymotherwarnedme 1181	Tired	11
4Mar88-	1Aqu	fst	6f	⊡:23⅖	:48	1:14⅘	ⒻClm 17500	6	2	21½	2½	21	3¾	Ortega P Jr5	b	111	3.10	69-18	Bearly 116nk Dancing Socks 116½ Miss Sherby 111hd	Weakened	7
8Feb88-	5Aqu	fst	1⅛	⊡:48⅕	1:14⅘	1:56⅖	ⒻClm 32500	3	1	2hd	41½	716	728¾	Ortega P Jr5	b	109	13.00	31-24	Devastated 116hd Ballet Birdie 111¾ Last Shower 1181	Gave way	7
30Jan88-	4Aqu	fst	6f	⊡:21⅘	:45⅗	1:12	ⒻClm c-25000	9	2	24	22	87½	88	Hernandez R	b	116	7.20	76-17	Fair and Frosty1162GoldenCreditCard1162BalletBirdie111no	Tired	10
15Oct87-	4Bel	fst	7f	:23⅕	:47⅕	1:26⅕	ⒻClm 70000	2	4	53½	66	57½	58	Santos J A	b	114	12.10	63-27	Roleplay 112nk Cute Move 114hd Bionaire 1126¾	Steadied turn	7

7–1

Flower de Noel

Own.—Garren M M

$16,500 **B. f. 3, by Sovereign Dancer—Fleur de Noel, by Chieftain**
Br.—Hershe Marty Jr (Fla)
Tr.—Garren Murray M

107^7

Lifetime 16 4 2 2 $25,981 — 1988 7 1 0 1 $6,160 — 1987 9 3 2 1 $19,821 — Turf 1 0 1 0 $3,111

27Apr88-	1Aqu	fst	7f	:22⅖	:45⅕	1:25⅖	ⒻClm 17500	10	1	1½	1hd	1114	1114	Pezua J M	b	116	34.00	60-18	PocketO'Swts116noPromistoYou112nkDncingSocks1181¾	Stopped	11
24Mar88-	1Aqu	fst	7f	:23	:46⅖	1:26⅕	ⒻClm 30000	4	4	2hd	2hd	55	717½	Pezua J M	b	112	11.70	52-25	ChangebleQueen114¾JessicPie109½DimondEvening1132¼	Stopped	7
21Mar88-	3Aqu	fst	6f	:23⅕	:48⅖	1:15	ⒻClm c-15500	1	8	818	811	817	820¾	Pagano S R	b	112	2.30	44-28	LuluDncr1082¼MissShrby1071½ChrmngIrsh1122½	Broke awkwardly	8
21Feb88-	9Suf	gd	6f	:22⅘	:48⅕	1:17⅕	ⒻAlw 10000	2	2	12½	31	32½	514	Pagano S R	b	122	3.40	41-43	Real Moony1143¼NewburyStreet1196¾LuckyMaid1192½	Sp'd, tired	6
10Feb88-	9Suf	fst	6f	:22⅖	:46⅕	1:12⅘	ⒻClm 15000	2	5	12½	13	12½	11¼	Pagano S R	b	114	*1.70	77-24	FlowerdeNoel1141¼NewburyStret1142¼GloriousCthy1091¾	Driving	6
31Jan88-	9Suf	gd	6f	:22⅖	:46⅖	1:14⅖	ⒻAlw 10000	1	2	1½	1½	1½	35½	Pagano S R	b	119	3.10	63-32	AmzingAngel1191¾GloriousCthy1193¾FlowerdNol1198½	Weakened	5
24Jan88-	9Suf	fst	6f	:22⅗	:46⅘	1:14⅕	ⒻAlw 10000	1	6	1½	3½	32	811	Pagano S R	b	119	7.70	59-34	SweetAlex1192Hven'tGotClue1161¾DncForRogr1191	Sp'd into str.	9
23Dec87-	4Suf	fst	6f	:23⅕	:47⅗	1:15⅖	ⒻClm 10000	5	1	13½	14	16	14½	Pagano S R	b	119	1.70	64-33	Flower de Noel 1194½DanceRoyDance1191¾Laughnot119nk	Driving	6
16Dec87-	6Suf	gd	6f	:23	:48⅕	1:17	ⒻClm 7500	4	1	12½	14	15	13	Pagano S R	b	119	*1.10	56-38	Flower de Noel 1193 Fast Treasure 119½ My Wave 1225¾	Driving	7
9Dec87-	6Suf	fst	6f	:23	:47⅘	1:15⅘	ⒻClm 10000	3	4	1hd	1hd	23	39	Pagano S R	b	119	2.70	53-40	Patty'sDayNHalf1228¾MyWave122nkFlowerdeNoel1191	Weakened	7

LATEST WORKOUTS ● Apr 21 Bel tr.t 5f fst 1:00⅘ h Apr 3 Bel tr.t 3f fst :36⅖ h ● Mar 17 Suf 4f fst :50⅖ b

20–1

(*Continued on following page*)

Second half of Daily Double. Exacta wagering. Quinella wagering.

Mymotherwarnedme

Own.—Twin Cedar Stables

B. f. 3, by El Baba—Mating Native, by Last Dance
$17,500   Br.—Beechwood Group I (Ky)
Tr.—Curtis William Jr

			Lifetime	1988 7 1 2 1	$19,190
	116		8 1 2 1	1987 1 M 0 0	
			$19,190		5—1

18Apr88- 5Aqu fst 6f	:22	:45⅖ 1:12⅗	ⒻClm 22500	1 10 8⁷¹10¹⁰10¹⁰ 9⁷¼	Peck B D⁵	b 109	14.90	70-20 Split Moment114¹¾CheekyToo114nkDiamondEvening116nk Outrun 11
2Apr88- 2Aqu fst 6f	:22⅖	:46⅖ 1:13⅘	ⒻClm 17500	3 2 1½ 2hd 11½ 2¹	Peck B D⁵	b 113	7.20	70-22 DncingSocks116¹Mymotherwarnedme113¹¾DeeGeSis116nk Gamely 12
20Mar88- 4Aqu fst 6f	:23	:47⅖ 1:12⅘	ⒻClm 25000	3 1 2½ 41 8⁷¼ 9¹⁹¼	Romero R P	b 118	15.10	57-27 First Gem 114¾ Smiling Tune 116hd Mine 109¼ Stopped 9
9Mar88- 4Aqu fst 6f	:23	:47⅕ 1:14⅖	ⒻClm 25000	7 2 3¹ 2¹ 2½ 3¹¼	Venezia M	b 118	9.60	71-26 Roleplay 114¹¼ Mine 111no Mymotherwarnedme 118¹ Ridden out 11
2Mar88- 9Aqu fst 6f	:23	:46⅖ 1:13⅘	ⒻMd 35000	6 3 11 11½ 13 15	Venezia M	b 121	*2.00	76-21 Mymotherwrndm121¹⁵CoolEmbrc110¹¼SoringOvr123¾ Ridden out 11
8Feb88- 4Aqu fst 6f	▣:23⅕	:47⅕ 1:14½	ⒻMd 50000	2 4 1½ 11 2²½ 47½	Venezia M	b 121	*1.20	65-24 Rajab's Tune 117⁶ Dats Ruby 117nk Senility 117¹¼ Weakened 11
25Jan88- 4Aqu fst 6f	▣:23	:46⅗ 1:12⅗	ⒻMd 50000	4 3 1hd 1hd 2²½ 24	Venezia M	121	*1.60	77-23 Smartn'Irish117⁴Mymotherwarnedme121⁴Tgett121¼ Second best 10
21Dec87- 4Aqu fst 6f	▣:22⅕	:45⅗ 1:11⅘	ⒻMd Sp Wt	2 1 2³ 2⁴ 3⁵¼ 5⁸¼	Santagata N	117	14.00	76-15 Anthenian Girl 117¼ Antiqua Winds 117hd Prattler 117³¼ Tired 9

LATEST WORKOUTS   Apr 13 Bel 5f fst 1:00⅘ h   Apr 8 Bel 4f gd :49⅕ b   Mar 30 Bel tr.t 3f fst :36 b

Int'l Guest

Own.—Black Gold Stable

Ch. f. 3, by Mr International—Honor Guest, by Bolero
$15,500   Br.—Evangelista T (NY)
Tr.—Meyer Jerome C

			Lifetime	1988 12 2 1 2	$28,290
	112		22 2 3	1987 10 M 1 1	$10,340
			$38,630		5—1

27Apr88- 1Aqu fst 7f	:22⅖	:45½ 1:25⅗	ⒻClm 17500	3 11 9⁷¼10⁹ 7⁸ 7⁵	Santagata N	b 116	6.50	69-18 PocketO'Swets116noPromistoYou112nkDncingSocks118¹¾ Outrun 11
20Apr88- 3Aqu fst 6f	:23	:47⅘ 1:12⅘	ⒻClm 17500	4 5 4¹½ 3½ 1½ 2¹½	Santagata N	b 116	12.90	75-26 Man She's Sweet116¹½Int'lGuest116⁴DancingSocks118² Game try 8
16Apr88- 6Aqu fst 1	:47⅗	1:13⅗ 1:39½	3+Ⓕ⒮Alw 31000	7 10 10⁸¾11¹¹ 8¹²¹⁰13¾	Krone J A	b 112	19.30	56-21 Daz's Who 121nk Maidwell 121³¼ Konnies Joy 121hd Outrun 11
28Mar88- 1Aqu fst 1⅛	:49⅖	1:15⅜ 1:56⅖	ⒻClm 25000	1 3 45½ 43 5¹⁴ 6²⁵	Krone J A	b 116	3.50	28-30 Kaikilani 116⁵¾ Mine 114³ Hollywood Barb 114nk Tired 7
17Mar88- 1Aqu fst 1⅛	:47⅘	1:13⅖ 1:53⅘	ⒻClm 25000	6 8 8¹⁶ 7⁷¼ 34½ 18½	Krone J A	b 116	17.20	57-27 Devastated 116⁷ Fay Gay 111¼ Int'l Guest 116⁴ P'ssd tired ones 8
12Mar88- 7Aqu fst 6f	▣:22⅖	:46½ 1:13	Ⓕ⒮Alw 31000	5 8 5³½ 54¼ 46½ 7¹⁰¼	Krone J A	b 116	10.20e	69-22 Unsanctioned 116no Victoria Creek 116¾ Talc Two 111⁶¼ Outrun 9
25Feb88- 7Aqu fst 6f	▣:47⅘	1:13⅗ 1:49⅘	Ⓕ⒮Alw 31000	3 7 5⁴ 3²½ 1hd 3²½	Krone J A	b 116	55.20	58-25 ElegantMoment121²¼FamilyFraud113noInt'lGuest116no Weakened 9
17Feb88- 3Aqu fst 6f	▣:22⅗	:45⅖ 1:12⅗	ⒻClm c-16500	8 2 2¹½ 2¹¼ 3¹½ 5⁴¼	Correa C J⁵	b 109	7.40	64-29 Roleplay 116¼ First Gem 111nk Weakened 7
10Feb88- 1Aqu fst 6f	▣:22⅗	:46⅖ 1:13⅗	Ⓕ⒮Alw 30000	4 6 7⁷¼ 7⁷¾ 6⁹¼ 5¹²¾	Correa C J⁵	b 111	30.20	64-29 AnthenianGirl116⁸¼VictoriCreek116¹¼ChngebleQueen109¹ Outrun 7
28Jan88- 1Aqu fst 6f	▣:23	:47⅘ 1:16	ⒻClm 15500	4 3 2⁴ 1½ 1½ 1¹¾	Correa C J⁵	b 109	*1.00	64-30 Int'l Guest 109¹¾ Auntie Gosh116²¼GoldenDistinctive107³ Driving 7

Promise to You

Own.—Garcia J I

Ch. f. 3, by Dunham's Gift—Dance Time, by Tarleton Oak
$17,500   Br.—Boone Mr-Mrs C M (Ky)
Tr.—Martin Jose

			Lifetime	1988 6 1 1 0	$13,020
	111⁵		8 1 1 0	1987 2 M 0 0	
			$13,020		8—1

4May88- 2Aqu fst 6f	:22	:45⅖ 1:11⅗	ⒻClm 22500	1 8 6⁵ 8⁷½ 6⁴¾ 9⁹¾	Antley C W	b 114	12.00	72-19 Jessica Pie 111nk SplitMoment116⁵ChangeableQueen116¼ Outrun 10
27Apr88- 1Aqu fst 7f	:22⅖	:45½ 1:25⅗	ⒻClm 15500	5 7 2½ 2hd 11½ 2no	Antley C W	b 112	39.30	74-18 PocktO'Swts116noPromstoYo112nkDncngScks118¹¼ Bobbled late 11
8Apr88- 3Aqu my 7f	:22⅖	:46⅖ 1:24⅖	ⒻClm 22500	7 3 1½ 2½ 69 6¹⁶½	Santos J A	b 118	8.80	63-17 Roleplay 109¹½ Split Moment 114⁵ Fencible 116²¼ Tired 7
21Mar88- 3Aqu fst 6f	:23½	:48⅖ 1:15	ⒻClm c-17500	7 3 2hd 3¹½ 37 46¼	Krone J A	b 118	4.10	59-28 Lulu Dancer108²¼MissSherby107½CharmingIrish112²¼ Weakened 8
11Mar88- 6Aqu fst 6f	▣:23	:46½ 1:13	ⒻClm 22500	4 5 5³¼ 46½ 69½ 7¹⁰¼	Venezia M	b 116	30.30	68-31 SaucyVoyage116nkGoldenSweetheart111³¾Naskr'sSong116³ Tired 8
2Mar88- 3Aqu fst 6f	▣:22⅖	:47 1:13⅘	ⒻMd 30000	7 5 11 12¼ 14¼ 17¼	Venezia M	113	4.10	75-21 Promise to You 117⁷¼ Senility 117²¼ Toy For Joy112¾ Ridden out 12
30Nov87- 3Aqu sly 7f	:23¼	:47⅘ 1:28⅕	ⒻMd 30000	11 7 41 5⁴ 10¹⁷ 9²⁰¼	Venezia M	113	7.00	40-30 Peggy's Prospect110²¼CatsandTigers113¹¼Brevolly113³ Gave way 14
14Nov87- 2Aqu gd 6f	:22	:45½ 1:12½	ⒻMd 45000	10 11 7⁹½ 8⁹¾ 8⁷½ 8⁶¼	Venezia M	113	3.50	74-13 Split Moment 117¼ Turn to Slew 117²¼ Fay Gay 115no Outrun 11

LATEST WORKOUTS   Apr 18 Bel tr.t 4f fst :49 b   ●Apr 6 Bel tr.t 3f fst :35 h   Apr 1 Bel tr.t 3f fst :36⅘ h

Irish Mistress

Own.—Ruben L

Dk. b. or br. f. 3, by Advocator—Irish Comedy, by Irish Castle
$16,500   Br.—Oak Manor Farm (Ky)
Tr.—Drogitis Michael

			Lifetime	1988 5 1 2 0	$13,008
	114		11 4 2 0	1987 6 3 0 0	$13,890
			$26,898		*
					6—5

23Mar88- 3Aqu fst 1⅛	:49⅕	1:13⅘ 1:55⅖	ⒻClm 50000	4 2 42½ 64¾ 714 715½	Santagata N	116	12.50	42-24 Naskra's Song 112hd Helga's Honey 116no Outshine 116³ Wide 7
5Mar88- 8GS fst 6f	:22	:45⅗ 1:13	ⒻⓇWoodcrest	2 6 5¹⁰ 5¹² 5¹⁰ 4¹¹½	Ferrer J C	118	6.80	65-23 Maria'sBrownEyes118²HaiPlateau120¾BubbDulyh122⁹ No menace 6
12Feb88- 9GS sly 1	:47⅕	1:14⅖ 1:43⅗	ⒻⒶAlw 11500	3 3 35 32 1hd 11½	Rocco J	116	*1.60	56-30 Irish Mistress 116¹½ Avatine 116¾ Helga's Honey 116⁴ Driving 5
31Jan88- 5Pha my 1	:47⅖	1:14⅖ 1:42⅘	ⒻAlw 13500	1 3 32 32¼ 2¹½ 2nk	Ferrer J C	116	3.40	60-25 PetitePinc116nkIrishMistrss116⁶GrndKnightsWif122¹⁹ Erratically 5
17Jan88- 1Pha fst 1⁷⁰	:47⅗	1:13⅘ 1:45⅕	ⒻClm c-18000	7 3 32¼ 31½ 2¹½ 23	Colton R E	116	*2.40	66-23 Peter's Gift 116³ Irish Mistress 116²¼ Sable Stop 112⁷ Gamely 8
15Dec87- 2Pha sly 1	:48½	1:14⅖ 1:43½	ⒻClm c-14000	6 5 52¼ 43½ 1½ 12½	Rocco J	116	*2.00	58-26 IrishMistress116²¼Ms.Strshine119nkIrishCeeG116³ Br in air, drvg 7
24Nov87- 5Med fst 6f	:23⅖	:47⅖ 1:12⅖	ⒻClm 40000	1 6 52 43½ 56¼ 58¼	Cordova D W	110	2.60e	70-23 ThLdyRls116¾SmmrBlssm113²¼GrndKnghtsWf113¹¼ Lacked rally 6
3Nov87- 5Med fst 6f	:23	:46⅖ 1:13	ⒻClm 35000	3 4 4½ 76 64½ 57½	Krone J A	111	7.70	69-21 Mnorhven115³NewYorkNncy112¹½Dⓗ Whispring Spring108 Outrun 7
22Oct87- 7Med fst 1	:47⅕	1:15⅕ 1:43⅖	ⒻClm c-16000	8 3 2¹ 44 43¼ 43¾	Krone J A	109	2.50	54-25 PtltOnMyBll108³MyMdnghtMrg115nkDsBoomBm110¼ Weakened 8
4Oct87- 7Del fst 6f	:22¼	:45½ 1:13⅗	Clm 13000	3 4 23 2¹½ 1hd 12	Intelisano G P Jr	110	5.60	73-30 Irish Mistress 110² Afterdeck 116¹ First Ode 119¹½ Driving 8

LATEST WORKOUTS   May 2 Bel 5f fst 1:03 b   Apr 22 Bel 5f fst 1:02 h   Apr 18 Bel 4f fst :49⅘ b   Apr 12 Pha 4f fst :49⅕ b

(9 Horses)

3 AQUEDUCT

START
7 FURLONGS
AQUEDUCT
FINISH

7 FURLONGS. (1.20⅕) CLAIMING. Purse $16,500. 4-year-olds and upward. Weight, 122 lbs. Non-winners of two races since April 1 allowed 3 lbs. Of a race since then 5 lbs. Claiming price $17,500; for each $1,000 to $15,500, 2 lbs. (Races when entered to be claimed for $14,000 or less not considered.)

Coupled—Bienestar and Talc Power; Weebok and Bold Mein; Ballyduggan and Empathetic.

Bienestar *

Own.—Gagliano S

Dk. b. or br. g. 7, by Cormorant—Jig Time Rose, by Jig Time
$15,500 Br.—Wind O'Hill Farm (Pa)
Tr.—Barrera Oscar S

106 7 — Lifetime 82 12 10 12 $231,818 — 1988 10 0 1 3 $10,140 — 1987 24 3 5 3 $70,050 — Turf 3 1 0 0 $6,000

23Mar88- 9Aqu fst 6f	:22⅕ :45⅘ 1:12	Clm 13000	3 9 109½ 98 75¾ 54¾	Walker E E7	b 108	6.50	75-24 Soleri 112½ Visible Force 117½ Luna Lula 1132	Rallied 12	
14Mar88- 1Aqu fst 6f	[•]:23 :46⅕ 1:10⅘	Clm 15500	2 5 63½ 56 45½ 34¾	Walker E E7	b 106	*1.40e	85-20 Straight Dancer 117hd Easton 1174¾ Bienestar 1061¾	Rallied 9	
7Mar88- 9Aqu fst 1 1/16	[•]:48⅘ 1:14⅘ 1:48⅗	Clm 14000	9 7 52¼ 63¼ 56 56¾	Boulanger G5	b 112	*2.60	59-25 Macho 1122 Ambassadorship 108nk Proverbial II 117½	Fin. early 12	
27Feb88- 2Aqu fst 6f	[•]:23 :46⅖ 1:12	Clm 12000	2 5 42½ 62¾ 41½ 21¼	Ortega P Jr5	b 108	5.30e	83-19 Equal Terms 1121¼ Bienestar 108nk StraightDancer119nk	Game try 6	
24Feb88- 3Aqu fst 6f	[•]:23⅗ :47⅖ 1:13⅗	Clm 14000	10 6 129½ 1212 1110 107¼	Antley C W	b 117	6.00	69-21 Flippant 117nk Mc Michael 1081 Saskatchwan 117hd	Outrun 12	6–1
21Feb88- 9Aqu fst 6f	[•]:22⅘ :47 1:12⅖	Clm 17500	12 2 64¾ 43½ 78 79½	Antley C W	b 117	13.60	72-21 Rocky Knave 1124¾ Askrano 1172¾ Too Tough to Beat117hd	Tired 12	
14Feb88- 9Aqu fst 1 1/16	[•]:47⅖ 1:13 1:46⅖	Clm 17500	4 3 35½ 33½ 49½ 36½	Antley C W	b 117	*3.30	70-16 Bold Mein 1171 Brave and Bright1175½Bienestar1171	Lacked rally 11	
27Jan88- 2Aqu fst 1 1/16	[•]:49⅕ 1:14⅖ 1:46⅗	Clm 20000	8 6 42 63¼ 47½ 310¼	Boulanger G5	b 108	2.00e	66-27 Effective Action 1157WarriorCountry1173¼Bienestar1081½	Evenly 12	
21Jan88- 2Aqu my 1 1/16	[•]:47⅕ 1:11⅖ 1:43⅘	Clm 30000	4 7 98¼ 1014 814 713¼	Kaenel J L	b 115	19.00	77-21 Romancer 1173½ Silky Appeal1103½LordWindemere1172½	Steadied 12	
16Jan88- 3Aqu fst 1⅛	[•]:47⅘ 1:12⅕ 1:52⅕	Clm 25000	12 4 46 64¾ 66¾ 68¾	Antley C W	b 117	16.10	72-22 Silky Appeal 1122½ Boutinierre 1173 Overbought 115nk	Tired 12	

LATEST WORKOUTS May 2 Bel tr.t 3f fst :37 b Apr 19 Bel tr.t 3f fst :37⅕ b

Test of Loyalty

Own.—Roth Joseph

Dk. b. or br. g. 5, by Fire Dancer—Call Her Joyce, by Up Spirits
$17,500 Br.—Newchance Farm (Fla)
Tr.—Pagano Frank X

112 5 — Lifetime 57 12 7 11 $98,163 — 1988 11 3 2 1 $28,850 — 1987 22 5 1 5 $32,790 — Turf 1 0 0 0 $610

28Apr88- 2Aqu sly 6f	:22 :45⅘ 1:11⅖	Clm 17500	5 4 62¾ 54 34 42¾	Santos J A	b 117	*1.60	80-17 Artimon 1151¾ [DH]Musial 113 [DH]Sass The Maitre d' 1141	Rallied 9	
18Apr88- 3Aqu fst 6f	:21⅘ :45⅗ 1:11⅕	Clm 17500	8 3 43 41¾ 22½ 32½	Santos J A	b 117	5.30	81-20 Straight Dancer 115¾ Bold Mein1171¾TestofLoyalty1172½	Blocked 10	
18Apr88-Awarded second purse money									
5Apr88- 2Aqu fst 6f	:22⅖ :46⅕ 1:11	Clm 22500	9 6 63¼ 62½ 64½ 56	Santagata N	b 115	17.50	79-23 Passing Thunder1171FattyBoy1171EffectiveAction1171¼	Even try 10	
26Mar88- 4Aqu sly 7f	:22⅗ :45⅕ 1:23	Clm 22500	4 11 54½ 45½ 37½ 410	Cruguet J	b 115	14.70	76-23 TruthBeTold1124Timperature1174¾SociallyInformed1171¼	Bore in 12	
14Mar88- 1Aqu fst 6f	[•]:23 :46⅕ 1:10⅘	Clm c-16500	3 7 42½ 33 34½ 46½	Migliore R	b 115	2.10	83-20 Straight Dancer 117hd Easton 1174¾ Bienestar 1061¾	Evenly 9	5–1
1Mar88- 3GS fst 6f	:23 :47⅕ 1:12	Clm 17000	3 3 42½ 52 31½ 32½	Castaneda K	b 117	*1.60	80-33 Aprils Son 1191½ Ro Bart G. 112¾ TestofLoyalty1176½	Stead'd str. 6	
21Feb88- 2Aqu fst 6f	[•]:23⅕ :47⅕ 1:12⅗	Clm 16500	7 7 4¾ 4nk 2hd 21¾	Krone J A	b 115	3.40	79-21 HoldYourMoney1101¾TestofLoyalty115¾EqualTerms112hd	Gamely 10	
14Feb88- 9Pha fst 6½f	:22⅕ :44⅖ 1:16⅗	Alw 6500s	8 7 4nk 21 24 47½	Castaneda K	b 122	*1.30	82-14 LuciteLight1196Gaylord'sShelter116½HighIndKing1221	Weakened 9	
29Jan88- 5Pha my 6f	:22⅗ :45⅗ 1:10⅕	Clm 17000	3 2 21 2½ 1hd 11½	Marquez A	b 116	*1.70	90-17 Test of Loyalty 1161½ Razzle 1092 Kona Way 1198½	Driving 5	
16Jan88- 7Pha fst 6f	:22 :44⅘ 1:10⅘	Clm 14000	4 3 5¾ 2½ 11 11	Castaneda K	b 119	*2.10	87-16 Test of Loyalty 1191 Saltine Warrior107hdRandomly1191½	Driving 12	

Bold Mein

Own.—Friends Only Stable

Ch. rig. 5, by Tyrant—Over the Moon, by Prince John
$17,500 Br.—Nielsen Joanne T (NY)
Tr.—Levine Bruce

117 — Lifetime 40 9 6 6 $119,212 — 1988 8 3 1 1 $37,200 — 1987 16 0 4 2 $12,964

18Apr88- 3Aqu fst 6f	:21⅘ :45⅗ 1:11⅕	Clm 17500	3 8 78½ 72¾ 33 2¾	Romero R P	b 117	9.40	83-20 Straight Dancer 115¾ Bold Mein 1171¾TestofLoyalty1172½	Rallied 10	
18Apr88-Awarded first purse money									
28Mar88- 4Aqu fst 1⅛	:48⅖ 1:13⅗ 1:53⅖	Clm 22500	2 1 12 1½ 54 912	Santagata N	b 115	15.30	56-30 Easton 1151¾ Road To Ponder 114nk Freedoms Edge 115hd	Tired 12	
16Mar88- 5Aqu fst 1⅛	:47⅗ 1:12⅕ 1:51⅕	Clm 25000	3 3 42½ 32½ 511 716½	Davis R G	b 117	2.50	62-26 Feldspar 1121 Timperature 1176½ Advance Plan 1152½	Tired 9	
22Feb88- 2Aqu fst 1⅛	[•]:49⅗ 1:14⅕ 1:54⅗	Clm c-17500	9 1 12½ 13½ 15 13¾	Davis R G	b 119	3.00	69-32 Bold Mein 1193¾ Print Money 1086½ Proverbial II1171	Drew clear 10	*
14Feb88- 9Aqu fst 1 1/16	[•]:47⅖ 1:13 1:46⅖	Clm 17500	11 2 21½ 2½ 13½ 11	Davis R G	b 117	6.20	77-16 Bold Mein 1171 Brave and Bright 1175½ Bienestar 1171	Driving 11	
6Feb88- 2Aqu fst 6f	[•]:22⅘ :47⅖ 1:13⅕	Clm c-14000	2 5 41 53 43 32½	Santagata N	b 117	*2.70	76-28 Soleri 1151¾ What Intensity 111½ Bold Mein 1173	Rallied 10	2–1
28Jan88- 2Aqu fst 6f	[•]:23 :47⅖ 1:13⅘	Clm 14000	7 11 63 62¾ 41½ 2hd	Santagata N	b 117	12.10	75-30 CsulPhysicin106hdBoldMin1172TooToughtoBt114nk	Broke slowly 11	
4Jan88- 2Aqu fst 6f	[•]:22⅕ :45⅖ 1:11⅕	Clm 16500	8 7 98 811 812 77½	Lovato F Jr	115	16.10	80-22 Truth Be Told 112nkEqualTerms112¾EffectiveAction1102¾	Outrun 11	
5Dec87- 6Aqu fst 1⅛	[•]:48⅗ 1:13⅘ 1:52⅘	3↑ Clm 22500	5 4 42 44½ 513 619½	Hernandez R	115	19.20	58-27 Boutinierre 1194½ Bienestar 1174½ Road To Ponder 1195	Tired 8	
30Nov87- 2Aqu sly 6f	:22⅘ :47 1:12⅖	3↑ Clm 22500	2 11 1012 1112 916 912½	Munoz O R7	108	13.80	67-30 Killer Joe 117½ Indian Licorice117½Dale'sFolly115nk	Broke poorly 11	

LATEST WORKOUTS May 2 Aqu 5f fst 1:01⅖ h Mar 12 Aqu 4f fst :48⅕ h ●Mar 7 Aqu [•] 4f fst :48 h

Fatty Boy

Own.—Tedrow Barbara

B. g. 4, by Full Out—Water Flume, by Turn and Count
$17,500 Br.—Crabtree & Lyster III (Ky)
Tr.—Lake Robert P

117 — Lifetime 38 7 4 7 $116,193 — 1988 7 0 1 0 $6,800 — 1987 22 4 3 7 $84,286 — Turf 1 0 0 0

28Apr88- 2Aqu sly 6f	:22 :45⅘ 1:11⅖	Clm 17500	1 7 85¾ 86 67½ 66¾	Maple E	b 117	2.70	76-17 Artimon 1151¾ [DH]Musial 113 [DH]Sass The Maitre d' 1141	Outrun 9	
15Apr88- 4Aqu fst 7f	:23 :46 1:24⅕	Clm 25000	4 9 107¾ 54 21½ 42½	Pezua J M	b 117	7.20	77-23 EffectivAction115½PssingThundr119nkGiuspp1171¾	Bid, weakened 10	
5Apr88- 2Aqu fst 6f	:22⅖ :46⅕ 1:11	Clm 25000	10 7 108¼ 83½ 42 21	Pezua J M	b 117	16.30	84-23 Passing Thunder 1171 FattyBoy1171EffectiveAction1171¼	Gamely 10	
26Mar88- 4Aqu sly 7f	:22⅗ :45⅕ 1:23	Clm 22500	11 2 32 34½ 611 512¼	Pezua J M	b 115	12.70	74-23 TruthBeTold1124Timperture1174¾SocillyInformd1171¼	Weakened 12	
19Mar88- 9Aqu fst 7f	:23⅕ :46⅘ 1:24⅘	Clm c-17500	5 5 2hd 2hd 77¾ 1012¼	Krone J A	b 117	*1.60	65-23 Squire Percival 115hd Galaxy Island1152¾Centurian1171¾	Faltered 12	
18Feb88- 9Aqu fst 6f	[•]:23 :46⅗ 1:11⅕	Clm 25000	1 12 128¾ 105¼ 69 47¼	Antley C W	b 117	6.50	81-23 Sports Medicine 1157DerbyJunior115nkSemaj117hd	Bumped start 12	4–1
17Jan88- 2Aqu fst 6f	[•]:22⅖ :46⅕ 1:11⅘	Clm 32500	7 6 56 42½ 41 53	Santagata N	b 115	8.70	82-23 Racer 117½ Ebony Rig 1171¾ Honored Counsel 113no	Weakened 12	
4Dec87- 5Aqu fst 1 1/16	[•]:47⅕ 1:13 1:45⅗	Clm 32500	7 4 2hd 51¼ 35 35¾	Krone J A	b 115	4.10	75-18 Target X. 1171¾ Super Scholar 1174 Fatty Boy 115½	Weakened 8	
28Nov87- 4Aqu fst 6f	:23 :47 1:12⅖	Clm c-25000	2 8 94 51¼ 12 13¼	Antley C W	b 117	4.90	79-23 Fatty Boy 1173¼ Hoss 'N Ryder117hdBigSpender1172½	Ridden out 10	
21Nov87- 9Aqu fst 7f	:23⅕ :47⅕ 1:25⅗	Clm 35000	9 3 84 65 78½ 614	Garcia J A	b 117	*2.90	59-30 Mixed Emotions1105¾MakeLemonade117noTemptSec1172	Outrun 11	

LATEST WORKOUTS Mar 15 Bel tr.t 3f fst :37⅕ b

(*Continued on following page*)

(Race 3 continued)

Ballyduggan — Dk. b. or br. g. 5, by Rollicking—Evening Kiss, by Saggy
$15,500 Br.—Rooney A & D & P & T (Md) — Tr.—Martin Gregory — 113
Own.—Martin G
Lifetime 31 5 2 4 $52,470 — 1988 5 0 0 1 $3,510 — 1987 19 3 2 1 $29,630 — Turf 6 1 0 0 $7,500

1Apr88- 2Aqu fst 7f :23 :46 1:24⅖ Clm 14000 10 5 94¼ 107¾ 97¾ 78¼ Antley C W b 117 3.30 71-24 Ideal Solution 1134 Weebok 113nk Artimon 103no No factor 13
24Mar88- 2Aqu fst 1 :45⅘ 1:11⅕ 1:37⅕ Clm 17500 3 8 87 88 55 46¾ Santos J A b 117 8.80 73-25 I'm Ahead 117¾ Easton 1176 Print Money 108hd Mild rally 13
9Mar88- 2Aqu fst 6f ⊡:23 :46⅘ 1:12⅕ Clm 17500 4 11 106¾ 96¼ 68 58¼ Correa C J5 b 112 6.70 75-26 Equal Terms1174SquirePercival1153Dusty'sDynamite1171¼ outrun 11
25Feb88- 4Aqu fst 1⅛ ⊡:48⅕ 1:13⅖ 1:53⅕ Clm 25000 5 3 23½ 22½ 58 513 Correa C J5 b 112 1.90 63-25 Brave and Bright 1151¾ Socially Informed 1106½Mr.J.V.1083 Tired 7
25Jan88- 9Aqu gd 6f ⊡:22⅖ :46 1:11⅗ Clm c-25000 1 11 107¾ 78½ 44 32 Lovato F Jr b 117 11.30 84-23 Dancing Drake 117hd Sports Medicine 1152 Ballyduggan 117nk 11
29Dec87- 2Aqu fst 6f ⊡:23 :46⅗ 1:11⅗ 3↑ Clm 32500 5 5 94¼ 99½ 710 57 Lovato F Jr b 115 26.50 79-23 ScottishMonk1194PssingThunder117nkHoss'NRyder1151¼ Outrun 10
14Dec87- 9Aqu fst 1 1/16 ⊡:47⅗ 1:12⅖ 1:44⅕ 3↑ Clm c-25000 1 8 1017 815 714 613¼ Santos J A 117 6.30 75-20 Sidi Bou Said 1176¼ Heama Zar 1111½ Sylson 1175¼ Showed little 12
3Dec87- 2Aqu fst 6f ⊡:22⅖ :46 1:11⅖ 3↑ Clm 17500 7 3 96¾ 86½ 54 24 Krone J A 117 7.50 83-19 Zonker Harris1174Ballyduggan117½FullofSpice1131¾ Lacked room 10
27Nov87- 8Aqu fst 1 :47⅗ 1:13 1:38⅗ 3↑ Alw 35000 5 6 86¾ 76¼ 78¾ 59¼ Krone J A 117 19.50 64-36 Native Wizard1174¾StrongPerformance117½Landyap115no Outrun 8
21Nov87- 6Aqu fst 1 :48⅖ 1:14⅘ 1:40⅘ 3↑ Alw 47000 7 5 4¾ 63½ 69 516¾ Venezia M b 115 33.50 45-30 Bowladrome 1151¾ Krul 1137¾ Racer 1152¼ Tired 7
LATEST WORKOUTS May 2 Bel tr.t 5f fst 1:01 h — Apr 17 Bel tr.t 4f fst :48⅗ h — Mar 20 Bel tr.t 3f fst :36⅕ b

7–2

Casual Physician — Gr. g. 4, by The Cool Virginian—Gun Cotton, by Hagley
$15,500 Br.—Church Melville III (Va) — Tr.—Galimi Paul — 1085
Own.—Chuckolow Stable
Lifetime 34 3 6 2 $52,430 — 1988 8 1 1 1 $14,430 — 1987 23 2 5 1 $37,520

26Mar88- 4Aqu sly 7f :22⅗ :45⅕ 1:23 Clm 20000 1 9 86½ 710 814 815¾ Davis R G b 113 7.60 70-23 Truth BeTold1124Timperature1174¾SociallyInformed1171¼ Outrun 12
23Mar88- 7Aqu fst 7f :22⅗ :45 1:25⅕ Alw 30000 5 3 21 1hd 2hd 62¼ Baird E T b 117 10.10 73-24 Knockon 117no Leave The Keys 112½ Homo Soho1171½ Weakened 10
13Mar88- 1Aqu fst 1 1/16 ⊡:49 1:13⅗ 1:46⅗ Alw 31000 8 1 11½ 1hd 31½ 54 Baird E T b 117 12.40 72-18 Feldspar 110¾ Knockon 117nk Target X. 117hd Clipped heels 8
29Feb88- 3Aqu fst 6f ⊡:22⅘ :46⅕ 1:11⅘ Clm 15500 8 3 42 2hd 2hd 21¼ Baird E T b 113 6.10 84-25 BillyWilbur1081¼CasulPhysicin1133¼SecretConclve1172¾ 2nd best 12
15Feb88- 3Aqu fst 6f ⊡:22⅗ :46 1:11⅘ Clm 12000 9 3 11½ 13½ 11½ 32 Termini C7 b 108 4.60 83-22 Askrano 1172 Soleri 119hd Casual Physician 1085 Weakened 10
12Feb88- 9Aqu my 6f ⊡:23 :46⅘ 1:12⅗ Clm 17500 2 8 22½ 53¼ 56 56¼ Termini C7 b 110 13.10 75-26 ShineDiulus1191½KeylineCredit1101¾Rprocssd1172¾ Saved ground 8
28Jan88- 2Aqu fst 6f ⊡:23 :47⅖ 1:13⅘ Clm 12000 3 8 52 31 3½ 1hd Termini C7 b 106 9.50 75-30 CasualPhysicin106hdBoldMein1172TooToughtoBet114nk Prevailed 11
15Jan88- 1Aqu fst 1 1/16 ⊡:48⅖ 1:14 1:46⅕ Clm 17500 6 2 2hd 2hd 715 824 Termini C7 b 112 10.90 54-19 MixedEmotions1125½BraveandBright117¾I'mAhed1121¾ Gave way 11
20Dec87- 2Aqu my 1 1/16 ⊡:47⅘ 1:12⅘ 1:46⅕ 3↑ Clm 15500 8 2 31 21½ 1hd 11½ Termini C7 b 104 17.80 78-15 CasualPhysician1041½PershingPach1071LedTheWy1104 Drew out 11
17Dec87- 9Aqu fst 6f ⊡:22⅗ :46⅘ 1:13⅕ Clm 15000 6 3 2hd 2hd 1hd 62 Garcia J A b 113 8.00 76-21 KylnCrdt1151¼HoldYourMony117nkCn'tPssthBck114hd Weakened 12
LATEST WORKOUTS May 2 Aqu 5f fst 1:03⅘ b — Apr 26 Aqu 5f fst 1:04⅖ b — Apr 15 Aqu 3f fst :37⅘ b — Mar 19 Aqu 3f fst :36 h

9–1

Sixth of May — Gr. g. 9, by Jacques Who—Fifth of May, by Five Strong
$15,500 Br.—Sedlacek Sue (NY) — Tr.—Sedlacek Sue — 1085
Own.—Sedlacek Sue
Lifetime 52 6 10 11 $141,360 — 1988 7 0 0 1 $1,980 — 1986 13 2 6 4 $42,640

30Apr88- 9Aqu fst 6f :22⅗ :46 1:10⅕ Clm 13000 2 11 52¾ 53¼ 53½ 55¾ Davis R G b 117 3.60 83-13 Empathetic 1132 Weebok 113¾ Tim Collins 1171 Stead'd late 12
18Apr88- 3Aqu fst 6f :21⅘ :45⅗ 1:11⅕ Clm 15500 6 7 55½ 51¾ 44 45 Velasquez J b 114 11.70 79-20 Straight Dancer 115¾ Bold Mein 1171¾TestofLoyalty1172½ Rallied 10
18Apr88-Awarded third purse money
9Apr88- 9Aqu fst 7f :23⅖ :47 1:25 Clm 12000 5 9 52½ 11 52½ 65¾ Romero R P b 113 9.90 70-19 Visible Force 113nk Wicked Wike 1172 Be Clever 113hd Tired 10
26Mar88- 4Aqu sly 7f :22⅗ :45⅕ 1:23 Clm 20000 2 10 76 56½ 510 612¼ Lopez V b 113 21.00 74-23 TruthBeTold1124Timperature1174¾SocillyInformed1171¼ Bore out 12
4Mar88- 3Aqu fst 6f ⊡:23⅗ :47⅖ 1:11⅗ Clm 14000 10 5 61½ 22 511 817¼ Lopez C b 117 7.50 69-18 [D]Straight Dancer 117½ Easton 1172¾ Centurian 1178¼ Tired 10
27Feb88- 4Aqu fst 6f ⊡:21⅕ :45⅖ 1:11⅖ Clm 20000 4 7 76¼ 57¼ 56½ 811½ Lopez C b 113 14.30 75-19 SportsMedicine1195¾DylightSving1121¾HoldYourMony108no Tired 9
30Jan88- 2Aqu fst 6f ⊡:22⅘ :46 1:11⅖ Clm 20000 9 12 1213 1212 1115 1014½ Lopez V b 113 14.50 72-17 TruthBeTold112nkDrrllWltrip1171¼RoylSlndr1131¾ Stumbled at st. 12
4Sep86- 2Bel fst 7f :23 :45⅗ 1:23⅗ 3↑ Clm 25000 5 5 54 44½ 21 3¾ Venezia M b 117 3.00e 83-18 Koffkoff 114hd Flying Skipper 119¾ Sixth of May 1172¼ Hung 7
13Aug86- 9Sar fst 6f :22⅕ :45⅗ 1:10⅗ 3↑ Clm 22500 7 10 44½ 32 21½ 23 Lopez V b 115 *2.90 84-17 FlyingSkipper1173SixthofMay115¾PledgeCap113no Best of others 11
16Jly86- 3Bel fst 7f :23⅘ :46⅘ 1:23⅖ Clm 22500 1 4 3½ 2½ 2hd 2½ Lopez V b 115 3.30 84-17 Flying Skipper 113½ Sixth of May 1153½ ArcticSong117no Gamely 7
LATEST WORKOUTS Apr 6 Aqu 4f fst :48⅖ h — Mar 23 Aqu 4f fst :50⅕ b

11–1

Phantom Fair — Gr. c. 4, by Fairway Phantom—Miss Phantom, by Gray Phantom
$17,500 Br.—Tackett E J & M J (Ky) — Tr.—Lee P O'Donnell — 117
Own.—Sylvan View Stable
Lifetime 20 2 0 0 $20,850 — 1988 5 0 0 0 $900 — 1987 11 1 0 0 $9,960 — Turf 1 0 0 0

18Apr88- 3Aqu fst 6f :21⅘ :45⅗ 1:11⅕ Clm 17500 2 5 89 85¼ 77 66 Lovato F Jr b 117 8.30e 78-20 Straight Dancer 115¾BoldMein1171¾TestofLoyalty1172½ No factor 10
29Mar88- 4Aqu fst 6f :22 :45⅘ 1:11⅖ Clm 17500 10 6 913 77 34 43 Maple E b 117 66.50 80-28 TiltThePocket1171StraightDancer1221¾SquirePercivl119nk Rallied 11
29Feb88- 3Aqu fst 6f ⊡:22⅘ :46⅕ 1:11⅘ Clm 17500 2 9 106¼ 84¼ 78½ 89¼ Maple E b 117 21.80 76-25 BillyWilbur1081¼CasualPhysician1133¼SecretConclve1172¾ Outrun 12
18Feb88- 9Aqu fst 6f ⊡:23 :46⅗ 1:11⅕ Clm 22500 5 11 115¾ 95¼ 917 920 Boulanger G5 b 110 81.50 68-23 Sports Medicine 1157 Derby Junior 115nk Semaj 117hd Wide 12
25Jan88- 9Aqu gd 6f ⊡:22⅖ :46 1:11⅗ Clm 25000 11 10 1111 1114 712 79¾ Maple E b 117 37.30 76-23 Dancing Drake117hdSportsMedicine1152Ballyduggan117nk Outrun 11
27Dec87- 1Aqu fst 1 1/16 ⊡:48⅖ 1:13 1:45⅘ Clm 47500 6 9 1016 1017 1023 1034¾ Hernandez R b 115 43.70 45-18 KingKoin117nkHeritnce1175¼VioIntRlunch1133½ Bmpd repeatedly 10
5Dec87- 9Aqu fst 6f ⊡:22⅗ :46⅗ 1:13⅕ Clm 17500 3 9 810 87¾ 53½ 1no Maple E b 117 15.30 78-27 Phantom Fair 117noSoleri1153RoyalPerformer119nk Very wide up 9
21Nov87- 9Aqu fst 7f :23⅕ :47⅕ 1:25⅗ Clm 32500 5 8 53½ 76 815 918½ Santagata N b 115 111.60 54-30 Mixed Emotions1105¾MakeLemonade117noTemptSec1172 Outrun 11
5Nov87- 9Aqu fst 7f :23⅕ :46⅗ 1:24⅘ 3↑ Alw 30000 1 9 83¾ 86¼ 67¾ 715 Santagata N b 115 95.00 62-29 Eclipso 1158¾ Sam the Lion 1152 Noble Ambition 1201¼ Outrun 10
16Sep87- 3Bel fst 1 1/16 :46 1:10⅘ 1:43 Clm 35000 1 11 1110 98 86½ 810¾ Bailey J D b 117 50.90 76-20 Proud Guy 1171¼ Tap Writer 1173SunriseService117nk Broke slow 12
LATEST WORKOUTS May 2 Bel tr.t 5f fst 1:02⅕ b — ●Apr 12 Bel tr.t 4f fst :47⅘ b — Mar 26 Bel tr.t 4f fst :50⅖ b — Mar 19 Bel tr.t 4f fst :48⅖ h

25–1

4 AQUEDUCT

(9 Horses)

TURF COURSE 1⅛ MILES AQUEDUCT

1⅛ MILES. (Turf). (1.47) MAIDEN SPECIAL WEIGHT. Purse $28,000. 3-year-olds and upward. Weight, 3-year-olds, 115 lbs. Older, 124 lbs.

Medieval Rival

Ch. c. 3, by Medieval Man—Miss Rival, by Riva Ridge
Br.—Live Oak Stud (Fla)
Own.—Live Oak Plantation
Tr.—Kelly Patrick J
115
Lifetime 3 0 0 1 $4,380
1988 3 M 0 1 $4,380
1987 0 M 0 0
Turf 1 0 0 1 $3,360

22Apr88- 7Aqu fm 1 1/16 Ⓣ:48⅕ 1:13⅖ 1:45⅘ 3↑Md Sp Wt 7 3 32 31 33 35¾ Hernandez R 115 3.60 71-21 Shalom'NSalam115nk Tin'sWorld1125½MedievlRivl1151¾ Weakened 7
10Apr88- 9Aqu fst 6f :23⅕ :48⅕ 1:13 3↑Md 50000 8 5 74¼ 74¼ 44 44¼ Hernandez R 115 24.60 71-26 Grumpy Miller 115hd Great Gypsy 1152¼ Valque 1122 Wide 9
2Apr88- 5Aqu fst 6f :22⅗ :46⅖ 1:11⅖ Md Sp Wt 7 7 118¾11131116 917¼ Belmonte J F 122 55.10 66-22 FiveStarCamp122½FoolishMacDuff1222½ScavengerHunt1224 Wide 12
LATEST WORKOUTS May 4 Bel tr.t 3f fst :36⅘ b Apr 29 Bel tr.t 3f fst :36⅖ h Apr 19 Bel tr.t 4f fst :48⅘ b Mar 24 Bel tr.t 4f fst :48⅘ hg

10–1

Goes So Fast

Ch. c. 3, by Johns Gold—Fleet Victory, by Vaguely Noble
Br.—Heubeck E & Harriet Jr (Fla)
Own.—Bazarian Aram
Tr.—Perez Ronald M
115
Lifetime 4 0 1 1 $4,420
1988 4 M 1 1 $4,420
1987 0 M 0 0

9Apr88-11Suf fst 170 :47⅗ 1:13⅘ 1:47⅗ Handicap 4 2 1hd 12½ 14½ 21½ Rivera L Jr b 110 37.30 60-29 Sharp Jason 1131½ Goes So Fast 110½ Tap Star 1143¾ Weakened 7
4Apr88- 2Suf fst 6f :22⅘ :46⅗ 1:13 Md Sp Wt 7 5 31 2hd 2hd 49¼ Bonilla R b 120 3.10 66-33 GrndpDominic1206¾WorthADnc1201¾FortMcHnry1201 Wide, tired 7
21Mar88- 5Suf fst 6f :24⅕ :48⅖ 1:15⅘ Md Sp Wt 4 1 1½ 21½ 35 512¾ Bonilla R b 120 3.60 49-40 Sharp Jason 1205 Grandpa Dominic 1201¾ Jay Power 1204 Tired 7
14Mar88- 4Suf fst 6f :23⅗ :47⅘ 1:14⅕ Md Sp Wt 4 2 41½ 43½ 33½ 34½ Baez R b 120 3.60 65-37 Ono Omer 1202 Sharp Jason 1202½ Goes So Fast 1201 Steadied 6
LATEST WORKOUTS May 4 Suf 4f fst :50 b Apr 1 Suf 5f fst 1:03⅗ b Mar 11 Suf 5f fst 1:06 bg

10–1

Damascus Gold

Dk. b. or br. c. 3, by Damascus—North Downs, by Hoist The Flag
Br.—Jones W L Jr (Ky)
Own.—Lions Head Farm
Tr.—Johnson Philip G
115
Lifetime 3 0 0 0 $3,000
1988 2 M 0 0 $1,620
1987 1 M 0 0 $1,380

24Mar88- 7Aqu fst 7f :22⅕ :45 1:24⅕ Md Sp Wt 9 8 98½ 99½ 78¾ 612¼ Correa C J5 b 117 3.80 68-25 Ali Shuffle 1221½ Rise Measure 1224¾ Bear Branch 1223¾ Outrun 9
4Mar88- 9Aqu my 6f ⊡:22⅘ :46⅘ 1:12⅘ Md Sp Wt 2 10 77¾ 68½ 54 41 Correa C J5 b 117 5.70 79-16 HotShwklit1221[DH]AdvncingEnsign122[DH]Mrshu'sLedr122hd Shied 11
1Aug87- 4Bel fst 6f :22⅘ :47⅕ 1:13⅗ Md Sp Wt 5 8 911 98¾ 55½ 46¼ Nuesch D5 113 5.70e 66-27 Three Engines 1185¼ Fancy Hoofer 118½DonHernando118½ Rallied 9
LATEST WORKOUTS May 2 Bel 6f fst 1:13⅘ h Apr 24 Bel 1 fst 1:37⅗ h Apr 18 Bel 7f fst 1:26⅖ h Apr 11 Bel 5f fst 1:01 h

4–1

Kanduit's Pride

Dk. b. or br. c. 3, by Proudest Roman—Kanduit, by Rugged Man
Br.—Cole Mrs C (Ky)
Own.—Cole Mrs C
Tr.—Watters Sidney Jr
115
Lifetime 11 0 0 2 $6,470
1988 8 M 0 1 $5,040
1987 3 M 0 1 $1,430
Turf 1 0 0 0

2May88- 4Aqu gd 1⅛ Ⓣ:48⅘ 1:14 1:53 3↑Md Sp Wt 11 12 12241215 813 613½ Pezua J M 115 34.30 56-24 Age of Gold 124no Shy Genius 115¾ Russian Affair1153 No factor 12
16Apr88- 2Aqu fst 1⅛ :48 1:13⅖ 1:53 3↑Md Sp Wt 8 8 716 813 512 610 Krone J A b 115 44.10 60-21 Country Playboy 1152½ My Word 1153½GreyBasque1243 No factor 8
17Mar88- 6Aqu fst 1 :47⅕ 1:12⅗ 1:38⅕ Md Sp Wt 2 10 10121012 714 718¼ Krone J A b 122 46.20 57-27 Parsimonious1227AdvancingEnsign1221½[D]BizarreStr122¾ Outrun 10
6Mar88- 5Aqu fst 1 1/16 ⊡:48⅖ 1:15⅕ 1:48⅘ Md Sp Wt 1 8 816 73¾ 44½ 49¼ Krone J A 122 25.10 56-20 Fancy Raja 1226¼ High Policy 1173 Egret 122hd No threat 8
12Feb88- 4Aqu my 170 ⊡:48⅗ 1:14⅘ 1:45⅘ Md Sp Wt 3 8 815 815 721 720 Krone J A 122 10.10 51-26 Crafty Ike 122nk Torvill 1223¼ Fancy Raja 1223½ Outrun 8
30Jan88- 1Aqu fst 1 1/16 ⊡:47⅗ 1:12⅗ 1:47⅕ Md Sp Wt 1 5 45½ 33½ 33 32¼ Krone J A 122 21.20 71-17 BullSluice1221½FunandGmes122¾Knduit'sPride122½ Saved ground 7
23Jan88- 6Aqu fst 6f ⊡:22⅗ :46 1:11⅕ Md Sp Wt 6 6 11111016 919 818 Hernandez R 122 63.90 70-13 Total Look 1223 Bullhorn 1224 Grumpy Miller1225 Ducked out st. 12
11Jan88- 6Aqu fst 6f ⊡:22⅗ :46⅗ 1:13⅕ Md Sp Wt 8 8 11121114 11131110 Krone J A b 122 13.60e 68-24 Winter Drive 122nk No Bondage 1223¼ Dance OnFire122hd Outrun 12
19Sep87- 1Med fst 6f :22⅘ :46⅗ 1:12 Md Sp Wt 8 3 31 43 56½ 68½ Rocco J b 118 3.70 73-12 Smart Bishop 1184 Ful Count Dancer1181½CloseUnion1181½ Tired 9
29Aug87- 4Mth gd 6f :23 :46⅗ 1:12⅖ Md Sp Wt 3 5 1hd 21 33½ 36½ Rocco J b 118 *2.00 71-17 Grande Jette1182½Harmonious1184Kanduit'sPride1184 Weakened 8
LATEST WORKOUTS Apr 26 Bel 3f fst :38⅖ b Apr 11 Bel 5f fst 1:01 h Mar 14 Bel tr.t 4f fst :49⅘ h

6–1

Armand

B. c. 3, by Nureyev—Road Princess, by Gallant Man
Br.—Elmendorf Farm (Ky)
Own.—Cooke J K
Tr.—Lukas D Wayne
115
Lifetime 1 0 0 1 $3,240
1988 1 M 0 1 $3,240
1987 0 M 0 0

23Apr88- 9Aqu fst 6f :22⅕ :45⅗ 1:10 Md Sp Wt 6 4 55 58 34½ 31¾ Santos J A 122 9.50 88-12 Gee Jamie 1221¼ Foolish MacDuff 122½ Armand 1224 Late bid 10
LATEST WORKOUTS Apr 18 Bel 3f fst :37 bg Apr 14 Bel 3f fst :37⅖ bg Apr 10 Bel 3f fst :37 bg Apr 4 Bel 5f fst 1:00⅕ h

*
3–5

Originally scheduled for the turf.
Switched to dirt at the same distance (two turns).
Exacta wagering. Quinella wagering.

(5 Horses)

5 AQUEDUCT

START
6½ FURLONGS AQUEDUCT
FINISH

6 ½ FURLONGS. (1.15) CLAIMING. Purse $32,000. 4-year-olds and upward. Weight, 122 lbs. Claiming price $100,000; for each $5,000 to $75,000 allowed 2lbs.

Scholars Task — 4–1

B. h. 6, by Naskra—College Bold, by Boldnesian
$80,000 Br.—Meadowhill (Ky)
Tr.—Clayton Marjorie
Own.—Nest Farms Stable
114
Lifetime 56 8 9 11 $251,025 | 1988 5 1 1 1 $36,420 | 1987 20 2 5 3 $102,760 | Turf 3 0 0 0 $210

28Apr88- 8Aqu my 1	:45⅗ 1:10⅕ 1:35⅕	3↑Alw 47000	2 5 64½ 54 58 48¾	Cordero A Jr	b 121	13.70	81-17 Fuzzy 121¾ Abject 124½ Pirate's Skiff 1216½	No excuse 6
7Mar88- 7Aqu fst 170	⊡:48 1:13 1:42	Clm 85000	3 3 33 41½ 47½ 413¾	Cordero A Jr	b 116	3.60	76-25 GoforCommdor1124¾Prt'sSkff1127AuthntcHro1222	Veered in late 8
13Feb88- 6Aqu fst 170	⊡:47⅘ 1:13⅕ 1:44⅖	Clm 85000	4 4 32 31 33½ 34	Cordero A Jr	b 116	2.60	74-25 Super Scholar 113hd Etat Major 1124ScholarsTask1165½	Even try 6
3Feb88- 6Aqu gd 1 1/16	⊡:48⅗ 1:12⅘ 1:45⅘	Clm 75000	5 2 21 2½ 34 1hd	Skinner K	b 117	7.60	80-18 Scholars Task 117hd Wild Wood 1131¾ King Koin 113nk	Driving 7
1Jan88- 5Aqu fst 170	⊡:47⅕ 1:12 1:42⅕	Clm 80000	2 2 2½ 1½ 1½ 24½	Skinner K	b 115	2.50	84-19 Belocolus 1124½ ScholarsTask1152½DonSanders1141¼	Second best 6
21Dec87- 1Aqu fst 1 1/16	⊡:48⅕ 1:12⅖ 1:43⅘	3↑Clm 75000	3 1 11 11 2hd 21½	Cordero A Jr	b 117	3.20	88-15 Rollodka 1171½ Scholars Task 117nk Britton's Mill 1132½	Gamely 6
22Nov87- 1Aqu fst 1⅛	:48⅘ 1:13⅘ 1:54⅕	3↑Clm 90000	6 2 21½ 31½ 47½ 414	Skinner K	b 118	2.10	50-32 Belocolus 1121½ Carjack 1129 Salvington 1143½	Tired 7
14Nov87- 6Aqu fst 1⅛	:46⅘ 1:11 1:48⅗	3↑Clm 75000	5 1 2½ 1hd 2hd 2½	Cordero A Jr	b 117	4.30	91-13 Slickster 113½ Scholars Task 1173 Belocolus 1173	Game try 9
21Oct87- 9Med fst 1 1/16	:47⅗ 1:12 1:45⅖	3↑Alw 25000	2 1 31½ 34 43½ 53¼	Santos J A	b 115	*1.10	73-31 Bowldrome1171RelForst115nkLordOfThNight115½	L'ckd solid bid 5
11Oct87- 7Bel gd 1	:47 1:10⅖ 1:36⅗	3↑Alw 47000	4 2 3½ 46½ 47 46¼	Cordero A Jr	b 115	19.60	76-22 Conventioneer 115nk OmarKhayyam1124FabulousFlight1152	Tired 6

LATEST WORKOUTS Apr 26 Bel 3f fst :36⅕ h | Apr 13 Bel 4f fst :48⅖ h | Apr 2 Bel tr.t 5f fst 1:02 b

Conventioneer — * 3–2

Ch. h. 5, by Key to the Mint—Cavort, by Foolish Pleasure
$75,000 Br.—Whitney Mrs J H (Ky)
Tr.—Barrera Oscar S
Own.—Barrera O S
105[7]
Lifetime 24 6 2 6 $137,540 | 1988 3 1 0 0 $13,200 | 1987 17 4 2 4 $104,300 | Turf 5 0 0 2 $8,700

30Apr88- 4Aqu fst 1	:45 1:09⅗ 1:34⅗	Clm 25000	6 2 11 11 12 11	Walker E E7	b 110	*1.70	93-13 Conventioneer 1101RoadToPonder1151¾IdealSolution117½	Driving 7
17Apr88- 6Aqu fst 1⅛	:47⅗ 1:12 1:51⅘	Clm 25000	9 3 21½ 2hd 2hd 52	Walker E E7	b 110	3.60e	74-25 SocillyInformd110noQundcllon1151½It'sAboutSvn117nk	Weakened 9
8Apr88- 1Aqu my 6f	:22⅖ :45⅕ 1:09⅗	Clm 32500	7 5 45 54½ 45 69	Belmonte J F	b 115	4.80	83-17 Truth Be Told 1151½ Hoss 'N Ryder 1174¼Timperature1081½	Wide 7
2Nov87- 9Aqu fst 1	:46⅕ 1:10⅖ 1:35⅖	3↑Handicap	3 2 1½ 1½ 2½ 53½	Pezua J M	b 112	13.20	85-21 Homebuilder 1121¾ AnotherReef1171EasyNDirty115no	Sp'd, wknd 10
30Oct87- 8Aqu fst 6f	:22⅖ :45 1:09⅗	3↑Alw 42000	3 4 54½ 44 45½ 46½	Pezua J M	b 122	2.30	87-25 Matthews Keep 1191 Pinecutter 1191½ Quick Call 1194	No threat 6
11Oct87- 7Bel gd 1	:47 1:10⅖ 1:36⅗	3↑Alw 47000	1 3 2½ 11½ 12½ 1nk	Antley C W	b 115	4.20	82-22 Conventioneer115nkOmarKhayyam1124FbulousFlight1152	Driving 6
7Oct87- 5Bel my 6f	:22⅗ :45⅗ 1:09⅗	3↑Alw 31000	3 4 42 2½ 22 25¼	Antley C W	b 119	4.60	86-22 StackedPck1145¼Conventioneer1192Vronsky1163½	Altered course 6
3Oct87- 7Bel fst 7f	:22⅕ :45⅖ 1:23	3↑Alw 30000	7 4 45½ 32½ 14 16	Antley C W	b 117	11.70	87-20 Conventioneer 1176 Ron Stevens 114½ NativeWizard117hd	Driving 10
30Sep87- 6Bel my 1 1/16	:46 1:10⅖ 1:42	3↑Alw 31000	7 2 32½ 22 1½ 2½	Antley C W	b 117	8.20	91-12 PlceMrch113½Conventioneer1172Gnom'sPlsur113¾	Ducked in late 8
26Sep87- 7Bel sf 1 1/16	Ⓣ:49 1:12⅘ 1:45⅗	3↑Alw 33000	5 4 53 32 32½ 43	Antley C W	b 117	17.00	70-25 Patlomat 114nk Double Alias 1191¾ Easton 1171	Hung 7

LATEST WORKOUTS Mar 29 Bel tr.t 5f fst 1:00 hg | Mar 22 Bel tr.t 3f fst :37⅗ b | Mar 19 Bel tr.t 3f fst :37⅖ b

Cost Conscious — 4–1

Dk. b. or br. h. 6, by Believe It—Pennygown, by Herbager
$85,000 Br.—Phipps O M (Ky)
Tr.—Shapoff Stanley R
Own.—Cohen R B
116
Lifetime 42 8 10 4 $289,671 | 1988 7 0 1 0 $6,400 | 1987 9 1 1 1 $55,913 | Turf 7 1 1 0 $41,120

25Apr88- 8Aqu fst 7f	:23 :46 1:23	3↑Alw 44000	1 5 58½ 511 67½ 68½	Samyn J L	121	44.90	77-24 MocitoFogoso121noPeppyLePew121noJazzingAround1217½	Outrun 6
14Apr88- 8Aqu fst 1	:45⅖ 1:09⅖ 1:34⅘	3↑Handicap	7 8 85½ 77¾ 911 810¾	Samyn J L	111	26.60	81-21 Royal Pennant 114hd LacOuimet1222¾CountOnRomeo113¾	Outrun 9
30Mar88- 8Aqu fst 7f	:23⅖ :46⅕ 1:23	3↑Alw 42000	5 7 52½ 32½ 42 53¾	Samyn J L	121	27.70	82-22 Prospctor'sHlo121hdJzzngArond1211½Dpsn1211½	Bumped, in tight 7
5Mar88- 9GP fst 7f	:22⅕ :44⅗ 1:21⅕	Alw 30000	5 3 77½ 66 513 518¾	Samyn J L	115	13.50	79-16 Lost Code 12215½ Carborundum1151¾I'llRaiseYouOne122¾	Outrun 8
14Feb88- 3GP fst 1 1/16	:47⅗ 1:11⅖ 1:42⅘	Alw 26000	6 2 2hd 1½ 1hd 21¾	Samyn J L	117	22.40	85-18 Silver Comet1171¾CostConscious117noNewYorkSwell1174	Held pl 7
2Feb88- 9GP fm *1 1/16	Ⓣ 1:43⅖	Alw 26000	9 8 83½ 62¼ 95 86½	Samyn J L	115	8.60	82-14 Kindly Court 119¾ LauriesWarrior1151QuickSnap115no	No mishap 11
9Jan88- 9GP fm 1	Ⓣ:46 1:10⅗ 1:35	3↑Appleton H	12 12 1413 1313 1214 1110¼	Samyn J L	113	24.70f	85-09 YankeeAffair1163PerformingPppy114nkKingsRiverII114nk	Outrun 14
9Jan88-Grade III								
13Dec87- 8Aqu fst 6f	⊡:22⅖ :45⅖ 1:09⅗	3↑Gravesend H	3 6 64 54¼ 67¼ 58	Maple E	112	23.40	88-16 Vinnie the Viper 116no King's Swan122noBestByTest1177½	Outrun 6
30Nov87- 8Aqu sly 7f	:22⅗ :45⅘ 1:23⅘	3↑Handicap	2 5 53½ 64½ 612 614¼	Kaenel J L	115	19.90	68-30 Another Reef 116nk Matthews Keep 1111½ I Rejoice 1102	Outrun 6
2Nov87- 9Aqu fst 1	:46⅕ 1:10⅖ 1:35⅖	3↑Handicap	4 5 42½ 44 68½ 68	Samyn J L	114	15.00	81-21 Hombuildr1121¾AnothrRf1171EsyNDirty115no	No further respnse 10

LATEST WORKOUTS ●May 3 Bel 5f fst :59⅕ h | Apr 21 Bel tr.t 5f fst 1:02 b | ●Apr 9 Bel 6f gd 1:12 h | Mar 29 Bel tr.t 3f fst :35⅘ h

Real Account — 2–1

B. c. 4, by Private Account—Unreality, by In Reality
$100,000 Br.—Vangeloff Karil (Ky)
Tr.—Gullo Thomas J
Own.—Pokoil L
122
Lifetime 20 4 5 3 $117,980 | 1988 7 2 1 2 $56,940 | 1987 13 2 4 1 $61,040

30Mar88- 8Aqu fst 7f	:23⅖ :46⅕ 1:23	3↑Alw 42000	7 1 74½ 74½ 62¾ 77½	Nuesch D3	121	17.00	78-22 Prospector's Halo121hdJazzingAround1211½Diapason1211½	Outrun 7
21Mar88- 8Aqu fst 7f	:23 :46⅕ 1:23⅘	Alw 38000	5 2 53 42½ 2½ 1¾	Nuesch D3	114	9.00	82-28 Real Account 114¾ Mt. Pleasant 1174½SlewCitySlew1174½	Driving 5
5Mar88- 5Aqu gd 6f	⊡:22⅖ :45⅘ 1:10	Alw 33000	2 6 61½ 52½ 64¼ 610½	Nuesch D3	114	12.20	83-11 Seattle Knight 1191½ Placid Waters 1173 Abject 1191½	No factor 8
25Feb88- 5Aqu fst 6f	⊡:22⅕ :45⅖ 1:11	Alw 33000	4 2 3½ 2hd 13 21½	Nuesch D3	114	2.60	87-25 SeattleKnight1171½RealAccount1146Patty'sGambit117nk	2nd best 6
14Feb88- 7Aqu fst 6f	⊡:22⅕ :45⅗ 1:10⅘	Alw 32000	8 1 2½ 1½ 14 12½	Nuesch D3	114	*2.40	90-16 RealAccount1142½SeattleKnight117½MenndCrfty1172¾	Ridden out 8
4Feb88- 5Aqu sly 6f	⊡:22⅗ :46⅖ 1:11⅖	Alw 32000	3 1 32 31 34 37¾	Nuesch D3	114	3.70	79-21 Tis Royal 1175¾ Mean and Crafty 1172 RealAccount1141	Even try 5
15Jan88- 5Aqu fst 6f	⊡:22⅕ :45 1:10⅖	Alw 32000	2 6 34 34 34½ 33½	Nuesch D3	114	11.50e	88-19 Pop John 1191¾ Tis Royal 1171¾ Real Account 1142½	Evenly 10
17Dec87- 7Aqu fst 6f	⊡:23⅕ :47 1:11⅕	3↑Alw 32000	3 3 21½ 31½ 22½ 22¾	Nuesch D3	112	7.60	85-21 Hibernation 1172¾ Real Account 1121½ Mawsuff1173½	best others 9
28Nov87- 5Aqu fst 7f	:23 :46⅖ 1:25	3↑Alw 32000	7 1 55 43½ 32 32	Nuesch D3	112	9.00	74-23 Forbes Way 115½ ⒹChyonofuji 1101½ RealAccount112nk	IMpeded 7
28Nov87-Placed second through disqualification								
18Nov87- 7Aqu fst 7f	:22⅘ :45⅖ 1:22⅗	3↑Alw 32000	5 6 52 61¼ 3½ 33¼	Nuesch D3	112	18.20	85-16 Irish Chili 1152 Eclipso 1201¼ Real Account 112nk	Wide 8

LATEST WORKOUTS ●Apr 27 Bel 6f fst 1:12⅖ h | Apr 21 Bel 6f fst 1:14⅖ h | ●Apr 15 Bel tr.t 3f fst :36 h | Apr 9 Bel tr.t 4f fst :51⅕ b

Young Blade — 6–1

Gr. h. 5, by Silent Dignity—Grey Axe, by The Axe II
$75,000 Br.—Conway James D (Ky)
Tr.—Martin Jose
Own.—Rantz F
107[5]
Lifetime 28 6 4 1 $96,855 | 1988 7 1 1 0 $32,060 | 1987 6 1 1 0 $27,402 | Turf 16 4 2 1 $37,393

28Apr88- 7Aqu sf 1⅛	Ⓣ:50 1:15⅕ 1:53⅗	Clm 75000	7 5 64¼ 65 45½ 510½	Santos J A	113	4.70	56-33 AllHndsOnDck1144¼MjstcRobrto1162RmntcTn116¾	Flattened out 9
16Apr88- 7Aqu fst 1	:46⅗ 1:12⅕ 1:36⅗	3↑Alw 47000	4 8 86½ 56 59 510½	Hernandez R	121	7.70	72-21 Prospector's Halo 1211 Abject 1245½ Pirate's Skiff 121hd	In close 8
6Apr88- 8Aqu fst 7f	:23⅕ :46⅖ 1:23⅘	3↑Alw 42000	8 4 64 74 65½ 44½	Hernandez R	121	5.30	77-25 Pirate's Skiff 1211 Native Wizard 1211 Say Hey 1212½	In tight 9
24Mar88- 8Aqu fst 1	:46⅖ 1:11⅖ 1:35⅘	Alw 47000	3 5 54 41 1hd 2½	Hernandez R	115	7.00	86-25 Conquer 115½ Young Blade 115no Pirate's Skiff 1155	Gamely 6
18Mar88- 6Aqu fst 1	:45⅖ 1:10⅖ 1:36⅕	Clm 70000	4 6 64¾ 62½ 11½ 14	Hernandez R	113	21.90	85-22 Young Blade 1134 Tempt Sec117nkPlacidWaters1132¾	Ridden out 6
26Feb88- 5Aqu fst 1 1/16	⊡:49⅕ 1:13 1:44⅖	Clm 75000	6 4 32 31½ 59¼ 613½	Kaenel J L	117	6.50	73-22 King Koin 118no Wild Wood1178MiracleWood1172½	Wide far turn 6
14Feb88- 6Aqu fst 6f	⊡:22 :45⅕ 1:09⅗	Alw 42000	4 6 64½ 53½ 512 614¼	Kaenel J L	115	25.30	82-16 Pinecutter 1176 Derby Hat 1151 Conquer 1221¼	Wide str 6
20Nov87- 9Grd fst 1	:46⅖ 1:11⅗ 1:38⅕	3↑Alw 24600	4 5 53 54 54 55	Ravera P P5	114	20.85	84-24 S. S. Enterprise 119no Dance Corps 117¾ Ice Over 1171½	10
8Nov87- 9Grd gd 1	:46⅖ 1:11⅗ 1:38⅖	3↑Autumn H	5 7 55½ 710 612 613	Clark D	115	9.45	75-27 Control Zone 120hd InTheEast1163MisterLorenzo1153½	No factor 8
8Nov87-Grade III-C								
24Oct87- 8WO sly 6½f	:23 :46⅖ 1:18⅖	3↑Alw 22400	2 5 44 54 44½ 45½	Attard L	117	*1.25	75-28 Dance Corps 1173 Mister Lorenzo 1171¼ Night Fight1191¼	Evenly 6

LATEST WORKOUTS Apr 24 Bel tr.t 4f fst :47⅗ h | Apr 13 Bel tr.t 4f fst :49 b | Apr 4 Bel tr.t 3f fst :50 h | Mar 13 Bel tr.t 4f fst :48 h

No exacta wagering.
First half of "Instant" Double, Races 5 and 6.

AQUEDUCT

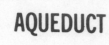

START / FINISH
7 FURLONGS
AQUEDUCT

7 FURLONGS. (1.20⅕) CLAIMING. Purse $24,000. Fillies and mares, 4-year-olds and upward. Weight, 122 lbs. Non-winners of two races since April 1 allowed 3 lbs. Of a race since then 5 lbs. Claiming price $50,000; for each $2,500 to $45,000, 2 lbs. (Races when entered to be claimed for $40,000 less not considered.)

Coupled—Too Bobees Return, Spiriting and Puddin Tane.

Tasma's Star

Ch. f. 4, by Star de Naskra—Tasma's Baby, by Tatan
Br.—Nuckols Bros (Ky)
Tr.—Barrera Oscar S
Own.—Gagliano S — $45,000

108⁵

Lifetime	1988	13	3	4	3	$66,915
27 5 7 5	1987	14	2	3	2	$29,765
$96,680	Turf	2	1	0	0	$9,000

7–1

28Apr88- 4Aqu sly 6f	:22	:45⅘ 1:11⅕	ⒻClm 45000	1 8 8⁸¾ 7⁵¼ 4⁴ 4⁴½	Peck B D⁵	108	*3.70	80–17 Peaceful Above 113²¼ Star Brilliant 109ⁿᵏ LauraJones117¼ Rallied 8
23Apr88- 2Aqu fst 7f	:22⅘	:45⅘ 1:23⅘	ⒻClm 35000	5 3 4⁴ 3¹½ 3¹½ 1ⁿᵏ	Peck B D⁵	114	*2.00	84–12 Tasma's Star 114ⁿᵏ Ain't That Wicked 117⁶ GladyH.113²¼ Driving 6
18Apr88- 1Aqu fst 1	:46⅘	1:11⅕ 1:36⅘	ⒻClm 35000	6 3 3¹ 2² 2²½ 2²½	Romero R P	117	*1.20	81–20 Mrs. Watters 108²¼ Tasma's Star 117³ Debo 113¼ Best of others 6
13Apr88- 5Aqu fst 6f	:22⅘	:46⅓ 1:11	ⒻClm 35000	2 4 4³½ 4³ 4²½ 1½	Krone J A	117	2.00	85–25 Tasma's Star 117½ Classical Ballad 117² Henna Girl108ⁿᵏ Driving 8
5Apr88- 5Aqu fst 6f	:22⅘	:47 1:12½	3↑Alw 32000	5 7 6⁶ 6⁴¼ 5²¼ 3½	Walker E E⁷	114	5.50	78–23 BoldMgestrte112¼ GoldnT.Dncr121ⁿᵏ Tsm'sStr114ʰᵈ Altered course 7
31Mar88- 7Aqu fst 1	:45⅘	1:10 1:36⅘	3↑Alw 33000	4 3 3⁴ 4²½ 4¹¼ 4¼	Walker E E⁷	114	13.40	79–30 Topicount 112ⁿᵏ OurGallamar113³¾ DearDusty113ⁿᵏ Altered course 7
25Mar88- 4Aqu fst 7f	:22⅘	:45⅘ 1:24⅘	ⒻClm 35000	4 10 8⁵¾ 5⁵¼ 2⁴ 2⁴	Davis R G	117	4.10	73–27 Morning Jo 1174 Tasma's Star 117¹ Miss Otani 112¼ Second best 14
10Mar88- 5Aqu fst 6f	:22⅘	:45⅘ 1:24⅘	ⒻClm 25000	2 6 6⁵¼ 5²¼ 3¹ 2¹¾	Romero R P	117	3.50	65–34 NativeCandy117¹¾ Tsm'sStr117ⁿᵏ Fteful Prospect115⁴ Up for place 8
28Feb88- 4Aqu fst 6f	:50	1:15⅘ 1:54⅘	ⒻClm 25000	2 3 3¹¼ 2ⁿᵈ 2¹ 2¹½	Correa C J⁵	112	5.70	66–25 Sunny Her 1172¼ Tasma's Star 112⁵ Sea Trip 1143½ Drifted out 8
20Feb88- 6Aqu gd 1¼	:48⅕	1:13½ 1:45⅘	3↑Alw 33000	5 6 7⁵¼ 7⁹¾ 5¹³ 5¹⁶	Krone J A	117	17.00	65–15 Adorable Angel 117¼ Suistina 1173½ Laura Jones 117¾ No factor 9

Too Bobees Return

B. f. 4, by Talc—Hasty Elegance, by Vertex
Br.—Peters & Spring Tree Stables (NY)
Tr.—Moschera Gasper S
Own.—Davis A — $50,000

117

Lifetime	1988	6	1	1	1	$25,440
24 4 10 1	1987	12	3	6	0	$106,220
$147,060						

*
3–2
(entry)

24Apr88- 1Aqu fst 6f	:22½	:45⅘ 1:10⅘	ⒻClm 70000	5 6 6⁸¾ 5⁵¼ 3⁴ 3²½	Santos J A	b 114	*1.00	85–17 SociallySet117¼ P.J.'sBlitzen114¼ TooBobeesReturn114²¼ Checked 6
15Apr88- 1Aqu fst 1	:46½	1:11½ 1:36½	ⒻClm 75000	3 6 5³¼ 4² 2²¼ 2ⁿᵏ	Santos J A	b 115	3.50	80–23 RoylDiscovery1171½ TooBobsRtrn115³ AdorblAngl107¾ Second best 6
6Apr88- 4Aqu fst 6f	:22⅘	:46½ 1:11⅘	ⒻClm c–50000	1 7 5³ 5²½ 3¹ 1¹½	Santos J A	b 115	*2.50	82–25 TooBbsRtrn117¹½ P.J.'sBlitzn111ⁿᵏ LdyAshInd113ⁿᵒ Blocked,driving 7
21Mar88- 5Aqu fst 7f	:22⅘	:46⅘ 1:25	ⒻAlw 33000	4 5 5⁵½ 6³¼ 7³½ 5⁵	Davis R G	117	8.50	71–24 Adorable Angel 114ⁿᵏ Bristlin' Belle117¾ SteadyGaze117²¾ Outrun 7
17Jan88- 8Aqu fst 170	:49⅘	1:13⅘ 1:44⅘	3↑ⒷroadwayH	2 3 8⁴¾ 6⁶¼ 7⁶¼ 710¼	Lovato F Jr	b 112	16.80	67–23 Anniron124¹½ OhHowWeDanced107²¼ ChseTheDrem112½ No factor 10
7Jan88- 8Aqu fst 6f	:22⅘	:46⅘ 1:12⅘	3↑ⒻAlw 42000	2 5 5² 5⁷¼ 410 511¼	Maple E	115	12.30	71–17 Royal Discovery 1171½ Nasherrico 1153½ Arunji 1165¾ Tired 7
20Dec87- 5Aqu my 6f	:22⅘	:46 1:11	3↑ⒻAlw 33000	1 7 6³¼ 7³¼ 5² 5²¼	Migliore R	b 115	5.20	86–15 Royal Discovery 114¼½ Yrmika 117ʰᵈ Fire Break 119½ No threat 8
5Dec87- 8Aqu fst 170	:47½ 1:13	1:44⅘	ⒻClm 45000	6 5 4³¾ 3³ 3⁴ 3⁷¼	Santos J A	b 114	4.70	68–27 Anniron 120ⁿᵏ La Polonaise 1206ⁿᵏ ChaseTheDream116¾½ Driving 8
15Nov87- 7Aqu fst 6f	:21⅘	:44⅘ 1:09⅘	3↑ⒻClm 45000	1 10 9⁹ 7⁷ 4⁴¼ 2¹¾	Davis R G	b 110	13.80	91–10 LPolonise112¼½ TooBobeesReturn110²¼ ChristyHill112¼ Slow start 10
7Nov87- 8Aqu fst 6f	:47½ 1:13	3↑ⒻAlw 34000	3 5 6⁵¼ 4⁴¼ 4¼ 1⁴¼	Santos J A	b 115	*1.60	76–26 TooBobeesReturn115⁴ FoundaJewel115ʰᵈ Ria'Mae115² Drew clear 8

LATEST WORKOUTS ● Mar 29 Aqu 3f fst :36⅘ b ● Mar 17 Aqu 3f fst :35⅘ b ● Mar 12 Aqu 6f fst 1:16⅘ b Mar 7 Aqu ▣ 5f fst 1:01⅘ h

Superb Time

Ch. m. 5, by Superbity—Timely Queen, by Olden Times
Br.—Lin-Drake Farm (Fla)
Tr.—Ferriola Peter
Own.—Riccio J — $45,000

113

Lifetime	1988	6	2	2	1	$46,220
34 7 5 6	1987	23	5	3	4	$80,925
$128,755	Turf	1	0	0	0	$320

2–1

2Apr88- 1Aqu fst 7f	:23	:46⅕ 1:23⅘	ⒻClm 35000	3 3 3¹ 3¹½ 3¹ 1³	Santagata N	b 117¼	2.10	82–22 DHPuddnTne117³ DHSuperbTime117³ PwnTheSilver119⁶ Driving 9
2Apr88—Dead heat								
23Mar88- 1Aqu fst 6f	:23½	:46 1:23⅘	ⒻAlw 32000	3 6 3² 4³ 3³½ 4⁴¼	Santagata N	b 117	3.60	78–24 Winsome Act 1223½ Socially Set 117ⁿᵒ SpankinSmart117¼ Evenly 8
12Mar88- 6Aqu fst 1⅛	:49	1:14½ 1:46⅘	ⒻAlw 33000	1 3 1½ 1¹ 2ʰᵈ 25½	Santagata N	b 117	2.60	71–22 Suistina 1175½ Superb Time 117¼ Tarnished Gold 117³ No match 7
7Feb88- 4Aqu fst 1⅛	:50 1:15 1:55	ⒻAlw 33000	5 2 1ʰᵈ 1ʰᵈ 3¹ 3¹½	Correa C J⁵	b 112	*.90	65–29 Larkridge 1171 Run Come See 117½ Superb Time 1129 Weakened 6
18Jan88- 4Aqu sly 1⅛	:47⅘ 1:12 1:53	ⒻAlw 33000	4 8 4⁵¼ 26 2¹¼ 2⁴	Correa C J⁵	b 110	5.90	73–24 Buck Magic 1194 Superb Time 1104¼ 2nd best 8
11Jan88- 4Aqu sly 1⅛	:49½ 1:14⅘ 1:55	ⒻClm 47500	4 3 3¹½ 4¹½ 1ʰᵈ 1³¾	Correa C J⁵	b 110	6.70	67–24 SuperbTime110³½ Fontine113⁵ PersonlProblem106¹ Brushed, clear 8
12Dec87- 6Aqu gd 6f	:22½	:44⅘ 1:10	3↑ⒻAlw 33000	1 7 7⁹ 713 6⁹ 5⁸¼	Migliore R	b 117	3.10	85–10 Wakonda 115½ Sharpening Up 1173 I'm Quite High 115½ Outrun 7
3Dec87- 3Aqu fst 1⅛	:48⅘ 1:13⅘ 1:47⅘	3↑ⒻClm c–47500	2 2 1ʰᵈ 3¹¼ 46	Bailey J D	b 117	*.80	66–19 ⒹPekina 115²¼ Glady H. 113¹½ Nc Place But Win 106³ Ridden out 7
16Nov87- 1Aqu fst 1⅛	:49 1:13⅘ 1:50⅘	ⒻClm 45000	2 2 2¹ 2ʰᵈ 15 13¾	Bailey J D	113	3.50	81–15 SuperbTime113³¾ NoPlceButWin106ⁿᵏ CupO'Cke112¹¼ Ridden out 7
25Oct87- 1Aqu fst 6f	:22½	:45⅘ 1:11	3↑ⒻClm 45000	1 6 56 713 611 117¾	Bailey J D	112	*1.00e	80–21 MoHuia114²¼ CherokeeChill118⁵ SuperbTime112ʰᵈ Pssd tired ones 8

LATEST WORKOUTS Apr 21 Aqu 7f fst 1:30⅘ b Mar 31 Aqu 3f fst :36 h Mar 10 Aqu ▣ 3f fst :36⅘ h

Spiriting

Gr. m. 5, by Forever Casting—Hattabs Spirit, by Al Hattab
Br.—Hart Mr-Mrs E C (Fla)
Tr.—Moschera Gasper S
Own.—Davis A — $45,000

108⁵

Lifetime	1987	16	1	1	1	$23,260
37 7 8 3	1986	15	5	5	2	$83,960
$118,660	Turf	1	0	0	0	$360

*
3–2
(entry)

22Oct87- 1Aqu fst 7f	:23½	:46⅘ 1:24⅘	3↑ⒻClm 25000	2 4 2ʰᵈ 2ʰᵈ 59 68¾	Antley C W	b 117	11.30	69–16 GldyH.112³¼ TurnpikePrincess115² TheZimmrmnNot115¹½ Stopped 7
30Oct87- 4Med sly 6f	:22⅘	:47 1:11⅘	3↑ⒻClm 25000	3 4 2ʰᵈ 2ʰᵈ 63¼ 918	Antley C W	b 116	4.20	65–21 Quint Star 1164 Adda Girl 116²¼ Mito's Touch 119¹ Tired 8
25Sep87- 8Med fst 6f	:22⅘	:45⅘ 1:11⅘	3↑ⒻClm 30000	8 2 2¹½ 2ʰᵈ 2³ 7⁵¼	Antley C W	b 114	9.60	81–18 Pawn The Silver 116ⁿᵏ Secluded 116ʰᵈ Are You Hot 116² Tired 8
12Sep87- 3Bel fst 7f	:23	:46 1:24⅘	3↑ⒻClm 35000	7 4 2¼ 3¹¼ 812 815¼	Cruguet J	b 117	11.00	62–19 GirlishGlee110ʰᵈ TheZimmermnNote115² ProudstBb117¼ Stopped 8
17Jly87- 1Bel fst 7f	:22⅘	:45¼ 1:25⅘	ⒻClm 35000	5 1 1² 1¹½ 1ʰᵈ 2²¼	Bailey J D	b 117	12.40	72–20 Mother Maloney 117½ Spiriting117¼ That'sFine117ⁿᵒ Drifted out 7
5Jly87- 1Bel fst 6f	:22	:45½ 1:11⅘	ⒻClm 35000	4 4 49¼ 4⁹ 1ʰᵈ 6¹²¼	Antley C W	b 117	6.50	71–24 Hula Zone 115²¾ Peace Keeper 117ʰᵈ Mother Maloney 117²¼ Tired 7
18Jun87- 6Bel fst 6f	:22⅘	:46 1:12	ⒻClm 45000	4 6 44¼ 3² 33¼ 78¾	Nuesch D⁵	b 108	*1.30e	71–23 Space Flower 117¼½ Anchorgram 113ⁿᵏ Forever Special117¼ Tired 7
29May87- 1Bel fst 6f	:22⅘	:45⅘ 1:11⅘	ⒻClm 45000	2 2 2¼ 2ʰᵈ 11 15¼	Nuesch D⁵	b 108	3.30e	81–15 Spiriting 108ⁿᵏ Lady Be Regal 1142½ Space Flower 117²¼ Driving 9
7May87- 1Bel fst 6f	:22⅘	:45⅘ 1:10⅘	ⒻClm 45000	8 4 3³ 65 814 819¼	Bailey J D	b 113	9.20	67–21 BabyChris108⁴ MerryWidowWaltz113ⁿᵏ GreatLdy117ⁿᵒ Raced wide 9
16Apr87- 1Aqu fst 6f	:22⅘	:45⅘ 1:11⅘	ⒻClm 45000	7 3 42 3¼ 54¾ 66¾	Correa A Jr	b 115	9.60	76–22 Peace Keeper115ⁿᵏ PeacefulAbove113ⁿᵏ BabyChris113⁵¼ Gave way 7

LATEST WORKOUTS May 3 Bel tr.t 3f fst :36 h Apr 27 Bel tr.t 4f fst :48⅘ h Apr 22 Bel tr.t 3f fst :36⅘ b

Star Brilliant ✻

B. m. 5, by Devoted Ruler—Brilliant Time, by Noholme II
Br.—Sasso L P (Md)
Tr.—Sedlacek Michael C
Own.—Friedman L — $45,000

108⁵

Lifetime	1988	10	1	3	1	$34,080
56 12 14 9	1987	13	4	0	3	$48,450
$163,215						

8–1

28Apr88- 4Aqu sly 6f	:22	:45⅘ 1:11⅘	ⒻClm 45000	2 4 3²¼ 3¹ 2¹½ 2²¼	Correa C J⁵	109	7.70	81–17 Peaceful Above 113²¼ Star Brilliant 109ⁿᵏ LauraJones117¼ Gamely 8
13Apr88- 5Aqu fst 6f	:22⅘	:46⅘ 1:11	ⒻClm c–30000	3 2 2ʰᵈ 3¹½ 3¹½ 3¹½	Migliore R	113	*1.80	82–25 Tasma's Star 117½ Classical Ballad 117²¾ HennaGirl108ʰᵈ Steadied 8
2Apr88- 1Aqu fst 7f	:23	:46⅕ 1:23⅘	ⒻClm 30000	4 5 2ʰᵈ 2¼ 2¼ 4³	Migliore R	119	5.50	79–22 DHPuddnTne119³ DHSuperbTime117³ PwnTheSilvr119⁶ Weakened 8
23Mar88- 1Aqu fst 6f	:22⅘	:46⅓ 1:11⅘	ⒻClm 35000	5 2 3¹½ 3² 22½ 2¼	Davis R G	119	*2.70	82–24 P. J.'s Blitzen 119½ Star Brilliant 1194¼ Henna Girl 117²¼ Fin. well 7
11Mar88- 2Aqu fst 6f	:22⅘	:46⅘ 1:13	ⒻClm 35000	3 5 2²¼ 2² 2ʰᵈ 12	Davis R G	113	5.50	79–31 Star Brilliant 113² P. J.'s Blitzen119¼ RunGenuine114ⁿᵏ Drew off 8
2Mar88- 1Aqu fst 6f	:22⅘	:46⅓ 1:13	ⒻClm 30000	4 5 2¼ 2¹½ 2¹ 2ⁿᵏ	Davis R G	113	8.80Ⓓ	79–21 P.J's Blitzen116ⁿᵏ ⒹStrBrillint113¹ MissilMgic117²¼ Bore in after st 7
2Mar88—Disqualified and placed seventh								
12Feb88- 2Aqu my 6f	:23½	:47½ 1:12⅘	ⒻClm 32500	2 4 1½ 1ʰᵈ 23 461½	Santos J A	b 115	6.70	73–26 Rick'sDelivery112⁴ PrinceofLdy117²½ SpcFlowr117¹½ Set pace, tired 8
3Feb88- 4Aqu gd 6f	:22⅘	:47½ 1:13	ⒻClm 35000	7 4 4¹¼ 3¹½ 5⁴¼ 6⁵¼	Ortega A Jr⁵	b 112	10.70	82–18 Space Flower 115²¾ Peaceful Above 115² RunGenuine110ⁿᵒ Wide 9
27Jan88- 2Aqu fst 6f	:23⅘	:47⅘ 1:13⅘	ⒻClm c–25000	8 2 12 1¹½ 1¹¼ 33	Antley C W	b 117	*1.20e	72–27 No Fools No Fun 108ⁿᵏ Keroky117²¼ StarBrilliant117ⁿᵏ Weakened 12
7Jan88- 9Aqu fst 6f	:23½	:47⅘ 1:13⅘	ⒻClm 35000	9 1 12 1¼ 2½ 2¼	Krone J A	b 115	*2.60	74–27 Daniella Drive 110½ StarBrilliant115³ Daddy'sSlugger115ⁿᵏ Gamely 11

LATEST WORKOUTS Apr 23 Aqu 4f fst :47⅘ h

Exacta wagering.
Second half of Instant Double.

(6 Horses)

7 AQUEDUCT

TURF COURSE
1⅛ MILES
AQUEDUCT

1⅛ MILES. (Turf). (1.47) ALLOWANCE. Purse $35,000. 3-year-olds and upward which ahve never won three races other than maiden or claiming. Weight, 3-year-olds, 115 lbs. Older, 124 lbs. Non-winners of two races other than maiden or claiming at a mile or over since April 1 allwoed 3 lbs.

Knockon — 7–2

Gr. c. 4, by Big Spruce—Bonnie Empress, by Young Emperor
Br.—Schwartz Arlene (Ky)
Tr.—Schwartz Scott M
Own.—Schwartz Arlene

121

Lifetime	1988	8	3	2	2	$76,940
19 3 5 3	1987	10	M	2	1	$17,810
$100,030	Turf	1	0	0	0	

24Apr88- 7Aqu	fst	1⅛	:49 1:13⅗ 1:50⅖	3↑ Alw 33000	4	1	11½	1hd	2hd	1hd	Davis R G	b	121	14.70	83-17	Knockon 121hd Chyonofuji 1162 Ask Not 114¾	Driving	7
23Mar88- 7Aqu	fst	7f	:22⅗ :45 1:25⅕	Alw 30000	8	1	63	55¼	32	1no	Davis R G	b	117	*2.50	75-24	Knockon117noLeveTheKys112½HomoSoho1171¼	Drifted out drvng	10
13Mar88- 1Aqu	fst	1 1/16	⊡:49 1:13⅘ 1:46⅗	Alw 31000	4	4	64½	64¾	42½	2¾	Davis R G	b	117	*2.10	75-18	Feldspar 110¾ Knockon 117nk Target X. 117hd	Steadied	8
4Mar88- 6Aqu	gd	1 1/16	⊡:48⅗ 1:13⅕ 1:44⅘	Alw 31000	6	3	32½	41¼	45	44¼	Santagata N	b	117	*.70	81-18	Alamour 112nk Brave and Bright117hdTargetX.1174	Lacked a rally	6
19Feb88- 7Aqu	fst	1⅛	⊡:48⅖ 1:13⅘ 1:54	Alw 31000	4	6	64¼	41¾	42½	2nk	Santagata N	b	117	*3.50	72-29	Shoreham 117nk Knockon 1172 Alamour 112½	Checked	11
8Feb88- 8Aqu	fst	1 70	⊡:49⅕ 1:13⅘ 1:43	Alw 31000	2	4	51¼	45½	38½	38	Santagata N	b	117	*.70	77-24	Nephrite 1177½ Willow Isle 117½ Knockon 1175	Lacked rally	5
28Jan88- 8Aqu	fst	1⅛	⊡:48⅕ 1:13⅗ 1:54	Alw 31000	2	5	56	52½	4nk	31	Santagata N	b	117	19.70	71-30	Nice Core 112nk Special Message 117¾ Knockon 1172¾	Rallied	12
21Jan88- 1Aqu	my	6f	⊡:21⅘ :45⅗ 1:11⅗	Md Sp Wt	1	9	59½	46½	32½	12¾	Santagata N	b	122	9.90	86-21	Knockon 1222¾ Just Great1221¼Where'sBilly122½	Slow start, clear	11
29Dec87- 6Aqu	fst	1 1/16	⊡:48⅕ 1:14⅗ 1:47	3↑ Md Sp Wt	4	7	65	72¾	27	28½	Santagata N	b	120	19.90	65-23	Divine Providence 1208½Knockon1204½BekaaValley120nk	2nd best	9
18Dec87- 1Aqu	fst	1⅛	⊡:49⅘ 1:15⅕ 1:53⅘	3↑ Md Sp Wt	7	4	31½	3½	47½	512	Santagata N	b	120	3.90	61-21	Shoreham1207½OfficerKrupke120hdWineMerchant1201¼	No factor	8

LATEST WORKOUTS Apr 19 Bel 5f fst 1:01 h

Dr. Carrington * — 5–2

Dk. b. or br. g. 3, by Mari's Book—Nurse Lulu, by Jacinto
Br.—Ferraro James (Ky)
Tr.—Ferraro James W
Own.—Ferraro T

107 5

Lifetime	1988	5	1	1	0	$64,242
13 3 1 2	1987	8	2	0	2	$37,480
$101,722	Turf	3	0	0	2	$5,080

9Apr88- 7Aqu	fst	1	:45 1:10 1:34⅘	Gotham	1	7	710	79	715	717¾	Santagata N		118	44.40	74-19	PrivteTerms126¾SeekingtheGold1145PrfctSpy1213	Wheeled start	8
9Apr88-Grade II																		
12Mar88- 8Aqu	fst	6f	⊡:21⅗ :44⅖ 1:10⅖	Swift	8	8	86½	76¼	88¼	79¼	Santagata N		120	29.20	83-22	AlohaProspector1202¾Pryett1141½ProudndVlid1171¾	Never factor	8
12Mar88-Grade III																		
5Mar88- 8Aqu	fst	1⅛	⊡:45⅘ 1:10 1:48⅖	Lucky Draw	1	1	1hd	21½	513	515¼	Santagata N		126	2.20	84-11	Dynaformer 1162¼ Cougarized1262¼John'sConcorde1149½	Faltered	8
12Feb88- 8Aqu	my	1 1/16	⊡:47⅗ 1:12⅗ 1:45	Whirlaway	1	1	11½	11	15	18½	Santagata N		117	2.30	84-26	Dr.Crrington1178½John'sConcord117hdCougrizd1232¼	Going away	5
18Jan88- 8Aqu	sly	1 70	⊡:47⅖ 1:12⅕ 1:42⅕	Count Fleet	3	3	2½	1hd	1hd	23	Santagata N		121	5.10	86-24	DlightfulDoctor1173Dr.Crrington1211½ChcotCounty121nk	2nd best	5
9Dec87- 7Aqu	fst	1 1/16	⊡:49⅕ 1:14 1:45⅗	Alw 31000	8	1	11½	11	1½	12	Carr D7		110	17.90	81-17	Dr. Carrington1102InnerIntensity1171½TimeMarching1175	Driving	8
31Oct87- 8Aqu	gd	1⅛	Ⓣ:47⅘ 1:13⅗ 1:53⅗	Pilgrim	7	1	11½	1½	56	720½	Bailey J D	b	113	13.60	46-32	Blew by Em 1152 Cefis 1131¾ Smart Lad 1133½	Stopped	8
31Oct87-Grade III																		
21Oct87- 7Aqu	fm	1 1/16	Ⓣ:48 1:13⅖ 1:45⅘	Alw 31000	4	1	15	12	2½	35½	Velasquez J	b	117	7.90	70-22	BlewbyEm1225¼Darby'sVenture117nkDr.Crrington1171¼	Weakened	10
6Oct87- 6Med	yl	1	[T]:47⅗ 1:13⅖ 1:41⅕	Alw 16000	6	5	55	74¼	68	310¾	Santagata N	b	120↓	6.10	61-28	MasterSpeker1174¾GoldenHonor1176[DH]SilkyCommnd117	Rallied	9
6Oct87-Dead heat																		
5Sep87- 4Bel	fst	6½f	:22⅗ :46 1:17⅖	Alw 28000	7	6	42	2hd	46½	510¾	Nuesch D5	b	112	11.20	77-15	Tsarbaby 1225¼ Digress 122¾ Red Scamper 1193	Wide, tired	10

LATEST WORKOUTS Apr 3 Aqu 3f fst :33⅘ h

Socially Informed — 16–1

B. g. 4, by Raised Socially—Embossed, by Info
Br.—Lavin A & K (Ky)
Tr.—Galluscio Dominick
Own.—Winbound Farms

116 5

Lifetime	1988	12	4	2	3	$66,380
35 8 6 6	1987	14	2	2	2	$40,005
$130,568	Turf	3	1	1	0	$18,575

25Apr88- 1Aqu	fm	1 1/16	Ⓣ:47⅘ 1:13 1:44⅗	Clm 45000	4	1	12½	1½	2½	26	Bermudez J E5	b	108	7.70	76-18	AllHandsOnDeck1176SociallyInformed108¾Eston113nk	Held place	9
17Apr88- 6Aqu	fst	1⅛	:47⅗ 1:12 1:51⅘	Clm c-22500	6	1	11½	1hd	1hd	1no	Peck B D5	b	110	14.00	76-25	SocillyInformed110noQuindcillion1151½It'sAboutSvn117nk	Driving	9
13Apr88- 1Aqu	fst	1	:46⅖ 1:12⅖ 1:38⅕	Clm c-17500	1	1	14	1hd	1½	1nk	Bermudez J E5	b	112	7.00	75-25	ScllyInfrmd112nkIdlSltn1137¾Dncr'sFnnyfc117nk	Long hard drive	10
7Apr88- 3Aqu	sly	1	:46 1:11⅖ 1:38	Clm 25000	1	2	11	32	47	517¾	Migliore R	b	117	7.20	58-26	Fast Jack 1171¼ Quindecillion 1171½ Easton 1174	Weakened	11
26Mar88- 4Aqu	sly	7f	:22⅗ :45⅕ 1:23	Clm 25000	10	1	2½	22½	27	38¾	Migliore R	b	117	13.90	77-23	TruthBeTold1124Timperture1174¾SocillyInformd1171¼	Weakened	12
5Mar88- 1Aqu	gd	1 1/16	⊡:48⅗ 1:13 1:56⅗	Clm 25000	3	1	12	12	2hd	33	Migliore R	b	117	2.40	91-11	PthsOfGlory117noPrintMoney1083SocillyInformed117¾	Weakened	8
25Feb88- 4Aqu	fst	1⅛	⊡:48⅕ 1:13⅖ 1:53⅕	Clm 22500	7	1	13½	12½	1½	21¾	Carr D7	b	110	*1.60	74-25	BravendBright1151¾SocillyInformed1106½Mr.J.V.1083	Second best	7
15Feb88- 9Aqu	fst	1 1/16	⊡:49⅖ 1:13⅗ 1:47	Clm 22500	11	1	1hd	1hd	1½	34	Carr D7	b	110	7.00	70-22	PppyLP1172DcrtdEmprr1172ScllyInfrmd1102	Set pace, weakened	12
5Feb88- 1Aqu	fst	1⅛	⊡:48⅕ 1:13⅗ 1:55⅗	Clm 20000	6	1	1½	11½	11	1nk	Carr D7	b	106	6.00	64-32	Socially Informed 106nk Sylson 1134½ Joe Allen 1154½	Lost whip	7
30Jan88- 9Aqu	fst	1⅛	⊡:47⅘ 1:12⅖ 1:52⅕	Clm 14000	11	1	12	12	1hd	1hd	Carr D7	b	110	6.00	81-17	Socially Informed 110hdWickedWike1175½MossPond114nk	Driving	12

LATEST WORKOUTS ●May 2 Aqu 4f fst :48⅘ h ●Apr 4 Aqu 4f fst :48⅕ h ●Mar 21 Aqu 4f fst :48 h Mar 14 Aqu 4f fst :48⅕ h

Go for Commadore — * 4–5

Dk. b. or br. g. 4, by Commadore C—Gofore Bull, by Winning Bull
Br.—Laurell Sally S (Fla)
Tr.—Ferriola Peter
Own.—Nagle K

116 5

Lifetime	1988	6	3	1	1	$95,160
33 8 1 2	1987	13	1	0	1	$14,785
$141,565	Turf	4	1	0	0	$11,910

23Apr88-10GS	fst	1¼	:49⅘ 1:39⅕ 2:04⅖	3↑ Trenton H	3	3	31	1hd	2hd	25	Nuesch D	b	114	4.60	77-19	Manzotti 1185 Go forCommadore1146CountOnRomeo114½	Rallied	5
23Apr88-Grade III																		
2Apr88- 8Aqu	fst	1	:44⅗ 1:08⅘ 1:34⅖	3↑ Westchtr H	9	4	69	69	813	814¾	Santagata N	b	111	11.30	79-22	Faster Than Sound 1138½RonStevens111noKing'sSwan133no	Tired	9
2Apr88-Grade III																		
13Mar88- 6Aqu	fst	1⅛	⊡:46⅘ 1:11⅗ 1:50⅕	Alw 47000	5	3	37	2½	14	15	Santagata N	b	115	*1.10	91-18	GoforCommdor1155MkADcison1151¾BoyshChrm1151¾	Ridden out	6
7Mar88- 7Aqu	fst	1 70	⊡:48 1:13 1:42	Clm 75000	1	2	21½	2hd	1½	14¾	Santagata N	b	112	*2.00	90-25	GoforCommdor1124¾Pirt'sSkiff1127AuthnticHro1222	Going away	8
2Mar88- 4Aqu	fst	1 1/16	⊡:48⅕ 1:12⅖ 1:44⅖	Clm 35000	7	4	11	13	15	18½	Davis R G	b	117	*2.30e	87-21	GoforCommdore1178½NicCor1131½LordWindmr1081½	Going away	8
29Jan88- 1Aqu	fst	1⅛	⊡:48 1:13⅕ 1:54⅖	Clm 45000	2	3	33½	31½	1½	35¾	Correa C J5	b	108	7.30	64-26	LovelyBons1132¾PthsOfGlory1063GoforCommdor108nk	Led, wknd	7
31Dec87- 4Hia	fst	1⅛	:48⅖ 1:13⅕ 1:52⅖	3↑ Clm c-20000	6	7	73¾	31	32½	44½	Danjean R	b	114	*2.00	64-30	Gallant Friend1182BoldScreen120hdPeacefulArab1162½	Weakened	7
19Dec87- 7Hia	gd	1 1/16	Ⓣ 1:45⅕	3↑ Alw 15700	1	1	31	1½	129½	1218	Torso M A7	b	107	16.60	54-26	Toh's Moment 1202 First Patriot 114¾ Pershing 114hd	Stopped	12
8Dec87- 8Hia	fst	7f	:22⅗ :45⅖ 1:22⅖	3↑ Clm 35000	6	7	53½	42	52½	65½	Danjean R	b	114	27.70	85-20	Sagittarian 116nk Huch 1152½ Ring for Peace 114hd	Weakened	12
25Nov87- 5Hia	fst	1 1/16	:48⅕ 1:12⅘ 1:45⅘	3↑ Clm 25000	1	7	51¾	3nk	2½	32½	Danjean R	b	114	22.50	70-27	[DH]CtchthPrnc1142½[DH]BlcLnnH1142½GfrCmdr1141¼	Wknd midstr.	8

LATEST WORKOUTS ●Apr 21 Aqu 1 fst 1:41 h

To be run at 1 1/8 miles on dirt.
Exacta wagering.
Track now called fast.

(8 Horses)

8 AQUEDUCT

START
7 FURLONGS
AQUEDUCT
FINISH

7 FURLONGS. (1.20⅕) 88th Running THE CARTER HANDICAP (Grade I). $250,000 added. 3–year–olds and upward. By subscription of $500 each which should accompany the nominaton; $2,000 to pass the entry box, $2,000 to start with $250,000 added. The added money and all fees to be divided 60% to the winner, 22% to second, 12% to third and 6% to fourth. Weight, Monday, May 2. Starters to be named at the closing time of entries. Trophies will be presented to the winning owenr, trainer an jockey. Closed April 20 with 17 nominations.

Prospector's Halo

Own.—Heath V H
B. c. 4, by Gold Stage—Rivenoak, by Halo
Br.—Hillbrook Farm (Ky)
Tr.—Lundy Richard J
113
Lifetime 13 6 2 0 $107,790
1988 5 4 0 0 $83,510
1987 3 1 0 0 $7,820
Turf 1 0 0 0 $950

16Apr88- 7Aqu fst 1 :46⅗ 1:12⅕ 1:36⅗ 3↑Alw 47000 6 3 2hd 1hd 1½ 11 Davis R G 121 *.50 83–21 Prospector's Halo 1211 Abject 1245½ Pirate's Skiff 121hd Driving 8
30Mar88- 8Aqu fst 7f :23⅖ :46⅕ 1:23 3↑Alw 42000 6 3 63 64 52¼ 1hd Davis R G 121 *1.50 86–22 Prospector'sHalo121hdJazzingAround1211½Diapason1211½ Driving 7
18Feb88- 9GP fst 7f :22⅗ :45⅖ 1:22⅖ Alw 20000 4 3 21 2½ 12 12¼ St Leon G 122 *1.90 92–26 Prospector's Halo 1222¼ Dub Nhoc 1171¼ Admit 119¾ Drew clear 7
30Jan88- 9GP fm *1⅟₁₆ Ⓣ 1:42⅖ Alw 19000 2 4 57 49½ 47½ 411 St Leon G 117 5.40 83–04 Iron Courage 11910 Holy Moldy 119nk Admit 117¾ No threat 10
2Jan88- 6Hia fst 7f :23⅗ :46⅖ 1:22⅘ Key West 1 5 1hd 1hd 11½ 11½ St Leon G 114 35.60 89–14 Prospector'sHlo1141½NoPoints114hd[DH]Bldski'sStr117 Drew clear 8
12Dec87- 7Hia fst 7f :23⅖ :46⅖ 1:24⅖ 3↑Alw 12000 11 1 72¾ 3nk 1hd 11 St Leon G 114 *2.20 81–18 Prospector'sHlo1141BshfulBrv1162NorthWrning114nk Drew clear 12
3Dec87- 8Hia fst 6f :22⅕ :45⅗ 1:10⅗ 3↑Alw 14100 3 6 42 62¾ 53¼ 45½ St Leon G 114 15.10 81–21 Johnny Fats 1203¼KeytoCandy1201½DiscoveredGold114½ Steadied 12
22Mar87- 8GP fst 6f :22⅕ :45⅘ 1:10⅘ Alw 14000 6 4 52¼ 54 33 58¼ Maple E b 117 25.90 77–24 Jade Hunter 122no Charalo 1225½ Shoot Fire 117nk Outrun 9
31Aug86-10Cby fst 6½f :22 :44⅖ 1:16⅘ Cby Juv 3 11 53½ 44¼ 44½ 56¾ Oldham J b 120 40.60 90–08 Staff Riot 120nk Sudden Dance 1204½ Texas Trio 120no 14
16Aug86- 9Cby fst 6f :22⅗ :46 1:11⅗ Alw 11000 2 4 43 53½ 52¾ 42½ Oldham J 117 3.40 86–07 Adam Bomb 112¾ Texas Trio 117¾ Saga 1171 6
LATEST WORKOUTS ●May 1 Bel 5f fst :58⅖ h Apr 25 Bel 4f fst :47 h Apr 14 Bel 3f fst :35⅖ b Apr 9 Bel 5f gd 1:01⅘ b

14–1

Afleet

Own.—Kennedy & Taylor Made Farm
Ch. c. 4, by Mr Prospector—Polite Lady, by Venetian Jester
Br.—Kennedy Richard R (Ont-C)
Tr.—England Phillip
124
Lifetime 11 7 2 0 $668,698
1988 1 1 0 0 $66,480
1987 10 6 2 0 $602,218

19Mar88- 8Aqu fst 6f :22⅗ :45⅘ 1:09⅕ 3↑Toboggan H 3 4 23½ 22 21 11¾ Stahlbaum G b 123 *1.50 94–23 Afleet 1231¾ Pinecutter 1152¾ Vinnie the Viper 1227½ Drew off 4
19Mar88-Grade III
21Nov87- 7Hol fst 1¼ :46⅖ 1:35⅖ 2:01⅖ 3↑Br Cp Class 7 6 75¼ 1217 1220 1027¼ Stahlbaum G b 122 9.60 58–12 Ferdinand 126noAlysheba1221¼JudgeAngelucci1261½ Bmpd 1st trn 12
21Nov87-Grade I
23Oct87- 9Med fst 1¼ :47 1:36⅕ 2:01⅘ 3↑Med Cup H 7 2 2½ 11 11½ 2no Stahlbaum G b 118 *1.70 93–16 Creme Fraiche 123no Afleet 1186 Cryptoclearance1203½ Sharp try 7
23Oct87-Grade I
4Oct87- 9Pha fst 1⅛ :47 1:10⅖ 1:48⅕ Pa. Derby 7 2 1hd 2½ 22½ 12¼ Stahlbaum G b 122 *1.40 94–17 Afleet 1222¼ Lost Code 1222 Homebuilder 1192 Drew out 8
4Oct87-Grade II
7Sep87- 8Bel fst 1 :45⅕ 1:09⅕ 1:33⅘ Jerome H 9 3 1hd 1½ 11 13¼ Stahlbaum G b 115 2.60 96–19 Afleet 1153¼ Stacked Pack 1098 Templar Hill 117hd Drew away 9
7Sep87-Grade I
19Jly87- 8WO fst 1¼ :45⅗ 1:37⅖ 2:03⅗ [S]Qn Plate 14 6 75¼ 1½ 1½ 23¼ Stahlbaum G b 126 *.60e 85–11 Market Control 1263¼Afleet1262OneFromHeaven1212½ No match 14
19Jly87-Grade I-C
5Jly87- 9WO fst 1⅛ :47 1:11⅘ 1:50⅕ [S]Plate Trl 10 1 2½ 1½ 1hd 12½ Stahlbaum G b 126 *1.30 89–19 Afleet 1262½ Bold Executive 1268 Duckpower 126nk Handily 13
5Jly87-Grade II-C
21Jun87- 9WO fst 1⅟₁₆ :48⅕ 1:12⅗ 1:44 Marine 1 3 32 63¾ 67 53 Stahlbaum G b 121 *.50 86–17 Duckpower 119¾ Steady Power119nkOrderofexcellence1211½ Tired 7
21Jun87-Grade II-C
23May87- 9WO fst 7f :23 :45 1:22⅘ [S]Queenston 6 3 31½ 3½ 11½ 14 Stahlbaum G b 121 *.75 95–24 Afleet 1214 Orderofexcellence 123no Bold Revenue 1261½ Handily 6
23May87-Grade III-C
9May87- 9WO fst 6f :22⅖ :45 1:09⅘ Friar Rock 3 2 21½ 2hd 1hd 11¾ Stahlbaum G 117 *.35 94–20 Afleet 1171¾ Pinecutter 1193½ Arctic Lord 1175¾ In hand 4
LATEST WORKOUTS May 4 WO 3f fst :36⅗ b Apr 30 WO 3f sly :37⅗ b Apr 26 WO 4f fst :49 b Apr 22 WO 4f fst :48⅗ b

*
4–5

Gulch *

Own.—Brant P M
B. c. 4, by Mr Prospector—Jameela, by Rambunctious
Br.—Brant P M (Ky)
Tr.—Lukas D Wayne
124
Lifetime 24 10 4 3 $1,858,981
1988 3 2 0 1 $124,300
1987 14 3 3 2 $1,297,171

16Apr88- 9OP gd 1⅛ :46⅗ 1:10⅗ 1:47 Oaklawn H 7 2 42 42½ 22 33¾ Delahoussaye E 120 5.70 94–12 Lost Code 126¾ Cryptoclearance 1223 Gulch 1204 8
16Apr88-Grade I
30Mar88- 8SA fst 6½f :21⅘ :44⅖ 1:15 Ptro Grnd H 3 1 1½ 21 21½ 11¼ Delahoussaye E 123 1.20 95–18 Gulch 1231¼ Very Subtle 1202¼ Gallant Sailor 111 3
18Mar88- 8SA fst 6f :22⅕ :45 1:08⅘ Alw 55000 6 3 41 2hd 1hd 11¾ Delahoussaye E 116 3.10 94–18 Gulch 1161¾ Sebrof 1183½ My Gallant Game 1163½ 6
21Nov87- 7Hol fst 1¼ :46⅖ 1:35⅖ 2:01⅖ 3↑Br Cp Class 11 8 87¾ 87½ 910 915¼ Santos J A 122 25.20 70–12 Ferdinand 126no Alysheba 1221¼ Judge Angelucci 1261½ 12
21Nov87-Grade I
21Oct87- 8Aqu fst 1 :45⅖ 1:09⅖ 1:34⅘ Jamaica H 1 7 711 65½ 33½ 2¾ Santos J A 123 *.80 91–19 Stacked Pack 110¾ Gulch 123¾ Homebuilder 1121¾ Rallied 8
21Oct87-Grade III
20Sep87- 8Bel gd 1¼ :48⅖ 1:36⅘ 2:01 3↑Marlboro H 2 4 58 34 32 43¼ Santos J A 117 4.80 90–14 Java Gold 1202¼ Nostalgia's Star 116nk Polish Navy 117¾ Hung 5
20Sep87-Grade I
5Sep87- 8Bel fst 1⅛ :46 1:09⅕ 1:47 3↑Woodward 8 6 88¾ 68½ 33 2¾ Santos J A 118 5.50 91–15 Polish Navy 116¾ Gulch 118nk Creme Fraiche 1192¾ Rallied 9
5Sep87-Grade I
22Aug87- 8Sar sly 1¼ :46⅕ 1:36⅖ 2:02 Travers 4 6 612 44 55 410¼ Santos J A 126 9.90e 80–16 Java Gold 1262 Cryptoclearance 1266¾PolishNavy1261½ No threat 9
22Aug87-Grade I
8Aug87- 8Sar fst 1⅛ :46⅖ 1:10⅖ 1:48⅖ 3↑Whitney H 1 6 58 42½ 12½ 2¾ Santos J A 117 3.40e 92–13 Java Gold 113¾ Gulch 1172¼ Broad Brush 127no Drifted out 7
8Aug87-Grade I
6Jun87- 8Bel fst 1½ :49⅖ 2:03 2:28⅕ Belmont 9 6 813 816 412 314 Day P 126 7.70e 65–15 Bet Twice 12614 Cryptoclearance 126no Gulch 126nk Wide str 9
6Jun87-Grade I
LATEST WORKOUTS Apr 29 Bel 6f fst 1:15⅕ b Apr 4 SA 6f fst 1:14 h Mar 26 SA 5f fst :59 h Mar 11 SA 5f fst 1:01⅗ h

2–1

(*Continued on following page*)

Exacta wagering. Late Daily Double (Race 8 plus Kentucky Derby).

(Race 8 continued)

King's Swan ×

Own.—Akman A
B. g. 8, by King's Bishop—Royal Cygnet, by Sea-Bird
Br.—Kerr Mrs D K (Ky)
Tr.—Dutrow Richard E
128
Lifetime 77 26 12 12 $1,507,216
1988 6 4 0 1 $366,441
1987 12 3 6 2 $477,218
Turf 6 1 0 0 $9,630

22Apr88- 8Aqu fst 6f :22⅖ :46 1:10⅕ 3↑Bold Ruler 3 6 7^{5} 6^{4} 5^{2} 1^{2} Antley C W 123 2.40 89-28 King'sSwan123^{2}SeattleKnight119^{nk}FasterThnSound$123^{1½}$ Driving 7
22Apr88-Grade II
2Apr88- 8Aqu fst 1 :44⅗ 1:08⅘ 1:34⅖ 3↑Westchtr H 7 3 $3^{7½}$ $4^{6½}$ $4^{9½}$ $3^{8½}$ Antley C W 133 1.70 85-22 FstrThnSound$113^{8½}$RonStvns111^{no}Kng'sSwn133^{no} Altered course 9
2Apr88-Grade III
6Mar88- 8Aqu fst 1⅛ ⊡:49 1:13 1:50⅗ 3↑Grey Lag H 3 2 2^{1} 2^{1} $1^{1½}$ 1^{5} Santos J A 130 *.90 89-20 King's Swan 130^{5} Palace March $113^{1½}$MatthewsKeep117^{9} Driving 4
6Mar88-Grade III
15Feb88- 8Aqu fst 1⅛ ⊡:49 1:13⅖ 1:51⅖ 3↑Stymie H 5 2 2^{1} $2^{½}$ $1^{1½}$ $1^{4½}$ Santos J A 126 *.50 85-22 King's Swan $126^{4½}$ Wind Chill $110^{3¾}$ FeelingGallant$116^{¾}$ Drew off 5
15Feb88-Grade III
23Jan88- 8Aqu fst 1⅛ ⊡:46⅗ 1:10⅕ 1:48⅘ 3↑Assault H 3 2 1^{1} $1^{½}$ 1^{2} $1^{4½}$ Santos J A 122 *.80 98-13 King'sSwan$122^{4½}$PalaceMrch$112^{3½}$ProudDebonir$113^{6½}$ Ridden out 6
23Jan88-Grade III
2Jan88- 8Aqu fst 1$\frac{1}{16}$ ⊡:49 1:13⅕ 1:45⅕ 3↑Aqueduct H 5 3 $3^{½}$ 1^{hd} $1^{½}$ $1^{½}$ Antley C W 121 *.50 D 83-30 D King's Swan $121^{½}$CleverSecret$112^{1¾}$ProudDebonair$114^{½}$ Bore in 9
2Jan88-Grade III; Disqualified and placed fourth
13Dec87- 8Aqu fst 6f ⊡:22⅖ :45⅖ 1:09⅗ 3↑Gravesend H 1 5 4^{2} $4^{1¾}$ $3^{1½}$ 2no Antley C W 122 *.80e 96-16 Vinnie the Viper 116no King's Swan122^{no}BestByTest$117^{7½}$ Rallied 6
22Nov87- 8Aqu fst 6f :22⅖ :46⅕ 1:10⅖ 3↑Sprt Pge H 7 2 $2^{1½}$ $2^{1½}$ 1^{hd} $2^{1¼}$ Santos J A 123 3.60 88-32 Vinnie the Viper $115^{1¼}$ King's Swan$123^{½}$Banker'sJet$118^{2¼}$ Gamely 10
22Nov87-Grade III
21Jun87- 8Bel my 6f :22 :44 1:07⅘ 3↑Tru Nrth H 2 2 $3^{1½}$ $3^{5½}$ 3^{5} $2^{5¾}$ Santos J A 120 3.60 95-10 Groovy $123^{5¾}$ King's Swan 120^{nk} Sun Master 117no Gained place 4
21Jun87-Grade II
6Jun87- 1Bel fst 6f :21⅗ :44 1:08⅖ 3↑Roseben H 6 5 $6^{9½}$ 6^{10} $4^{8½}$ $3^{6¼}$ Santos J A 121 2.60 92-15 Groovy $119^{4½}$ Love That Mac 118^{2} King's Swan $121^{3½}$ No menace 6
6Jun87-Grade III
LATEST WORKOUTS Apr 18 Aqu 5f fst 1:01 b Apr 12 Aqu 5f fst 1:01⅖ b ●Mar 29 Aqu 6f fst 1:13⅘ b

5–1

Seattle Knight

Own.—Tayhill Stable
Dk. b. or br. c. 4, by Seattle Slew—Gueniviere, by Prince John
Br.—Seminole Stable (Ky)
Tr.—Hertler John O
111
Lifetime 20 4 7 1 $152,776
1988 9 2 2 1 $91,616
1987 10 2 4 0 $56,320
Turf 1 0 0 0

22Apr88- 8Aqu fst 6f :22⅖ :46 1:10⅕ 3↑Bold Ruler 4 4 $6^{4½}$ $7^{6½}$ $6^{2¼}$ 2^{2} Krone J A 119 45.40 87-28 King'sSwn123^{2}SettlKnight119^{nk}FstrThnSound$123^{1½}$ Gained place 7
22Apr88-Grade II
2Apr88- 8Aqu fst 1 :44⅗ 1:08⅘ 1:34⅖ 3↑Westchtr H 4 7 7^{17} 7^{10} 7^{12} $7^{13¼}$ Samyn J L 110 39.80 81-22 Faster ThanSound$113^{8½}$RonStevens111^{no}King'sSwan133^{no} Outrun 9
2Apr88-Grade III
16Mar88- 8Aqu fst 7f :23⅕ :46⅖ 1:23⅘ Alw 42000 3 8 8^{7} $7^{6¼}$ $6^{6½}$ 3^{4} Krone J A 122 3.00 78-26 Abject $122^{1½}$ Peppy Le Pew $115^{2½}$ Seattle Knight 122^{nk} Rallied 8
5Mar88- 5Aqu gd 6f ⊡:22⅖ :45⅘ 1:10 Alw 33000 5 5 $8^{7½}$ $8^{5¼}$ $5^{2¼}$ $1^{1¼}$ Krone J A 119 3.20 94-11 Seattle Knight $119^{1¼}$ Placid Waters 117^{3} Abject$119^{1½}$ Ridden out 8
25Feb88- 5Aqu fst 6f ⊡:21⅕ :45⅖ 1:11 Alw 33000 5 1 $4^{7½}$ $4^{6½}$ 3^{3} $1^{1½}$ Krone J A 117 3.90 89-25 SeattleKnight$117^{1½}$RealAccount114^{6}Ptty'sGmbit117^{nk} Ridden out 6
14Feb88- 7Aqu fst 6f ⊡:22⅕ :45⅗ 1:10⅘ Alw 32000 2 8 8^{11} $7^{8¾}$ $5^{6½}$ $2^{2½}$ Krone J A 117 8.00e 87-16 RealAccount$114^{2½}$SeattleKnight$117^{½}$MeanndCrfty$117^{2¾}$ Reared st. 8
4Feb88- 5Aqu sly 6f ⊡:22⅗ :46⅖ 1:11⅖ Alw 32000 1 5 $5^{7¼}$ 5^{8} 5^{10} $4^{8¾}$ Antley C W 117 14.60 78-21 Tis Royal $117^{5¾}$ Mean and Crafty 117^{2} Real Account 114^{1} Outrun 5
15Jan88- 5Aqu fst 6f ⊡:22⅕ :45 1:10⅖ Alw 32000 6 7 8^{9} 9^{14} 6^{14} $7^{11¼}$ Antley C W 117 10.30e 81-19 Pop John $119^{1¾}$ Tis Royal $117^{1¾}$ Real Account $114^{2½}$ Outrun 10
2Jan88- 7Aqu fst 1$\frac{1}{16}$ ⊡:48⅗ 1:13⅖ 1:46⅖ Alw 33000 3 2 $2^{2½}$ $2^{2½}$ 8^{14} $7^{16¾}$ Antley C W 117 7.60 60-39 D Placid Waters $112^{¾}$ Darn Smart $117^{2¾}$ Stalking 117^{2} Tired 8
17Dec87- 7Aqu fst 6f ⊡:23⅕ :47 1:11⅕ 3↑Alw 32000 5 8 $8^{4¼}$ $7^{4¼}$ $6^{9½}$ $5^{7½}$ Davis R G 115 4.10 80-21 Hibernation $117^{2¾}$ Real Account $112^{1¼}$ Mawsuff$117^{3½}$ Wide in str. 9
LATEST WORKOUTS May 1 Bel 5f fst :59⅕ b Mar 29 Bel tr.t 3f fst :37 b

35–1

Stacked Pack *

Own.—Phipps O
B. c. 4, by Majestic Light—Con Game, by Buckpasser
Br.—Phipps O (Ky)
Tr.—McGaughey Claude III
112
Lifetime 9 5 1 0 $171,438
1988 1 0 0 0
1987 7 4 1 0 $153,238

22Apr88- 8Aqu fst 6f :22⅖ :46 1:10⅕ 3↑Bold Ruler 7 3 $4^{2½}$ 4^{2} $3^{1½}$ 5^{4} Romero R P 119 7.90 85-28 King'sSwn123^{2}SettleKnight119^{nk}FsterThnSound$123^{1½}$ Weakened 7
22Apr88-Grade II
22Nov87- 8Aqu fst 6f :22⅖ :46⅕ 1:10⅖ 3↑Sprt Pge H 4 4 4^{2} $5^{2¼}$ $8^{7¼}$ $8^{11½}$ Romero R P 113 *1.80 77-32 Vinnie theViper$115^{1¼}$King'sSwan$123^{½}$Banker'sJet$118^{2¼}$ No excuse 10
22Nov87-Grade III
21Oct87- 8Aqu fst 1 :45⅖ 1:09⅖ 1:34⅘ Jamaica H 7 2 2^{1} $1^{½}$ $1^{2½}$ $1^{¾}$ Romero R P 110 1.50 92-19 Stacked Pack $110^{¾}$ Gulch $123^{¾}$ Homebuilder $112^{1¾}$ Driving 8
21Oct87-Grade III
7Oct87- 5Bel my 6f :22⅗ :45⅗ 1:09⅗ 3↑Alw 31000 5 1 1^{1} $1^{½}$ 1^{2} $1^{5¼}$ Romero R P 114 *.40 91-22 Stacked Pack $114^{5¼}$ Conventioneer 119^{2}Vronsky$116^{3½}$ Ridden out 6
7Sep87- 8Bel fst 1 :45⅕ 1:09⅕ 1:33⅘ Jerome H 7 4 3^{2} $2^{½}$ 2^{1} $2^{3¼}$ Guerra W A 109 16.20 93-19 Afleet $115^{3¼}$ Stacked Pack 109^{8} Templar Hill 117^{hd} 2nd best 9
7Sep87-Grade I
22Aug87- 7Sar sly 7f :22⅖ :45⅕ 1:23 King Bishop 1 5 $4^{1¼}$ $5^{5½}$ $5^{4¼}$ $6^{9¼}$ Romero R P 115 5.80 78-16 Templar Hill 119^{nk} Mister S. M.119^{5}Homebuilder115^{nk} Weakened 8
22Aug87-Grade III
1Aug87- 5Bel fst 1 :45⅘ 1:11⅕ 1:37 3↑Alw 28000 2 1 $1^{1½}$ 1^{4} $1^{2½}$ $1^{4½}$ Romero R P 112 *.60 80-27 Stacked Pack $112^{4½}$ JohnMuir117^{5}Gnome'sPleasure$114^{5½}$ Driving 6
9Jly87- 3Bel my 6f :22 :45⅘ 1:10⅘ 3↑Alw 26000 5 7 $4^{4½}$ 1^{hd} $1^{½}$ $1^{1¼}$ Romero R P 113 *.80 86-24 StckedPck$113^{1¼}$RelAccount$108^{4½}$BillyWilbur$117^{½}$ Slow strt,drvng 7
15Sep86- 4Bel fst 6f :22⅗ :46 1:10⅖ Md Sp Wt 11 5 1^{2} $1^{2½}$ 1^{5} $1^{8¾}$ Romero R P 118 2.20 90-15 Stacked Pack $118^{8¾}$ Its Acedemic $118^{3½}$ Yucca $118^{1¾}$ Ridden out 12
LATEST WORKOUTS May 3 Bel 4f fst :48⅗ b Apr 21 Bel 3f fst :35 h Apr 14 Bel 4f fst :47 h ●Apr 5 Bel 4f fst :46⅕ h

18–1

Its Acedemic

Own.—Vogel M
Ch. c. 4, by Sauce Boat—After School, by Arts and Letters
Br.—Vogel Hortense & M (Ky)
Tr.—Barrera Luis
108
Lifetime 18 4 4 5 $114,920
1988 7 3 1 1 $70,100
1987 3 1 0 1 $21,060

20Apr88- 8Aqu fst 7f :22⅕ :45⅖ 1:24 3↑Alw 33000 8 3 6^{9} 5^{5} 2^{1} $1^{1¾}$ Pezua J M 124 9.80 81-26 Its Acedemic $124^{1¾}$ Proud andValid$112^{1¼}$ForbesWay$121^{2½}$ Driving 8
11Apr88- 7Aqu fst 1 :46⅗ 1:11⅕ 1:35⅕ 3↑Alw 35000 5 5 $4^{2½}$ $3^{1½}$ $2^{2½}$ 2^{6} Pezua J M 121 11.70 84-23 Talinum 121^{6} Its Acedemic $121^{4½}$ Fast Lead 121^{2} Second best 10
6Apr88- 5Aqu fst 1 :45⅗ 1:10⅗ 1:36⅖ 3↑Alw 33000 2 5 3^{3} 2^{hd} $1^{2½}$ 1^{3} Migliore R 121 2.40 84-25 Its Acedemic 121^{3} Bucket Shop121^{2}Aristocount$115^{2½}$ Ridden out 7
30Mar88- 5Aqu fst 1 :46⅕ 1:10⅖ 1:35⅗ Clm 45000 7 5 4^{3} 4^{2} $4^{2½}$ 3^{2} Migliore R 113 6.90 86-22 Wild Wood $115^{1½}$ Lord Windemere $113^{½}$ ItsAcedemic$113^{½}$ Rallied 7
25Mar88- 6Aqu fst 7f :22⅕ :44⅗ 1:23⅗ Clm 50000 1 5 $6^{4½}$ $7^{7½}$ $4^{7½}$ $4^{5¾}$ Belmonte J F 119 14.20 77-27 Say Hey $113^{3½}$ Arctic Beat 117^{2} Tis Royal 117^{nk} Mild bid 7
16Mar88- 7Aqu fst 7f :23⅕ :46⅗ 1:23⅗ Alw 32000 5 2 $6^{3¼}$ 6^{5} $6^{5¾}$ $8^{8¼}$ Belmonte J F 122 6.80 75-26 RichesToRiches117^{1}OurHappyWrrior$117^{3¾}$BucketShop$117^{1½}$ Wide 9
3Mar88- 7Aqu fst 6f ⊡:23 :46⅗ 1:11⅗ Alw 30000 2 2 3^{2} $2^{1½}$ $1^{1½}$ $1^{4¾}$ Belmonte J F 117 17.20 86-22 Its Acedemic $117^{4¾}$ High Rex$117^{¾}$LilKell'sBrother117^{1} Ridden out 8
11Dec87- 6Aqu gd 6f ⊡:22⅘ :46⅗ 1:11⅖ 3↑Md Sp Wt 1 3 $4^{5½}$ 4^{5} 3^{1} 2^{hd} Krone J A 120 *1.40 87-16 D Shoreham 120^{hd} Its Acedemic $120^{1¾}$ Flickering $120^{7½}$ Bumped 7
11Dec87-Placed first through disqualification
3Dec87- 1Aqu fst 6f ⊡:22⅕ :45 1:11 3↑Md Sp Wt 1 4 3^{1} 3^{1} 3^{5} $3^{9½}$ Krone J A 120 10.90 79-19 Hiberntion$122^{3¾}$DivineProvidence$120^{5¾}$ItsAcedmic$120^{2½}$ Even try 8
21Nov87- 1Aqu fst 6f :23 :47⅖ 1:12⅖ 3↑Md Sp Wt 2 4 $5^{2½}$ 6^{4} 5^{8} $4^{12¼}$ Krone J A 120 12.40 67-30 CoastalVoyage120^{4}Hiberntion122^{nk}DivineProvidence120^{8} Outrun 6
LATEST WORKOUTS ●May 3 Bel tr.t 5f fst 1:01 h Apr 29 Bel tr.t 4f fst :48⅖ h Apr 18 Bel tr.t 4f fst :50 b Mar 23 Bel tr.t 4f fst :48⅘ b

65–1

(17 Horses)

(Odds are given for Churchill Downs)

9 AQUEDUCT

Simulcast of The Kentucky Derby, 8th Race at Churchill. See Page 62.

1 1/4 Miles. Three-year-olds.

Risen Star — Dk. b. or br. c. 3, by Secretariat—Ribbon, by His Majesty
Own.—Roussel L & Larmarque RacSta — Br.—Hancock A B III & Peters L J (Ky) — Tr.—Roussel Louie J III
126 — Lifetime 8 6 2 0 $262,425 — 1988 5 4 1 0 $190,948 — 1987 3 2 1 0 $71,477 — Turf 1 1 0 0 $5,040 — **5–1**

16Apr88- 8Kee	fst	1 1/16	:48 1:12⅖ 1:42⅘	Lexington	5	5	53½	53½	2½	1hd	Vasquez J	118	3.20	92-18	Risen Star 118hd Forty Niner 12112 Stalwars 1182	Driving	5
16Apr88-Grade II																	
13Mar88-11FG	fst	1 1/16	:47⅗ 1:12 1:43⅕	La Derby	1	6	67½	67	42½	11¾	Romero S P	120	2.60	96-14	Risen Star 1201¾ Word Pirate 118¾ Pastourelles 1181¾	Driving	7
13Mar88-Grade III																	
27Feb88-10FG	fst	1 40	:46⅕ 1:12⅖ 1:40	Dby Trl H	11	9	914	55½	22	11	Romero S P	120	*1.10	93-20	Risen Star 1201 Pastourelles 1153½ Jim's Orbit 1221	Driving	12
6Feb88-10FG	gd	1 1/16	:47⅗ 1:12⅘ 1:46⅗	Lecomte H	7	5	55	21	21	21¼	Romero S P	122	*.30e	78-21	Pastourelles 1131¼ Risen Star 1223 Run Paul Run1141	Held place	7
2Jan88- 8FG	gd	1 1/16	:49 1:14⅕ 1:47⅗	Alw 9200	5	5	52½	11	14	110	Romero S P	119	*.30	74-26	Risen Star 11910 Mr. Buttercup 1161 Proper Duty 1194½	Easily	7
6Dec87- 9FG	fm	*7½f Ⓣ	:24⅕ :48⅕ 1:34⅕	Alw 8400	10	12	914	65¼	13	14	Romero S P	120	*.40	78-18	Risen Star 1204 Quick Bob 1174½ Jacumlea 1201	Easily	12
11Oct87-10LaD	fst	7f	:23⅕ :46⅖ 1:22⅗	S O King Fut	5	3	31½	32	36	215	Snyder L	121	2.40	80-21	Success Express 12115 Risen Star 1212¾ Big Snoz 12113	Tired	6
24Sep87- 9LaD	fst	6½f	:22⅖ :45⅗ 1:19	Minstrel	3	9	53½	66¼	43½	11	Walker B J Jr	112	*.90	80-27	RisenStar1121BoldChadra1151½SholSercher115½	Soundly bumped.	9

LATEST WORKOUTS ●May 3 CD 6f fst 1:13 b — Apr 15 Kee 3f fst :37⅕ b — ●Apr 11 Kee 5f fst :59⅘ h — ●Mar 27 FG 6f fst 1:12⅖ b

Regal Classic — Ch. c. 3, by Vice Regent—No Class, by Nodouble
Own.—Sam-SonFarms&WindfieldsFrm — Br.—Sam-Son Farms (Ont-C) — Tr.—Day James E
126 — Lifetime 10 4 4 2 $848,863 — 1988 2 0 1 1 $36,363 — 1987 8 4 3 1 $812,500 — Turf 4 2 2 0 $189,923 — **17–1 (field)**

28Apr88- 8Kee	fst	1⅛	:48⅗ 1:13 1:52⅕	Blue Grass	6	6	67½	76	55	33¾	Day P	121	*.90	69-22	Granacus 1213 IntensiveCommand121¾RegalClassic121no	Mild bid	9
28Apr88-Grade I																	
13Apr88- 8Kee	fm	1 1/16 Ⓣ	:48⅕ 1:12⅗ 1:43⅘	Alw 38500	2	5	64	42½	2hd	2nk	Cordero A Jr	123	*.30	110 —	Posen 114nk Regal Classic 1234 Denomination 1152	Just failed	10
20Dec87- 8Hol	fst	1	:45 1:09⅕ 1:34⅗	Hol Fut	7	7	63½	42	33	34	Day P	121	*1.80	86-08	Tejano 1212¼ Purdue King 1211¾ Regal Classic 1215½	Evenly late	8
20Dec87-Grade I																	
21Nov87- 5Hol	fst	1	:44⅘ 1:09⅖ 1:35⅕	Br Cp Juv	4	11	73¾	44	23	21¾	Penna D	122	3.60	85-12	SuccessExpress1221¾RegalClassic1221¾Tejno122hd	Boxed in turn	13
21Nov87-Grade I																	
25Oct87- 8WO	fst	1⅛	:47⅗ 1:13 1:53⅘	[S]Crnt'n Fut	5	3	44	32½	11½	13¼	Penna D	122	*.20e	71-24	Regal Classic 1223¼ Gotitall 122nk Regal Intention 1222	Handily	7
25Oct87-Grade I-C																	
12Oct87- 9WO	fst	1 1/16	:46⅗ 1:11⅘ 1:45	Grey	7	4	45½	4¾	11½	14½	Penna D	123	*.55	84-19	Regal Classic 1234½ Air Worthy 115¾ Moosejaw 1161½	Handily	12
12Oct87-Grade III																	
26Sep87- 9WO	gd	1 1/16 Ⓣ	:47⅘ 1:12⅗ 1:44⅕	[S]Cup Saucer	4	6	63¼	62¾	13	17	Penna D	122	*.75	83-17	Regal Classic 1227 Granacus 1221 Gotitall 1224	Handily	10
26Sep87-Grade I-C																	
13Sep87- 7WO	sf	1 [T]	:47 1:13⅗ 1:39⅘	Summer	7	7	69½	32	2½	16½	Penna D	122	*1.35	78-36	Regal Classic 1226½ Deputize 1223½ Riding Master 1223	In hand	8
13Sep87-Grade III																	
4Sep87- 4WO	fm	*7f [T]	:24⅕ :47⅗ 1:26⅗	Alw 26000	8	6	75	74¾	11½	2no	Penna D	117	*.60e	83-12	Gallant Mel 117no Regal Classic 117nk Deputize 1176	Gamely	9
22Aug87- 9WO	fst	6f	:22⅕ :45⅕ 1:11	[S]Bull Page	2	7	64½	57	36	22¾	Lauzon J M	115	3.10	85-25	HighlandRuckus1242¾RegalClassic115nkBelle'sRuckus1176	Rallied	8

LATEST WORKOUTS May 4 CD 4f fst :49⅗ b — Apr 25 Kee 4f fst :48⅘ b — Apr 20 Kee 1 fst 1:40⅖ b — ●Apr 9 Kee 5f fst :59 h

Kingpost * — Ch. g. 3, by Stalwart—Flaxen, by Graustark
Own.—Warner M — Br.—Warnerton Farm (Oh) — Tr.—Carpenter Dianne
126 — Lifetime 13 3 4 4 $452,010 — 1988 4 1 2 0 $314,030 — 1987 9 2 2 4 $137,980 — **16–1**

30Apr88- 9CD	fst	1	:47⅕ 1:12⅕ 1:38⅗	Derby Trial	5	6	65¾	55	64¼	2no	Velasquez J	122	5.80	76-23	Jim's Orbit 122no Kingpost 122no Lover's Trust 119no	Wide finish	7
30Apr88-Grade III																	
2Apr88-11TP	my	1⅛	:46⅗ 1:11⅖ 1:50⅘	Jim Beam	9	8	53½	2½	1hd	1hd	Sipus E J Jr	121	21.20	91-15	Kingpost 121hd Stalwars 121no Brian's Time 121½	Driving	11
2Apr88-Grade II																	
19Mar88- 9TP	fst	1	:46⅗ 1:12⅕ 1:37⅘	J Battaglia	7	11	95½	53	66¼	510	Moran M T	b 114	*1.90	76-21	Glory Afar 1127 Double Walt 1152 Cannon Dancer 121hd	No rally	11
9Mar88- 8Crc	fst	1 1/16	:48⅗ 1:13⅘ 1:47⅗	Alw 16700	1	4	67½	48½	35½	24	McCauley W H	115	1.30	77-19	Primal 1154 Kingpost 1152 Pricey Mac 11211	Second best	8
30Oct87- 8Med	fst	1 1/16	:46⅗ 1:11⅕ 1:45	Yng America	1	4	55½	85½	74¾	32½	Pincay L Jr	119	5.90	75-23	Firery Ensign 1191¼ Cherokee Colony 1191¼ Kingpost119¾	Rallied	10
30Oct87-Grade I																	
20Oct87- 8Kee	fst	*7f	1:26⅕	Alw 34500	1	7	78½	76¾	41¾	32½	Sipus E J Jr	112	3.00	89-16	Key Voyage 1171¾ Delightful Doctor 112¾ Kingpost 1129	Rallied	7
3Oct87-10TP	fst	1	:45⅘ 1:11 1:37⅘	In Memorm	11	9	78½	62¾	2½	2¾	Sipus E J Jr	120	17.20	85-20	Jim's Orbit 120¾ Kingpost 1209 Delightful Doctor 1201½	Rallied	11
7Sep87-10RD	fst	1 1/16	:47 1:11⅕ 1:44⅗	Mil Hgh Lfe	8	5	44½	32½	2hd	21½	Sipus E J Jr	120	12.00	84-18	Cannon Dancer 1201½ Kingpost 1201½HouseAccount1202½	Held pl.	11
7Sep87-Grade III																	
26Aug87- 7RD	fst	1	:47⅕ 1:12⅗ 1:40	Alw 15000	8	5	44½	34	1hd	11	Sipus E J Jr	117	*.50	84-20	Kingpost 1171 Waite for Action 114hd Schmada 1174	Driving	8
16Aug87- 6RD	fst	5½f	:22⅗ :45⅘ 1:05⅗	Md Sp Wt	11	1	63½	44½	22	13	Sipus E J Jr	118	*.90	87-19	Kingpost 1183 King's Banner 1182 LordNelsonsWay118nk	Driving	12
21Jun87- 9CD	fst	6f	:21 :45⅕ 1:11⅘	B Manor	5	9	107½	107	76	53¾	Cooksey P J	114	28.60	80-17	Blair's Cove 1143 Endurance 118nk Mr. Igloo 116½	Rallied	11
13Jun87- 5CD	fst	5f	:22⅘ :47 :59⅘	Md Sp Wt	7	7	76½	76	52¾	32	Miller S E	119	5.60	88-19	Jake the Bear 119no Glory Afar 1192 Kingpost 1193	Rallied	10
6Jun87- 5CD	fst	5f	:22⅗ :46⅖ :58⅘	Md Sp Wt	2	1	67	66	54½	34	Cooksey P J	121	6.70	91-13	Funzy 1214 Speaker's Dance 121hd Kingpost 1212	Mild bid	8

LATEST WORKOUTS May 5 CD 4f my :49⅗ b — Apr 24 CD 5f fst 1:00⅗ h — ●Apr 13 CD 5f fst :59⅗ h — ●Mar 30 TP 4f fst :47⅗ h

Brian's Time — B. c. 3, by Roberto—Kelley's Day, by Graustark
Own.—Phillips J — Br.—Phillips Mr-Mrs J W (Ky) — Tr.—Veitch John M
126 — Lifetime 8 3 1 1 $391,619 — 1988 5 2 0 1 $368,599 — 1987 3 1 1 0 $23,020 — **8–1**

23Apr88- 8Aqu	fst	1⅛	:46⅘ 1:10⅖ 1:47⅕	Wood Mem	3	10	1015	89	65½	55	Cordero A Jr	126	3.00	94-12	PrivteTerms1261½SeekingtheGold126noCherokColony126½	Rallied	10
23Apr88-Grade I																	
2Apr88-11TP	my	1⅛	:46⅗ 1:11⅖ 1:50⅘	Jim Beam	5	11	1116	117	54	3hd	Romero R P	121	*2.00	91-15	Kingpost 121hd Stalwars 121no Brian's Time 121½	Fast finish	11
2Apr88-Grade II																	
5Mar88-10GP	fst	1⅛	:46⅗ 1:10⅘ 1:49⅘	Fla Derby	4	9	912	811	42½	1nk	Romero R P	118	32.80	83-16	Brian's Time 118nk Forty Niner 1223 Notebook 122nk	Driving	10
5Mar88-Grade I																	
15Feb88-10GP	fst	1 1/16	:46⅗ 1:10⅘ 1:43⅕	Fountin Yth	1	7	89½	89¾	67¾	43	Bailey J D	112	15.80	82-21	Forty Niner 122no Notebook 1221 Buoy 1192	Rallied	9
15Feb88-Grade II																	
16Jan88- 7GP	fst	1 1/16	:49⅕ 1:13⅗ 1:45⅖	Alw 17000	2	5	55½	43¼	2hd	14½	Bailey J D	119	*.80	74-20	Brian's Time 1194½ GrayGardner1222MasteryPlay1171	Ridden out	12
9Dec87- 5Aqu	fst	1 1/16 [•]	:48⅘ 1:13⅘ 1:45⅗	Alw 31000	5	6	52¾	52¼	3nk	2hd	Bailey J D	117	4.80	81-17	Chicot County 117hd Brian's Time 1173 Dynaformer 117no	Sharp	9
28Nov87- 6Aqu	fst	7f	:23⅗ :47⅖ 1:26	Md Sp Wt	6	6	54½	42½	1hd	13½	Velasquez J	118	7.70	71-23	Brian's Time1183½John'sConcorde1131½Buckbean118½	Drew clear	8
30Aug87- 2Sar	my	6f	:22⅕ :45⅘ 1:11⅕	Md Sp Wt	9	11	68	56¼	55	57	Bailey J D	118	12.10	77-16	Appiello 1185 Lucy's Hill 118nk Grumpy Miller 1181½	No factor	11

LATEST WORKOUTS May 5 CD 4f my :50 b — May 1 CD 4f fst :50⅖ b — Apr 22 Bel 3f fst :35⅗ h — Apr 17 Bel 5f fst :59⅗ h

(*Continued on following page*)

Second half of Late Double. Exacta wagering. Triple wagering.

Seeking the Gold

B. c. 3, by Mr Prospector—Con Game, by Buckpasser
Br.—Phipps Ogden (Ky)
Tr.—McGaughey Claude III
126
Lifetime 6 4 2 0 $260,430
1988 5 3 2 0 $253,230
1987 1 1 0 0 $7,200
Own.—Phipps O

23Apr88- 8Aqu fst 1⅛ :46⅘ 1:10⅖ 1:47⅕ Wood Mem 1 3 34½ 2½ 1hd 2½ Romero R P 126 *2.30 97-12 PrivteTrms126½SkingthGold126noChrokColony126½ Held gamely 10
23Apr88-Grade I
9Apr88- 7Aqu fst 1 :45 1:10 1:34⅘ Gotham 3 5 45 42 32½ 2¾ Romero R P 114 *.60 91-19 PrivteTerms126¾SeekingtheGold1145PrfctSpy1213 Altered course 8
9Apr88-Grade II
5Mar88- 8GP fst 7f :22⅕ :46⅕ 1:21⅗ Swale 7 1 41½ 2hd 1hd 1nk Romero R P 114 *.70 96-16 SeekingtheGold114nkAboveNorml1149½PrfctSpy1222¼ Ridden out 7
13Feb88- 8GP fst 7f :22⅕ :45⅖ 1:23⅘ Alw 17000 11 3 52 43½ 11½ 11½ Romero R P 122 *.30 85-25 Seeking theGold1221½RocketPrince1172RedGetAlong1222¼ Easily 12
17Jan88- 6GP fst 6f :22 :45 1:09⅕ Alw 16000 2 8 31½ 2½ 1½ 14½ Romero R P 122 *.30 93-19 Seeking the Gold 1224½ Red Get Along 1174Eon117nk Ridden out 9
26Dec87-11Hia fst 6f :22⅕ :45⅖ 1:09⅘ Md Sp Wt 5 4 2½ 11½ 15 112 Romero R P 120 *.90 91-19 SeekingtheGold12012KnightlyProspect1201½Eronele120hd Handily 12
LATEST WORKOUTS May 6 CD 3f fst :36 b May 1 Bel 5f fst 1:01⅖ b Apr 22 Bel 3f fst :35 b Apr 17 Bel 5f fst :59⅖ h

15–1

Winning Colors

Ro. f. 3, by Caro—All Rainbows, by Bold Hour
Br.—Echo Valley Horse Farm Inc (Ky)
Tr.—Lukas D Wayne
121
Lifetime 6 5 1 0 $470,150
1988 4 3 1 0 $438,750
1987 2 2 0 0 $31,400
Own.—Klein E V

9Apr88- 5SA fst 1⅛ :45⅗ 1:09⅗ 1:47⅘ S A Derby 5 1 11½ 12½ 17 17½ Stevens G L 117 *2.60 90-13 Winning Colors1177½LivelyOne1221¼MiPreferido1222½ Ridden out 9
9Apr88-Grade I
13Mar88- 8SA fst 1$\frac{1}{16}$:45⅘ 1:10 1:42 ⒻS A Oaks 1 1 11 11 15 18 Stevens G L 117 2.10 91-15 WinningColors1178JeanneJones1171¼GoodbyeHlo1179 Ridden out 4
13Mar88-Grade I
20Feb88- 8SA fst 1 :46⅕ 1:11 1:36⅘ ⒻL Virgenes 4 2 12½ 11 1hd 2nk Stevens G L 119 *.70 84-18 GoodbyeHalo123nkWinningColors1198SadieB.Fst1157½ Just failed 5
20Feb88-Grade I
20Jan88- 8SA fst 1 :45⅘ 1:11 1:36⅗ ⒻⓇLa Cntla 2 1 11½ 12½ 14 16½ Stevens G L 114 *.70 85-22 Winning Colors1146½LittlePassword1143Forewarning1161 Handily 7
27Dec87- 3SA fst 6f :21⅘ :44⅘ 1:09⅘ ⒻAlw 32000 1 5 12½ 12½ 13½ 13½ Stevens G L 114 *1.30 89-17 WnnngClrs1143½FlrlMgc1182¾CnstntlyRght1161½ Slw st, veered in 6
13Aug87- 3Sar fst 7f :22⅕ :45⅗ 1:24⅕ ⒻMd Sp Wt 9 3 1½ 11½ 14 12½ Romero R P 117 *1.90 81-14 Winning Colors 1172½ Epitome 1174 Bippus 1171½ Ridden out 11
LATEST WORKOUTS May 3 CD 4f fst :49 b Apr 26 CD 6f fst 1:13⅕ b Apr 19 Hol 5f fst 1:01⅘ b ●Apr 5 Hol 4f fst :47⅖ h

3–1

Proper Reality

Dk. b. or br. c. 3, by In Reality—Proper Princess, by Nodouble
Br.—Winn Mrs J A (Fla)
Tr.—Holthus Robert E
126
Lifetime 5 4 0 0 $357,840
1988 4 3 0 0 $352,020
1987 1 1 0 0 $5,820
Own.—Winn Mrs James A

23Apr88- 9OP fst 1⅛ :46⅖ 1:11 1:48⅖ Ark Derby 1 6 62¾ 61¼ 41½ 11¼ Bailey J D 118 3.20 91-14 Proper Reality 1181¼ Primal 1151¼ Sea Trek123½ Boxed in 2nd trn 8
23Apr88-Grade I
2Apr88- 9OP fst 1$\frac{1}{16}$:45⅗ 1:10⅖ 1:42⅗ Rebel 2 5 42 73¾ 54½ 43 Bailey J D 119 2.30 85-16 Sea Trek 1121 Din's Dancer 114¾ Notebook 1221¼ Boxed 2nd trn 10
5Mar88- 9OP fst 1 :46⅖ 1:10⅗ 1:36⅘ So West 8 6 54 21 11½ 11½ Bailey J D 113 *1.40 88-18 ProperRelity1131½LongviewAshly119½Morgn'sLv1194½ Wide early. 8
19Feb88- 6OP gd 6f :22⅖ :45⅘ 1:10⅘ Alw 16000 1 6 63¼ 31½ 11 18 Bailey J D 115 *.70 86-27 Proper Reality 1158 Total Look 1202½ Avenger G. 1152¼ Driving 6
10Oct87- 7LaD fst 6f :22⅕ :46 1:11⅗ Md Sp Wt 1 6 1½ 12 15 115 Valovich C J 119 *1.30 84-20 ProperReality11915VolcnicMn1191GoldenRumor1192½ Ridden out 12
LATEST WORKOUTS May 6 CD 3f fst :36⅕ b May 2 CD 5f fst 1:03 b Apr 22 OP 3f fst :38⅗ b Apr 18 OP 5f sly 1:01⅖ b

27–1

Private Terms *

Dk. b. or br. c. 3, by Private Account—Laughter, by Bold Ruler
Br.—Janney Mr-Mrs S S Jr (Ky)
Tr.—Hadry Charles H
126
Lifetime 7 7 0 0 $742,328
1988 5 5 0 0 $726,128
1987 2 2 0 0 $16,200
Own.—Locust Hill Farm

23Apr88- 8Aqu fst 1⅛ :46⅘ 1:10⅖ 1:47⅕ Wood Mem 6 5 56½ 54½ 41 11½ Antley C W 126 3.60 99-12 PrivteTerms1261½SekingthGold126noChrokColony126½ Strng ride 10
23Apr88-Grade I
9Apr88- 7Aqu fst 1 :45 1:10 1:34⅘ Gotham 7 4 35 31½ 12 1¾ Antley C W 126 10.50 92-19 Private Terms 126¾ Seeking the Gold1145PerfectSpy1213 Driving 8
9Apr88-Grade II
12Mar88- 9Pim fst 1$\frac{1}{16}$:47⅗ 1:12⅕ 1:44⅗ F Tesio 7 4 43½ 21 11½ 14½ Santos J A 122 *.40 81-20 PrivteTerms1224½MichelJosh1133½RoylLgnd1143½ Bumped, drvng 7
12Mar88-Grade III
15Feb88-11Lrl fst 1 :47 1:13⅕ 1:38⅘ Gen. George 4 8 76¼ 51¼ 51¼ 11½ Desormeaux K J 116 *1.60 78-21 PrivateTerms1161½Dynaformer122½DelightfulDoctor122nk Driving 13
30Jan88- 9Lrl fst 7f :23 :46⅗ 1:24⅘ Alw 15000 3 5 44½ 3nk 31 1¾ Bracciale V Jr 117 *1.00 87-14 Private Terms 117¾ Royal Legend 1203 Sir Riddle 117nk Driving 6
15Dec87- 6Lrl sly 1 :47⅗ 1:13 1:39⅕ Alw 14500 5 4 43 11 11½ 11 Desormeaux K J 114 *.70 76-25 Private Terms 1141 Prince Stanley 1145½ Artbelt 115hd Driving 6
26Nov87- 7Lrl fst 6½f :22⅖ :46⅖ 1:18⅖ Md Sp Wt 2 9 710 48½ 22½ 16 Desormeaux K J 120 *1.40 89-18 Private Terms 1206 Sir Riddle 1202½FullSecurity120nk Drew clear 12
LATEST WORKOUTS May 6 CD 3f fst :39⅕ b Apr 30 Pim 5f fst 1:04⅘ b Apr 22 Pim 3f fst :37⅗ b Apr 17 Pim 5f fst 1:02⅘ b

*3–1

Forty Niner *

Ch. c. 3, by Mr Prospector—File, by Tom Rolfe
Br.—Claiborne Farm (Ky)
Tr.—Stephens Woodford C
126
Lifetime 11 7 3 0 $921,880
1988 5 2 3 0 $286,972
1987 6 5 0 0 $634,908
Own.—Claiborne Farm

16Apr88- 8Kee fst 1$\frac{1}{16}$:48 1:12⅖ 1:42⅘ Lexington 4 2 31 21½ 1½ 2hd Day P 121 *.40 92-18 Risen Star 118hdFortyNiner12112Stalwars1182 Stead'd st. gamely 5
16Apr88-Grade II
8Apr88- 8Kee fst 7f :23 :45⅖ 1:22 Lafayette 7 2 42½ 3½ 11 15 Day P 121 *.50 96-21 Forty Niner 1215 Buoy 12210 Aloha Prospector 1215 Ridden out 8
5Mar88-10GP fst 1⅛ :46⅗ 1:10⅘ 1:49⅘ Fla Derby 9 1 1½ 11½ 12 2nk Maple E 122 3.00 83-16 Brian's Time 118nk Forty Niner 1223 Notebook 122nk Just missed 10
5Mar88-Grade I
15Feb88-10GP fst 1$\frac{1}{16}$:46⅗ 1:10⅘ 1:43⅕ Fountin Yth 7 1 1hd 1hd 1hd 1no Maple E 122 *.80 85-21 Forty Niner 122no Notebook 1221 Buoy 1192 Driving 9
15Feb88-Grade II
3Feb88- 9GP fst 7f :21⅘ :44⅗ 1:23 Hutcheson 5 2 2hd 2½ 21½ 21 Maple E 122 *.70 88-24 Perfect Spy 1141 Forty Niner 122½ Notebook 1224 Couldn't gain 7
3Feb88-Grade III
30Oct87- 8Kee fst 1$\frac{1}{16}$:46⅘ 1:11 1:43⅘ Brd Fut 2 1 21 2hd 2hd 1no Maple E 121 *.40 87-18 Forty Niner 121no Hey Pat 1212½ Sea Trek 1213 Driving 7
30Oct87-Grade II
17Oct87- 8Bel fst 1 :46⅘ 1:10⅘ 1:36⅘ Champagne 7 2 31½ 2hd 11½ 14¼ Maple E 122 3.30 81-20 Forty Niner 1224¼ Parlay Me 1221¼ Tejano 1225½ Drew away 11
17Oct87-Grade I
20Sep87- 6Bel gd 7f :22⅕ :45⅖ 1:22⅗ Futurity 1 2 11½ 11½ 13 13 Maple E 122 4.50 89-14 Forty Niner 1223 Tsarbaby 1222¼ Crusader Sword1224 Ridden out 5
20Sep87-Grade I
19Aug87- 8Sar sly 6f :21⅘ :44⅗ 1:10 Sanford 3 3 22 21½ 1hd 13½ Maple E 115 6.10 90-15 Forty Niner 1153½ Once Wild 1153 Velvet Fog 1155½ Driving 6
19Aug87-Grade II
7Aug87- 8Sar fst 6f :21⅘ :45 1:10⅕ Sar Special 2 4 1½ 2hd 31 610 Maple E 117 3.40 79-17 Crusader Sword 117nk Tejano 1175½ Endurance 1194 Tired 8
7Aug87-Grade II
17Jly87- 5Bel fst 6f :22⅖ :46 1:11⅗ Md Sp Wt 8 4 1½ 11½ 13 13¼ Maple E 118 *1.40e 82-20 Forty Niner 1183¼ Dyna Former 1182¾ Tsarbaby 1181½ Ridden out 13
LATEST WORKOUTS May 5 CD 4f my :50 b May 1 CD 1 fst 1:38⅗ h Apr 28 CD 4f fst :51⅗ b Apr 24 CD 5f fst 1:02⅘ b

9–2

10 AQUEDUCT

1⅛ MILES AQUEDUCT START FINISH

(10 Horses)

1 ⅛ MILES. (1.47) MAIDEN SPECIAL WEIGHT. Purse $28,000. 3-year-olds and upward foaled in New York State and approved by the New York State-bred registry. Weight, 3-year-olds, 115 lbs. Older, 124 lbs.

Coupled—Pine Island Pat and Dial A King.

Don't Give In

B. g. 3, by Compliance—Bold Cosmic, by Bold Reason
Br.—Goldberg Gertrude & Susan (NY)
Tr.—Schulhofer Flint S
Own.—Letsbelucky Stable
115
Lifetime 4 0 0 0 $3,240 — 1988 3 M 0 0 $3,240 — 1987 1 M 0 0

30Mar88- 6Aqu fst 7f :23 :46⅗ 1:24⅗ 3↑ⓈMd Sp Wt 1 13 107¾ 76¾ 45 412 Romero R P 115 4.80 66–22 CavanaghSpecial115¾PennsylvaniPride1157PourMoi1154¼ Rallied 14
5Mar88- 4Aqu gd 6f ⊡:22⅗ :47 1:11⅖ ⓈMd Sp Wt 7 11 74¼ 64¼ 44¼ 46¼ Belmonte J F 122 18.90 81–11 Rack It Up 1224 Bold Result 1172 My Palooka 122nk No factor 12
18Feb88- 6Aqu fst 1⅟₁₆ ⊡:48⅗ 1:14⅗ 1:47⅗ Md Sp Wt 7 2 59¼ 912 921 924¾ Belmonte J F 122 88.40 46–23 Torvill 122no Parsimonious 12213 Fun and Games122¾ Slow start 9
21Sep87- 4Bel fst 6f :22⅘ :46⅖ 1:12 ⓈMd Sp Wt 11 9 76 1011 1010 107 Martens G 118 25.10 72–15 Whodam1181¾EnjoyTheMoment118noThreeGifts118hd Raced wide 14
LATEST WORKOUTS May 2 Bel 4f fst :49⅖ b — Apr 27 Bel 4f fst :49⅖ b — Apr 22 Bel 4f fst :49⅖ b — Apr 17 Bel 4f fst :47⅘ h

7–1

Duly Rebuked

Gr. c. 3, by Fio Rito—Tall Coin, by Alto Ribot
Br.—Spielman Michael (NY)
Tr.—Zito Nicholas P
Own.—Spielman M
108[7]
Lifetime 12 0 0 1 $5,340 — 1988 9 M 0 1 $5,340 — 1987 3 M 0 0

27Apr88- 9Aqu fst 1 :46⅕ 1:11⅕ 1:37⅗ 3↑ⓈMd Sp Wt 11 8 51¾ 21½ 47½ 410½ Lawless W7 b 108 25.00 67–18 Mr. Walter K. 1152 Pine Island Pat 1151 Agnoble1157½ Weakened 12
20Apr88- 7Aqu fst 6f :23 :47 1:12 3↑ⓈAlw 32000 4 7 63¾ 65½ 68½ 69 Lawless W7 b 105 91.50 71–26 I Knew That 112nk My Palooka 1156 ClearCataracts121nk Outrun 7
15Apr88- 9Aqu fst 1⅛ :48⅘ 1:13⅗ 1:53⅗ 3↑ⓈMd Sp Wt 1 2 31 53¾ 814 817½ Maple E b 115 51.30 49–23 Paolino 1154 Pour Moi 1152 Shi Bri 1243 Tired 12
21Mar88- 9Aqu fst 7f :23⅕ :47⅘ 1:27⅖ ⓈMd Sp Wt 8 12 129½ 129¾ 1214 915¼ Antley C W b 122 27.20 49–28 Try Much 1172 Del Guercio 122¾ Brave Beast 1192 Pinched back 12
7Mar88- 2Aqu fst 6f ⊡:23 :47⅗ 1:14⅗ Clm 16500 10 4 34 32½ 22¾ 34¾ Graell A b 115 138.70 66–25 Super Pal 1141¼ John One Four1173DulyRebuked115hd Weakened 11
22Feb88- 9Aqu fst 1⅛ ⊡:50⅖ 1:16 1:59⅕ ⓈMd Sp Wt 4 7 88 98¾ 812 814½ Belmonte J F b 122 40.00 31–32 Wingate Arch 117¾ My Palooka 1152 Pine IslandPat122hd Outrun 12
5Feb88- 9Aqu fst 1⅟₁₆ ⊡:49⅕ 1:15⅘ 1:49⅘ ⓈMd Sp Wt 8 9 55 31½ 37¾ 411 Belmonte J F b 122 65.30 49–32 UltimtAuthority1177PourMo122½HorsplyrJoy122¾ Wide far turn 12
9Jan88- 1Aqu fst 6f ⊡:23⅕ :47 1:13⅘ Clm 20000 8 5 85¾1013 713 613 Termini C7 b 106 80.50 62–26 Cy Quad Louis 1124½ClotheTheDorDor1193¼Lummox110hd Outrun 11
4Jan88- 4Aqu fst 1⅟₁₆ ⊡:48 1:13 1:47⅖ ⓈMd Sp Wt 11 9 918 1124 1130 1131¾ Termini C5 117 62.00 40–22 Nessuno 122½ Paolino 1225 La Jazz Hot 1221 Outrun 12
14Nov87- 4FL fst 5½f :22⅖ :46⅗ 1:07⅘ ⓈMd Sp Wt 10 1 32 56¾ 67½ 65 Holm A A 120 13.20e 73–24 GoldStark120½JollyAgenda120½ClssicMistril120nk Showed little 10
LATEST WORKOUTS Apr 13 Bel 3f fst :38 b — Mar 28 Bel tr.t 3f fst :37 h

49–1

Fleche

Ch. c. 4, by Sharpen Up—Moonlight Serenade, by Dictus
Br.—Gallagher's Farm Inc (NY)
Tr.—Martin Jose
Own.—Brody J
119[5]
Lifetime 6 0 0 0 — 1988 3 M 0 0 — 1987 3 M 0 0 — Turf 3 0 0 0

29Apr88- 9Aqu fst 1⅛ :47⅗ 1:12 1:52⅘ 3↑Md 30000 4 11 1112 64¾ 31 62¾ Correa C J5 115 34.80 69–17 For the Motion113½HighPolicy1152TopoftheRidge108no Bid, hung 12
15Apr88- 9Aqu fst 1⅛ :48⅘ 1:13⅗ 1:53⅗ 3↑ⓈMd Sp Wt 4 11 108¾ 911 713 713½ Antley C W 124 11.50 53–23 Paolino 1154 Pour Moi 1152 Shi Bri 1243 Outrun 12
4Apr88- 9Aqu gd 6f :22⅘ :46 1:12⅘ 3↑Md 35000 5 11 1217 1215 917 811 Estrada J C 124 45.60 67–21 Passabell 113no Agnoble 1151½ Tandis Que 115nk Outrun 12
12Jun87♦7Chantilly(Fra) yl*1⅞ 3:24⅖ ⓣ Prix de Lamorlaye(Mdn) 920 Legrix E b 124 41.00 — — Hoppner 1282 Talamsan 1173 New Dude 1281½ No factor 13
4Jun87♦2Chantilly(Fra) yl*1½ 2:40⅕ ⓣ Prix duConnetable(Mdn) 12 Mongil W b 122 64.00 — — Ashumet 1282 Hoppner 1282 Delegant 1244 No factor 15
22May87♦5StCloud(Fra) sf*1½ 2:46⅖ ⓣ Prix Mistral 13 Mongil W b 116 99.00 — — Prince Forest 121¾ Thrifty Lad 1211½ Delegant 1181 No factor 24
LATEST WORKOUTS Apr 24 Bel tr.t 4f fst :48⅗ h — Mar 25 Bel tr.t 5f fst 1:03⅕ b — Mar 19 Bel tr.t 5f fst 1:03⅘ b

9–1

Pine Island Pat

B. c. 3, by Pat's Victory—Isle of Pines, by Wajima
Br.—Bailie Sally A (NY)
Tr.—Bailie Sally A
Own.—Bailie Sally A
115
Lifetime 7 0 2 1 $18,700 — 1988 4 M 2 1 $17,140 — 1987 3 M 0 0 $1,560

27Apr88- 9Aqu fst 1 :46⅕ 1:11⅕ 1:37⅗ 3↑ⓈMd Sp Wt 1 6 31½ 32 22 22 Lovato F Jr b 115 2.50 76–18 Mr. Walter K. 1152 Pine Island Pat 1151 Agnoble 1157½ Came out 12
30Mar88- 4Aqu fst 7f :22⅘ :45⅗ 1:25⅘ 3↑ⓈMd Sp Wt 4 4 52½ 54 41½ 21½ Lovato F Jr b 115 18.80 70–22 Brave Beast 1151½ Pine Island Pat 1151 Knick Press 115¾ Gamely 10
9Mar88- 6Aqu fst 1⅟₁₆ ⊡:49⅕ 1:15 1:49⅗ 3↑ⓈMd Sp Wt 5 6 75½ 66½ 58 413½ Baird E T b 122 9.30 47–26 Swift n' Lucky 1226 Active Wear 122¾ Cousteau 1225 Outrun 12
22Feb88- 9Aqu fst 1⅛ ⊡:50⅖ 1:16 1:59⅕ ⓈMd Sp Wt 5 4 42¾ 31½ 32 32¾ Lovato F Jr b 122 24.20 43–32 Wingate Arch 117¾ My Palooka 1152PineIslandPat122hd Even try 12
10Sep87- 4Bel fst 6f :22⅘ :47 1:12⅗ ⓈMd Sp Wt 12 5 52½ 58½ 913 1013¾ Maple E b 118 8.40 62–19 Poster Run 1133 Ultra Care 1181½ Classi Whip 1182½ Outrun 14
14Aug87- 3Sar fst 6f :22⅘ :47⅖ 1:13⅖ ⓈMd Sp Wt 9 4 63½ 32 31½ 53¼ Davis R G b 118 *3.20 70–21 Del Viking 118hd Ultra Care 1181¾ Pour Moi 1181½ Weakened 14
24Jly87- 4Bel fst 6f :22⅗ :47⅕ 1:12⅘ ⓈMd Sp Wt 2 2 43½ 67 58 410½ Belmonte J F5 113 38.60 66–26 Brother's Pal 1189 Stockport 1181½ Novel Nashua 118no Steadied 10
LATEST WORKOUTS May 4 Bel 4f fst :47⅕ h — Apr 18 Bel tr.t 4f fst :52 b — Apr 9 Bel tr.t 4f fst :51 b — Mar 16 Bel tr.t 4f fst :51 b

2–1

Agnoble

Ch. c. 3, by Noble Nashua—Piedmont Agnes, by Anticipating
Br.—Somerset Breeding Association & Fly (N.Y.)
Tr.—Meyer Jerome C
Own.—Black Gold Stable
115
Lifetime 8 0 1 1 $8,615 — 1988 3 M 1 1 $6,440 — 1987 5 M 0 0 $2,175

27Apr88- 9Aqu fst 1 :46⅕ 1:11⅕ 1:37⅗ 3↑ⓈMd Sp Wt 4 7 61¾ 46 32½ 33 Santagata N b 115 6.60 75–18 Mr.WalterK.1152PineIslandPat1151Agnoble1157½ Slow st,checked 12
15Apr88- 9Aqu fst 1⅛ :48⅘ 1:13⅗ 1:53⅗ 3↑ⓈMd Sp Wt 5 5 42 32½ 57 513 Santagata N b 115 4.60 54–23 Paolino 1154 Pour Moi 1152 Shi Bri 1243 Gave way 12
4Apr88- 9Aqu gd 6f :22⅘ :46 1:12⅘ 3↑Md 35000 7 10 97½ 76¾ 34 2no Carter T b 115 35.70 78–21 Passabell 113no Agnoble 1151½Tandis Que 115nk Pinched back 12
3Dec87- 6Med fst 170 :47⅗ 1:12⅘ 1:44⅘ Md Sp Wt 4 4 33¾ 65½ 67 716¾ Santagata N b 118 22.60 58–16 Gallantmister 1182 HoldYourHeadup1183½MajesticReef118½ Tired 8
24Nov87- 6Med fst 170 :47⅘ 1:14⅕ 1:45 Md Sp Wt 2 2 31½ 21½ 59¼ 511½ Santagata N b 118 38.80 59–23 Grey's Ferry 118nk Gallantmister1181½Harmonious1183 Weakened 9
12Nov87- 5Med sly 1⅟₁₆ :47⅖ 1:13⅖ 1:47⅗ Md Sp Wt 7 3 33½ 36 315 423¾ Santagata N b 118 9.60 41–28 Boldly Daring 11814 Grey'sFerry1187DarbyJet1182½ Wide 1st turn 7
31Oct87- 4Med fst 1 :48⅘ 1:14⅘ 1:40⅘ Md Sp Wt 5 1 1hd 2½ 41½ 411¼ Santagata N b 118 76.50 60–21 Hasty Words 118noHarmonious1185¾WoodyAsbury1186 Weakened 11
12Oct87- 4Med fst 1⅟₁₆ :48 1:14 1:48⅕ Md Sp Wt 6 7 87 97½ 89¼ 915¾ Pezua J M b 118 18.40 46–22 One Loud Laugh 118hdT.V.Broadcast1183RuntheColony1183 Tired 12
LATEST WORKOUTS Apr 23 Bel tr.t 4f fst :50⅕ b — Mar 30 Bel tr.t 6f fst 1:17⅖ b — Mar 19 Bel tr.t 5f fst 1:07 h

5–1

Mr. Frosty

Dk. b. or br. g. 3, by Just Right Classi—Always Cold, by Ever On
Br.—Karutz W S (NY)
Tr.—O'Brien Leo
Own.—Bertolino F
115
Lifetime 2 0 1 0 $5,940 — 1988 2 M 1 0 $5,940 — 1987 0 M 0 0

21Apr88- 4Aqu fst 6f :23⅗ :48⅘ 1:13⅘ 3↑ⓈMd Sp Wt 11 5 71¾ 2hd 11½ 23 Samyn J L b 115 5.90 71–26 Atom Blade 1153 Mr. Frosty 1151¾ Classi Whip 115¾ Game try 13
11Apr88- 6Aqu fst 6f :22⅘ :47 1:12⅘ 3↑ⓈMd Sp Wt 1 11 96 78½ 68¾ 65½ Samyn J L b 115 10.70 70–23 Drums in the Night 115¾ Ogle 115½ Ahsonoble1151½ Lacked room 12
LATEST WORKOUTS May 2 Bel 5f fst 1:00 h — Apr 4 Bel 5f fst 1:01⅘ h — Mar 29 Bel tr.t 6f fst 1:14⅘ h — Mar 24 Bel tr.t 4f fst :49⅕ hg

8–1

Sunshiner

B. c. 4, by Mr Sunshine—Shadblow, by Bravo
Br.—Karutz W S (NY)
Tr.—Trovato Joseph A
Own.—Holmwood Stable
124
Lifetime 11 0 1 1 $12,355 — 1988 6 M 1 1 $12,355 — 1987 5 M 0 0

27Apr88- 5Aqu fst 1 :46⅕ 1:11 1:37⅘ 3↑ⓈMd Sp Wt 5 10 1013 89 43½ 2¾ Velasquez J 124 4.30 76–18 Pour Moi 115¾ Sunshiner 1243 Classi Whip 115¾ Wide 12
4Apr88- 6Aqu fst 1⅛ :48⅗ 1:13⅗ 1:52 3↑ⓈMd Sp Wt 5 7 64½ 46 49 411 Harvey B 124 5.50 64–21 Horseplayer Joy 1156Paolino1153½DelGuercio1151½ Bumped start 12
19Mar88- 4Aqu fst 1 :47⅕ 1:12⅘ 1:37⅖ Md Sp Wt 7 6 62¾ 63½ 59 412¾ Harvey B 122 31.80 66–23 Yankee Fan 1224¾ Leave The Bar 1225½ McKim 1222½ Evenly 7
4Mar88- 7Aqu gd 1⅛ ⊡:47 1:12⅘ 1:51⅘ ⓈMd Sp Wt 5 9 98 75½ 56 47¾ Harvey B 122 21.10 75–18 Le Serre 122¾ H. J.'s Babe 1224¾ Piccadilly Prince115nk Late bid 11
17Feb88- 3GS fst 6f :22⅘ :46 1:11⅘ Md Sp Wt 9 4 75 57½ 611 710¾ Harvey B 122 2.70 72–24 Rosen Warrior 122nk Gabbie's Boy 1222 BergenStreet1225 Outrun 10
9Feb88- 3GS fst 6f :22⅘ :46 1:11⅕ Md Sp Wt 4 7 79½ 45 44½ 34½ Castaneda K 122 7.10 81–15 I'm A Cruiser 1222 Romaneck 1222½ Sunshiner 1223 Wide 7
18Dec87- 1Aqu fst 1⅛ ⊡:49⅘ 1:15⅕ 1:53⅘ 3↑Md Sp Wt 4 7 79 710 824 — Ortega P Jr5 b 115 49.70 — — Shoreham 1207½ Officer Krupke 120hd WineMerchant120½ Eased 8
8May87- 9Bel fst 7f :23⅕ :46⅗ 1:26 3↑Md 30000 3 7 99¼ 98¼ 713 712¼ Nuesch D5 b 104 45.00 60–24 Fair Rex1134½ComputerCode1131½DoubleFreckleKid1131¾ Outrun 11
14Apr87- 2Aqu fst 1⅛ :49⅖ 1:14⅖ 1:53⅘ 3↑Md 35000 4 4 62¾ 32½ 69¾ 815¾ Migliore R b 113 36.40 50–23 Proud Harry1205MarketProphet1084InspectorClouseau1033 Tired 12
20Mar87- 6Aqu fst 1⅛ :49⅘ 1:15 1:53⅕ ⓈMd Sp Wt 8 11 109½ 109¾ 920 923 Murphy D J b 122 110.10 46–27 DucdeVl122 12¾StrikeAndSpr122¾ActAccordingly122½ Steadied st. 12
LATEST WORKOUTS Apr 25 GS 3f fst :37⅘ b — Apr 22 GS 4f fst :50 b — Apr 1 GS 4f fst :49⅕ b — Mar 15 GS 3f fst :35⅘ b

*

2–1

Exacta wagering. Triple wagering.

AQUEDUCT ANALYSIS

Before giving the results of each race, I have made a few comments on how you should have used the selection principles set forth in this book.

RACE ONE

A race with only three horses! If you are the type who begins by eliminating losers, you will never, except in a match race, have less work to do.

The final odds made it clear that the crowd at the track and in the New York City Off-Track Betting parlors (the mutuel pool is a combination of betting on and off the track) threw out the bottom two horses immediately.

But what a poor 2–5 favorite Quindecillion is. True, he had just won in good time, far superior to Jig Time Dixie's (who had very little to show for it in terms of speed or class and *should* have been thrown out), and had a good race on an off track.

Nevertheless, he still has to beat Paris Office, who had demonstrated his ability to win at a distance in the slop and had been running against superior horses prior to his long layoff.

How do we know this? The *Racing Form* gives the purse for an allowance race in the past-performance charts but it doesn't give the conditions. You should always assume in a win-restricted allowance race such as this (did you read the conditions?) that a horse coming off a win is now meeting better horses. Quindecillion is, therefore, rising in class, facing a horse that has competed in stakes races.

The only "if" in this race comes from the long time Paris Office has been away from the races. *If* he is in condition, as his five-furlong bullet in the slop indicates, Paris Office should win easily. He makes a great bet for daily doubles.

RACE TWO

This race is a clear example of why we have to look for more than just high speed ratings in a sprint race. Every horse listed has some speed indicator.

Three horses are within one point of each other in their last races. Two have better times in their next-to-last races, and all the horses have run even faster in the past.

The way to handle a race like this is to eliminate horses with negative factors, and then see which horses have something going for them in addition to speed.

It is highly unusual for a trainer to run a horse on only three days rest. In this race we have two such horses! Although both are dropping in claiming price, both have to be eliminated. Promise to You's awful mud form and Miss Sherby's atrocious recent form make them doubtful win bets.

Similarly, Flower de Noel's poor recent form, poor consistency, and novice jockey count far more negatively than her drop in weight and her off-track form.

Of the horses left, Irish Mistress is clearly the horse to beat. Most horsers are never claimed. This horse has been claimed three times, indicating it has the kind of winning spirit that trainers look for. It has an excellent win consistency, good back time at Delaware, and has shown a great love for off tracks.

Is she a standout favorite, one we should never bet against? Not at all. Although she has run at higher claiming prices and won a cheap allowance in Pennsylvania, this filly has never *won* at this claiming price. Even more important, after a layoff of forty-five days, her best workout is mediocre. The horse may not be sharp enough to win after a layoff.

Clever But Costly had a good race last time out and has run the fastest race of them all in terms of speed ratings adjusted according to track variants.

International Guest ran fairly well in its last race, finishing only three lengths behind Clever But Costly, and went off at considerably lower odds. She has two things going for her: the best time in the past thirty days and a drop in claiming price. (This is not actually a drop in class, since she is running against the same type of horses, but it does show the stable's willingness to risk a claim for $2,000 less in order to drop four pounds in weight.)

If the favorite is going to be beaten, Clever But Costly and International Guest seem the likeliest candidates.

If you are "alive" with these two horses in the doubles, make no win bets. If not, International Guest is the play to win because of her bigger possible payoff. Because of her odds, International Guest should be reversed in exactas with the favorite and with Clever But Costly.

RACE THREE

The track, still rated as good, is getting even more difficult to fathom. The second race was run in 1:12, an 80 speed rating. If you will check, you will see that this is faster than any of these horses have ever run.

Is the track off, or isn't it?

One thing that is clear is that Bold Mein is not an outstanding favorite. He has the best time in the past thirty days, but that was better than he had ever run before, and six horses have run even faster in the past. If the track is truly off, he might even be eliminated because of his poor past race in the slop.

There is no question that Bienestar and Casual Physician can be dismissed. Both have class and workout knocks. Phantom Fair had a poor last race and has a top time that, when adjusted for track variant, is a point higher than the best recent time, but that was his only swift race and his consistency (2/20) is poor. These horses should probably have not even made it to your worksheet.

If the track were definitely favoring off-track horses, Test of Loyalty, with his best race ever run in the mud, would be a clear choice. He is dropping five pounds off a race in which he was a beaten favorite.

Fatty Boy has the best time in the past thirty days at seven furlongs. When the seven-furlong adjustment is made, he becomes tied with Bold Mein for top recent time, when Bold Mein's rating is dropped to 82 because of the 20 track variant.

Sixth of May is rising in class, but he is taking a huge drop in weight. His best back time is the best of all at seven furlongs. He apparently had a bad trip in his last race. If the track were fast, he would be the clear choice.

The only way this race can be handled is to declare it too hard to come up with a single winner. Sixth of May must be played at the odds, and Test of Loyalty and Fatty Boy should be bet lightly so that you can break even on the race if Sixth of May can't handle the track.

With so many contenders, it would be foolish to try to come up with a reasonable number of exacta combinations.

RACE FOUR

Almost all of the horses with turf experience were scratched when this race was put on the dirt. Two of the remaining horses had experience running around two turns, but their times were dismal.

Damascus Gold has extraordinary workouts and must be bet on that basis. If the track were definitely off, he would be a Best Bet at the odds.

Armand, with only one start and an excellent closing fraction, deserves to be the favorite. But 3–5 for a horse that has never run around two turns?

In his last race at Suffolk Downs, Goes So Fast finished in front of horses that had already won. His time was poor, but he is the only front-runner and might upset. He deserves a saver bet and also an exacta underneath Armand.

RACE FIVE

Conventioneer seems to be taking a sharp rise in class, but he had won for the highest purse last year and has beaten some of the horses he is meeting today. His overwhelming six-furlong rating in his winning mile race and the very light weight he is asked to carry make him a clear choice, especially on this track which is still called "good."

Real Account has fine workouts but has poor off-track form. At odds of 2–1, he is a poor risk against Conventioneer, who is in top form and can run on any kind of track.

There is no exacta wagering, and as you will see, the choice in the sixth race is also a 3–2 favorite, so only a token double should be placed.

As a matter of fact, this is probably a good time to go for a late lunch and collect your thoughts on who is going to win the Kentucky Derby.

RACE SIX

Too Bobees Return, with a drop in class after her last race, in which she posted the top time of the month, looks like a solid favorite. Superb Time, whose best speed rating was done at the seven-furlong distance of today's race, might be a threat, but her slow, single work after a layoff makes her readiness to win questionable. Tasma's Star won a quick race on April 23, but she has never finished in the money at this claiming price.

RACE SEVEN

Go for Commadore finished second in his last race, a graded stakes, has an outstanding back time, and worked a mile bullet for this race. The handicapper can ask for no more.

Dr. Carrington, a three-year-old tackling older horses, won a stakes (ungraded) in the mud in January, but his last three races have been very poor. The stewards have now changed the track to "fast," so his excellent mud form seems to be no advantage.

You have to either bet Go for Commadore at the odds, skip the race, or put longshot Socially Informed underneath the public choice for an exacta. He is going up in class, but he has a bullet work and not bad back time, when adjusted.

RACE EIGHT

Sixty percent of handicap races for older horses and classified allowance ("money") races are won by one of the horses showing the best or next best earnings per start. When these horses lose, they are beaten by horses that are in superb condition, as shown by a very fast last race or super workouts, especially long ones.

In this race there are three horses with top earnings per start: Gulch (83G), King's Swan (61G), and Afleet (60G). (Did you remember to calculate the earnings per start and did you do it correctly?)

None of the other horses show the kind of quickness that makes for an upset.

King's Swan, as a top money earner, has very enticing odds, but his lack of a workout for such an important race may indicate that his winter racing has taken its toll.

Afleet does have multiple workouts, but his best work is mediocre. Unless his trainer has been conserving him for a great effort, he is unlikely to beat Gulch, who has a good last race, a long (if not exceptional) workout, and the highest earnings per start.

Gulch looks like a solid favorite and should be bet like one. A saver should be put on King's Swan, and he should be reversed with Gulch for a small exacta.

RACE NINE:
SIMULCAST OF THE KENTUCKY DERBY

Every type of race presents a different series of questions. Ask the right questions, get the right answers, and you come up with a winner.

The key questions for the Kentucky Derby over the past twenty years have been:

1. Which horse has a top time last out at a mile and one eighth?
2. Which horse has an excellent workout at Churchill Downs, preferably at six furlongs or longer?
3. Which horse has a good closing time in its last race?

Last year, Alysheba, the winner at 8–1, was one of two horses that could answer "Yes" to all three questions. The other was the favorite, Demons Begone, who ran very poorly.

This year no horse qualifies on all three conditions, primarily because Private

Terms' last race in the Wood Memorial at Aqueduct was so exceptional. He not only came within one fifth of a second of equaling a track record that has stood for fifteen years, but he closed unusually well.

That super race excluded everyone but Seeking the Gold from qualifying as having a speed rating within five points of the top time, and Seeking the Gold has no other qualifications.

The race was so fast that it introduced another serious question. Had it taken too much out of Private Terms?

There are no absolutes in racing, but a long-standing commandment has been: "Do not bet a horse that has equaled or come close to equaling a track record unless it has been given time to rest."

Only those human athletes involved in distance races can fully appreciate the dulling effect an incredibly fast race has on the body. They know well how long it takes for their muscles and their spirit to recover. Horses are no different.

Private Terms had never worked swiftly, even before his sensational race in the Wood, but his prep for the Derby was so slow that we have to conclude his best race was behind him. He cannot be totally dismissed, but he can only be considered a favorite that will be used as a saver over some longshots, which have a chance to come in second.

We must look for our major bet someplace else.

Of the horses with the next best speed ratings, Brian's Time had a fine closing fraction. Can he make his scintillating close from very far back in a field of seventeen horses? Probably he will fare like some of the other famous closers in the Derby. They made their usual late surge, but it was either too late because of the wall of horses in front of them, or they had to go too wide. With a large field, we will have to bypass Brian's Time and go with a front-runner or presser.

Three horses have good times and good workouts, but these horses present other questions.

Risen Star has never raced more than a mile and one sixteenth. Can he get the distance?

Can the filly Winning Colors beat the boys as Genuine Risk had done? Her last race was excellent, and her superb workout makes her fitness clear, but would she be allowed to take an easy, uncontested lead as she had done in that race?

Forty Niner, an ace as a two-year-old and the favorite in the early polls to win the Derby, has the best workout of all. He is definitely ready, but his closing times make him very questionable as a mile-and-one-quarter horse.

In the chapter on distance racing, it was noted that a novel system for picking

Derby winners has become famous during the past few years. This so-called Dosage Index does indeed have an amazing record over the past couple of decades and so some attention should be paid to the selections using that method.

Leon Rasmussen, the *Racing Form* writer who was most responsible for making the system well known, picked the Derby in this order: Forty Niner, Kingpost, and Risen Star. Forty Niner does not seem as if he can get the distance, despite his great breeding. Kingpost ran well last time out but in very slow time. His very slow closing fractions do not inspire confidence. Risen Star? He is already on our list of probable contenders.

But the list is not long at all. Risen Star and Winning Colors must be bet because of their good last races and bullet works. These should have been hooked with Gulch in the late double.

These two horses should be reversed in exactas, and Brian's Time and Forty Niner should be played underneath each of our win picks.

One saver exacta should be made with Private Terms. The only horse that will pay the minimum $30 we look for is Brian's Time, so we will place him underneath the favorite.

RACE TEN

This is a race limited to horses bred in New York State. "State-bred" horses race almost exclusively against each other. The better horses slowly graduate, and the rest have a chance to win.

Consequently, the first group of contenders should be those with a good last race at any distance. Fleche (best at the actual distance), Pine Island Pat, Agnoble, and Sunshiner all qualify.

"Trip" handicappers would have no trouble separating these horses. Agnoble had to check in his last race. This "bad trip" undoubtedly cost him speed rating points and possibly a chance for his first victory.

Another time-honored trainer method is to run maiden horses in sprints until they are in shape, give them a sharpening bullet work, and then run them at the "wrong" distance to get a better price in the mutuels. Mr. Frosty, with only two lifetime races at six furlongs and the only horse in the race with an excellent work, five furlongs in an even minute, certainly rates as a put-over horse.

The inside post is a definite advantage in a two-turn race. Don't Give In has one poor two-turn race, but he has been given three works in fifteen days, surely significant in a race that contains horses that can hardly be considered outstanding.

Because of his odds, Mr. Frosty should be bet to win. He should be played in a three-horse exacta box with Agnoble and Don't Give In, and he should be played underneath favorite Sunshiner as a saver.

Aqueduct Results

RACE ONE

Horse	Finish	Prices		
Paris Office	1hd	7.40	—	—
Quindecillion	2¹⁶		—	—
Jig Time Dixie	3			—

(Win wagering only)

It wasn't easy at all. Paris Office stalked the pace to the turn, battled head to head with Quindecillion from that point on, and after a half-mile struggle finally notched victory by a head. Class prevailed, but barely, in one of the most thrilling races of the day.

RACE TWO

Horse	Finish	Prices		
International Guest	1¹	13.80	4.80	4.20
Irish Mistress	2³³⁄⁴		3.00	2.60
Miss Sherby	3nk			3.20

$2 Exacta paid $50.40
$2 Quinella paid $20.60
$2 Daily Double paid $45.00

The winner may have been a trifle lucky. Clever But Costly was up near the leaders for the first quarter mile, got caught in tight quarters, dropped back to dead last, got going again, and rallied strongly to just miss the show spot.

Irish Mistress may have shown her racing staleness by dropping back to last after a fair start. She made a late move, slipping through on the rail, but couldn't overtake International Guest, who stalked the early pace, split horses, and got a clear lead in the stretch.

Notice the good exacta price for the third choice in the betting with a 6–5 favorite coming in second.

Flower de Noel quit badly after leading for half a mile, and the others showed nothing.

RACE THREE

Horse	Finish	Prices		
Sixth of May	1^{nk}	25.40	11.80	8.00
Ballyduggan	$2^{43/4}$		5.80	5.00
Fatty Boy	3^{nk}			4.20

$2 Exacta paid $194.00

After the race there was no doubt that Ballyduggan was both ready to win and the best horse in the race. He got trapped behind horses on the turn, waited and waited to get through, finally went to the outside, and finished fastest of all, just missing at the wire.

RACE FOUR

Horse	Finish	Prices		
Armand	$1^{43/4}$	3.40	2.80	2.20
Medieval Rival	2^2		5.80	4.00
Kanduit's Pride	3no			3.00

$2 Exacta paid $23.40
$2 Quinella paid $20.20

Goes So Fast did go fast—but only for six furlongs. He led by four but quit going around the far turn and finished next to last. Damascus Gold left his race on the training track. He never entered contention. Armand smashed them like a 3–5 shot should, winning with only the mildest of urging.

RACE FIVE

Horse	Finish	Prices		
Conventioneer	1$^{3/4}$	5.00	3.20	2.60
Scholar's Task	2$^{21/4}$		3.60	2.60
Cost Conscious	3$^{1/2}$			2.80

(No exacta wagering)

Conventioneer quickly went to the lead, opened up by almost three at the head of the stretch, and was never really threatened.

The race was run in fast but not sensational time. The interesting thing was that Real Account, the strong second choice, with poor off-track form, couldn't seem to handle the track. He finished a dismal last, twelve lengths behind.

On the other hand, the top two finishers were the only horses with off-track form.

RACE SIX

Horse	Finish	Prices		
Spiriting	1$^{3/4}$	5.00	2.60	2.20
Superb Time	2$^{53/4}$		3.00	2.20
Tasma's Star	3$^{3/4}$			3.00

$2 Exacta paid $12.40
$2 Double paid $14.00

We tend to remember the bad luck in racing and to quickly forget the times that fortune smiled.

Too Bobees Return had no closing punch and finished a distant fourth. Meanwhile, stablemate Spiriting led by four lengths at the half and cruised to an easy win.

Those who bet the favorite luckily won for the wrong reasons.

RACE SEVEN

Horse	Finish	Prices		
Go for Commadore	1^4	3.80	2.60	2.10
Dr. Carrington	2^4		3.20	2.20
Knockon	3^{hd}			2.10

$2 Exacta paid $10.80

Go for Commadore let Dr. Carrington take a big lead (six lengths), bided his time, swept by him as they came down the stretch, and won going away.

Socially Informed was no match for Dr. Carrington for the place, but he did run second most of the way, and just missed holding on for the show spot.

RACE EIGHT

Horse	Finish	Prices		
Gulch	$1^{1¼}$	6.40	2.80	2.60
Afleet	2^2		2.60	2.40
It's Acedemic	$3^{1¾}$			7.20

$2 Exacta paid $14.00
$2 Pick Six paid $2,466.00 (Six wins)
(Five wins paid $19.00)

Gulch led all the way and drew out a bit in the stretch. Afleet had some traffic problems, dropped from third to fifth, and ran well once he got clear, but he was no match for the winner. King's Swan ran well off the pace early, went very wide into the stretch and lacked hustle when his jockey called for it.

The Pick Six was unusual in that five of the six races were won by favorites. Four of these favorites were standouts. In the fourth race, three horses should have been bet, since the favorite was risky. Although we won the third race betting three horses, that race really should have included the four possibilities. And so, for $24 (or $48, if King's Swan were played as a saver in the eighth) the Six could have been Picked.

Do not be misled. Normally, the Pick Six is very difficult. But, on this day, four standout favorites held up and the other two races ran according to form.

Meanwhile, you are alive with Gulch, but which horses did you hook him with in the Kentucky Derby, which forms the second half of the late double at Aqueduct?

RACE NINE

Horse	Finish	Prices		
Winning Colors	1^{nk}	9.80	6.00	5.20
Forty Niner	2^3		6.20	4.80
Risen Star	3$^{1/2}$			7.40

$2 Exacta paid $69.80
$2 Quinella paid $34.80
$2 Triple paid $457.00
$2 Double paid $35.40

The Derby had two big surprises. Winning Colors was allowed to take an easy lead after a half mile and was even allowed to increase the lead between the quarter pole and the stretch call.

The other surprise? The closing surge that Forty Niner made simply could not be predicted from the charts. Having failed to last over Risen Star and Brian's Time in the past, he seemed the candidate least likely to be cutting down the lead enjoyed by Winning Colors and to narrowly miss in one of the closest Derbies in years.

No surprises: Private Terms ran poorly. Brian's Time made up more ground than anyone, finished faster than everyone, but still couldn't get up for the win.

RACE TEN

Horse	Finish	Prices		
Agnoble	1no	12.60	7.00	5.40
Don't Give In	2^1		9.00	7.00
Duly Rebuked	3^{hd}			17.60

$2 Exacta paid $124.20
$2 Triple paid $2,282.00

Sunshiner threw in a bad race. Running last most of the way, the favorite beat only three horses.

Mr. Frosty made a good move on the outside around the turn, got within a half length of the leader, and then flattened out.

Agnoble split horses to take the lead in deep stretch and then just lasted over Don't Give In, who came within a nose of taking all the money.

Before moving on to the California practice session, you should examine your selecting and betting methods.

You are now aware that no single method works in every race. Some methods work better in certain types of races, but you can never simply take the top time in the past thirty days *or* the best time ever *or* a class drop *or* a trainer move and say, "*This* is the winner."

Although handicapping is never a matter of numerically adding positive factors and subtracting negative ones, all of our winners had more than one thing going for them. And except for odds-on-favorite Armand, none of the horses that beat us had been excluded because of negative factors.

This will not always happen. In fact, in three races, horses with negative factors came very close to beating us out. On the other hand, a few of our winners were still selected despite having negative factors. (Most notably, the filly Winning Colors.)

We had a very high percentage of winners, primarily because all of our favorites, including one won by the lesser half of an entry, stood up. This too cannot be expected to always happen.

If you did not have the horses we selected according to the principles of this book, review your methods.

Did you read the conditions of the races? They were the keys to Races 1, 7, 8, and 10.

Did you compare recent time *and* back time?

Did you apply the track variant properly?

Did you calculate the earnings per start as the first step in analyzing Race 8?

Did you distinguish the solid favorites from the risky ones?

Did you notice which of the contenders were dropping in weight? Except possibly for King's Swan, high weight did not affect the outcome of any race, but weight off (the trainer's delight) was a forceful positive factor in a number of races.

In races where horses had run against each other, did you compare their finishes and their odds?

Did you look for bullet workouts and attempt to find excellent but nonbullet works? Did you notice which horses had gone too long a time after their last races with no workouts?

Did you pay attention to the pace indicators? This was clearly a key factor in the Derby.

Finally, if you had a winner, did you have it for the right reason?

Reminder: At Hollywood Park you will be using a different track variant range (16–20) and a slightly different set of figures for calculating workouts (see page 198).

When comparing speed ratings for different sprint distances, the average six-furlong rating at both major California tracks is 1½ points lower than the average six-and-one-half-furlong rating. The point added to six-furlong ratings will make a negligible difference in most races, but if you are making a very difficult final choice you might want to keep it in mind.

Since the Hollywood Park meeting had only recently begun, almost all of the horses will show only Santa Anita races in their most recent past-performance lines. When you are analyzing distance races, keep in mind that races at one mile at Santa Anita are run around two turns.

California has a large county fair circuit. Speed ratings attained at these small tracks should generally be ignored. "Best evers" should be restricted to races run at Santa Anita (SA) or Hollywood Park (Hol).

1st Hollywood

START — 6 FURLONGS — HOLLYWOOD PARK — FINISH

6 FURLONGS. (1.08⅖) CLAIMING. Purse $16,000. Fillies and mares. 4-year-olds and upward. Weight, 122 lbs. Non-winners of two races since March 22 allowed 3 lbs.; a race since then, 6 lbs. Claiming price $16,000; if for $14,000, 2 lbs. (Races when entered for $12,500 or less not considered.)

Coupled—Cabrolee and Miss San Diego.

Iron Lark Miss — 3–1

PEDROZA M A — **116**
Own.—Belmonte-Lewis-Weisberg

Gr. m. 5, by Iron Warrior—To a Skylark, by T V Lark
Br.—Moore & Fletcher (Wash) — 1988 6 0 1 0 $5,750
Tr.—Mitchell Mike — $16,000 — 1987 14 3 0 3 $30,970
Lifetime 31 7 3 4 $66,625

23Apr88-2SA	6f	:211	:443	1:111sy	9½	116	12	12	1½	44½	Pedroza M A7	Ⓕ 16000	77-15	FoxiesEgo,DancersOrbit,JolieMdme	9
16Apr88-1SA	6f	:214	:452	1:11 gd	4¾	1115	1½	2hd	22½	812¼	ShermanAB2	Ⓕ c12500	71-16	KnightTraker,Hoofer'sBrew,Brdell	11
16Apr88—Bobbled start															
19Mar88-2SA	6½f	:214	:451	1:173ft	*2¾	116	21	21	22½	67¼	Stevens G L11	Ⓕ 20000	75-18	TmiUBr,HevyWether,LefkdinSrnd	12
5Mar88-1SA	6f	:213	:444	1:104ft	8¾	116	87	119	1217	1218¾	Black C A2	Ⓕ 25000	65-14	PlyngThrgh,FghtngMrtt,LdBrncrd	12
5Mar88—Bumped, steadied start															
14Feb88-2SA	6f	:214	:454	1:12 ft	9¼	116	2½	2½	1hd	23	Black C A4	Ⓕ 25000	75-20	FelThMusic,IronLrkMiss,P-isinLc	10
14Feb88—Bobbled start															
13Jan88-2SA	6f	:212	:442	1:111ft	8	118	21½	21½	33½	88¾	VlenzuelPA3	Ⓕ c32000	73-20	ChmpgnGold,OkPortl,Prsc'l'sCrwn	11
13Jan88—Rough start															
30Dec87-8BM	6f	:221	:451	1:111m	7¼	112	11	2hd	43	58	Camargo T5	ⒻHcp0	75-29	ChipOfDrems,VelvetEcho,OurBstTll	5
18Dec87-6BM	6f	:223	:453	1:11 gd	*2e	1115	2hd	21	32	36	Camargo T1	Ⓕ 50000	78-25	VelvetEcho,Kurbstone,IrorLrkMiss	8
19Nov87-6BM	6f	:22	:451	1:094ft	13	1115	11½	12	13	15	Camargo T1	Ⓕ 32000	90-21	IronLrkMiss,LdyTsch,Hylnd'sHHop	7
10Oct87-9Lga	6½f	:223	:452	1:163ft	3¼	1155	1½	1hd	11	61¾	Camargo T5	Ⓕ 40000	84-18	SprklingBubbls,IslndMst,BrrDLRos	6

May 5 Hol 3f ft :353 h — Apr 8 SA 5f ft 1:003 h — Mar 27 SA 5f ft :593 h — Mar 14 SA 5f ft 1:004 h

Weather Eye Open — 15–1

SOLIS A — **116**
Own.—Mamakos J L

B. f. 4, by Good Counsel—Hidden Reef, by Cohoes
Br.—Gentry T (Ky) — 1988 3 0 0 1 $2,550
Tr.—McAnally Ronald — $16,000 — 1987 3 1 0 0 $4,400
Lifetime 6 1 0 1 $6,950

1Apr88-7SA	6f	:214	:453	1:113ft	20	117	21½	43½	1215	1219¾	Pincay L Jr12	Ⓕ 25000	60-21	BoldVegas,DiamondADy,LceyLinn	12
1Apr88—Wide into stretch															
10Feb88-8GG	1	:453	1:103	1:361ft	4¾	118	11½	32½	614	628¾	HummlCR3	ⒻAw17000	58-19	SmmrGlow,Grfnggrvton,SmmyDncr	6
28Jan88-6GG	1	:461	1:102	1:36 ft	14	118	11½	11	1hd	33½	HummlCR5	ⒻAw17000	84-16	Vlr'sDlght,SummrGlow,WthrEyOpn	6
16Dec87-5BM	6f	:221	:451	1:094ft	19	116	2½	2hd	32	68¼	Johnson B G4	Ⓕ 25000	82-10	PrncssGodWn,SprmSplndr Prmssbl	7
13Nov87-6BM	6f	:221	:451	1:10 gd	21	116	2½	32	612	719¼	McHargueDG4	Ⓕ 40000	70-19	MissPso,RiverBelle,Kitty'sVlentine	7
9Oct87-9BM	6f	:222	:453	1:112ft	6½	117	1½	11	12	14	McHargue DG6	M20000	82-16	WetherEyeOpen,NovZmbl,PrtFrnch	8

Apr 22 SA 6f gd 1:122 h — Apr 16 SA 5f gd 1:001 h — Apr 10 SA 4f ft :473 h — Mar 29 Hol 5f ft 1:021 h

Sunlight Miss — * 3–1

BLACK C A — **116**
Own.—Cooke J K

Ch. m. 5, by Topsider—Sister Glass, by Olympiad King
Br.—Headley H P Jr (Ky) — 1988 3 0 0 0 $3,450
Tr.—Mandella Richard — $16,000 — 1987 6 1 0 1 $22,400
Lifetime 12 3 1 1 $51,858 — Turf 2 1 0 0 $16,783

24Apr88-1SA	6½f	:213	:444	1:164ft	*3	116	52¾	54	34	48½	Stevens G L4	Ⓕ 25000	77-14	LadyHelch,UnBelDi,GreySeptember	8
1Apr88-7SA	6f	:214	:453	1:113ft	4½	116	84¾	86¼	75½	43¼	Stevens G L11	Ⓕ 25000	77-21	BoldVegas,DiamondADy,LceyLinn	12
23Jan88-1SA	6f	:213	:443	1:102ft	6	116	98¾	913	1010	87½	Stevens G L8	Ⓕ 40000	78-14	TimeToSwp,OkPortl,OnLuckyRod	11
23Jan88—Bobbled start															
5Dec87-8Hol	1 1/16	:47	1:12	1:453m	12	1105	31½	33½	59½	614	Gryder AT1	ⒻAw40000	61-17	HollywoodGlittr,SrosBrg,MyVrgnRl	8
29Oct87-8SA	6½f	:213	:442	1:163gd	4¼	117	31½	33½	35½	35½	Toro F3	ⒻAw33000	81-16	IrshLrd'sMss,WndTrplK.,SnlghtMss	8
11Sep87-3Dmr	6f	:22	:444	1:091ft	7½	115	41½	55	56½	513½	Toro F1	ⒻAw27000	78-13	Flying Julia, Alydariel, Jell	6
22Feb87-3SA	a6½f Ⓣ	:214	:443	1:162fm	*3	120	31	31	43	53¾ ♦	Toro F2	ⒻAw34000	73-22	MissBevrlyHills,Rkindling,Aromcor	9
♦22Feb87—Dead heat															
25Jan87-5SA	a6½f Ⓣ	:213	:441	1:154fm	2¾	117	2½	2½	11½	1nk	Toro F5	ⒻAw30000	80-18	SunlightMiss,Missen,Sir'sNewHope	9
25Jan87—Bumped crossing dirt															
1Jan87-3SA	6f	:213	:451	1:111ft	*9-5	120	2½	32	52¾	63½	Toro F4	ⒻAw29000	78-19	BlconyPss,SeDoubyRun,LuckySilvr	9
1Jan87—Steadied															
13Dec86-6Hol	6f	:213	:45	1:102ft	*7-5	120	21½	21	2½	11¾	Toro F10	ⒻAw22000	91-09	SunlightMiss,QueenMrlen,Bmblor	10

May 5 Hol 5f ft 1:01 h — Apr 23 SA 3f ft :383 h — Apr 19 SA 4f ft :481 h — Apr 14 SA 4f ft :482 h

Hoofer's Brew * — 5–1

MEZA R Q — **116**
Own.—Semple D M

Gr. f. 4, by Sharp Hoofer—Home Timer, by Terresto
Br.—Cossack Farms (BC-C) — 1988 4 0 2 0 $6,400
Tr.—Baze Jeffrey A — $16,000 — 1987 9 4 0 1 $39,450
Lifetime 13 4 2 1 $45,850

23Apr88-2SA	6f	:211	:443	1:111sy	2½	116	32½	46	79½	713½	Meza R Q3	Ⓕ 16000	68-15	FoxiesEgo,DancersOrbit,JolieMdme	9
16Apr88-1SA	6f	:214	:452	1:11 gd	*4-5	116	31	32½	33½	26½	Stevens G L6	Ⓕ c12500	76-16	KnightTraker,Hoofer'sBrew,Brdell	11
18Mar88-5SA	6f	:214	:453	1:103ft	*9-5	116	12	11	2hd	22¼	Stevens G L10	Ⓕ 16000	83-19	LdyHelch,Hoofer'sBrew,JolieMdm	11
2Jan88-2SA	6f	:214	:451	1:114gd	*3	115	2½	42	85¾	86¾	Stevens G L7	Ⓕ 25000	72-15	WtchOutForM,GrySptmbr,OurMrg	12
19Dec87-1Hol	6f	:22	:45	1:10 gd	9-5	115	1hd	1hd	31½	75	Stevens G L7	Ⓕ 32000	87-10	PromisingNot,BuyMor,LdyBrunicrd	8
16Nov87-3SA	6½f	:212	:444	1:174ft	*7-5	116	1½	1hd	33	713¼	Gryder A T3	Ⓕ 40000	68-22	AlisNin,OnLuckyRod,BeutifulBrook	9
1Nov87-2SA	6f	:213	:443	1:102m	2¾	1115	12	12	11½	12	Gryder A T3	Ⓕ 32000	86-12	Hfr'sBrw,ChmpgnGld,Lt'sDrnkDnnr	7
20Jun87-6Hol	6f	:213	:45	1:102ft	7	116	1½	1hd	12	14	Stevens G L1	Ⓕ 40000	91-11	Hoofer's Brew,Folia,MyProperGal	10
6May87-7Hol	7f	:213	:442	1:234ft	3¼	116	13	13	26	511½	ValenzuelPA4	Ⓕ 50000	74-18	Ambra'sBeat,DandyRuth,RomnGem	9
10Apr87-1SA	6½f	:214	:45	1:172ft	2¾	118	11½	11½	12	14½	Stevens G L2	Ⓕ 25000	83-21	Hoofer'sBrew,Superelle,Slade'sLdy	8

May 3 SA 4f ft :523 h — Apr 10 Hol 5f ft 1:022 h — Apr 4 Hol 5f ft 1:014 h — Mar 30 Hol 5f ft 1:023 h

(*Continued on following page*)

No exacta wagering. First half of Daily Double.

Unassailable

B. f. 4, by Well Decorated—Pass The Cask, by Buckpasser
ORTEGA L E 116
Br.—Tilly Foster Farms (Ky) 1988 5 1 0 0 $12,050
Tr.—Young Gregory $16,000 1987 14 3 1 2 $36,750
Own.—Bell M A & M R
Lifetime 20 4 1 2 $48,800
11–1

Entered 6May88- 1 HOL
22Apr88-3SA 1 :462 1:113 1:38 gd 14 116 1½ 2hd 11 55¼ Ortega L E6 Ⓕ 16000 73-20 DoYouMind,DrmticElegnce,Aspirte 7
22Apr88—Lugged out
25Mar88-3SA 1 1/16 :463 1:113 1:451ft 25 118 21 910102010333¾ Velasquez J7 Ⓕ 20000 41-18 OurMrge,Nicholov,DelightfulTwist 10
25Mar88—Lugged out 7/8
12Mar88-9SA 1 1/16 :471 1:121 1:452ft 22 116 21 55 11191224¼ Toro F12 Ⓕ 25000 50-19 Let'sDrinkDinnr,SprucsIn,BoldVgs 12
10Feb88-9SA 1 :464 1:122 1:393ft 6 114 1hd 1hd 1hd 1no Velasquez J8 Ⓕ 20000 70-23 Unssilble,B.A.Sport,MybeMybenot 10
10Feb88—Wide 7/8 turn
14Jan88-1SA 7f :221 :453 1:25 ft 7½ 115 2hd 1½ 3½ 68¾ Meza R Q3 Ⓕ 20000 66-21 SwtExpcttons,HvyWthr,HolySmks 10
29Dec87-1SA 6½f :22 :46 1:19 sy 9½ 116 41½ 52¾ 53¼ 52¾ Solis A2 Ⓕ 25000 72-24 WildDrive,Holderm,SwtExpcttions 12
29Dec87—Wide into stretch
26Nov87-7Hol 1 1/16 :47 1:112 1:443ft 11 116 21½ 34 918 924¾ Olivares F9 Ⓕ 32000 55-18 FirstSilverHwk,Divest,DoubleDent 10
30Oct87-9SA 1 :473 1:12 1:374gd 7 116 3½ 3nk 1hd 22½ Meza R Q7 Ⓕ 32000 76-21 FirstSilverHwk,Unssilble,CelticLdy 9
30Oct87—Bumped 3/16
8Oct87-9SA 1 :46 1:112 1:391ft *2¾ 117 2hd 11 13½ 31 Meza R Q4 Ⓕ c25000 71-19 SignTheCard,Radiantly,Unassilble 10
14Sep87-3Dmr 1 :462 1:121 1:384ft 3 1115 1hd 2hd 23 32¾ Patton D B1 Ⓕ 32000 71-19 CelticLady,Believablee,Unassailable 6
14Sep87—Lugged out
May 2 SA 5f ft :594 h Apr 16 SA 5f gd 1:002 h ● Mar 23 SA 3f ft :35 h

Hidden Past

B. m. 6, by Historically—Knowledgeable Lady, by Tree of Knowledge
CORRAL J R 1115
Br.—Dollase & Hanson (Cal) 1988 1 0 0 0
Tr.—Bernstein David $16,000 1987 9 1 0 2 $18,150
Own.—Giuliano–Jackson–WalkerEtl
Lifetime 37 9 3 3 $86,045 Turf 1 0 0 0
5–1

30Apr88-4Hol 6f :22 :451 1:11 ft 69 1105 53¾ 53½ 76 64 Olguin G L11 Ⓕ 20000 83-14 Jingle, Buy More, Fancy Fogarty 12
1Aug87-1Dmr 6½f :22 :451 1:18 ft 9½ 116 51¾ 44½ 58 68¼ PedrozMA11 Ⓕ[S] 16000 74-15 RedFrenchy,DlightfulTwist,IrishVl 12
6Jun87-2Hol 7f :221 :452 1:244ft *3¼ 1115 75½ 97¾ 99¼ 812¾ Gryder A T7 Ⓕ 16000 67-17 Oh Marie, Safeera, St. Moritz 9
6Jun87—Wide 3/8 turn
29May87-5Hol 6f :221 :453 1:11 ft *8-5 116 52 58 69½ 611¾ Stevens G L8 Ⓕ 20000 76-16 IndinFlowr,GrySptmbr,QunDimggio 8
29May87—Wide 3/8 turn
5Apr87-3SA 6f :213 :443 1:103ft *3-2 116 42 35 25 33½ Stevens G L3 Ⓕ 25000 81-16 FightingMritt,LovlyCndy,HiddnPst 8
18Mar87-7SA 6½f :214 :444 1:17 ft *2½ 118 31 21½ 22½ 32 Stevens G L8 Ⓕ 25000 83-17 PeggyDee,Ms.CrookdRod,HiddnPst 8
20Feb87-7SA a6½f Ⓣ:214 :4411:153fm 19 117 42 52¼ 75¼ 68¼ Black C A9 ⒻAw27000 73-19 InConcert,Jerry'sGoldmine,Phylell 10
30Jan87-3SA 6½f :214 :444 1:174ft 3¼ 116 108½10101214129¾ Stevens G L7 Ⓕ 40000 71-20 Velveteen, Wine Girl, My Tara 12
30Jan87—Wide final 3/8
19Jan87-7SA 6½f :214 :444 1:173ft 4¾ 118 32 33 33 12¾ Stevens G L4 Ⓕ 32000 82-25 HiddenPst,PrimroseKitchns,Vlvtn 10
4Jan87-6SA 6f :22 :452 1:114sy 6 116 86¼1112 912 912¾ Stevens G L8 Ⓕ 40000 66-22 IrishKristin,ThirdMarrige,WineGirl 12
4Jan87—Wide 3/8
Apr 17 SA 4f ft :48 h Apr 10 SA 4f ft :483 h Apr 1 Hol 5f ft 1:021 h Mar 21 Hol 4f ft :472 h

Promise Me Luck

Gr. m. 5, by Bolger—Pammy's Luck, by Lucky Gray
GRYDER A T 116
Br.—Shahan E H (Cal) 1988 4 0 0 1 $750
Tr.—Wheeler Robert L $16,000 1987 5 0 0 2 $4,360
Own.—Zubow I
Lifetime 22 3 4 5 $55,035
16–1

23Apr88-11TuP 5½f :223 :464 1:074sl 11 113 12 12½ 2½ 33½ Guerra V J 5 Aw7500 65-49 BoldCmbro,C.K.'sOrphn,PrmsMLck 6
3Apr88-9TuP 6f :212 :44 1:09 ft 21 114 2hd 3nk 44¼ 613¼ Gomez E A 7 ⒻAw7500 76-19 Why NotTell,GinMill,HighAppraisal 7
13Mar88-9TuP 6f :22 :442 1:091ft 9¼ 114 3½ 55½ 58½ 710 Guerra V J3 ⒻAw7500 78-18 OneMorLdy,WhyNotTll,DrconicCod 7
4Mar88-10TuP 6f :213 :443 1:10 ft 7 114 1½ 3nk 61 77½ MartinezFIII5 Ⓕ 25000 76-22 TretMeRight,ForvrABlurr,ClssyPirt 7
15Sep87-9Bmf 5½f :212 :443 1:024ft 4½ 115 11 1hd 31½ 58½ Doocy T T 3 ⒻAw16000 89-14 MissPso,SprklPlntyToo,Codx'sBrid 6
15Sep87—Bumped start
10Jun87-8Aks 6f :222 :46 1:121m *2-3e 118 11 1½ 31½ 718¼ CordovDW 7 ⒻAw13600 58-31 DremPolicy,LooseAnnie,Redecortd 8
7May87-7Aks 6f :222 :453 1:111ft *4-5 115 11 1hd 2hd 32¾ Cordova DW 1 Aw18100 78-27 MyDbutnt,I'mEnchntd,PromsMLck 7
29Apr87-8Aks 5½f :213 :484 1:041ft *9-5 112 31 21½ 33 35 Doocy T T 7 ⒻAw22600 84-25 NobleScrtry,MyMris,Prom'sMLuck 7
1Jan87-3SA 6f :213 :451 1:111ft 7¾ 116 1½ 2hd 2½ 94½ Kaenel J L 9 ⒻAw29000 77-19 BlconyPss,SeDoubyRun,LuckySilvr 9
1Jan87—Veered out start
2Nov86-5SA 6f :212 :441 1:102ft 28 117 12 1½ 1½ 52¼ Solis A 4 ⒻAw28000 84-10 StridingEsy,LoversNtive,FlyingJuli 9
2Nov86—Lost whip 1/8
Apr 9 TuP 5f ft 1:014 h

Coron Miss

Ch. f. 4, by Irish Stronghold—Love to Reason, by Hail to Reason
SIBILLE R 116
Br.—Bruce & J Ehret Syndicate (Cal) 1988 7 2 0 0 $8,850
Tr.—Jordan James $16,000 1987 8 3 1 0 $35,525
Own.—Bruce–Campbell–Johnson
Lifetime 16 5 2 0 $44,975
7–1

15Apr88-9SA 1 1/16 :47 1:132 1:471m 7¾ 116 11½ 1hd 42¼ 412½ Black C A 5 Ⓕ 20000 52-21 Mapleton, Vindolanda, Pribor 6
1Apr88-7SA 6f :214 :453 1:113ft 11 1165 12111211109 98¼ Banderas AL 5 Ⓕ 25000 72-21 BoldVegas,DiamondADy,LceyLinn 12
1Apr88—Wide into stretch
19Mar88-9AC 6f :232 :453 1:094ft 8-5 117 2hd 21½ 2hd 13 GrciLopzJH 2 ⒻAw6000 90-16 CoronMiss,ConvivilMiss,It'sLovble 6
6Mar88-9AC 6f :224 :451 1:092ft *6-5 114 3½ 31½ 2hd 13½ EnriquezHF 5 ⒻAw6000 92-14 Coron Miss,Debilyn,CoralCockatoo 7
26Feb88-2SA 6f :22 :45 1:12 ft 4¼ 115 31 52½ 53¼ 65½ PedrozMA 3 Ⓕ[S] 16000 72-23 ThirdMrrige,MostDrmtic,Slde'sLdy 9
26Feb88—Bumped start
14Feb88-2SA 6f :214 :454 1:12 ft 9 115 74¾ 74¼ 96¾ 911¾ Pedroza MA 10 Ⓕ 25000 66-20 FelThMusic,IronLrkMiss,PrisinLc 10
4Feb88-5SA 6f :213 :45 1:104ft 9 115 55 — — — Meza R Q 3 Ⓕ 32000 — — StEpcttns,Prscll'sCrn,FghtngMrtt 12
4Feb88—Pulled up; Broke in, bumped
4Jly87-6Hol 6f :214 :443 1:101ft 3¾ 116 32 712 724 — Meza R Q 1 Ⓕ 50000 — — DowryIndex,PlesurBntKris,TriHolly 7
4Jly87—Eased
30Apr87-7Hol 6f :214 :452 1:104ft 8½ 116 31 87¾ 815 823½ VlenzulPA 5 ⒻAw22000 65-13 MissSprinklet,PlesureBntKris,Aflot 8
30Apr87—Took up 5/16
11Apr87-3SA 6f :214 :45 1:104ft 2½ 118 21½ 2½ 2½ 11½ Meza R Q6 Ⓕ 40000 84-16 CoronMiss,FoxiesEgo,LefkdinSrnd 6
● May 6 SA 3f ft :341 h Apr 30 SA 5f ft 1:011 h Apr 24 SA 5f m :592 h Apr 11 SA 4f ft :473 h

2nd Hollywood

(10 Horses)

6½ FURLONGS. (1.15⅗) CLAIMING. Purse $14,000. 4-year-olds and upward. Weight, 121 lbs. Non-winners of two races since March 22 allowed 3 lbs.; a race since then, 6 lbs. Claiming $12,500; if for $10,500, 1 lbs. (Races when entered for $9,000 or less not considered.)

Classy Vigors

3–1

CORRAL J R 1105
Own.—Plato G W
Gr. g. 4, by Vigors—Lot of Class, by Home Guard
Br.—Hawn W R (Ky) 1988 1 0 0 0
Tr.—Lage Armando $12,500 1987 7 0 2 0 $13,800
Lifetime 16 2 2 1 $38,070

28Apr88-2Hol 6f :213 :444 1:10 ft 5¾ 1095 75½ 87 77½ 75¾ Corral J R 3 14000 86-18 FllThDncr,Lrk'sLgcy,Exbrrt'sImg 12
28Apr88—Bobbled start
6Jun87-1Hol 6f :22 :452 1:12 ft *7-5 1105 64½ 44 55 54¾ Gryder A T 2 25000 78-17 ShrewdSteve,HerrHeinz,RoyalAgori 7
7May87-5Hol 6f :214 :45 1:101ft 2½ 116 99 77½ 57½ 47 Stevens G L 8 32000 85-13 PrimConcord,ExubrntFling,Somshn 9
22Apr87-5Hol 1 :452 1:102 1:36 ft *1 117 11½ 1½ 33 510¼ Pincay L Jr 2 50000 73-18 NvrMssT.V.,SprActon,BooBo'sBckr 5
3Apr87-3SA 6f :214 :452 1:111ft *1 115 76½ 54 42¼ 21 Ortega L E 3 c40000 81-17 Nourished,ClassyVigors,NtiveReply 7
3Apr87—Broke slowly
22Mar87-2SA 6f :213 :45 1:10 gd 17 116 77 75¾ 55½ 35¼ Ortega L E 4 Aw29000 83-23 Lookinforthbgon,‡Jmok,ClssyVgors 7
22Mar87—Broke in a tangle; bumped, took up start; Placed second through disqualification
19Feb87-7SA 6f :213 :443 1:093ft 2¾ 114 62¾ 52 41½ 42½ Stevens G L 5 50000 87-13 Rconnotrng,SoclDmnd,ImprssvRsn 9
19Feb87—Broke slowly
16Jan87-5SA 1 1/16 :464 1:111 1:433ft 9¾ 114 66½ 79 714 818½ Baze G 8 Aw28000 64-18 Hot AndSmoggy,Reland,JustBobby 9
31Dec86-3SA 1 :452 1:104 1:372ft 9 116 17 15 11 35¾ ValenzuelPA 4 Aw28000 75-20 RedAndBlue,LightSbre,ClssyVigors 6
14Dec86-4Hol 7f :214 :45 1:241ft 11 115 75½ 62½ 95¼ 96½ Baze G 3 Aw22000 76-18 OrchardSong,Reland,HoustonBrgg 11
14Dec86—Lacked room 1/4
●Apr 24 Hol 4f gd :453 h Apr 17 SA 5f ft 1:00 h Apr 8 SA 5f ft 1:001 hg Apr 2 SA 5f ft :593 h

Roll A Natural

5–1

SIBILLE R 115
Own.—Teichner S & Phyllis
B. g. 8, by L'Natural—Happy Dunce, by Fleet Nasrullah
Br.—Warwick & West (Cal) 1988 6 0 0 1 $3,550
Tr.—Dorfman Leonard $12,500 1987 3 0 0 0 $1,175
Lifetime 63 8 9 3 $143,425 Turf 4 0 0 1 $4,900

27Apr88-1Hol 6f :214 :452 1:113ft 23 116 85¼ 52½ 73¾ 4½ Sibille R 12 [S] 10000 83-17 Rimmou, End Play, HoustonBragg 12
13Apr88-1SA 6f :213 :443 1:104ft 9 116 78 1012 912 89½ Black C A2 [S] 12500 74-22 IrishIllusion,Pyrmiding,MrkThLrk 12
13Apr88—Broke slowly, lugged out backside, 3/8 turn
9Mar88-3SA 7f :223 :453 1:231ft 5½ 116 64 88 811 912½ DelahoussayeE8 12500 71-19 Premiere, Rock EnSam,Gossarone 10
9Mar88—Wide into stretch
25Feb88-7SA 1 1/16 :471 1:122 1:452ft 3½ 116 21½ 22½ 33½ 58¼ Sibille R2 12500 66-22 BngBngBng,AlotNoise,Vulnerbility 7
25Feb88—Lugged out
12Feb88-1SA 7f :222 :452 1:251ft 4 116 84½ 85¼ 63½ 3hd DelahoussayeE4 12500 74-24 LndseerII,WestL'Ouest,RollANturl 12
12Feb88—Lugged out backstretch, 3/8 turn
22Jan88-5SA 6½f :213 :443 1:163ft 8 116 56 66 45¼ 78½ DelahoussayeE1 14000 78-17 GoldenBeu,ClssicQuickie,BumBRy 12
22Jan88—Lugged out
20Mar87-3SA 6f :212 :443 1:093ft 14 116 95½ 96 99½ 58¾ McHargue D G3 32000 81-17 ElPrsdntUno,DshonorblGst,Donsprt 9
1Feb87-2SA 6½f :213 :441 1:163ft 15 116 63¼ 76¼ 78 53 Toro F2 40000 84-16 Romaxe,LuckyMasadado,C-cksmn 12
17Jan87-2SA 6f :214 :45 1:103ft 4½ 116 75¾ 1011 98½ 77¼ DelahoussayeE5 40000 78-18 Ondarty, Romaxe, Rivets Factor 11
17Jan87—Took up 5/8
15Nov86-3Hol 6f :221 :452 1:10 ft 3½ 117 2hd 21 21½ 21¼ DelahoussayeE4 40000 92-14 Cracksman,RollANturl,PtriotGloves 6
May 5 Hol 3f ft :37 h Apr 25 SA 3f ft :354 h Apr 10 SA 5f ft 1:02 h Apr 4 SA 5f ft 1:013 h

Hijo El Toro *

* 5–2

BANDERAS A L 1135
Own.—Aubrey B H
B. g. 5, by High Places—Busher's Lark, by Mr Busher
Br.—Gregg C E (Ore) 1988 3 1 0 0 $9,125
Tr.—Longden Eric J $12,500 1987 22 6 3 2 . $34,783
Lifetime 45 10 6 5 $71,238

29Apr88-1Hol 6f :214 :45 1:104ft 5 117 88½ 56½ 53 1hd Pincay L Jr 6 12500 88-17 Hijo ElToro,Devil'sIce,Don'tFightIt 9
14Apr88-5SA 6½f :212 :442 1:171gd 4 117 1010 1112 1112 1014¼ Pincay L Jr 10 16000 70-21 PssAnotherTb,Gossrone,Lrk'sLgcy 12
16Jan88-1SA 6f :212 :442 1:11 ft 5½ 116 65½ 79 56½ 43¾ Valenzuela P A 8 20000 79-20 Subito, Rising Pine, Agua Russo 10
23Dec87-2Hol 6f :222 :461 1:114ft 3½ 1125 107¾ 75¼ 76½ 52¾ Gryder A T 3 c16000 80-19 ElDiamonte,GranTerresto,Melchip 11
23Dec87—Steadied, ran up horse's heels at 1/4
11Dec87-9Hol 1 :452 1:10 1:363ft 7¾ 1115 54¾ 54½ 62¾ 51¼ ♦ Gryder A T 3 20000 79-18 Sasebo, Moro Bay, Fairly Omen 11
♦11Dec87—Dead heat
4Dec87-5Hol 6f :221 :451 1:103ft 8½ 116 31 31 42 75¼ Cordero A Jr 11 25000 84-21 RdwoodBoy,BolgrMgic,CuttingLin 11
22Nov87-1Hol 6f :22 :444 1:101ft 30 117 108½ 911 67 45¼ Castanon A L 3 32000 86-14 MeYouAndQ.,NtiveRelity,KniDncr 10
15Nov87-9SA 1 1/16 :47 1:113 1:431ft 14 115 31½ 3½ 77 811¼ Castanon A L 3 32000 74-18 Bedouin, Shigamba, Air Alert 10
15Nov87—Lugged out
31Oct87-7BM 6f :223 :454 1:113sl 9¾ 117 77 711 88½ 85 Hansen R D 8 c25000 76-28 FinlConflict,‡AckAck'sJoy Pollinir 11
7Sep87-7Lga 6½f :213 :442 1:153ft *2¾ 120 76¾ 53½ 54½ 2no Hansen R D3 c16000 91-16 Vnton'sDoni,HijoElToro,HotHomr 10
Apr 28 SA 3f ft :361 h Apr 10 SA 5f ft :594 h Apr 4 SA 7f ft 1:291 h Mar 30 SA 5f ft 1:002 h

Quick Roundtrip

17–1

CASTANON A L 114
Own.—Garvey-Higman-Kent
B. g. 6, by Flight to Glory—Fleet Ali, by Fleet Mel
Br.—Garcia W G & Anne (Cal) 1988 4 0 0 0
Tr.—DiFiore Leslie $10,500 1987 13 6 2 1 $48,275
Lifetime 39 8 4 4 $75,265

27Apr88-1Hol 6f :214 :452 1:113ft 7½ 115 74¼ 95¾ 84¾ 82¾ Castanon AL5 [S] 10000 81-17 Rimmou, End Play, HoustonBragg 12
26Feb88-1SA 6f :22 :453 1:103ft 4½ 118 61¾ 84½ 98½ 813¾ Valenzuela P A 4 12500 71-23 BoldAndGreene,GrnPierre,HerrHinz 9
26Feb88—Steadied 3/8; bumped, steadied 3/16; lame after finish
31Jan88-1SA 6f :22 :453 1:11 ft 13 116 52½ 85¼ 85¾ 98 Stevens G L 1 20000 75-21 Melchip, Bum Bee Ray, Crack'n It 12
15Jan88-1SA 6f :214 :451 1:11 ft 8½ 116 42 32½ 43½ 86¾ Hawley S2 [S] c16000 76-20 CourgeRuler,ShowerDecre,Mlchip 12
26Dec87-1SA 7f :221 :451 1:234ft 4 117 21½ 21½ 2½ 11¾ Hawley S1 [S] 12500 81-16 QuckRoundtrp,Numpkns,P:fulImg 12
29Nov87-2Hol 6f :214 :45 1:102ft 5¾ 118 54 43½ 54½ 56¾ Castanon A L8 12500 83-12 Move Free, Savio,ElectricMoment 12
19Nov87-9Hol 6f :222 :453 1:104ft *2 115 31 2½ 2hd 11½ Higuera AR7 [S] c10000 88-14 QckRondtrp,AnothrBlom,BThnkfl 10
24Oct87-2SA 6f :214 :45 1:101gd 9¾ 116 94½ 87¾ 89 818 Higuera A R1 16000 69-17 MeYouAndQ.,Doodlesck,Inquisitiv 10
24Oct87—Broke slowly
27Sep87-12Fpx 6f :22 :453 1:112ft 3 119 43½ 32½ 32 1no Higuera A R5 12500 90-13 QuickRoundtrip,Witching,JulioNMe 9
6Sep87-3Dmr 6½f :22 :451 1:17 ft 3¾ 116 32 2hd 11½ 3¾ Higuera A R4 16000 86-17 Pegus, Moro Bay, Quick Roundtrip 7
Apr 19 Hol 5f ft 1:013 h Apr 13 Hol 5f ft 1:043 h ●Apr 6 Hol 5f ft 1:002 h

No exacta wagering.

Second half of Daily Double.

(*Continued on following page*)

(Race 2 continued)

Rimmou

B. c. 4, by To-Agori-Mou—Rimarking, by Ribot

MEDERO F — 1165 — Br.—Pascoe W T III (Cal) — 1988 5 3 1 0 $21,520 — **4–1**

Own.—Sinclair Throughbreds Inc — Tr.—Miyadi Steve — $12,500 — 1987 9 1 3 0 $16,825

Lifetime 14 4 4 0 $38,345

27Apr88-1Hol 6f :214 :452 1:113ft 4¼ 1165 42 63½ 52½ 1½ Corral J R2 [S] c10000 84-17 Rimmou, End Play, HoustonBragg 12
16Apr88-9SA 6½f :214 :45 1:164gd 5¼ 115 2½ 3nk 43 710¾ Castanon A L6 15000 75-16 AguRusso,Peppy'sConsul,WstBoyII 9
2Apr88-1SA 6f :213 :45 1:112ft 6¼ 121 1½ 1hd 1hd 1½ Castanon A L5 10000 81-19 Rimmou,Lrk'sLegcy,SoonToEscpe 12
18Mar88-1SA 6½f :214 :45 1:18 ft 15 116 2½ 11 12 1½ Castanon AL5 [S] 10000 80-18 Rimmou, El Ancon, Maso Blue 11
21Feb88-8AC 6f :223 :441 1:092ft 9-5 117 2½ 2½ 21 22 Lopez A D5 6250 90-13 T'Jill, Rimmou, Panuco 7
13Aug87-7LA 6½f :22 :462 1:161ft 2½ 117 21 21 22½ 26¾ Warren R J Jr4 20000 89-12 SundncSqr,Rmmo,Wnd'sOfWndsor 6
1Aug87-3Dmr 6f :214 :452 1:104ft 46 1115 62½ 74 43½ 46½ Gryder A T8 25000 77-15 ChrlieZee,DelJunco,PddyMuldoon 12
23Jly87-5Hol 1 1/16 :471 1:114 1:443ft 4¼ 116 42½ 53 57 610 Pedroza M A6 25000 76-15 HonorFlag,BigBuckie,ReglSecretrit 6
15Jly87-3Hol 1 :444 1:102 1:382ft *6-5e 1075 2½ 2½ 1hd 42½ Patton D B2 28000 68-14 RoyalAgori,Earthdust,Mr.Edelweiss 8
5Jly87-5Hol 6f :221 :452 1:102ft 13 112 2hd 2½ 21½ 46 Pedroza M A2 28000 85-11 CharlieZee,GrandVizier,Tissr'sBbe 10

Apr 10 SA 4f ft :482 h   Mar 27 SA tr.t 4f ft :51 h

Angle Arc

Ch. g. 5, by Angle Light—Hurry Countess, by Hurry to Market

MEZA R Q — 114 — Br.—Dickey M (Ky) — 1988 4 0 0 0 $475 — **8–1**

Own.—Belmonte-Popovich-Weisbrg — Tr.—Mitchell Mike — $10,500 — 1987 8 0 3 0 $18,475

Lifetime 33 3 7 2 $61,470 — Turf 2 0 0 1 $1,650

28Apr88-2Hol 6f :213 :444 1:10 ft 13 116 1212 99 99 97¾ McCarron C J 4 16000 84-18 FllThDncr,Lrk'sLgcy,Exbrnt'sImg 12
28Apr88—Steadied start
14Apr88-5SA 6½f :212 :442 1:171gd 9¼ 116 78¼ 88¼ 65½ 74¾ McCarron C J 2 16000 79-21 PssAnotherTb,Gossrone,Lrk'sLgcy 12
14Apr88—Wide into stretch
19Mar88-6SA 6f :211 :44 1:093ft 20 116 912 1014 1011 810¼ DelahoussayeE 9 25000 80-18 Fuzzy Bear, Bizeboy, Savio 11
12Mar88-2SA 6f :213 :442 1:092ft 13 116 911 89 69 57½ DelahoussyeE 5 c20000 83-19 Bizeboy, Alitak, Bold And Greene 12
28Jun87-5Hol 1 :454 1:11 1:363ft 7¾ 117 64 75 64 610¼ Vergara O 7 32000 70-12 QulityJet,VisibleAsset,BoldBtterUp 9
17May87-7Hol 6½f :221 :45 1:172ft 20 116 1010 1011 109½ 88¼ DelahoussayeE 1 40000 85-15 Auntie Rose,Pialor,GrowlerSandue 11
17May87—Bumped late
30Apr87-5Hol 7f :214 :444 1:224ft 7 116 66½ 67½ 78¾ 77 McHargue D G 1 50000 83-13 NorthernPolicy,Bizeboy,JttingHom 8
29Mar87-3SA 7f :223 :451 1:221ft 2 117 66 67 47½ 49¾ DelhoussyeE 3 Aw29000 79-18 Decore,NorthernVlor,TimeForSkrto 6
29Mar87—Broke stride 1/2
15Mar87-2SA 6½f :214 :452 1:172ft *3 117 118¼ 109¾ 87¾ 55¾ DelhoussyeE 5 Aw28000 77-20 Don'sIrshMlody,Dvl'sIc,TmFrSkrt 11
15Mar87—Wide final 3/8
28Feb87-9SA 6½f :213 :441 1:163ft 3 116 711 79½ 55 2no DelhoussyeE 4 Aw27000 87-17 Extranix, Angle Arc, Devil's Ice 7

Apr 26 Hol 3f ft :354 h   Apr 21 Hol 3f ft :361 h   Apr 8 Hol 5f ft 1:013 h   Apr 2 Hol 3f ft :362 h

Hovering Presence *

Gr. g. 5, by Dust Commander—Puss in Cahoots, by The Axe II

ORTEGA L E — 115 — Br.—Franzheim Susan Beth (Ky) — 1988 10 0 1 1 $5,425 — **59–1**

Own.—Forster & Rodriguez — Tr.—Rodriguez Hugo — $12,500 — 1987 18 3 1 4 $29,359

Lifetime 53 6 7 7 $79,514 — Turf 2 0 0 1 $1,060

30Apr88-2Hol 1 :461 1:114 1:38 ft 24 116 1213 913 912 916¼ Ortega L E2 12500 57-14 D.D.TheKid,Polysemous,GreyWritr 12
14Apr88-5SA 6½f :212 :442 1:171gd 53 116 1113 99¾ 75¼ 64¼ Ortega L E1 16000 79-21 PssAnotherTb,Gossrone,Lrk'sLgcy 12
6Apr88-9SA 1⅛ :464 1:111 1:494ft 22 1115 44 78½ 916 921¼ Banderas A L4 16000 59-17 Shafy, Amatar, Bigbadandmean 10
26Mar88-1SA 6f :211 :44 1:094ft 7¼ 116 1114 1014 911 910 Olivares F11 c12500 79-17 And Justice, CleverCoin,MasoBlue 12
12Mar88-7GG 6f :214 :443 1:09 ft 12 117 95¼ 87¾ 84¼ 53½ Schacht R3 16000 90-10 CuttingLin,StrtchItOut,BiscynBoy 11
2Mar88-7GG 6f :214 :444 1:102ft 5¾ 117 79¼ 69¾ 56 3½ Schacht R1 12500 86-18 TrojnTrick,Witching,HovringPrsnc 8
20Feb88-5GG 6f :22 :443 1:092ft 9¼ 117 66 74¼ 97¾ 74¾ Hummel C R 5 16000 87-12 Park Road, Witching, Walt 12
6Feb88-3GG 6f :214 :443 1:083ft 7¼ 115 77¾ 78¼ 68 49 Hummel C R 1 22500 87-09 Mr.Medi,AckAck'sJoy,GentlemnJov 7
6Feb88—Wide on turn
26Jan88-7GG 6f :214 :45 1:101ft 16 116 78¼ 65½ 54¼ 21½ Hummel C R 6 18000 86-15 Mr.Medi,HoveringPrsnc,NvdSwingr 7
1Jan88-8BM 1 1/16 :463 1:113 1:444gd 5 115 77 66 58½ 59 Fox W I Jr 3 c14000 59-26 RisedOnStge,IronLdr,OlimpicBingo 8

Apr 26 Fpx 4f ft :583 h

Supreme Legend

Ch. g. 4, by Northern Supremo—Jennis Whistle, by Whistling Kettle

MEZA R Q — 115 — Br.—Heerensperger D (Wash) — 1988 1 0 0 1 $1,500 — **14–1**

Own.—DeMeo Mr-Mrs J — Tr.—Hess R B Jr — $12,500 — 1987 15 2 3 3 $15,920

Lifetime 17 2 3 4 $17,420

16Apr88-7GG 6f :211 :434 1:092ft 46 117 34 45½ 46 43¼ Nicolo P 6 12500 89-13 FrOutPlsr,‡ScootrWfr,MnOfThHor 8
16Apr88—Placed third through disqualification; Bumped 4 1/2
10Dec87-3BM 1 1/16 :47 1:123 1:471m *7-5 119 32½ 33 36 54¾ Castaneda M 1 12500 51-30 GoldenSheng,SwetKing,SpcilBonus 7
29Nov87-5BM 1 1/16 :461 1:101 1:423ft 3¼ 116 54½ 43½ 35 48½ Castaneda M 7 16000 70-15 CourtWizrd,AlDeNskr,SlpyBrigdir 11
29Nov87—Bumped start
7Nov87-6BM 1 :453 1:102 1:36 ft 8¼ 116 44 54¾ 67 57 Castaneda M 2 25000 81-15 LuckyEdton,CrclErly,RllyRndThFlg 7
7Nov87—Stumbled start
22Oct87-6BM 1 1/16 :453 1:102 1:42 ft *2¼ 117 32 54½ 56½ 57 Baze R A 3 c20000 75-15 LuckyEdition,OurStrDncer,NleesPc 8
12Oct87-9BM 1 1/16 :461 1:103 1:431ft 24 117 32 31½ 1hd 13 Castaneda M 11 12500 76-18 SupremeLegend,GoldnShng,Johmr 11
27Sep87-2Lga 6½f :222 :453 1:163ft 4 115 85¾ 910 1015 109½ Hansen R D 1 12500 76-19 Ken'sImge,SpiritOfArch,PepeLGry 12
30Aug87-2Lga 6½f :214 :451 1:17 ft 3¼ 114 913 88¼ 45 22 Hansen R D 11 12500 82-17 Miod'Shib,SuprmLgnd,D.T Exprss 11
23Aug87-1Lga 1 1/16 :483 1:13 1:454ft 3¼ 114 41¾ 41¼ 53½ 31¾ Lamance C 1 12500 68-18 MeridinDncr,RthrOdd,SuprmLgnd 10
9Aug87-6Lga 1⅛ :474 1:13 1:523ft *8-5 114 31½ 31½ 2hd 21½ Lamance C 7 12500 68-21 MeridinDncer,SuprmLgnd,DockStrt 8

Apr 18 GG 6f ft 1:14 h   Apr 4 GG 6f ft 1:164 h   Mar 30 GG 5f ft 1:023 h   Mar 18 GG 5f ft 1:03 h

Special Wagering On Kentucky Derby

Past Performances on Page D-34.

3rd Hollywood (8 Horses)

START — 1 MILE — HOLLYWOOD PARK — FINISH

1 MILE. (1.32⅗) CLAIMING. Purse $33,000. 4-year-olds and upward. Weight, 122 lbs. Non-winners of two races at a mile or over since March 15 allowed 3 lbs.; such a race since then, 6 lbs. Claiming price $50,000; for each $2,500 to $45,000 allowed 2 lbs. (Races when entered for $40,000 or less not considered.)

Scrapbook — 5–1

MCCARRON C J — **116**
Own.—Whiting Mr-Mrs P J

B. g. 5, by Flying Paster—Lady Teela, by Tentam
Br.—Whiting Mr-Mrs P J (Cal)
Tr.—Headley Bruce — **$50,000**
Lifetime 22 4 4 4 $111,325

1988	6	1	0	1		$24,400
1987	3	1	1	0		$28,675
Turf	3	0	0	0		$2,750

25Apr88-9SA	1¼ Ⓣ:463 1:371 2:032 gd	42	115	21½ 85¾ 108¼ 1010	Patterson A12	62500	60-24	Danielli, Point D'Artois, Ataghan	12
9Apr88-9SA	1 1/16 :461 1:104 1:424 ft	4½	115	46 55 67 612	Meza R Q7	62500	75-13	Spacecapiat, Armin, Aloma's Tobin	7
12Mar88-3SA	1 1/16 :471 1:114 1:434 ft	3¾	115	32 41½ 52¾ 33¼	Meza R Q6	62500	79-19	Armin, Bugarian, Scrapbook	8
12Mar88—Crowded 3/8-1/16									
13Feb88-9SA	1 1/16 :464 1:114 1:443 ft	3½	116	44 3½ 2hd 1¾	Meza R Q6	50000	78-22	Scrapbook, Move Free, TokyoBoy	10
23Jan88-6SA	1 1/16 :461 1:102 1:421 ft	18	1105	43½ 53½ 68½ 612	Gryder A T7	Aw44000	78-14	Crimson Slew,CaptainValid,HillsBid	9
2Jan88-7SA	1 1/16 :463 1:103 1:421 ft	13	1115	63¼ 65½ 814 828	Gryder A T3	Aw44000	62-15	PowerForwrd,GrndVizier,CptinVlid	8
2Jan88—Bobbled start									
4Apr87-7SA	1 :47 1:111 1:362 ft	8½	116	64 42 22 1½	ShoemkerW7	Aw35000	86-17	Scrapbook, PrinceO'Fire,Centenary	8
4Apr87—Crowded 1/4									
20Mar87-8SA	1 1/16 :463 1:103 1:414 ft	3¾	116	51¾ 53¼ 55½ 48¼	McCarronCJ6	Aw35000	84-17	JudgeAngelucci,Centenary,October	7
20Mar87—Wide 7/8 turn									
8Mar87-3SA	1 1/16 :452 1:094 1:431 ft	10	116	48½ 56¾ 54½ 23	ShoemkerW3	Aw34000	82-15	Midwest King, Scrapbook, ReEnter	7
25Oct86-7SA	1 1/16 :47 1:12 1:43 ft	2¾	113	73½ 63¾ 68½ 616¾	Meza R Q6	Aw30000	69-17	Magyar, Passer II, Grecian Wonder	8
25Oct86—Lugged out late									

●Apr 22 SA 4f gd :464 h Apr 6 SA 4f ft :484 h ●Apr 1 SA 7f ft 1:253 h Mar 27 SA 7f ft 1:271 h

Claramount * — 4–1

GRYDER A T — **112**
Own.—Gray E S

B. c. 4, by Policeman—Fifties Galore, by Cornish Prince
Br.—Kinderhill Fm & Breeding (NY)
Tr.—Sinne Gerald M — **$45,000**
Lifetime 24 9 6 2 $73,250

1988	7	2	2	1		$37,600
1987	14	5	3	1		$26,812
Turf	2	0	0	0		

27Apr88-5Hol	1 1/16 :464 1:104 1:43 ft	3	116	1½ 2hd 2½ 21¾	Pedroza M A3	40000	83-17	SiberianHero,Clarmount,TokyoBoy	9
16Apr88-5SA	6½f :213 :442 1:161 gd	8	116	2hd 1½ 13 12¾	Pedroza M A10	25000	89-16	Clrmount,SlpprySlvr,SuprbMomnt	12
30Mar88-3SA	6½f :22 :444 1:16 ft	*2½	116	— — — —	Sibille R7	c18000	— —	SocilDimond,BlzingZulu,MstrNvjo	10
30Mar88—Lost rider									
13Mar88-10TuP	1 Ⓣ:463 1:103 1:36 fm	9¼	118	96¾ 84½ 73¼ 75¾	MalgariniTM7	Gvnrs H	95 —	Cpt.BillyBoogi,MnrsvllBluff,Fnncr	11
28Feb88-9SA	1 1/16 :463 1:11 1:434 gd	*2½	115	1hd 21 21 2nk	Sibille R1	32000	82-18	Bananas, Claramount, Jazz Player	8
17Feb88-5SA	6f :213 :443 1:102 ft	15	115	3½ 2hd 2hd 3½	Sibille R6	40000	85-23	LodThWgon,RoylBluEys,Clrmount	12
6Feb88-2SA	6f :214 :444 1:101 ft	5¾	115	31 33 31½ 1nk	Sibille R8	c16000	87-18	Clrmount,Pppy'sConsl,RockEnSm	12
26Sep87-11Fpx	1 1/16 :452 1:103 1:431 ft	9-5	117	45 65¾ 59½ 69¼	Black CA1	Ⓡ Derby Trl	86-11	DistntPl,TempttionTime,Nourishd	10
17Sep87-11Fpx	6½f :204 :443 1:161 ft	32	114	74¾ 74¾ 46 21¼	Stevens S A4	Foothill	94-12	HotAndSmggy,Clrmnt,HppyInSpc	10
5Sep87-5Dmr	1 1/16 Ⓣ:471 1:121 1:43 fm	12	117	68½ 64½ 66½ 67¾	Sibille R3	80000	77-13	CrosLove,ContctGme,PrcDesPrincs	9

●Apr 11 Fpx 5f ft 1:004 h Mar 7 TuP 7f ft 1:26 h

Bugarian — 8–1

SOLIS A — **116**
Own.—Sasselli & Onesian

Dk. b. or br. g. 5, by Fleet Barbarian—Bugscuffle, by British Roman
Br.—Dellinger J C (Cal)
Tr.—Murphy Marcus J — **$50,000**
Lifetime 43 3 5 8 $121,725

1988	5	0	1	0		$11,875
1987	15	1	1	3		$38,875
Turf	3	0	0	1		$4,950

27Mar88-9SA	1 1/16 :462 1:104 1:433 ft	5¾	116	68½ 66¼ 66½ 57¾	Toro F8	50000	75-16	Spacecapiat, Shigamba,OnoGummo	9
12Mar88-3SA	1 1/16 :471 1:114 1:434 ft	20	115	57½ 53 31½ 21	Toro F4	62500	81-19	Armin, Bugarian, Scrapbook	8
12Mar88—Wide, lugged in stretch									
13Feb88-9SA	1 1/16 :464 1:114 1:443 ft	[illegible]	116	910 75¾ 43½ 42½	Ortega L E8	c50000	75-22	Scrapbook, Move Free, TokyoBoy	10
13Feb88—Broke in, bumped									
31Jan88-4SA	1 :462 1:11 1:372 ft	26	115	65½ 56¼ 67¾ 610¾	Meza R Q5	50000	70-21	MoveFree,LastCommnd,QuickTwist	9
31Jan88—Bumped start									
6Jan88-7SA	1 :461 1:104 1:353 ft	22	116	87¼ 65 65¾ 59	Ortega L E3	50000	81-19	GoodTste,LstCommnd,HisHighness	8
6Jan88—Broke in a tangle									
13Dec87-9Hol	1 1/16 Ⓣ:471 1:111 1:422 fm	28	113	96¾ 96¾ 95¾ 88¾	Ortega L E2	55000	73-16	Pinstripe II, Kensof, Centenary	12
18Nov87-3Hol	1 1/16 :464 1:11 1:43 ft	16	116	510 45 34½ 33½	Ortega L E4	50000	84-12	LastCommnd,PowerForwrd,Bugrin	6
1Nov87-9SA	1 1/16 :46 1:10 1:414 m	27	119	31½ 33 54½ 67¾	Ortega L E2	62500	84-12	Sidersell, Gallant Sailor, Bedouin	10
27Sep87-10Fpx	1 1/16 :46 1:103 1:43 ft	8	122	64 56 58 58½	KenlJL4	Ⓡ C B Aflbgh	87-13	ForignLgion,Rcognizd,LstCommnd	9
19Sep87-10Fpx	1 1/16 :48 1:133 1:451 ft	*2¼	121	52¾ 31½ 2hd 12	Kaenel J L2	Aw27000	85-18	Bugarian, Proving Spark, Shrewdy	10

●May 2 Hol 5f ft :582 h ●Apr 26 SA 5f ft :581 h ●Apr 21 SA 4f sy :473 h (d) Apr 16 SA 4f gd :472 h

(Continued on following page)

Shigamba * — PEDROZA M A — 116 — Own.—Sofro D I — * 2–1

Dk. b. or br. g. 5, by Marshua's Dancer—Kinnard, by Verbatim
Br.—Thompson Enterprises (Ky) — 1988 5 0 4 0 $29,200
Tr.—Canani Julio C — $50,000 — 1987 9 2 2 1 $44,800
Lifetime 14 2 6 1 $74,000

20Apr88-7SA	1	:454	1:101	1:353sy	*1	116	11	1hd	1hd	2nk	Stevens G L4	50000	90-17	Rakaposhi, Shigamba, Tres Suave	7
27Mar88-9SA	1 1/16	:462	1:104	1:433ft	5	116	11½	11½	12½	21¼	Stevens G L9	50000	82-16	Spacecapiat, Shigamba,OnoGummo	9
27Feb88-5SA	1⅛	:464	1:112	1:504ft	4	116	11	1hd	24	69	Stevens G L1	Aw38000	66-17	Reland, Millero YMedio,ProudCat	10
7Feb88-5SA	1 1/16	:453	1:103	1:433ft	3¼	119	33	31	2½	22½	Stevens G L8	Aw38000	80-16	Fancy Oats, Shigamba,RedAndBlue	9
17Jan88-7SA	1⅛	:461	1:11	1:504sy	*7-5	118	11½	11½	11½	2¾	Stevens G L4	Aw38000	74-17	Rupperto,Shigamba,MilleroYMedio	9
16Dec87-7Hol	1 1/16	:47	1:113	1:433sy	3¾	115	21	1hd	14	13½	Pedroza MA4	Aw36000	85-21	Shigamb,SpruceSkipper,FstRomeo	7
6Dec87-7Hol	1	:45	1:101	1:371gd	3½	116	1hd	1hd	21½	31¾	Cordero AJr6	Aw35000	75-17	Fanticola, Barnhart, Shigamba	7
15Nov87-9SA	1 1/16	:47	1:113	1:431ft	4¼	117	1½	1hd	11½	22	Pincay L Jr5	32000	83-18	Bedouin, Shigamba, Air Alert	10
28Oct87-2SA	6½f	:214	:444	1:161ft	13	120	1hd	1hd	41½	74	Patterson A3	c25000	85-16	AirAlert,MischivousMtt,WstBoyII	10
28Oct87—Broke in, bumped															
9Oct87-5SA	6f	:213	:443	1:091ft	16	118	52	65	710	714	Patterson A3	40000	78-17	Pialor, Athlone, Native Reality	9

May 4 Hol 4f ft :472 h — Apr 28 Hol 5f ft 1:013 h — ●Apr 12 SA 5f ft :584 h — Apr 6 SA 4f ft :481 b

Extranix — MEZA R Q — 116 — Own.—L 4 Stable–Ustin–Ustin — 7–1

Ch. g. 5, by Transworld—Little Evil, by Tompion
Br.—Elmendorf Farm (Ky) — 1988 3 0 0 0 $3,000
Tr.—Mitchell Mike — $50,000 — 1987 12 3 2 1 $67,755
Lifetime 23 4 5 2 $95,030 — Turf 5 0 0 0 $2,925

9Apr88-9SA	1 1/16	:461	1:104	1:424ft	6	112	1½	1hd	42	46¼	Day P 3	55000	81-13	Spacecapiat, Armin, Aloma's Tobin	7
9Apr88—Lugged out backside															
3Apr88-5SA	a6½f Ⓣ	:212	:44	1:144fm	8	116	22	34	77½	88¼	McCarron C J 1	62500	77-15	Mrvn'sPlcy,GldnGntlt,BmTwnChrl	11
19Mar88-5SA	a6½f Ⓣ	:211	:432	1:141fm	13	118	66½	1012	1112	95¾	Pincay L Jr6	80000	82-10	Illuminux,BigChill,H'sADncingMn	12
19Mar88—Bumped 3/8															
4Oct87-11Fpx	a1⅛	:454	1:104	1:493ft	7	119	85¼	117¾	911	611	Black C A9 Pom Inv H		84-12	He'sASaros,QuickTwist,Emperdori	11
19Sep87-11Fpx	1 1/16	:453	1:113	1:444ft	*9-5	122	910	99½	917	927½	Black C A3 P D Shpd		59-18	He's A Saros, Don B. Blue, Rufjan	9
22Aug87-10LA	1⅛	:463	1:11	1:48 ft	*3-5	121	2½	2½	12	11¾	Black C A4 Ong Cty H		96-11	Extranix,Emperdori,ThalssinoAsteri	4
13Aug87-8LA	1 1/16	:452	1:101	1:413ft	*6-5	118	12	13	18	118	Black C A2 Ⓡ Carrillo		101-12	Extranix, Don Diege, Bugarian	5
8Aug87-10LA	6f	:211	:442	1:101ft	4½	116	811	711	67½	2¾	Black C A2 Ⓡ Dn Bnto		91-13	StepSon,Extranix,He'sADncingMn	10
20Jun87-7Hol	7f	:22	:442	1:224ft	14	119	41½	65½	78½	712	ValenzuelPA5	Aw25000	78-11	TommyTheHwk,FleetSudn DonDieg	8
11Jun87-8Hol	6f	:22	:451	1:093ft	8¼	116	56	66½	710	813½	ValenzuelPA2	Aw25000	81-18	HonkyTonkDancer,Pilor,ThunderCt	8
11Jun87—Bumped start															

May 3 Hol 4f ft :484 b — Apr 28 Hol 5f ft 1:003 h — Apr 23 Hol 5f ft 1:013 h — Mar 28 Hol 5f ft 1:002 h

Fanticola — TORO F — 116 — Own.—Pearlstein L — 7–2

Ro. c. 4, by Hatchet Man—Promising Gal, by Blade
Br.—Pearlstein L (Ky) — 1988 2 0 1 0 $7,000
Tr.—Cross Richard J — $50,000 — 1987 13 3 3 1 $61,025
Lifetime 15 3 4 1 $68,025 — Turf 5 1 0 0 $13,400

23Jan88-7SA	a6½f Ⓣ	:214	:444	1:163fm	4¾	118	88¼	911	911	98¾	Toro F6	Aw35000	67-28	King Hill,Illumineux,JazzMusician	12
10Jan88-5SA	7f	:222	:444	1:221ft	7	117	32	42	32	22	Toro F 7	Aw35000	87-15	ReEnter,Fanticola,Buckland'sHalo	10
6Dec87-7Hol	1	:45	1:101	1:371gd	4	115	56¼	33	32½	11	Toro F 1	Aw35000	77-17	Fanticola, Barnhart, Shigamba	7
22Nov87-6Hol	1	:453	1:10	1:353ft	*2	116	11	1½	1½	1¾	Toro F 7	50000	85-14	Fanticola, Teddy Bear Hug, Darion	7
29Oct87-3SA	1 1/16	:46	1:101	1:42 gd	3½	116	12½	11½	2hd	2½	Toro F 7	50000	90-16	El Tremblor, Fanticola,PatientKing	8
7Oct87-7SA	1	:442	1:093	1:334ft	17	115	611	86¼	713	617¾	Toro F 5	Aw30000	81-10	Salud Y Pesetas, Unicopia Chinati	10
7Oct87—6-wide into drive															
9Sep87-7Dmr	1 1/16 Ⓣ	:48	1:123	1:441fm	3	120	86¾	64¼	62¾	43	Toro F 6	Aw24000	76-21	WishfulThinkr,JohnVgors,BrdDncr	10
23Aug87-9Dmr	1⅛ Ⓣ	:473	1:121	1:493fm	13	1105	1hd	1hd	33	59¼	Gryder A T 2	Aw24000	76-13	Sobek, Feraud, Euphrates	10
12Aug87-7Dmr	1⅛ Ⓣ	:474	1:122	1:50 fm	12	120	1014	1010	85	74½	DelhoussyeE 6	Aw23000	78-17	PoltclAmbtn,CntctGm,LckyHrldH.	10
12Aug87—Hopped in air															
24Jly87-4Hol	1 1/16 Ⓣ	:464	1:112	1:433fm	*2¾	116	74¾	53¼	31½	21¼	Delahoussaye E 2	Mdn	75-20	‡DefiniteSigns,Fnticol,BstOBunch	11
24Jly87—Placed first through disqualification															

May 5 Hol 4f ft :482 hg — Apr 30 Hol 6f ft 1:17 h — Apr 25 Hol 5f ft 1:033 h — Apr 12 SA 6f ft 1:152 h

(12 Horses)

4th Hollywood

START
7 FURLONGS
HOLLYWOOD PARK
FINISH

7 FURLONGS. (1.20⅘) CLAIMING. Purse $18,000. 4-year-olds and upward. Weight, 122 lbs. Non-winners of two races since March 22 allowed 3 lbs.; a race since then, 6 lbs. Claiming price $20,000; if for $18,000 allowed 2 lbs. (Races when entered for $16,000 or less not considered.)

Fairly Omen

Ch. g. 6, by Fairly Certain—Aegean's Omen, by Aegean Isle
Br.—Watarida F (Cal) 1988 2 0 0 1 $3,000
NORTH M J 1115 **Tr.—Neumann Julie** $20,000 1987 13 2 5 2 $34,035 **15–1**
Own.—Okuda & Yaghlegian Lifetime 31 6 6 6 $74,710

16Apr88-9SA 6½f :214 :45 1:164gd 3 116 1½ 2hd 2hd 56½ Stevens G L 1 c16000 79-16 AguRusso,Peppy'sConsul,WstBoyII 9
31Mar88-5SA 6f :214 :443 1:094ft *3½ 116 64½ 56 35 35¾ Stevens G L 6 16000 83-20 ClssicQuicki,RockEnSm,FirlyOmn 12
31Mar88—Broke in a tangle, bumped
11Dec87-9Hol 1 :452 1:10 1:363ft 5¼ 116 3nk 2½ 2hd 3hd Sibille R 11 20000 80-18 Sasebo, Moro Bay, Fairly Omen 11
11Dec87—Bumped late
7Nov87-10BM 1 1/16 :451 1:091 1:412ft 5½ 114 1hd 13 13 22 SchvnevldtCP 1 c18000 83-15 Palestiglio, Fairly Omen, Renzo 8
31Oct87-7BM 6f :223 :454 1:113sl *2¾ 117 43½ 44½ 55 97½ SchvneveldtCP 7 25000 73-28 FinlConflict,‡AckAck'sJoy,Pollinir 11
10Oct87-6BM 6f :223 :451 1:092ft 5½ 117 22 21½ 2½ 21 SchvneveldtCP 2 25000 91-16 Crack'n It,FairlyOmen,AckAck'sJoy 6
26Sep87-6BM 6f :224 :453 1:093ft *8-5 117 42¼ 3½ 1½ 41¾ Diaz A L 5 c20000 89-13 BargainPower,NotbleHost,Crck'nIt 6
6Jun87-7GG 1 :453 1:092 1:351ft 7 116 1½ 1½ 11 21 Diaz A L 4 25000 91-07 BrginStndrd,FirlyOmen,IvrPhillips 10
17May87-7GG 1 :453 1:093 1:35 ft 7½ 114 21 2½ 1½ 33½ Diaz A L 7 22500 89-11 AckLikeM,TommyThoms,FirlyOmn 8
3May87-10GG 6f :211 :44 1:092ft 3¼ 119 76 63¾ 32 24 Diaz A L 2 20000 88-15 ThBrgnHuntr,FrlyOmn,RoylBluEys 10
3May87—Crowded 1/4
Apr 29 Hol 5f ft :593 h Apr 14 SA 3f ft :38 h Apr 9 SA 4f ft :513 h Mar 27 SA 5f ft 1:00 h

*Breu

B. h. 7, by Kuryakin—A Tempo, by Aurreko
Br.—Souza & Quiroz Sras (Brz) 1988 5 0 0 1 $8,375
BANDERAS A L 1115 **Tr.—Stute Melvin F** $20,000 1987 10 1 1 3 $35,475 **5–1**
Own.—Just 4 Fun Lifetime 35 6 3 8 $57,725 Turf 10 1 0 3 $3,439

24Apr88-2SA 6f :22 :451 1:104ft 3¾ 1115 42 42½ 33 31¼ Banderas A L 6 20000 83-14 RockEnSm,FbulousPretender,Breu 8
13Mar88-2SA 6½f :213 :442 1:162ft 12 116 45½ 57 67 56¼ McHrgueDG 11 c32000 82-15 MschvosMtt,TmToSmok,Clff'sPlc 11
28Feb88-5SA 6f :214 :443 1:094gd 12 116 115½108½ 55½ 44¾ McHargue D G 4 32000 84-18 SundnceSqur,RulrOfFlts,NtivRlity 12
28Feb88—Bumped hard start
7Feb88-9SA 1 1/16 :47 1:113 1:434ft 7 116 31½ 31 33½ 45¼ Solis A12 32000 77-16 OnoGummo,SavorFire,SuperPunk 12
7Feb88—Wide 7/8 turn
21Jan88-5SA 1 :461 1:102 1:361ft 11 118 77½ 66¼ 57 510¾ Solis A3 Aw34000 76-19 In Toto, Saker, Great Negotiator 10
21Jan88—Stumbled start
30Dec87-7SA 6f :213 :45 1:103m 5¾ 118 88¼ 54 34 33¾ Solis A4 Aw32000 81-23 Golden Gauntlet, Wily, Breu 9
20Dec87-4Hol 6½f :221 :45 1:163ft 7 117 68 66¾ 63¼ 42 Solis A1 40000 93-08 RisAPound,LuckyMsddo,MjstcIslnd 7
18Jly87-6Hol 1 1/16 :46 1:102 1:421ft 17 116 3½ 31 21½ 21½ Solis A5 50000 96-07 He's A Saros, Breu, PowerForward 8
31May87-5Hol 1 :452 1:103 1:363ft 3½ 117 42 42 21½ 1¾ Pincay L Jr5 40000 80-18 Breu, Nordicus, Lo Card 10
9May87-3Hol 6f :221 :45 1:083ft 4 117 32½ 42¾ 34 47¼ Pincay L Jr5 50000 93-10 MyFvrtMmnt,LckyMsdd,EghtyBlZr 6
May 2 SA 5f ft 1:032 h Apr 19 SA 5f ft 1:003 h Apr 6 SA 6f ft 1:15 h Mar 29 SA 5f ft 1:013 h

Cojak Man *

Dk. b. or br. g. 5, by Cojak—Madinus, by Bupers
Br.—Robertson & Miller (Ky) 1988 4 2 0 0 $15,400
CORRAL J R 1095 **Tr.—Cross David C Jr** $18,000 1987 11 0 2 2 $17,650 **5–1**
Own.—Cross Jr & Garber Lifetime 30 7 4 2 $81,599

21Apr88-9SA 7f :223 :452 1:23 m *2¼ 116 61¾ 41¼ 11½ 15 Sibille R9 c12500 85-17 Cojak Man, Del Junco, Bovig 11
21Apr88—Wide into stretch
15Apr88-1SA 6f :214 :452 1:11 m 4¾ 116 74½ 21½ 21½ 1½ Sibille R11 c10000 83-21 CojkMn,CoursingEgl,BoldTopsidr 12
24Jan88-10SA 1 1/16 :471 1:114 1:434ft 17 116 63¾ 67 914 815¾ Fernandez A L8 32000 66-18 ExoticMotion,L.A.Fire,SiberinHro 10
15Jan88-5SA 6f :213 :45 1:111ft 67 117 87½ 97½ 67 65¼ FernndezAL5 Aw32000 77-20 Yobbo, Chinati, Devil's Ice 12
26Dec87-9SA 1 :454 1:111 1:381ft 18 116 78½ 912 911 89 Castanon AL8 Aw34000 68-16 Syrian Wind,LuckyAdvance,BooW. 10
28Nov87-8Hol 1 1/16 :47 1:112 1:432ft 22 116 3½ 32 23½ 53 Solis A1 Aw35000 83-12 Captain Valid, Be Scenic, Rupperto 7
13Nov87-3SA 7f :223 :453 1:242ft 8¾ 117 1hd 2hd 21 44½ Solis A2 Aw28000 73-22 TimeForSakarto,TokyoBoy,ElCorzo 6
13Nov87—Bumped 1/8
6Nov87-5SA 6f :214 :442 1:102m 33 116 21½ 32½ 32 33 Solis A3 40000 83-24 RaiseAPound,IdealQuality,CojakMn 8
26Mar87-3SA 6½f :221 :452 1:164ft 5¼ 118 2hd 1hd 21½ 24½ McHargue D G8 20000 81-22 SwordPrince,CojakMan,Cmill'sBoy 8
4Mar87-9SA 1 1/16 :463 1:112 1:441ft 5¾ 116 1hd 1½ 21½ 35¼ Kaenel J L1 c16000 75-16 Idol, Oak Tree II, Cojak Man 8
Apr 10 Hol 5f ft 1:01 h Apr 5 Hol 4f ft :482 h Mar 31 Hol 6f ft 1:154 h Mar 25 Hol 5f ft 1:032 h

Urbana Cowboy *

Ch. g. 5, by Raja Baba—Dancing Hostess, by Sword Dancer
Br.—Warner M L (Ky) 1988 5 0 0 1 $6,000
MCCARRON C J 116 **Tr.—Luby Donn** $20,000 1987 21 3 1 1 $41,687 **9–2**
Own.—Salvatore Dr R L Lifetime 47 7 4 5 $95,752 Turf 2 0 0 1 $2,025

10Apr88-2SA 6½f :22 :443 1:16 ft 7½ 116 813 714 711 36½ McCarron C J 1 20000 83-18 SoclDmond,FblosPrtndr,UrbnCwby 8
10Apr88—Wide into stretch
19Mar88-6SA 6f :211 :44 1:093ft 15 116 11171114 89¼ 46¼ McCarron C J 10 25000 84-18 Fuzzy Bear, Bizeboy, Savio 11
19Mar88—Wide into stretch
14Feb88-1SA 7f :223 :453 1:242ft 8¼ 114 1016 912 88¼ 74¼ Ortega L E 3 c18000 74-20 CrystlCutter,Melchip,StrOfAmeric 10
22Jan88-5SA 6½f :213 :443 1:163ft 4 116 12181112 89¼ 44½ Sibille R 8 16000 82-17 GoldenBeu,ClssicQuickie,BumBRy 12
22Jan88—6 wide into drive
16Jan88-1SA 6f :212 :442 1:11 ft 8¾ 116 1014 911 77¾ 64¾ Sibille R 9 20000 78-20 Subito, Rising Pine, Agua Russo 10
16Jan88—Steadied late
11Dec87-9Hol 1 :452 1:10 1:363ft 16 116 1112 66 72¾ 51¼ ‡ Ortega L E 4 20000 79-18 Sasebo, Moro Bay, Fairly Omen 11
‡11Dec87—Dead heat
4Dec87-5Hol 6f :221 :451 1:103ft 21 116 118½119¼118¼ 87¼ Ortega L E 4 25000 82-21 RdwoodBoy,BolgrMgic,CuttingLin 11
4Dec87—Wide
6Nov87-9SA 6½f :213 :444 1:18 m 7 116 816 810 32 14 Ortega L E 6 16000 80-24 UrbnCowboy,RellyHopful,ElDimont 8
6Nov87—Wide into stretch
31Oct87-10SA 1 1/16 :474 1:121 1:443sy 28 1115 911109¼ 910 917½ Sherman A B 2 20000 60-25 Passer II, Bruli's Ante, Tic Nino 10
14Oct87-9SA 6½f :22 :45 1:171ft 23 116 12131211 83¾ 62¾ Ortega L E 12 16000 81-16 RdwoodBoy,FblsPrtndr,MVAndQ. 12
Apr 27 Hol 5f ft 1:01 h Apr 5 SA 4f ft :483 h Mar 28 SA 5f ft 1:004 h Mar 12 SA 5f ft 1:011 h

Exacta wagering.

(Continued on following page)

(Race 4 continued)

Premiere

B. g. 5, by Rare Performer--So What, by Iron Ruler
Br.—Stevens Herbert K (Ky) 1988 7 3 1 0 $30,150 *
OLIVARES F 116 Tr.—Canani Julie C $20,000 1987 3 1 0 0 $7,700
Own.—Gleason L Lifetime 24 8 3 3 $88,549 **8–5**

22Apr88-3GG 6f :231 :44 1:083ft 4¼ 117 54½ 52¾ 3½ 41½ Diaz A L2 32000 94-14 DoctorDkot,SuperbMomnt,ZrMoro 5
22Apr88—Forced wide into drive
2Apr88-9SA 6f :214 :45 1:101ft *9-5 117 64½ 44½ 44½ 21¾ Pincay L Jr4 c25000 85-19 SuperbMoment,Premir,SurdncSqur 8
2Apr88—Wide into stretch
17Mar88-1SA 6½f :22 :451 1:164ft 2¾ 116 53 31½ 11 14 Olivares F4 c16000 86-20 Premiere,WestL'Ouest,MasterNvjo 9
17Mar88—Checked 5/16
9Mar88-3SA 7f :223 :453 1:231ft 6 118 32 33 22½ 11¾ Olivares F10 12500 84-19 Premiere, Rock EnSam,Gossarone 10
12Feb88-1SA 7f :222 :452 1:251ft 6 118 98 98¼ 74 41¾ Olivares F9 12500 72-24 LndseerII,WestL'Ouest,RollAMturl 12
22Jan88-5SA 6½f :213 :443 1:163ft 4¼ 116 1114 99½ 79¼ 66¾ Olivares F7 16000 80-17 GoldenBeu,ClssicQuickie,BumBRy 12
22Jan88—Wide into stretch
9Jan88-1SA 6f :214 :452 1:111ft 14 116 1110 87 63¼ 11¼ ♦ Olivares F4 12500 82-17 Premir,AcksLikRulr,Pppy'sConsul 11
♦ 9Jan88—Dead Heat; Troubled trip
23Dec87-1Hol 7f :231 :471 1:261ft *3 118 84¼ 910 1115 1217¼ McHrgueDG12 c10000 56-19 Zac K., Snappy Band, East Tulip 12
6Dec87-2Hol 6f :222 :453 1:113gd 7½ 116 52¾ 42¾ 42½ 1hd McHargue DG10 10000 84-17 Premier,BoldAndGrn,CoursingEgl 11
17Jan87-1SA 6f :22 :454 1:12 ft 28 117 74¼ 129¼ 126½ 118 McHargue DG11 16000 70-18 West Boy II, Unagloshi, AirPirate 12
Apr 17 SA 5f ft 1:003 h ●Apr 11 SA 4f ft :463 h Mar 27 SA 4f ft :473 h

A Little Speed

Dk. b. or br. c. 4, by Fast—P'Tite Na Na, by Maribeau
Br.—Kochan W H & N J (BC-C) 1988 8 0 2 1 $13,025
SOLIS A 116 Tr.—Mascari James E $20,000 1987 8 2 1 1 $44,260 **18–1**
Own.—Mascari J E Lifetime 22 3 5 4 $68,235

24Apr88-5SA 1 1/16 :46 1:103 1:433ft 16 116 21 52½ 64 69¾ Solis A 9 25000 73-14 Imperious Spirit,‡Shafy,HighTouch 9
16Apr88-3SA 1 1/16 :46 1:104 1:443gd *2¾ 116 12 2hd 21 34 Castanon A L 2 20000 74-16 SensationalStar,Shfy,ALittleSpeed 7
2Apr88-9SA 6f :214 :45 1:101ft 15 116 53 32½ 34½ 45½ Castanon A L 7 25000 81-19 SuperbMoment,Premir,SundncSqur 8
19Mar88-9SA 1 1/16 :46 1:11 1:442ft 45 116 1hd 2hd 11½ 2nk Castanon A L 4 20000 79-18 LmmonJuic,ALttlSpd,ImprousSprt 11
9Mar88-9SA 1 1/16 :464 1:12 1:444ft 8¼ 116 52 54 78½ 79¼ Pedroza M A 9 c16000 68-19 BangBangBang,BlazingZulu,Shafy 12
9Mar88—Wide 7/8 turn; bumped 1/2
21Feb88-9SA 1 1/16 :472 1:122 1:451ft 10 115 2hd 1½ 2hd 22¾ Pedroza M A 2 16000 72-21 EarlieFires,ALittleSpeed,Plestiglio 12
21Feb88—Steadied at 7 1/2
10Feb88-2SA 6f :212 :443 1:102ft 26 115 64½ 55 66 76¾ Pedroza M A 6 25000 79-23 RulrOfFlts,SundncSqur,SmoothBd 10
10Feb88—Wide into stretch
17Jan88-2SA 6f :21 :434 1:093sy 13 1105 66¼ 68½ 811 812½ Gryder A T 6 c20000 77-17 GrowlerSndue,Bizeboy,ElDimonte 10
17Jan88—Veered in start
26Jly87-8EP 1 1/8 :454 1:103 1:492ft 23 122 64½ 62¼ 515 512½ LcrsrLJ 2 [S]AscotSoph 82-13 ReveDu,Snugamish,CaptainShadow 7
11Jly87-8EP 1 1/16 :462 1:11 1:434ft 11 118 54 43½ 68 69 KrasnerS 7 Dogwood H 83-16 Reve Du, Uncle Blan, Snugamish 10
May 2 SA 4f ft :501 h Apr 10 SA 5f ft :593 h Mar 27 SA 5f ft :592 h

Peppy's Consul

B. g. 5, by Cannonade—Blue Clarion, by Proud Clarion
Br.—Little & Hatfield (Ky) 1988 7 1 3 2 $26,825
MCCARRON C J 116 Tr.—Wright Robert $20,000 1987 14 3 3 1 $31,175 **7–1**
Own.—Aldekman—Goldstein—Zamost Lifetime 21 4 6 3 $58,000

16Apr88-9SA 6½f :214 :45 1:164gd *2 118 3½ 1hd 1hd 22½ Pincay L Jr 9 c16000 83-16 AguRusso,Peppy'sConsul,WstBoyII 9
8Apr88-7GG 6f :212 :434 1:092ft 3½ 119 65 69 68½ 44¼ Schacht R 2 Aw17000 88-13 Biscayne Boy, Strelnikoff, Walt 7
5Mar88-2SA 6f :213 :444 1:092ft *8-5 115 43 2½ 21½ 23½ Stevens G L 12 c25000 87-14 ChynnTrpc,Pppy'sCnsl,DshnrblGst 12
10Feb88-7SA 6½f :213 :444 1:171ft *2½ 116 22½ 22 11½ 13 DelahoussyeE 1 c16000 84-30 Pppy'sConsul,RoylAgori,PcfulImg 10
6Feb88-2SA 6f :214 :444 1:101ft 19 116 41½ 43 41½ 2nk DelahoussyeE 10 16000 87-18 Clrmount,Pppy'sConsl,RockEnSm 12
6Feb88—Bumped start
24Jan88-1SA 6½f :221 :453 1:174ft 8 116 63½ 53 32½ 34 Velasquez J 8 16000 77-18 Crck'nIt,RoylAgori,Peppy'sConsul 12
9Jan88-1SA 6f :214 :452 1:111ft *8-5 116 2hd 2hd 1hd 31¼ Sibille R 2 c12500 81-17 Premir,AcksLikRulr,Pppy'sConsul 11
23Dec87-2Hol 6f :222 :461 1:114ft 12 115 65 98¼ 68½ 63¼ Black C A 4 14000 80-19 ElDiamonte,GranTerresto,Melchip 11
23Dec87—Bumped hard start
28Nov87-1Hol 6f :222 :453 1:101ft 2½ 115 1hd 2½ 2hd 1nk Black C A 5 10000 91-13 Peppy'sConsul,BoldAndGrn,GrnPirr 7
22Sep87-13Fpx 6f :222 :462 1:114ft 9½ 116 32½ 51¾ 41¾ 12 Vergara O 4 10000 88-15 Peppy's Consul, Pico P., Valcreon 10
Mar 31 SA 4f ft :473 h

(9 Horses)

5th Hollywood

TURF COURSE
1 MILE
HOLLYWOOD PARK
FINISH
START

1 MILE. (Turf). (1.32⅘) 10th Running of THE SPOTLIGHT HANDICAP (1st Division). $75,000 added. 3-year-olds. By subscription of $100 each, which shall accompany the nomination, $750 additional to start, with $75,000 added, of which $15,000 to second, $11,250 to third, $5,625 to fourth and $1,875 to fifth. Weights, Monday, May 2. Starters to be named through the entry box by closing time of entries. Highweights preferred. A trophy will be presented to the owner of the winner. Closed Wednesday, April 27, with 31 nominations.

*Impatient Charlie

SHERMAN A B — **112** — 32–1

Own.—Armato P

B. c. 3, by Son of Shaka—Dublin Rock, by Dublin Taxi
Br.—Blackwell C A (Eng) — 1988 2 0 0 0 $3,150
Tr.—Cole Peter — 1987 9 2 1 1 $7,581
Lifetime 11 2 1 1 $10,731 — Turf 11 2 1 1 $10,731

6Apr88-8SA a6½f Ⓣ:21 :433 1:15 fm 9¼ 115 1½ 2hd 89 915¼ Sibille R5 Baldwin 69-13 Dr.Brent,AccomplishRidg,GldMusic 9
6Apr88—Run in divisions
16Mar88-8SA 1 Ⓣ:452 1:10 1:354fm 60 115 15 14 1hd 46¼ Sibille R6 Aw42000 90-08 Roberto'sDncer,BlAirDncr,Contmpt 9
16Mar88—Bumped hard start
30Oct87♦5Newmarket(Eng) 5f 1:03 gd 11 98 Ⓣ 2½ Hills G Pottr Nsy H Viviend,ImptientChrlie,MerMlody 17
23Sep87♦1Sandown(Eng) 5f 1:032gd 25 98 Ⓣ 1hd Hills G Oxsht Appr Sny H ImptntChrl,SchlCncrt,ChmmysGrl 14
24Aug87♦4Windsor(Eng) 5f 1:02 gd 16 112 Ⓣ 10 Dawson S Rssl Nsy H ElaYinniMou,MissHys,BrnbyMoor 10
7Aug87♦1Lingfield(Eng) 5f :581gd 10 105 Ⓣ 1113 Fox R Crts Hlt Nrsy H LonelyBech,BllCptin,ProudAndKn 11
15Jly87♦4Yarmouth(Eng) a5f 1:034fm 2¾ 123 Ⓣ 65½ McGloneA Clm 16370 FoxyMusic,ShrpPip,Dolichocephlic 8
10Jly87♦2Lingfield(Eng) 5f :581gd 50 123 Ⓣ 14 Rouse B Fstr Sllng ImpatientChrlie,Ucnbid,NtionsGme 6
25Jun87♦5Goodwood(Eng) 5f 1:031gd 80 123 Ⓣ 7 Rouse B Crvn Sllng TheBurden,KsKyD,FirAndBrimston 7
May 1 SA 5f ft :594 h — Apr 24 SA 1m 1:414 h — Apr 17 SA 4f ft :472 h — Apr 2 SA 4f ft :492 h

White Mischief

MCCARRON C J — **116** — 5–2

Own.—Brant P M

Ch. c. 3, by Roberto—Arachne, by Intentionally
Br.—Brant & Claiborne Farm (Ky) — 1988 3 0 0 0 $1,406
Tr.—Lukas D Wayne — 1987 4 1 0 0 $70,370
Lifetime 7 1 0 0 $71,776 — Turf 3 1 0 0 $70,156

6Apr88-8SA a6½f Ⓣ:21 :433 1:15 fm 7¼ 122 74¾ 65 45 54¼ Pincay L Jr6 Baldwin 80-13 Dr.Brent,AccomplishRidg,GldMusic 9
6Apr88—Run in divisions; 5-wide into drive
16Mar88-8SA 1 Ⓣ:452 1:10 1:354fm *9-5 117 67¾ 77 78 68½ Pincay L Jr3 Aw42000 87-08 Roberto'sDncer,BlAirDncr,Contmpt 9
11Feb88-7SA 1 :463 1:114 1:372ft 3¾ 117 53 85¾ 811 817 Pincay L Jr3 Aw34000 64-23 AllTheePower,JdTrd,GoForBrodwy 8
11Feb88—Bumped start; rank, steadied at 7 1/2
20Nov87-8Hol 1 Ⓣ:462 1:102 1:352fm 17 115 53 53 21½ 13½ SantosJA3 Hst Th Flg 90-11 WhitMischif,KngAlobr,TxsTyphoon 8
20Nov87—Grade III; Run in divisions
8Nov87-4SA 1 :473 1:13 1:41 gd 6 117 52½ 43½ 75 68¾ Shoemaker W7 Mdn 54-25 KingAlobar,PureExpense,GldMusic 8
8Nov87—Broke out, bumped
26Oct87-4Aqu 7f :224 :454 1:252ft 10e 118 94 98¾ 56½ 41¾ Cordero A Jr 7 Mdn 72-21 TemperteBlnce,‡IntrpidVoygr,Syrt 13
14Sep87-5Bel 6f :221 :452 1:084gd 18 118 610 79 712 615 Cordero A Jr4 Mdn 80-13 SuccssExprss,SunrsShowr,ZWorld 10
May 2 Hol 5f ft 1:003 h — Apr 17 SA 5f ft 1:013 h — Mar 11 SA 5f ft 1:013 h

Bel Air Dancer

GRYDER A T — **117** — * 9–5

Own.—Sultan A

B. g. 3, by Sovereign Dancer—Choke Cherry, by Connaught
Br.—Byrne J J (Ky) — 1988 6 2 2 0 $52,375
Tr.—Lewis Craig A — 1987 4 M 1 2 $11,550
Lifetime 10 2 3 2 $63,925 — Turf 1 0 1 0 $8,400

23Apr88-8GG 1⅛ :46 1:101 1:482gd 4½ 115 43½ 42½ 34 28 † Sibille R 3 Calif Dby 83-19 AllTheePower,‡BelAirDncer,Slwbop 9
23Apr88—Grade II; Drifted out 3/16; drifted in late; †Disqualified and placed ninth
9Apr88-8GG 1¹⁄₁₆ :46 1:092 1:402ft 3 115 22 33 34 23½ Doocy T T 3 Sausalito 93-09 Charlie'sNotes,BelAirDncer,Chillon 5
16Mar88-8SA 1 Ⓣ:452 1:10 1:354fm 2½ 120 57½ 34½ 2hd 2hd Stevens G L 1 Aw42000 96-08 Roberto'sDncer,BlAirDncr,Contmpt 9
16Mar88—Rank, bumped
6Mar88-6SA 1 :452 1:104 1:363ft 7 119 43½ 1½ 11½ 11 Stevens G L 8 Aw34000 85-13 BlArDncr,Smb'sGold,GoForBrodwy 8
24Jan88-4SA 1¹⁄₁₆ :472 1:124 1:443ft 13 1125 42 42 12½ 19 Gryder A T 9 Mdn 78-18 Bel AirDancer,Addie'sBro,SkyHigh 12
24Jan88—Rough trip
18Jan88-4SA 6f :22 :451 1:112m *1 118 53 64¼ 55 56¼ DelhoussyeE 7 Mc40000 75-17 Nskrem,CrverRod,GodKnowsWho 12
18Jan88—Wide late
6Dec87-6Hol 6f :214 :452 1:10 gd 3¾ 118 55½ 44½ 58½ 515¼ Delahoussaye E6 Mdn 77-17 Sam Who, All Thee Power Stalwars 8
6Dec87—Lugged in
15Nov87-6SA 7f :223 :46 1:234ft *2¾ 117 11½ 1hd 2hd 21¼ Pincay L Jr4 Mdn 80-18 AbbyB.Runnr,BlArDncr,OurNtvWsh 8
1Nov87-6SA 6f :213 :45 1:11 m 4¾ 119 33 22½ 34½ 34 Stevens G L9 Mdn 79-12 GrnMusico,SweetNGo,BelAirDncr 10
1Nov87—Steadied 5 1/2
17Oct87-6SA 6f :221 :453 1:103ft 32 117 77¼ 55½ 47 37 Baze R A5 Mdn 78-16 ProspctorsGmbl,Ovrbrok,BlArDncr 9
17Oct87—Took up start
May 1 Hol 5f ft 1:014 h — Apr 16 GG 5f ft :592 h — Apr 2 SA 5f ft 1:003 h — Mar 25 SA 6f ft 1:131 h

Exacta wagering.

(Continued on following page)

(Race 5 continued)

Blade Of The Ball Dk. b. or br. c. 3, by Highland Blade—Tusi Bella, by Better Bee
ORTEGA L E 113 Br.—King H G III (Ky) 1988 4 0 0 0
Tr.—Stute Melvin F 1987 9 2 2 2 $64,375 **50–1**
Own.—Abtahi(Lse)-Brown-Brown Lifetime 13 2 2 2 $64,375 Turf 2 0 0 1 $14,625
6Apr88-5SA a6½f Ⓣ:212 :4341:142fm 30 114 77½ 76¾ 78¾ 89 Ortega L E 7 Baldwin 78-13 ExclsvNryv,ProspctrsGmbl,Mhmtsk 9
6Apr88—Run in divisions
10Feb88-8SA 1 1/16 :472 1:123 1:432ft 84 114 76 76¾ 611 618¼ VelsquzJ 7 Ⓡ Sta Ctlna 66-23 Lively One, Stalwars, Havanaffair 9
10Feb88—Wide into stretch
24Jan88-8BM 1 1/16 :451 1:091 1:392ft 21 117 67½ 710 917 923 CstnAL 5 El Cm Rl Dy 72-15 Ruhlmann,Havanaffair,ChineseGold 9
24Jan88—Grade III
13Jan88-8SA 1 :46 1:104 1:371ft 5 114 76 66 88 810¼ VelasquezJ 9 Ⓡ Los Flz 72-20 PleaseRemit,SweetNGo,GldMusic 10
20Nov87-5Hol 1 Ⓣ:4741:1121:36 fm 10 115 411 47½ 45¾ 34½ OrtegLE 3 Hst Th Flg 82-11 PurdueKing,ChinesGold,BldOfThBll 6
20Nov87—Grade III; Run in divisions
8Nov87-9BM 1 1/16 :47 1:11 1:422ft 2¾ 114 86 73¾ 44 47 Ortega LE 7 Cal Juv 73-14 FlyingVictor,Skr'sJourny,Cougrizd 11
8Nov87—Grade III
18Oct87-10BM 1 :463 1:113 1:37 ft 11 115 811 74 32 21 OrtegLE 9 Sn Mto Mle 82-18 ChineseGold,BldeOfThBll,Rb'sNturl 9
24Sep87-11Fpx 6½f :21 :452 1:183ft *6-5 122 55½ 55½ 44½ 33¾ Black C A 4 Beau Brml 79-16 SureSwift,ChiefSol,BladeOfTheBall 6
18Sep87-7Fpx 6½f :21 :46 1:184ft *4-5 114 41¾ 1hd 1hd 13½ Black C A 1 Aw24000 82-18 BldeOfTheBll,RdHrbor,Brbrin'sOwn 9
19Aug87-9LA 6½f :213 :462 1:18 ft *4-5 114 31 1hd 11 2no OrtegaLE 6 Saddleback 87-12 WellPlnned,BldeOfTheBll,Winnrwld 6
May 5 Hol 4f ft :462 h ●Apr 25 Hol 6f ft 1:131 h ●Apr 19 Hol 6f ft 1:132 h Apr 13 Hol 5f ft 1:022 h

Balote Dk. b. or br. c. 3, by Fappiano—Toque Rouge, by Tarboosh
SIBILLE R 115 Br.—Waldemar Fms Inc & Robins (Fla) 1988 2 2 0 0 $18,700 **8–1**
Tr.—Drysdale Neil 1987 4 1 1 1 $21,150
Own.—Universal Stable Lifetime 6 3 1 1 $39,850
15Apr88-8GG 6f :212 :441 1:091ft *1-3 120 77 52¾ 32 12½ Baze R A7 Aw18000 93-20 Balote,Haveasilverbullet,ValleyLnd 7
25Mar88-7GG 6f :214 :441 1:091ft *2-5 117 2½ 1hd 11½ 16 Baze R A7 Aw16000 93-12 Balote,ChristmasHelp,Gunnabesint 7
8Nov87-7SA 7f :22 :452 1:243gd 4½ 116 2½ 44 56½ 510½ DelhoussyeE7 Fly Pstr 66-25 Tsarbaby, Jeanne Jones, SureSwift 7
8Nov87—Wide into stretch
28Oct87-7SA 6f :214 :444 1:10 ft *4-5 120 31 2½ 21 34½ DelhoussyeE7 Aw27000 83-16 Mr.GamePlayer,HardToMiss,Blote 10
7Oct87-6SA 6f :22 :444 1:092ft *3-5 117 2½ 1½ 12 14 Delahoussaye E3 Mdn 91-10 Balote, Toughness, Jet Pro 10
7Oct87—Crowded, bumped hard at 3 1/2
18Jly87-4Hol 6f :221 :453 1:102ft *2-3 117 41½ 11½ 12 22 Delahoussaye E8 Mdn 89-07 Bold Second, Balote, Running Over 8
Apr 10 Hol 6f ft 1:144 h Apr 5 Hol 6f ft 1:144 h Mar 31 Hol 3f ft :372 h Mar 21 Hol 5f ft 1:004 h

Greager ✕ B. g. 3, by Peleax—Candy Canyon, by Canyonland
LAMBERT J 116 Br.—Arterburn & Jackson (Cal) 1988 6 3 0 0 $53,950 **7–1**
Tr.—Arterburn Jack 1987 4 2 0 1 $17,950
Own.—ArterburnorArterburn&Wong Lifetime 10 5 0 1 $71,900 Turf 1 1 0 0 $13,200
23Apr88-6GG 1 Ⓣ:4811:1241:383yl 3 121 53½ 54 32½ 12 Lambert J 6 HcpO 74-30 Greager, Chillon, A Perfect Sham 6
9Apr88-8GG 1 1/16 :46 1:092 1:402ft 7 119 56½ 58½ 511 512¼ Lambert J 4 Sausalito 85-09 Charlie'sNotes,BelAirDncer,Chillon 5
12Mar88-8GG 1 :451 1:091 1:342ft 8-5 123 64¼ 54¾ 54½ 55¼ LmbrtJ 5 Ⓡ Lafyte Iv H 91-10 Chrlie'sNotes,Chillon,ProveSplndid 7
12Mar88—Steadied 1st turn
15Feb88-6GG 1 :45 1:091 1:351ft 3¾ 120 56½ 42¼ 11½ 19 Lambert J 3 HcpO 92-10 Greager, Distant Blade, Chillon 6
24Jan88-8BM 1 1/16 :451 1:091 1:392ft 6 117 813 812 715 619 LmbertJ 7 El Cm Rl Dy 76-15 Ruhlmann,Havanaffair,ChineseGold 9
24Jan88—Grade III
2Jan88-10BM 1 :451 1:11 1:371sy 3¼ 116 56½ 42½ 13 17 Lambert J 3 Determine 82-26 Greager, Blue Guy, Sweet N Go 8
10Dec87-8BM 1 :462 1:123 1:384m 3 117 68½ 42½ 21 12 Lambert J 4 Aw17000 74-30 Greager, Officer'sChoice,SilverSass 7
10Dec87—Fractious gate
21Nov87-8BM 6f :221 :452 1:113gd *6-5 117 74¾ 54¾ 32 3nk Lambert J 7 Aw17000 81-19 OverDuePlesure,HeirToGold,Greger 7
28Oct87-6BM 6f :221 :453 1:104sy 7½ 118 68 25 1½ 17 Lambert J 6 M32000 85-26 Greager, First David, Co Ack 8
27Sep87-9BM 6f :223 :452 1:103ft 21 118 98 86¼ 76¼ 76½ Lambert J 9 Mdn 79-10 HndsomHsIt,OvrDuPlsur,SlfTught 12
27Sep87—Broke in a tangle; lugged out on turn
May 5 Hol 4f ft :511 h Apr 21 GG 4f gd :493 h Apr 4 GG 5f ft 1:014 h Mar 29 GG 5f ft 1:012 h

Prospectors Gamble Ro. c. 3, by Crafty Prospector—Fannie C, by Sunny South
PEDROZA M A 117 Br.—Happy Valley Farm (Fla) 1988 6 2 3 0 $64,850 **3–1**
Tr.—Mayberry Brian A 1987 5 1 2 0 $22,925
Own.—Siegel Jan-M-Samantha Lifetime 11 3 5 0 $87,775 Turf 1 0 1 0 $11,250
27Apr88-8Hol 7f :213 :442 1:221ft 3½ 117 52¼ 52 42 23 McCrronCJ5 Debonair 90-17 Claim, ProspectorsGamble,Dr.Brent 7
27Apr88—Rough start
6Apr88-5SA a6½f Ⓣ:212 :4341:142fm*8-5 117 1hd 2hd 1hd 21¾ Solis A9 Baldwin 85-13 ExclsvNryv,ProspctrsGmbl,Mhmtsk 9
6Apr88—Run in divisions
16Mar88-8GG 6f :212 :433 1:082ft *4-5 120 32½ 32 2hd 14 Castaneda M6 HcpO 97-13 ProspctrsGmbl,LckySn'S,HrdTMss 6
15Feb88-8GG 6f :213 :434 1:074ft 2¾ 119 12 1½ 2hd 21½ Solis A5 Gldn Bear 98-10 Chrl'sNots,PrspctrsGmbl,HstyPsty 5
24Jan88-8SA 6f :212 :442 1:093ft 14 118 2hd 1½ 12½ 13½ Solis A10 Aw32000 90-18 PrspctrsGmbl,SmWh,GryLnExprss 10
8Jan88-5SA 6f :212 :441 1:094ft 7 118 63¼ 78½ 67½ 69¾ ShoemkerW6 Aw32000 79-19 Overbrook, Gran Musico,TemperT. 10
18Nov87-7Hol 6½f :214 :442 1:164ft 3½ 119 2½ 22 24 24½ Vasquez J1 Aw25000 89-12 Bolsure, Prospectors Gamble, Pain 9
28Oct87-7SA 6f :214 :444 1:10 ft 24 120 63½ 66 56½ 57½ Espino G G6 Aw27000 80-16 Mr.GamePlayer,HardToMiss,Blote 10
28Oct87—Broke slowly; lugged in stretch
17Oct87-6SA 6f :221 :453 1:103ft 12 117 11 12½ 13 14½ Espino G G6 Mdn 85-16 ProspctorsGmbl,Ovrbrok,BlArDncr 9
17Oct87—Hopped in air
7Sep87-4Dmr 6f :22 :451 1:10 ft 3 117 11½ 3½ 31½ 48½ McHargue D G6 Mdn 79-14 ScrtMtng,SwtchCods,MonMdnssl 11
7Sep87—Lugged out 1/4
Apr 17 SA 5f ft 1:004 h Mar 31 SA Ⓣ 4f fm :513 h Mar 12 SA 4f ft :482 b

Copyright © 1989, by DAILY RACING FORM, INC.
Reprinted with permission of copyright owner.

(8 Horses)

6th Hollywood

1 1/16 MILES. (1.40) ALLOWANCE. Purse $34,000. 4-year-olds and upward which have not won $3,000 other than maiden, claiming or starter. Weight, 120 lbs. Non-winners of a race other than claiming at a mile or over since March 15 allowed 3 lbs.; such a race since February 15, 6 lbs.

Northern Valor

Ro. h. 5, by Northern Jove—Valarris, by Jerry Crow
PEDROZA M A 114 **Br.—Nor Joanne H (Ky)** 1988 1 0 1 0 $7,200 — **5–2**
Tr.—Nor Fabio 1987 9 1 1 2 $24,050
Own.—Nor Joanne H **Lifetime 18 2 3 4 $51,150** **Turf 2 0 0 0**

13Apr88-7SA 1 :452 1:111 1:373ft 8¾ 116 67¼ 53 51¾ 22½ Velasquez J 7 Aw36000 77-22 Rfel'sDncer,NorthrnVlor,DsrtClssic 7
13Apr88—Lugged in
6Sep87-9Dmr 1 1/16 :451 1:092 1:414ft 10 116 58 33½ 2½ 11¾ McHargue D G 2 40000 91-17 NorthernValor,PowerForwrd,LeCid 9
6Sep87—Lugged in stretch
16Aug87-9Dmr 1 1/16 :452 1:101 1:424ft 20 116 32 2½ 22½ 33½ McHargue D G 6 32000 82-11 Convncng,PowrForwrd,NorthrnVlor8
29Jly87-7Dmr 6½f :22 :45 1:162ft 51 116 96¾ 98¾ 811 811 McHargue D G 1 40000 79-17 Pialor, Mondanite, Lo Card 12
27Jun87-7GG 6f :212 :44 1:093ft 14 119 86¾ 99 118¾116½ WarrenRJJr 12 Aw15000 84-10 LodThWgon,NotblHost,PruvinBld 12
3May87-5Hol 7f :22 :45 1:231ft 6¾ 116 1hd 2hd 53¼ 58½ ValenzuelPA 3 Aw22000 79-15 Fracoza, Baby Slewy, Mondanite 7
24Apr87-7Hol 6f :221 :452 1:091ft 7 116 31 32½ 23 38 ValenzuelPA 6 Aw22000 89-12 Superoyale, Athlone,NorthernValor 6
24Apr87—Bumped 1/2; lugged in
9Apr87-5SA a6½f Ⓣ:213 :4341:142fm 4½ 118 43 44 45½ 65 Toro F 9 Aw29000 82-09 Rinnegato, Recognized, Mondanite 9
29Mar87-3SA 7f :223 :451 1:221ft 5¼ 117 31½ 32 22 25 ValenzuelPA 4 Aw29000 84-18 Decore,NorthernVlor,TimeForSkrto 6
15Mar87-2SA 6½f :214 :452 1:172ft 95 117 54 66 45 66 Solis A 2 Aw28000 77-20 Don'sIrshMlody,Dvl'sIc,TrrFrSkrt 11
May 5 Hol 3f ft :371 h Apr 28 Hol 5f ft 1:003 h Apr 22 Hol 3f ft :362 h Apr 7 Hol 7f ft 1:294 h

Old Shanty Town

Dk. b. or br. c. 4, by Kennedy Road—Silverthrill, by Successor
CASTANON A L 114 **Br.—Wacker & Whittingham (Cal)** 1988 6 0 0 0 $5,100 — **27–1**
Tr.—Murphy Marcus J 1987 12 2 1 2 $31,400
Own.—Blau-Sigband-Willis Etal **Lifetime 18 2 1 2 $36,500** **Turf 2 0 0 0**

24Apr88-5SA 1 1/16 :46 1:103 1:433ft 10 1115 89 77½ 76¼ 712¼ Sherman A B 4 c25000 70-14 Imperious Spirit,‡Shafy,HighTouch 9
12Mar88-3SA 1 1/16 :471 1:114 1:434ft 15 1085 68 65 86¾ 89¼ Sherman A B 1 55000 73-19 Armin, Bugarian, Scrapbook 8
12Mar88—Bumped start; wide into stretch
25Feb88-5SA 1⅛ Ⓣ:4611:1041:504fm 9¾ 117 89½ 97 107 96¾ Pincay L Jr 9 Aw34000 66-27 All Cat, Sharp Choice, Dernis D. 12
25Feb88—Lugged in 3/8turn
17Feb88-7SA 1 1/16 :462 1:113 1:444ft 21 117 119¾ 75¾ 53½ 44½ Pincay L Jr 3 Aw34000 72-23 Saker,CarolinaNorth,DesertClassic 12
30Jan88-7SA 1¼ Ⓣ:46 1:3812:044fm 20 1115 21 31½ 57 712¼ Sherman AB 8 Aw34000 51-30 ProudCat,HotStge,StelliteExpress 12
21Jan88-5SA 1 :461 1:102 1:361ft 39 1125 88½ 76¼ 45½ 48¼ Sherman AB 7 Aw34000 79-19 In Toto, Saker, Great Negotiator 10
21Jan88—Lugged in stretch
16Dec87-5Hol 1 :451 1:111 1:374sy 3½ 116 614 58 66½ 55½ Black C A 5 50000 68-21 Boo W., Splendor Catch, Darion 7
2Dec87-9Hol 1 1/16 :46 1:112 1:442ft 6 1085 79¾ 52½ 12½ 14½ Sherman A B 7 35000 81-16 OldShntyTown,Gunbrst,Yo'rGloros 8
19Nov87-5Hol 1 1/16 :463 1:113 1:444ft 19 1145 31½ 31½ 21 2¾ Sherman A B 8 32000 78-14 ExotcEgl,OldShntyTown,P.T.Hustlr 9
19Nov87—Wide 7/8 turn
15Oct87-4SA 1 1/16 :463 1:113 1:45 ft 9½ 1125 31 31½ 11 11¼ Sherman AB 11 M32000 76-19 OldShntyTown,RoylRinger Ludwig 12
●May 5 Hol 3f ft :341 h Apr 30 Hol 5f ft 1:004 h Apr 18 SA 6f ft 1:163 h Apr 12 SA 5f ft 1:03 h

Desert Classic

Dk. b. or br. h. 5, by Damascus—Classic Perfection, by Never Bend
BLACK C A 114 **Br.—Winchell V H (Ky)** 1988 6 0 0 3 $20,850 — **7–1**
Tr.—Gosden John H M 1987 2 0 0 0 $600
Own.—V H W Stables (Lessee) **Lifetime 12 1 0 3 $36,275** **Turf 1 0 0 0**

13Apr88-7SA 1 :452 1:111 1:373ft 10 116 55¾ 42½ 41¾ 32¾ Black C A 5 Aw36000 77-22 Rfel'sDncer,NorthrnVlor,DsrtClssic 7
19Mar88-7SA 1 1/16 :462 1:111 1:433ft 5 117 32 32½ 34½ 44¼ Black C A 6 Aw36000 79-18 Thirty Grand,Canaide,CrystalCutter 7
19Mar88—Bumped start
2Mar88-5SA 1 1/16 :463 1:11 1:43 gd 15 117 96¼ 95¾ 65½ 35¾ Black C A 8 Aw34000 80-17 Rakaposhi,ExoticEgle,DesertClssic 9
17Feb88-7SA 1 1/16 :462 1:113 1:444ft 45 117 97¾ 96¾ 75 34¼ Black C A 11 Aw34000 72-23 Saker,CarolinaNorth,DesertClassic 12
30Jan88-7SA 1¼ Ⓣ:46 1:3812:044fm 6 118 43½10111118112¼ McCarronCJ 7 Aw34000 37-30 ProudCat,HotStge,StelliteExpress 12
30Jan88—Lugged in backstretch
6Jan88-5SA 1 1/16 :472 1:122 1:453ft 7 118 54½ 52¾ 32¼ 4½ Toro F 2 Aw34000 72-19 DnceForLee,NoblNthn,CirclViwDriv 8
26Dec87-9SA 1 :454 1:111 1:381ft 13 116 67 77½ 88½ 77¼ Toro F 3 Aw34000 70-16 Syrian Wind,LuckyAdvance,BooW. 10
12Jly87-5Hol 1 :45 1:093 1:35 ft 9½ 118 22 43½ 57 59 Toro F 5 Aw24000 79-09 CIticRlity,MrkChip,PoliticlAmbiton 7
14May86-7Hol 1 :452 1:104 1:354ft 2½e 120 76¾ 53¼ 35 46½ Toro F 3 Aw22000 77-14 Buckland'sHalo,RaiDen,Hlo'sSword 7
14May86—Bumped, pinched back start
4May86-6Hol 1 :444 1:103 1:371ft *2½ 122 89¾ 79 38½ 46½ McCarronCJ 6 Aw22000 70-18 Tourismo,SouthernHalo,CutByGlss 8
May 2 SA 5f ft 1:012 h Apr 26 SA 4f ft :49 h Apr 10 SA 4f ft :49 h Apr 4 SA 4f ft :48 h

No exacta wagering.

(*Continued on following page*)

(Race 6 continued)

Delegant

SHERMAN A B	**120**	Gr. c. 4, by Grey Dawn II—Dahlia, by Vaguely Noble
Own.—Hunt N B		Br.—Hunt N B (Ky)
		Tr.—Whittingham Charles

	1988	1 1 0 0	$16,500
	1987	5 M 0 2	$7,009
Lifetime 6 1 0 2 $23,509	Turf	5 0 0 2	$7,009

1—1 ⭑

17Apr88-6SA 1¹⁄₁₆:46 1:11 1:43²ft 23 118⁵ 87½ 2² 11½ 1⁴ Sherman A B² Mdn 84-17 Delegant,Exceller'sSpecil,Dupond 10
  17Apr88—Veered in, bumped; bore out 7/8
28Jly87◆2StCloud(Fra) a1½ 2:40 gd 13 121 ⓣ 8¹¹ DbrocqG Px Mntenon ThriftyLd,NorthernDisciple,Mirnshr 8
21Jun87◆5Toulouse(Fra) a1½ : gd — 117 ⓣ 11 Lee C G P Vlle dTou Soldouna, Meteil, Ashumet 12
  21Jun87—No time taken
4Jun87◆2Chantilly(Fra) a1½ 2:40¹yl 6 124 ⓣ 3⁴ Lee C Px dCntble(Mdn) Ashumet, Hoppner, Delegant 15
22May87◆5StCloud a1½ 2:46²sf 15 118 ⓣ 3⁴ Lee C Px Mistral Prince Forest,ThriftyLad,Delegant 24
3May87◆2Longchamp(Fra) a1¼ 2:11²gd 7 120 ⓣ 4³½ Lee C Px dGblns(Mdn) Jalaajel,ShrpYouth,ProspectF>ture 9
May 4 Hol 5f ft 1:01⁴ h   **Apr 28 Hol 6f ft 1:14³ h**   **Apr 23 SA 3f ft :35¹ h**   **Apr 14 SA 4f ft :49⁴ h**

Wily

CORRAL J R	**109⁵**	Dk. b. or br. g. 4, by On the Sly—Miss Dottie Bee, by West Coast Scout
Own.—Landers A W		Br.—Jenkins Brothers (Ky)
		Tr.—Morris Bill

1988	7 0 1 0	$7,600
1987	6 1 2 1	$22,125
Lifetime 13 1 3 1 $29,725		

10—1

23Apr88-8SA 7f :22¹ :45¹ 1:23 m 23 112⁵ 87 63¾ 45½ 2¾ Corral J R³ Aw34000 84-15 CheyenneTropic,Wily,PrimConcord 8
13Mar88-2SA 6½f :21³ :44² 1:16²ft 50 116 77¾11¹⁵101⁵101⁶¾ Ortiz M F Jr⁵ 32000 71-15 MschvosMtt,TmToSmok,Cliff'sPlc 11
3Mar88-7SA 6½f :21³ :44⁴ 1:16⁴ft 24 118 77¾ 85½ 67½ 68½ Castanon AL² Aw32000 78-19 Penasco, Everso, Vysotsky 10
19Feb88-7SA 6½f :21³ :44⁴ 1:16⁴ft 33 117 7¹² 78½ 56½ 57¾ Castanon AL¹ Aw32000 78-23 L. B. Jaklin, UnderAndOver,Chinati 7
  19Feb88—Bumped start; wide in drive
3Feb88-7SA 1¹⁄₁₆:46² 1:10⁴ 1:44 ft 21 116 6¹⁰ 69½ 68½ 6¹²½ Castanon AL⁶ Aw32000 68-20 Relnd,KentuckyStr,CircleViewDrive7
  3Feb88—Lugged out, wide
21Jan88-5SA 1 :46¹ 1:10² 1:36¹ft 14 117 10¹³ 88½ 79½ 7¹²½ Hawley S⁸ Aw34000 75-19 In Toto, Saker, Great Negotiator 10
  21Jan88—Broke slowly
15Jan88-5SA 6f :21³ :45 1:11¹ft 4½ 116 12¹⁰12¹⁰11¹¹ 76½ Hawley S⁹ Aw32000 75-20 Yobbo, Chinati, Devil's Ice 12
30Dec87-7SA 6f :21³ :45 1:10³m 44 116 9¹⁴ 97 45½ 21¾ Castanon AL³ Aw32000 83-23 Golden Gauntlet, Wily, Breu 9
  30Dec87—Bobbled start, steadied at 1/8
21Mar87-7SA 1¹⁄₁₆:47 1:11⁴ 1:43⁴sy 7½ 115 55 67½ 59 59½ Sibille R¹ Aw31000 72-16 Candi's Gold, Reland, Rakaposhi 6
19Feb87-4SA 1¹⁄₁₆:46¹ 1:10⁴ 1:43²ft 6 118 4² 3½ 1hd 11½ ValenzuelaPA⁵ M50000 84-13 Wily, Gold Room, Exotic Eagle 7
  19Feb87—Stumbled at start
● **Apr 20 SA 3f sy :36¹ h (d)**   **Apr 16 SA 4f gd :49² h**

Fleetspur

OLIVARES F	**114**	B. g. 4, by Fleet Twist—Ronnie S, by Outing Class
Own.—Bronson Mr–Mrs M M		Br.—Reilly J H (Cal)
		Tr.—Canani Julio C

1988	2 1 0 0	$11,000
1987	0 M 0 0	
Lifetime 2 1 0 0 $11,000		

13—1

23Apr88-8SA 7f :22¹ :45¹ 1:23 m 6½ 117 2¹ 31 68½ 6¹³½ Olivares F⁴ Aw34000 72-15 CheyenneTropic,Wily,PrimConcord 8
25Mar88-4SA 6f :21³ :45¹ 1:10¹ft 3½ 118 2¹ 2½ 11½ 12½ Olivares F⁵ ⓢM45000 87-18 Fleetspur, Eagle Dive, Adios Girl 12
● **Apr 22 SA 3f gd :34³ h**   **Apr 14 SA 6f ft 1:15² h**   **Apr 8 SA 5f ft 1:00¹ h**   **Mar 20 SA 6f ft 1:14³ h**

Willie N Waylon

SIBILLE R	**114**	Dk. b. or br. c. 4, by Master Willie—Street Ballet, by Nijinsky II
Own.—Aubin G J (Lessee)		Br.—Taylor E P (Md)
		Tr.—Moreno Henry

1988	3 1 0 0	$18,100
1986	0 M 0 0	
Lifetime 3 1 0 0 $18,100		

7—1

23Apr88-8SA 7f :22¹ :45¹ 1:23 m 3½ 120 43 74½ 7¹⁶ 72⁴½ Pedroza MA¹ Aw34000 61-15 CheyenneTropic,Wily,PrimConcord 8
13Apr88-7SA 1 :45² 1:11¹ 1:37³ft *8-5 116 1hd 11 2hd 44 Pedroza MA³ Aw36000 76-22 Rfel'sDncer,NorthrnVlor,DsrtClssic 7
30Mar88-6SA 6½f:22 :45 1:16⁴ft 8 120 2hd 1½ 12½ 12½ Pedroza M A³ Mdn 86-18 WllNWylon,ExcptnlTlnt,MrkOfCzr 10
May 5 Hol 4f ft :49⁴ h   **Apr 29 Hol 3f ft :37 h**   **Apr 5 SA 1f ft 1:41² h**   **Mar 28 SA 3f ft :35³ hg**

(9 Horses)

7th Hollywood

TURF COURSE
1 MILE
HOLLYWOOD PARK
FINISH START

1 MILE. (Turf). (1.32%) 10th Running of THE SPOTLIGHT HANDICAP (2nd Division). $75,000 added. 3-year-olds. By subscription of $100 each, which shall accompany the nomination, $750 additional to start, with $75,000 added, of which $15,000 to second, $11,250 to third, $5,625 to fourth and $1,875 to fifth. Weights, Monday, May 2. Starters to be named through the entry box by closing time of entries. Highweights preferred. A trophy will be presented to the owner of the winner. Closed Wednesday, April 27, 1988, with 31 nominations.

Cash In Store — 35–1

BLACK C A 114
Own.—Spelling A & Candy
Ch. c. 3, by Key to the Mint—Lauromee, by Gallant Romeo
Br.—Klein LaDonna (Fla)
Tr.—Gosden John H M
Lifetime 8 2 0 2 $7,938
1988 2 0 0 0 $1,875
1987 6 2 0 2 $6,063
Turf 6 2 0 2 $6,063

10Feb88-8SA 1 1/16 :472 1:123 1:432ft 99 114 8 6½ 6 6¼ 59 517¾ Black CA 9 Ⓡ Sta Ctlna 66-23 Lively One, Stalwars, Havanaffair 9
13Jan88-8SA 1 :46 1:104 1:371ft 15 115 65½ 1012 1010 1013 McCrronCJ8 Ⓡ Los Flz 69-20 PleaseRemit,SweetNGo,GldMusic 10
13Aug87 ♦6Salisbury(Eng) 6f 1:151gd 2¼ 133 Ⓣ 33½ StrkeyG Ogbrn Nsy H Reformdo,GoodMedicine,CshInStor 8
18Jly87 ♦6Lingfield(Eng) 7f 1:271sf 4 133 Ⓣ 1nk StrkeyG Plbrgh Nsy H CshInStr,KnwnChrtr,MrSndySprt 11
23Jun87 ♦1Brighton(Eng) 6f 1:133gd 8-5 126 Ⓣ 12 StrkeyG Eastbrn (Mdn) CshInStore,Lobric,BoldAndHrdsom 7
3Jun87 ♦5Epsom(Eng) a6f 1:093gd 10 123 Ⓣ 56¾ StarkeyG Woodcote CottonAuction,Lpierre,BorderGurd 9
23May87 ♦5Haydock(Eng) 5f 1:004gd 3 126 Ⓣ 37½ StrkeyG Sklmrsdl (Mdn) SpceCruiser,MgnTrville,CshInStor 12
8May87 ♦4Lingfield(Eng) 5f :592gd 2½ 126 Ⓣ 813 StrkyG AsocBrnds(Mdn) Jeronime, RedDollar, DanRoyal 14
May 2 Hol 5f ft 1:004 h ● Apr 25 Hol 7f ft 1:274 h Apr 18 Hol 7f ft 1:292 h Apr 12 Hol 6f ft 1:164 h

Dr. Brent — 4–1

MCCARRON C J 119
Own.—Braverman & Colvin
Dk. b. or br. g. 3, by Naevus—Renata's Love, by Nantequos
Br.—Colvin R (Cal)
Tr.—Soriano Morris
Lifetime 14 4 3 2 $105,607
1988 6 3 0 2 $87,512
1987 8 1 3 0 $18,095
Turf 1 1 0 0 $30,262

27Apr88-8Hol 7f :213 :442 1:221ft 12 119 42 62½ 3½ 38 Solis A2 Debonair 85-17 Claim, ProspectorsGamble Dr.Brent 7
6Apr88-8SA a6½f Ⓣ:21 :4331:15 fm 7½ 117 43½ 31½ 1hd 11½ Solis A8 Baldwin 84-13 Dr.Brent,AccomplishRidg,GldMusic 9
6Apr88—Run in divisions
17Mar88-7SA 6½f :214 :451 1:164ft *3-5 116 54½ 31 11½ 12¾ DlhoussyE3 Ⓢ Aw34000 86-20 Dr.Brent,GoForBroadway,Vancealot 8
17Mar88—Bumped hard start
4Mar88-5SA 6f :213 :443 1:10 ft 6 116 41½ 43 31 12¾ DelahoussayeE5 50000 88-19 Dr. Brent, Hard To Miss, Ekahi 10
5Feb88-5SA 6f :22 :451 1:113ft 7½ 116 1hd 2hd 11½ 3¾ Shoemaker W3 50000 79-20 Temper T., Hard To Miss,Dr.Brent 12
5Feb88—Bumped twice start
24Jan88-8SA 6f :212 :442 1:093ft 30 116 54½ 69 69 511¼ ShoemkerW7 Aw32000 79-18 PrspctrsGmbl,SmWh,GryLnExprss 10
24Jan88—Wide 3/8 turn
11Nov87-3SA 6½f :22 :453 1:174ft 3½ 117 42 2½ 11 22¼ Pincay L Jr2 40000 79-18 Rullah's Sky, Dr. Brent, Alandvon 7
11Nov87—Broke in a tangle
29Oct87-1SA 6f :213 :45 1:11 gd 5½ 118 52½ 2½ 21½ 2¾ DelahoussyeE10 32000 82-16 Dear John, Dr. Brent, Gaelic Bid 10
8Oct87-4SA 6f :214 :453 1:121ft 3½ 118 31 31½ 21 13½ DelahoussyeE9 M32000 77-19 Dr. Brent,LuckyTryst,ParOfCourse 11
3Oct87-6Fpx 6f :223 :461 1:121ft 2½ 118 813 816 716 716 Solis A8 Ⓢ M32000 70-10 Bttrynotincludd,Flpr,SnoritDmond 10
3Oct87—Lugged out
● Apr 17 SA 6f ft 1:13 h Apr 1 SA HC 5f fm :592 h (d) Mar 27 SA 4f ft :482 h Mar 15 SA 4f ft :463 h

Kamikaze Sam — 23–1

PEDROZA M A 110
Own.—Siegel Jan
Ch. c. 3, by Singular—Petite Jolie, by Jig Time
Br.—Siegel Jan (Fla)
Tr.—Ellis Ronald W
Lifetime 7 3 1 0 $34,462
1988 3 2 0 0 $27,100
1987 4 1 1 0 $7,362
Turf 1 0 0 0 $1,000

23Apr88-6GG 1 Ⓣ:4811:12411:383yl 5¾ 115 2½ 32 54 42¼ Sibille R 3 HcpO 72-30 Greager, Chillon, A Perfect Sham 6
11Feb88-3SA 1 :462 1:12 1:384ft 5 116 65 1hd 1½ 1nk DelahoussayeE 8 50000 74-23 KamikzeSm,Rullh'sSky,Mehmetski 8
11Feb88—Altered course 5/16; erratic in stretch
24Jan88-5BM 1 :451 1:101 1:36 ft 4 117 513 45 33½ 11½ Baze R A 1 Aw19000 88-15 Kamikaze Sam, Falpar, Coul Trip 8
26Dec87-8BM 1 :461 1:111 1:364ft 15 117 58½ 76¼ 56½ 45 Maple S 3 Aw14500 79-14 Distant Blade, Rencoo, HeirToGold 7
5Dec87-2BM 1 1/16 :464 1:122 1:482sy 14 118 88½ 33 1hd 12 Lamance C 7 M20000 50-22 KamikazeSam,TrojanWar,MyNskr 10
28Oct87-6BM 6f :221 :453 1:104sy 5¼ 118 43½ 610 718 721¾ McHargue DG 7 M32000 63-26 Greager, First David, Co Ack 8
9Oct87-5BM 6f :222 :454 1:11 ft 4¾ 118 31½ 31 2hd 22½ McHargue DG 7 M20000 81-16 DistantBlade,KamikzeSm,BoldNTn 8
May 3 Hol 4f ft :50 h Apr 17 SA 6f ft 1:141 h Apr 11 SA 1 ft 1:44 h Apr 5 SA 7f ft 1:293 h

Glad Music — 9–2

SOLIS A 116
Own.—Hunt N B
Dk. b. or br. c. 3, by I'm Glad—Laughing Music, by Luthier
Br.—Hunt N B (Ky)
Tr.—Whittingham Charles
Lifetime 12 1 2 4 $66,713
1988 5 0 1 2 $37,238
1987 7 1 1 2 $29,475
Turf 1 0 0 1 $8,438

20Apr88-8SA 1⅛ :462 1:103 1:504sy 2 117 48 35½ 32½ 2hd PncyLJr3 Ⓡ La Puente 75-17 Winnerwld,GldMusic,SunriseSrmon 5
20Apr88—Bumped start
6Apr88-8SA a6½f Ⓣ:21 :4331:15 fm 6½ 114 912 911 55½ 31¼ ShoemkerW 4 Baldwin 83-13 Dr.Brent,AccomplishRidg,GldMusic 9
6Apr88—Run in divisions
9Mar88-8SA 1⅛ :474 1:12 1:491ft 5½ 115 68 68 611 611½ ShoemkerW 5 Ⓡ Brdbry 71-19 Stalwars,AllTheePower,Havanaffair 6
9Mar88—Wide into stretch
28Jan88-7SA 1 :454 1:103 1:363ft 2½ 118 1016 713 611 47½ ShoemkerW 9 Aw34000 77-23 Din'sDncr,AllThPowr,GrnwichGold 10
28Jan88—Broke in, bumped
13Jan88-8SA 1 :46 1:104 1:371ft 5½ 114 1014 78 54½ 3nk ShomkrW 10 Ⓡ Los Flz 82-20 PleaseRemit,SweetNGo,GldMusic 10
13Jan88—Wide into drive
27Dec87-6SA 1 1/16 :464 1:121 1:444ft *8-5 117 810 53¾ 31½ 16 Shoemaker W 2 Mdn 77-17 GladMusic,Freeskate,RecittionSpin 9
9Dec87-6Hol 1 1/16 :464 1:122 1:454ft *9-5 117 96½ 63½ 43 21¾ Shoemaker W 5 Mdn 72-16 SpottdRj,GldMusic,SouthrnSpruc 11
8Nov87-4SA 1 :473 1:13 1:41 gd 3½ 117 63½ 54 31½ 32¼ Toro F 6 Mdn 61-25 KingAlobar,PureExpense,GldMusic 8
8Nov87—Broke slowly
10Oct87-6SA 1 :46 1:111 1:374ft 5 117 67½ 54½ 33½ 32½ Toro F7 Mdn 76-17 CrestingWter,KingAlobr,GldMusic 10
6Sep87-4Dmr 1 :463 1:113 1:374ft 5½ 117 86½ 65 43½ 44¾ Toro F8 Mdn 74-17 Cougrzd,WhtADplomt,OurMtvWsh 10
May 4 Hol 5f ft :594 h ● Apr 28 Hol 4f ft :47 h Apr 17 SA 6f ft 1:142 h Mar 31 SA 6f ft 1:114 h

Exacta wagering.

(Continued on following page)

(*Race 7 continued*)

Winnerwald Gr. c. 3, by Private Account—Promised Woman, by Promised Land
CASTANON A L Br.—Gentry T (Cal) 1988 4 1 2 0 $59,675 **19–1**
116 Tr.—Aguilera Humberto 1987 11 M 2 3 $36,525
Own.—Wald & Winner Lifetime 15 1 4 3 $96,200
20Apr88-8SA 1⅛ :46^2 1:10^3 1:50^{4}sy 15 114 5^9 5^8 4^4 1^{hd} Solis A^2 [R]La Puente 75-17 Winnerwld,GldMusic,SunriseSrmon 5
20Apr88—Bumped start
10Apr88-4SA 1 :46^2 1:12^3 1:39^{2}ft 3 117 75¾ 2½ 2^{hd} 2no Pincay L Jr 5 [S]Mdn 71-18 RcklssOn,Wnnrwld,Knndy'sKnockt 8
10Apr88—Bumped start; lugged out 7/8, wide stretch
20Mar88-6SA 1 1/16 :46^4 1:12^2 1:44^{3}ft 7 117 85¾ 4^1 2½ 22¼ Solis A 5 Mdn 76-15 Zachanie, Winnerwald, Attesa 11
20Mar88—Veered in start, wide throughout
13Mar88-6SA 1 :46^1 1:11^3 1:37^{4}ft 3 117 9^{11} 7^8 56½ 48¼ Pincay L Jr 9 [S]Mdn 71-15 Keepmeinstitchs,RcklssOn,MjorMn 9
13Mar88—Very wide
19Dec87-7Hol 1 1/16 :47^4 1:12^1 1:43^{1}gd 3 118 45½ 4^4 3^5 35½ Pincay L Jr 6 Mdn 81-10 Jade Trade, Stalwars, Winnerwald 8
19Dec87—Lugged out
29Nov87-4Hol 1 1/16 :47^2 1:12^1 1:44^{3}ft 3 117 63¾ 52½ 55½ 59¼ Solis A 8 Mdn 71-12 Lively One, SpottedRaj,Wcrryation 8
14Nov87-8SA 1 :46^4 1:12^1 1:38^{2}ft 42 114 87¾ 65½ 45½ 35¾ Solis A 4 [S]B J Rddr 70-22 PurdueKing,Mr.GmePlyr,Winnrwld 8
8Nov87-9BM 1 1/16 :47 1:11 1:42^{2}ft 25 114 11^{16}11^{11} 8^8 5^9 HnsenRD 11 Cal Juv 71-14 FlyingVictor,Skr'sJourny,Cougrizd 11
8Nov87—Grade III
24Oct87-6SA 1 1/16 :46^2 1:11^4 1:45^{3}gd 4½ 117 6^{15} 5^{10} 33½ 2^2 Pincay L Jr 5 Mdn 71-17 Propost, Winnerwald, Freeskate 8
24Oct87—Wide into stretch
10Oct87-6SA 1 :46 1:11^1 1:37^{4}ft 7½ 112^5 5^6 44½ 5^6 67¾ Gryder A T 5 Mdn 71-17 CrestingWter,KingAlobr,G'dMusic 10
10Oct87—Wide final 3/8
May 5 Hol 3f ft :36 h May 1 Hol 6f ft 1:17^2 h Apr 18 SA Ⓣ 3f fm :40^4 h (d) Apr 5 Hol 6f ft 1:16^3 h

Exclusive Nureyev Dk. b. or br. c. 3, by Nureyev—Balcony Dancer, by Gallant Romeo
MEZA R Q Br.—Carl W A (Ky) 1988 4 2 0 0 $58,537 **5–2**
118 Tr.—Palma Hector O 1987 1 M 0 0
Own.—Yasuda G Lifetime 5 2 0 0 $58,537 Turf 1 1 0 0 $39,162
20Apr88-8SA 1⅛ :46^2 1:10^3 1:50^{4}sy *7-5 120 1½ 1½ 2^{hd} 4^6 StvnsGL^5 [R]La Puente 69-17 Winnerwld,GldMusic,SunriseSrmon 5
6Apr88-5SA a6½f Ⓣ:21^2 :43^{4}1:14^{2}fm 5¾ 116 41½ 31½ 31½ 11¾ DelhoussyeE^3 Baldwin 87-13 ExclsvNryv,ProspctrsGmbl,Mhmtsk 9
6Apr88—Run in divisions
6Mar88-6SA 1 :45^2 1:10^4 1:36^{3}ft 12 117 8^{10} 76½ 7^{10} 716¾ ShoemkerW^2 Aw34000 68-13 BlArDncr,Smb'sGold,GoForBrodwy 8
6Mar88—Broke slowly, bore out, bumped entering stretch
20Feb88-6SA 7f :22^2 :45^3 1:24^{3}ft 13 118 2^{hd} 1^1 11½ 12¾ Valenzuela P A^5 Mdn 77-18 EclsvNryv,Allthkngsdncrs,MyBllyB 9
26Dec87-6SA 6f :22^2 :45^2 1:10^{3}ft 13 113^5 64¾ 79½ 9^{13} 913¾ Gryder A T^8 Mdn 71-16 Joe Nasr, Peace, Din's Dancer 12
26Dec87—Fractious gate
Apr 30 Hol 5f ft 1:00^4 h Apr 16 SA 5f gd 1:01^4 h Apr 1 SA HC 5f fm :58^3 h (d) ●Mar 25 SA 1 ft 1:39^2 h

Prove Splendid Dk. b. or br. g. 3, by Prove Out—Splendid Size, by Ambehaving
OLIVARES F Br.—Meadowbrook Farms Inc (Fla) 1988 6 2 0 2 $30,975 **15–1**
113 Tr.—La Croix David 1987 1 M 0 0
Own.—Meadowbrook Farm Inc Lifetime 7 2 0 2 $30,975
9Apr88-8GG 1 1/16 :46 1:09^2 1:40^{2}ft 17 115 3^2 43½ 4^7 48¼ Hansen R D 1 Sausalito 89-09 Charlie'sNotes,BelAirDncer,Chillon 5
23Mar88-7GG 1 :46^1 1:11^1 1:37^{3}ft *4-5 117 66½ 3^3 1^{hd} 12½ Baze R A 9 Aw17000 80-20 ProveSplndid,KingSkippr,LkrMgic 10
12Mar88-8GG 1 :45^1 1:09^1 1:34^{2}ft 14 113 3^2 31½ 42½ 3^4 DcyTT 3 [R]Lafyte Iv H 92-10 Chrlie'sNotes,Chillon,ProveSplndid 7
12Mar88—Bumped start
27Feb88-3GG 6f :22 :44^4 1:10 ft 3½ 120 41¼ 42½ 32½ 3¾ Lambert J 2 Aw16000 88-15 ChrlesTheGret,SePrid,ProvSplndid 6
27Feb88—Bumped 3 1/2
15Feb88-5GG 6f :21^4 :44^2 1:09^{3}ft 3¾ 118 2^{hd} 2^{hd} 1^{hd} 11½ Doocy T T 6 Mdn 91-10 ProvSplndd,KngSkppr,Drn'sDscvry 8
16Jan88-7BM 6f :22^2 :46^2 1:12^{2}sy 7¾ 118 77¾ 6^6 64¼ 46½ Doocy T T 6 Mdn 70-29 It'sCourtingTim,Tsfox,APrfctShm 10
24Dec87-2Hol 6f :22 :44^3 1:09^{1}ft 59 117 9^{11} 9^{16} 9^{19} 6^{14} Sibille R 1 Mdn 82-10 AllThPowr,KnghtRgnt,MonMdnssI 10
May 2 Hol 6f ft 1:13^4 h Apr 2 GG 7f ft 1:31^1 h Mar 7 GG 6f ft 1:14^4 h

Roberto's Dancer Dk. b. or br. c. 3, by Roberto—Witch Dance, by Northern Dancer
TORO F Br.—Evans T M (Va) 1988 2 1 0 0 $24,975 *****
117 Tr.—Speckert Christopher 1987 7 2 1 2 $32,900
Own.—Buckland Farm Lifetime 9 3 1 2 $57,875 Turf 5 3 0 1 $53,210 **9–5**
16Mar88-8SA 1 Ⓣ:45^{2}1:10 1:35^{4}fm 4½ 116 9^{11} 5^6 31½ 1^{hd} DelhoussyeE^8 Aw42000 96-08 Roberto'sDncer,BlAirDncr,Contmpt 9
16Mar88—Lugged in stretch, bumped late
27Jan88-8SA 7f :22 :44^1 1:22^{3}ft 16 113 5^9 5^{11} 5^{12} 517½ Black CA^4 Sn Vcnt 69-19 MPrfrdo,NoCmmtmnt,SccssExprss 5
27Jan88—Grade III; Broke slowly
19Dec87-8Aqu 1 1/16 ⊡:48 1:13 1:46 ft 14f 114 8^4 86¾10^{17}1021¼ McClWH^9 Nashua 58-20 Cougrized,BlwbyEm,ChicotCounty 12
19Dec87—Grade II
1Nov87-9Lrl 1 1/16 Ⓣ:48^{4}1:14^{1}1:46 fm 12 122 31½ 41½ 6^5 54¾ Lloyd J S^{10} Lrl Fut 62-32 Antiqu,MisterModsty,KohrWithK. 14
1Nov87—Grade I; Bumped 1/8
13Oct87-9Pim 1 Ⓣ:45^{2}1:09^{4}1:36^{2}fm 9¼ 114 1^2 12½ 1^2 1¾ Lloyd J S^1 Aw20000 98-04 Robrto'sDncr,CmoTyp,MistrModsty 8
13Oct87—Drifted, driving
26Sep87-9Pha 1 1/16 Ⓣ:47^{2}1:11^{4}1:44^{1}fm 2½ 116 51¼ 3^2 23½ 36¼ Allen K K^3 Dragoon 93-13 KohnWthK.,ContErntt,Rbrt'sDncr 11
26Sep87—Bore out
4Sep87-3Atl 1 Ⓣ:48 1:12^{3}1:38^{2}fm*8-5 116 2^2 2½ 1^{hd} 1^4 Chavez S N^7 Aw8200 79-17 Robrto'sDncr,SnstonlBlz,ContErntt 9
20Aug87-7Mth 6f :22^3 :46^1 1:12 ft 9 118 7^7 47½ 3^8 3^9 Terry J^4 Mdn 71-24 KohnWthK.,WhrlngAsh,Rbrt'sDncr 8
5Aug87-1Del 6f :22^3 :46^2 1:12^{4}ft *9-5 118 1^{hd} 2½ 21½ 2^3 Fielding R D^1 Mdn 74-25 FrontPg,Robrto'sDncr,SssyShnnon 8
May 5 SA 4f ft :47^1 h Apr 30 SA 5f ft 1:00 h Apr 25 SA Ⓣ 7f fm 1:27^1 h (d) ●Apr 18 SA Ⓣ 3f fm :36 h (d)

(9 Horses)

8th Hollywood

START
7 FURLONGS
HOLLYWOOD PARK
FINISH

7 FURLONGS. (1.20⅘) 10th Running of THE TRIPLE BEND HANDICAP (Grade III). $75,000 added. 3-year-olds and upward. By subscription of $100 each which shall accompany the nomination, $750 additional to start, with $75,000 added, of which $15,000 to second, $11,250 to third, $5,625 to fourth and $1,875 to fifth. Weights, Monday, May 2. Starters to be named through the entry box by closing time of entries. Highweights preferred. A trophy will be presented to the owner of the winner. Closed Wednesday, April 27, 1988, with 16 nominations.

*Sylvan Express — 15–1

B. h. 5, by Baptism—Folle Remont, by Prince Tenderfoot
MEZA R Q 120 **Br.—Lodge Park Stud (Ire)** 1988 5 2 1 2 $114,340
Tr.—Fulton John W 1987 12 3 0 1 $95,851
Own.—Johnson Rosemary A Lifetime 32 9 3 4 $274,723 Turf 25 6 2 2 $130,133

23Apr88-5SA 6½f :22^1 :45 1:15^{2}m *6-5 121 2^1 2^{1½} 2^2 3^{1¾} DlhssyE^3 Sn Smn H 91-15 CblloDeOro,GllntSilor,SylvnExpress 5
23Apr88—Grade III
6Mar88-11TuP 6f :21^2 :43^3 1:08 ft 9-5 126 5^{5½} 3^{3½} 3^4 3^2 Baze RA^7 Phx Gd Cp 92-14 Faro,Reconnoitering,SylvanExpress 7
6Mar88—Grade III
13Feb88-8SA 5½f :22 :45^1 1:03^{4}ft 3½ 119 4^3 5^4 4^3 1^{hd} DlhssyE^5 El Conejo H 92-22 Sylvan Express, Carload, HighBrite 8
6Feb88-8GG 6f :21^4 :44^1 1:08^{1}ft *6-5 118 1^{hd} 1^{hd} 1^1 1^{nk} Baze RA^3 Albany H 98-09 SylvnExpress,Reconnoitring,BidUs 7
16Jan88-7SA 1 :45^2 1:10 1:36 ft 2¼ 116 3^{3½} 3^{2½} 3^3 2^{¾} DelhoussyeE^7 Aw55000 87-20 FstrThnSnd,SlvnEprss,MstrflAdvct 7
31Dec87-7SA 6½f :22 :44^3 1:15^{4}gd 4½ 118 5^2 5^{2½} 2^2 1^{¾} DelhoussyeE^9 Aw55000 91-19 SylvnExprss,BndlOfIron,CptnVgors 7
21Nov87-1Hol 6f :21^1 :44 1:08^{4}ft 67f 126 10^{8¾}11^{12}10^{9¾} 8^{9¼} CuthenS^9 Br Cp Sprnt 89-12 VerySubtl,Groovy,ExclusivEnough 13
21Nov87—Grade I; Poor start
31Oct87♦1Newmarket(Eng) 1 1:42^{1}gd 20 133 Ⓣ 4^{5½} StarkeyG FlrcrbnMrshll ShadyHeights,Azyaa,CrestaAuction 9
11Oct87♦6Munich(Ger) a6½f 1:18 gd *9-5 129 Ⓣ 1^{½} StarkeyG GrsrSprntPr SylvnExpress,BelByou,HomePlese 14
4Sep87-8AP 1 Ⓣ:50 1:14^{4}1:37^{2}gd 7¾ 121 3^{1½} 3^2 4^2 5^{6¼} EddryP^4 Bud Brd Cup 82-23 PersianMews,MisterC.,VernonCstle 7
Apr 19 SA 4f ft :47 h

Don's Irish Melody * — 7–1

Dk. b. or br. g. 5, by The Irish Lord—Don's Music, by Don B
CASTANON A L 115 **Br.—Coelho & Valenti (Cal)** 1988 1 0 1 0 $11,800
Tr.—Sadler John W 1987 6 5 1 0 $124,150
Own.—Coelho & Valenti Lifetime 10 5 3 1 $142,775

15Apr88-7SA 6f :21^4 :45 1:10 m 3 117 3^3 3^{3½} 3^1 2^{nk} Pincay L Jr^5 Aw55000 88-21 Rconnotrng,Don'sIrshMlody,PsnPt 6
15Apr88—Broke slowly, bumped start
7Jun87-10Cby 6½f :22^2 :44^4 1:16^{1}ft 6 115 3^{½} 2^{½} 1^{hd} 1^{¾} CstnonAL^8 Chcr Cp H 100-07 Don'sIrshMlody,Suproyl,ChfStwrd 14
2May87-3Hol 6f :22^2 :45^1 1:09 ft 2½ 116 1^1 1^{½} 1^{½} 1^1 ValenzuelPA^4 Aw35000 98-12 Dn'sIrshMldy,LnclnPrk,GrndAllgnc 5
23Apr87-8Hol 6f :21^2 :44^3 1:09^{1}ft 3¼ 121 1^{½} 1^{½} 1^1 1^1 Pincay L Jr^4 Aw25000 97-09 Don'sIrshMlody,BoldSmochr,REntr 5
23Apr87—Drifted out late
15Mar87-2SA 6½f :21^4 :45^2 1:17^{2}ft 5¾ 120 2^{½} 2^1 1^{hd} 1^3 Pincay L Jr^4 Aw28000 83-20 Don'sIrshMlody,Dvl'sIc,TmFrSkrt 11
27Feb87-6SA 6f :21^3 :44^2 1:09^{2}ft *9-5 119 2^{hd} 1^{½} 1^{hd} 1^{hd} Pincay L Jr^6 Mdn 91-16 Don's Irish Melody, Decore, Ahica 12
8Jan87-6SA 6f :22 :45^4 1:11^{2}m *6-5 119 2^{1½} 2^{3½} 2^{3½} 2^{4½} Pincay L Jr^7 Mdn 76-30 Svnfvndchng,Dn'sIrshMldy,Mndnt 10
8Jan87—Bumped start
19Dec86-1Hol 6f :22 :45^4 1:11 ft *9-5 120 1^{½} 1^{½} 2^{hd} 2^3 Stevens G L^3 Mdn 85-17 GretYnkee,Don'sIrishMlody,Dtctor 7
19Dec86—Fractious gate; steadied start
23May86-3Hol 6f :22^2 :46^1 1:10^{1}ft *9-5 117 5^3 3^3 4^{6½} 4^{10¾} Pincay L Jr^3 ⓈMdn 82-23 BoldBrawley,PrinceOFire,MrkChip 12
11May86-6Hol 6f :22^1 :45^3 1:09^{4}ft 2¾ 120 1^{hd} 2^{hd} 2^{1½} 3^{3¾} Pincay L Jr^3 Mdn 91-15 Mrvn'sPlcy,PrncOFr,Dn'sIrshMldy 10
May 2 Hol 6f ft 1:13^1 h Apr 26 Hol 4f ft :48^1 h Apr 8 SA 5f ft :59^4 h ●Apr 2 SA 6f ft 1:11^4 h

Reconnoitering * — 14–1

B. g. 4, by Naskra—Track Jester, by Jeff D
GRYDER A T 115 **Br.—George Arakelian Farms Inc (Cal)** 1988 5 1 2 0 $70,570
Tr.—Marikian Charles M 1987 18 5 2 4 $131,450
Own.—Arakelian Fm &KradidanEtal Lifetime 27 6 4 5 $205,040 Turf 1 0 0 0

15Apr88-7SA 6f :21^4 :45 1:10 m 5 114 4^{4½} 4^{3½} 2^1 1^{nk} Gryder A T 6 Aw55000 88-21 Rconnotrng,Don'sIrshMlody,PsnPt 6
15Apr88—Wide 3/8 turn
23Mar88-10FG 6f :21^1 :44^1 1:09^{1}ft 5 116 5^6 5^7 4^{6½} 4^{4½} Hansen R D 7 Sprnt H 94-17 Wyne'sCrne,IrishOpen,CreoleDncer 8
6Mar88-11TuP 6f :21^2 :43^3 1:08 ft 5 115 7^{7½} 6^{4¼} 5^{4¼} 2^{1½} HnsnRD 4 Phx Gd Cp 92-14 Faro,Reconnoitering,SylvanExpress 7
6Mar88—Grade III
6Feb88-8GG 6f :21^4 :44^1 1:08^{1}ft 3 115 5^{2¾} 4^{3½} 2^1 2^{nk} HnsnRD 1 Albany H 98-09 SylvnExpress,Reconnoitring,BidUs 7
9Jan88-8SA 7f :22^1 :44^1 1:22 ft 24 113 6^{9½} 6^{9½} 6^{7½} 7^{5½} OlivaresF 1 Sn Crls H 84-17 Epidurus,SuperDimond,LordRuckus 7
9Jan88—Grade II; Off slowly
26Dec87-8SA 7f :22^1 :44^2 1:21 ft 18 114 4^2 2^{1½} 2^5 4^{8¾} Gryder AT 1 Malibu 86-16 OnTheLine,TemperteSil,Crdi'sGold 9
26Dec87—Grade II
12Dec87-9Hol 6f :21^3 :44 1:09^{3}ft 12 112 6^{3½} 6^{3½} 2^{½} 2^{½} GrydrAT 2 Nt Sprt Ch 93-18 HilcoScamper,Reconnoitering,Zblet 6
12Dec87—Grade III
25Nov87-7Hol 6½f :21^2 :43^4 1:15^{3}ft 4½ 109^5 4^{3½} 4^{1½} 3^{½} 1^{½} Gryder A T 3 Aw28000 100-13 Reconnoitering,Fracoz,OrchrdSong 7
25Nov87—Boxed in 3/16
11Nov87-7SA 6½f :21^3 :44 1:16^{1}ft 17 109^5 4^{2¼} 3^2 3^2 1^1 Gryder A T 8 62500 89-18 Reconnoitering,SilvrHro,SilntImpct 8
11Nov87—Fanned wide 3/8
1Nov87-5SA 6½f :21^3 :44^2 1:16 m 15 115 6^{2¼} 3^{1½} 5^4 5^{3½} Gryder A T 8 Aw30000 86-12 BoldArchon,WindwoodLne,MiBeso 8
1Nov87—Wide 3/8 turn
May 6 SA 3f ft :36 h Apr 30 SA 5f ft 1:00 h Apr 8 SA 4f ft :47^4 h Mar 16 SA 4f ft :48 h

Exacta wagering. (*Continued on following page*)

(*Race 8 continued*)

Gallant Sailor

B. g. 5, by Gallant Best—Sailing Joy, by Sailing Along

OLIVARES F 112 — Br.—Jones K & Sheryl (Wash) — Tr.—Jones Kenneth G — **25–1**

Own.—Jones K G — Lifetime 41 3 8 5 $107,150

1988 6 0 3 1 $42,850
1987 16 0 2 3 $35,960
Turf 10 0 0 2 $19,100

23Apr88-5SA 6½f :22¹ :45 1:15²m 4½ 112 43½ 42½ 43 21½ ShmrW5 Sn Smn H 92-15 CblloDeOro,GllntSilor,SylvnExpress 5
23Apr88—Grade III
30Mar88-8SA 6½f :21⁴ :44² 1:15 ft 8½ 111 34½ 34 33½ 33½ OlivresF2 Ptro Grnd H 91-18 Gulch, Very Subtle, Gallant Sailor 3
23Mar88-7SA 6½f :21² :43⁴ 1:15²ft 6 1105 510 59½ 34½ 2no Banderas AL1 Aw43000 93-18 Fracoza, GallantSailor,RightRudder 5
23Mar88—Broke slowly
4Feb88-8SA 6½f :21² :44 1:15²ft 55 1105 67½ 67 55½ 23 Gryder A T1 Aw40000 90-20 Sebrof, Gallant Sailor,RightRudder 7
4Feb88—Wide into stretch
23Jan88-6SA 1 1/16 :46¹ 1:10² 1:42¹ft 38 116 74¾ 88½ 913 817½ McHrgueDG5 Aw44000 72-14 Crimson Slew,CaptainValid,HillsBid 9
23Jan88—Lugged out 3/8
14Jan88-8SA 1⅛ Ⓣ:47¹1:11⁴1:49²fm 34 115 42 74 1010 912½ Sibille R10 Aw44000 68-20 Light Sabre, Mazilier, Gorky 10
23Dec87-8Hol 1 1/16 Ⓣ:48⁴1:13 1:43³fm 26 1115 42 52 3½ 32½ Banderas AL5 Aw45000 73-24 FiveDddyFive,RufusDwes,GllntSilor 8
12Dec87-10Hol 1 Ⓣ:47 1:11⁴1:36³fm 15 1115 57½ 53 41¾ 31 Banderas AL7 Aw45000 83-14 KingBlldeer,Uptothehilt,GllntSilor 10
29Nov87-9Hol 1 1/16 Ⓣ:47¹1:11 1:41²fm 15 1115 31 43½ 64½ 63 Banderas AL4 Aw39000 84-11 Samario, Il Miracolo, Dark Promise 8
19Nov87-8Hol 6f :22² :45² 1:10 ft 23 1105 65¾ 66 65 44¾ Banderas AL7 Aw31000 87-14 BoldArchon,CblloDOr,TmmyThHwk 7
May 3 Hol 3f ft :35³ h — Apr 19 Hol 3f ft :36⁴ h — Apr 15 Hol 6f gd 1:15² h — Apr 9 Hol 5f ft 1:01¹ h

Very Subtle *

Ch. f. 4, by Hoist the Silver—Never Scheme, by Never Bend

SOLIS A 120 — Br.—King J H (Ky) — Tr.—Stute Melvin F — * **4–5**

Own.—Rochelle B — Lifetime 21 11 4 3 $1,410,660

1988 5 1 2 1 $135,800
1987 12 6 2 2 $947,135

30Mar88-8SA 6½f :21⁴ :44² 1:15 ft *1-2 120 2½ 11 11½ 21½ McCrrCJ1 Ptro GrndH 94-18 Gulch, Very Subtle, Gallant Sailor 3
21Feb88-8SA 1⅛ :46³ 1:11² 1:50²ft *3½ 120 1½ 1hd 2hd 42¼ McCrrCJ2 ⒻStMrgIvH 75-21 FlyingJul,HollywoodGlttr,ClbbrGrl 10
21Feb88—Grade I
6Feb88-8SA 1⅛ :46¹ 1:10¹ 1:49¹ft *2½ 126 43 33 34 35¾ ShmrW2 ⒻLa Cnda 77-18 HollywoodGlttr,ByLndByS,VrySbtl 7
6Feb88—Grade I; Returned bleeding from right nostril
23Jan88-8SA 1 1/16 :45⁴ 1:09² 1:41³ft *2-3 122 2½ 1hd 1hd 2½ CstnAL3 ⒻEl Encino 92-14 ByLndBySe,VerySubtl,Annoconnor 8
23Jan88—Grade III
2Jan88-8SA 7f :22⁴ :45³ 1:21³ft *2-5 124 11 12 17 19 VlnzlPA4 ⒻLa Brea 92-15 Very Subtle,SarosBrig,FoldTheFlag 6
2Jan88—Grade III
21Nov87-1Hol 6f :21¹ :44 1:08⁴ft 16 121 1½ 11½ 13½ 14 VlnlPA11 Br Cp Sprnt 98-12 VerySubtl,Groovy,ExclusivEnough 13
21Nov87—Grade I
31Aug87-9AP 7f :22 :44² 1:22⁴ft *2-5 120 31 3nk 22 23½ SlsA1 ⒻBud Brd Cp H 84-27 LzerShow,VrySubtl,MoonbmMcQun 6
6Aug87-8Sar 7f :21³ :43³ 1:21 ft 3½ 121 2½ 1hd 14 15¼ VlnzulPA6 ⒻTest 97-14 VerySubtle,UptheAplch,SilntTurn 14
6Aug87—Grade II
12Jly87-8Hol 1⅛ :46¹ 1:10¹ 1:48³ft 8-5 121 2hd 1hd 31½ 47½ McCrrCJ2 ⒻHol Oaks 86-09 PerchnceToDrem,Schuist,PenBlLdy 6
12Jly87—Grade I
20Jun87-8Hol 1 1/16 :45³ 1:10¹ 1:43 ft *4-5 122 3½ 41½ 33½ 31½ ShmrW6 ⒻPrincess 92-11 RnsomedCptive,Schuist,VerySubtle 6
20Jun87—Grade II; Wide 7/8 turn
●May 6 Hol 3f ft :34³ h — ●Apr 29 Hol 5f ft :58⁴ h — Apr 19 SA 5f ft :59³ h — Apr 12 SA 6f ft 1:15 h

Sebrof

Dk. b. or br. c. 4, by Bold Forbes—Jamila, by Graustark

MCCARRON C J 116 — Br.—Jones A U (Ky) — Tr.—Barrera Lazaro S — **5–2**

Own.—Jones A U — Lifetime 11 5 2 0 $138,763

1988 5 2 2 0 $78,000
1987 6 3 0 0 $60,763
Turf 3 0 0 0 $6,563

27Mar88-7SA 1 :46² 1:10¹ 1:35²ft *8-5 116 1½ 1½ 11½ 11¾ Stevens G L 1 Aw60000 91-16 Sebrof, Talinum, Nostalgia's Star 6
18Mar88-8SA 6f :22¹ :45 1:08⁴ft *6-5 118 1½ 1hd 2hd 21¾ Stevens G L 3 Aw55000 92-18 Gulch, Sebrof, My Gallant Game 6
18Mar88—Bumped hard start
27Feb88-7SA 1 :45³ 1:10² 1:37¹ft 9-5 116 2½ 1hd 1hd 2½ Stevens G L 4 Aw60000 81-17 StaffRiot,Sebrof,Masterful'Advocte 5
4Feb88-8SA 6½f :21² :44 1:15²ft 2½ 114 32 32½ 21½ 13 Stevens G L 2 Aw40000 93-20 Sebrof, Gallant Sailor,RightRudder 7
22Jan88-7SA 6½f :21⁴ :44² 1:15²ft *3-2 115 41½ 31½ 63¾ 65½ Stevens G L 7 Aw40000 87-17 WindwoodLn,CblloDOro,CrystlRun 8
11Sep87-8Dmr 1 1/16 :45² 1:09³ 1:41 ft 7½ 114 23 11 11½ 11 StevnsGL 5 ⓇEl Cajon 95-13 Sebrof,EarnYourStripes,LightSabre 7
23Aug87-8Dmr 1⅛ Ⓣ:47¹1:11¹1:48²fm 7½ 114 1½ 1hd 52½ 77¾ StnsGL 2 Dmr Dby H 83-13 DeputyGovernor,SttelyDor,ThMdic 9
23Aug87—Grade II
9Aug87-8Dmr 1 1/16 Ⓣ:47²1:11¹1:42¹fm 23 114 94 63½ 53 41 StevnsGL 6La Jolla H 88-12 ThMdic,SomthingLucky,SvonTowr 11
9Aug87—Grade III; Pinched at start
29Jly87-5Dmr 1 Ⓣ:46³1:11¹1:36³fm 5 114 89¾ 86¾ 77 54¾ StvnsGL 6 ⓇOceanside 83-13 KindlyCourt,MagnPlus,MountLgun 8
29Jly87—Run in divisions; Pinched at start
5Jly87-7Hol 6f :22 :45¹ 1:10³ft 4½ 116 1½ 1hd 1½ 1½ Stevens G L 1 Aw22000 90-11 Sebrof, Penasco, Five Shy 1/
●May 4 Hol 5f ft :58³ h — Apr 26 Hol 5f ft 1:00¹ h — Mar 15 SA 4f ft :47 h — Mar 9 SA 4f ft :48¹ h

Perfec Travel

B. g. 6, by Inverness Drive—Native Ruler, by Home Ruler

BLACK C A 115 — Br.—Pumphrey J (Okla) — Tr.—Sherman Art — **36–1**

Own.—Matar S J — Lifetime 39 9 6 4 $269,325

1988 6 2 1 1 $49,900
1987 7 0 0 1 $7,825
Turf 12 3 0 2 $140,775

13Apr88-8GG 1 :45⁴ 1:09⁴ 1:34²ft *6-5 117 42 31½ 31 13 Kaenel J L3 HcpO 96-10 PerfecTrvel,Verbotn,LuckyHroldH.
13Apr88—Crowded mid-drive
26Mar88-8GG 1 Ⓣ:47¹1:11 1:36²fm 17 115 1hd 1hd 31½ 66½ Maple S6 S F Mle H 79-15 Ifrad, The Medic, Blanco
26Mar88—Grade III
27Feb88-8GG 1 :45⁴ 1:10¹ 1:35³ft 3½ 116 31 31 21½ 41½ Maple S6 Berkeley H 88-15 SngrChf,LckyHroldH.,PowrForwrd
13Feb88-6GG 1 :44⁴ 1:08² 1:33 ft 3 117 31½ 2½ 2½ 23½ Maple S5 HcpO 99-10 CarosLove,PerfecTrvel,FstAccount
23Jan88-10BM 1 1/16 :45⁴ 1:09² 1:40¹ft 6½ 115 12 1½ 11½ 12¼ MplS2 ⓇH B P A Iv H 91-19 PerfecTrvel,LuckyHroldH.,Spcecpit
10Jan88-10BM 1 :47 1:11³ 1:37 m 5 112 21½ 21½ 23 34¼ Aragon V A1 Bart H 79-28 SpeedyShnnon,BreWithM,PrfcTrvl
10Jan88—Drifted out 1/16
22Nov87-9BM 1 :45¹ 1:10 1:36 gd 30 112 67 54 54½ 54½ ArgnVA7 ⓇSbsct Iv H 83-21 Sidersell, Sanger Chief, JustInCase 9
7Nov87-8BM 1 1/16 Ⓣ:45⁴1:10³1:42⁴fm 32 112 2½ 11 21 53½ ShrmnAB3 Spr Mnt H 85-11 ClvryChrg,RufusDws,ChuckNLuck 10
7Nov87—Drifted in 3/16
18Oct87-7SA 1 :45³ 1:10⁴ 1:36¹ft 8½ 115 79 77 89 817¾ Baze G8 Aw45000 69-15 Midwest King, Joel, Good Taste 9
18Oct87—Pinched back, steadied start
8Oct87-8SA a6½f Ⓣ:22 :44⁴1:15²fm 13 116 73¾ 64½ 21½ 51½ DelhoussyeE4 Aw45000 80-18 Sabona, Lord Ruckus, Pokare 9
May 2 GG 7f ft 1:25² h — Apr 25 GG 5f ft 1:01¹ h — ●Apr 7 GG 5f ft :59³ h — ●Mar 17 GG 1f ft 1:39⁴ h

(9Horses)

9th Hollywood

TURF COURSE
1 1/4 MILE
HOLLYWOOD PARK
START
FINISH

1¼ MILES. (Turf). (1.59) CLAIMING (Chute Start). Purse $43,000. 4-year-olds and upward. Weight, 122 lbs. Non-winners of two races at a mile or over since March 15 allowed 3 lbs.; such a race since then, 6 lbs. Claiming price $80,000; for each $5,000 to $70,000 allowed 2 lbs. (Races when entered for $62,500 or less not considered.)

Danielli

*
2–1

B. h. 5, by Private Account—Jawn, by Graustark
TORO F 116 **Br.—Hawn W R (Ky)** **Tr.—MacDonald Mark** **$80,000**
Own.—Hawn W R **Lifetime 21 4 4 2 $91,075**
1988 4 1 0 1 $28,750
1987 9 1 1 0 $19,150
Turf 13 3 1 1 $62,675

25Apr88-9SA 1¼(T):463 1:371 2:032gd 5¼ 115 77 74¾ 63¼ 1½ Toro F6 62500 70-24 Danielli, Point D'Artois, Ataghan 12
10Apr88-5SA 1⅛(T):463 1:104 1:484fm 14 116 74¾ 73½ 5¾ 31 Toro F9 80000 82-12 MinutesAway,RndomRover,Dnielli 11
19Mar88-5SA a6½f (T):211 :432 1:141fm 13 118 88 911 89 75½ Toro F8 80000 82-10 Illuminux,BigChill,H'sADncingMn 12
26Feb88-3SA 1 :463 1:111 1:37 ft 14 117 42½ 54½ 78¼ 712¼ Stevens G L5 80000 71-23 Armin, Syrian Wind, Red And Blue 7
16Aug87-5Dmr 1 1/16(T):493 1:132 1:432fm 9 115 63½ 62¾ 74 73 ValenzuelPA7 Aw28000 80-12 Individualist, Kohaylan, Samarid 8
16Aug87—Crowded final 1/4
2Aug87-7Dmr 1 1/16(T):48 1:121 1:424fm 41 116 106¼ 106 63½ 54 ShoemkerW8 Aw28000 82-13 Santella Mac, A New Era,Samarid 10
2Aug87—Steadied late
12Jly87-11Pln 1⅛ :452 1:103 1:473ft 10 112 43½ 21½ 59½ 512½ Tohill K S2 Almdn H 84-13 GrandExchnge,Spcecpit,RetsinRun 6
6Jun87-6GG 1 (T):49 1:121 1:364fm 5½ 119 42½ 32½ 41¾ 42½ Lambert J2 Aw17000 80-20 Havildar,CoastingCougr,Kingsbury 7
6Jun87—Crowded 1/4, steadied 1/8
2May87-6GG 1⅜(T):494 1:394 2:182fm 12 114 34 21 43 65¾ Tohill K S1 HcpO 67-26 SalvateTel,PairOfAces,ShadowsFall 6
17Apr87-8GG 1 (T):49 1:132 1:38 fm *1 117 32½ 31½ 2hd 11 Baze R A1 Aw20000 77-23 Dnielli,ExoticMotion,SensitiveCopy 6
Apr 21 SA 5f sy 1:024 h (d) **Apr 4 SA 4f ft :483 h** **●Mar 17 SA 4f ft :463 h**

*Feraud

22–1

B. h. 5, by Lefty—Fair Share, by Indian Chief
CASTANON A L 112 **Br.—Haras Las Ortigas SAAG (Arg)** **Tr.—Russell John W** **$70,000**
Own.—Haras Senoita **Lifetime 17 2 3 3 $52,422**
1988 4 0 0 1 $6,650
1987 8 1 2 1 $35,300
Turf 12 1 2 2 $42,645

6Mar88-7SA 1¼(T):482 1:381 2:042fm 6¾ 118 76 87¾ 911 911½ Velasquez J7 80000 53-30 InFocs,HowVryTochng,RndomRvr 12
27Feb88-5SA 1⅛ :464 1:112 1:504ft 16 116 712 811 917 1020¾ McCarronCJ3 Aw38000 54-17 Reland, Millero YMedio,ProudCat 10
27Feb88—Bumped start; wide into stretch
14Feb88-7SA 1¼(T):464 1:371 2:024fm 5 116 49 22½ 32½ 32½ McCarronCJ2 Aw38000 70-23 Uptothehilt, Nilambar, Feraud 10
29Jan88-8SA 1⅛(T):473 1:122 1:511fm 19 117 31½ 42 42 56 McHrgueDG8 Aw38000 65-29 Fiction, Be Scenic, L'Empire 12
29Jan88—Bumped start; erratic backstretch
16Nov87-5SA 1⅛(T):472 1:12 1:504fm 6¾ 118 1010 97½ 64½ 33¾ McCarronCJ5 Aw33000 69-34 Chess Set, L'Empire, Feraud 12
28Oct87-5SA 1⅛(T):48 1:133 1:512fm 2¾ 118 85½ 94¾ 61¾ 11¾ McCarronCJ7 Aw29000 70-30 Feraud, L. A. Fire, The GreatPrize 10
14Oct87-5SA 1¼(T):492 1:374 2:041fm 3¼ 118 65½ 45 31 2½ McCarronCJ7 Aw30000 65-34 Rough Passage, Feraud, Dhaleem 9
14Oct87—Wide throughout
6Sep87-7Dmr 1 1/16(T):471 1:12 1:424fm 3 118 56¼ 75¼ 43½ 43 Toro F9 Aw24000 83-16 Rufus Dawes, Ima Bullet,ChiefPal 10
23Aug87-9Dmr 1⅛(T):473 1:121 1:493fm 8¼ 118 44 41¾ 11½ 2hd McCarronCJ6 Aw24000 85-13 Sobek, Feraud, Euphrates 10
23Aug87—Bumped 3/8
10Aug87-5Dmr 1⅛(T):474 1:122 1:493fm 2½ 118 912 911 68 66 ShoemkerW 3 Aw23000 79-11 L'Empire, Ima Bullet, First Dibs 9
10Aug87—Lugged in drive
May 1 Hol 7f ft 1:281 h **Apr 25 Hol 6f ft 1:152 h** **Apr 19 Hol 7f ft 1:271 h** **Apr 13 Hol 7f ft 1:292 h**

Coasting Cougar

9–2

B. g. 5, by Coastal—Wild Cougar, by Cougar II
BLACK C A 119 **Br.—Cloverfield Farm Inc (Md)** **Tr.—Thomas John R** **$80,000**
Own.—Everett D R **Lifetime 26 4 7 1 $81,260**
1988 2 1 1 0 $15,250
1987 14 1 4 0 $32,080
Turf 21 3 6 1 $70,100

9Apr88-6GG 1⅜(T):474 1:384 2:171fm*8-5 115 12 11 12 2nk Chapman T M 2 HcpO 79-23 ScurII,CostingCougr,PirdAndPintd 6
9Apr88—Drifted out late
18Mar88-8GG 1 (T):463 1:112 1:364fm 10 117 32½ 31½ 1½ 11½ ChapmanTM 3 Aw19000 83-17 CostingCougr,PeterMoon,Snowcrk 8
23Dec87-8Hol 1 1/16(T):484 1:13 1:433fm 40 116 52¼ 31 73¼ 85½ Solis A 8 Aw45000 70-24 FiveDddyFive,RufusDwes,GllntSilor 8
10Oct87-5SA 1¼(T):471 1:372 2:022fm 9 1115 2½ 77 814 812½ Banderas A L 6 80000 62-25 Clanrallier, Keyala, Migrator 9
10Oct87—Bumped start
13Sep87-5Dmr 1 1/16(T):474 1:122 1:431fm 8 118 88¾ 73¾ 52¼ 21 Shoemaker W 1 80000 83-17 Clanrallier,CoastingCougar,AvitorII 8
31Aug87-8Dmr 1 (T):471 1:112 1:363fm 23 115 811 77 53½ 53¼ Sibille R 7 85000 85-18 Pokare, Fabulous Sound,Emperdori 8
16Aug87-5Dmr 1 1/16(T):493 1:132 1:432fm 6 115 52½ 51¾ 53 63 Sibille R 2 Aw28000 80-12 Individualist, Kohaylan, Samarid 8
31Jly87-5Dmr 1 1/16(T):471 1:114 1:43 fm 14 117 96½ 52½ 33½ 32½ Sibille R 6 80000 82-15 Clnrllier,‡He'sASros,CostirgCougr 10
31Jly87—Placed second through disqualification; Steadied 1/16
12Jly87-9Hol 1 1/16(T):462 1:102 1:412fm 36 118 64½ 63 53¼ 54 Sibille R 6 Aw30000 83-13 GrtCommunctor,WorldCort,Cntnry 7
1Jly87-8Hol 1 1/16(T):464 1:102 1:402fm 33 118 1hd 2hd 76 713½ Sibille R 5 Aw30000 78-08 Rufjan, Rai Den, Centenary 7
May 3 Hol 5f ft 1:004 h **Apr 25 Hol 5f ft 1:034 h** **Mar 31 Hol 6f ft 1:14 h** **Mar 15 Hol 5f ft 1:002 h**

Exacta wagering.

(*Continued on following page*)

(Race 9 continued)

Narghile — B. h. 6, by Foolish Pleasure—Nonoalca, by Nonoalco — **5–2**
OLIVARES F — 116 — Br.—Societe Aland (Ky) — 1988 2 0 1 0 $3,200
Own.—Bronson Mr-Mrs M — Tr.—Russell John W — $80,000 — 1987 9 1 2 2 $112,000
Lifetime 27 6 7 5 $214,618 — Turf 27 6 7 5 $214,618

29Apr88-8Hol 1 1/16 Ⓣ:4541:09 1:402fm 9¾ 115 816 810 710 69½ Olivares F7 Aw50000 82-08 SkpOtFront,FoolThExprts,ArtFrncs 8
20Feb88-7SA 1 Ⓣ:4641:1021:354fm *2½ 117 97¼ 86 44½ 22¾ Pincay L Jr3 100000 93-05 Rufjan, Narghile, Peter Moon 10
20Feb88—Bumped, steadied at start
10Dec87-9Hol 1⅛Ⓣ:4821:12 1:49 fm 9 115 41½ 42 52½ 42¾ Cordero AJr6 Aw55000 80-17 Bruiser, Gorky, Rich Earth 6
10Dec87—Steadied late
27Nov87-9Hol 1⅛Ⓣ:4841:1311:49 fm 4½ 114 33½ 1½ 11½ 2nk Cordero AJr8 Aw52000 83-14 Havildar, Narghile, Bello Horizonte 8
7Nov87-8BM 1 1/16 Ⓣ:4541:1031:424fm 10 114 77½ 95¾ 99¼ 89½ SchldtCP7 Spr Mnt H 79-11 ClvryChrg,RufusDws,ChuckNLuck 10
15Oct87-8SA 1⅛Ⓣ:4421:10 1:474fm 3½ 116 716 58½ 34½ 32½ Olivares F4 Aw48000 85-12 OverTheOcn,NorthrnProvidr,Nrghil 7
15Oct87—Wide in stretch
16Sep87-7Dmr 1 Ⓣ:47 1:1121:354fm 9 116 87¼ 74¼ 52½ 21¼ Olivares F4 Aw40000 91-13 HopefulWord,Narghile,Bestebreuje 8
16Sep87—Bumped start
16Feb87-8SA 1½Ⓣ:4612:0142:282gd 19 117 42½ 87½ 815 825¾ OlivresF2 Sn Lus Ob H 47-27 Louis Le Grand, Zoffany, Schiller 8
16Feb87—Grade II
1Feb87-11TuP 1⅛Ⓣ:4631:1121:48 fm 15 116 911 41 1hd 12 Olivares F13 Tu P H 108 — Narghile,SirNaskra,‡SkipOutFront 14
22Jan87-8SA 1⅛Ⓣ:4721:1131:49 fm 3¾ 117 55½ 41 21½ 31¼ Pincay L Jr5 Aw45000 81-18 Corridor Key, Catane, Narghile 7
Apr 25 Hol 6f ft 1:152 h — Apr 4 Hol 6f ft 1:152 h — Mar 29 Hol 6f ft 1:144 h — Mar 22 Hol 6f ft 1:154 h

Khalil — B. g. 4, by Plum Bold—Peachtree's Belle, by My Dad George — **34–1**
PEDROZA M A — 114 — Br.—Plemmons J H (Ky) — 1988 8 0 0 0 $6,750
Own.—Hoffman-Kruse-Strugar — Tr.—Sweeney Brian — $75,000 — 1987 16 2 5 1 $52,150
Lifetime 24 2 5 1 $58,900 — Turf 7 0 0 0 $3,900

25Apr88-9SA 1¼Ⓣ:4631:3712:032gd 56 115 1212 96¾ 75¾ 74 Baze R A11 62500 66-24 Danielli, Point D'Artois, Ataghan 12
10Apr88-5SA 1⅛Ⓣ:4631:1041:484fm 45 115 1110 107¼ 117¼ 95¼ Baze R A11 75000 78-12 MinutesAway,RndomRover,Dnielli 11
25Mar88-8SA 1⅛Ⓣ:4631:1131:482fm 84 116 105 105¾ 76½ 56¼ Solis A2 Aw42000 79-15 RoiNormnd,Eliminnte,Dfin'tSigns 10
11Mar88-5SA 1⅛Ⓣ:4611:1041:482fm 53 1115 1016 1014 98½ 710 Banderas AL5 Aw38000 75-15 PleasantVriety,Eliminnte,ProudCt 10
27Feb88-5SA 1⅛:464 1:112 1:504ft 42 115 68¼ 68¾ 69 810½ Solis A4 Aw38000 64-17 Reland, Millero YMedio,ProudCat 10
7Feb88-5SA 1 1/16:453 1:103 1:433ft 17 116 913 88¼ 76½ 48½ Solis A3 Aw38000 74-16 Fancy Oats, Shigamba,RedAndBlue 9
7Feb88—Wide into stretch
17Jan88-7SA 1⅛:461 1:11 1:504sy 9½ 114 49 35½ 45 43¼ Solis A1 Aw38000 72-17 Rupperto,Shigamba,MilleroYMedio 9
3Jan88-9SA 1 1/16:463 1:104 1:43 ft 9¾ 116 710 712 713 714¼ Hawley S2 Aw38000 72-17 ‡VlntCougr,LckyHroldH.,Ircndrtor 8
3Jan88—Altered course sharply at 3 1/2 to avoid fallen rider
26Dec87-7SA 1⅛Ⓣ:4631:1121:494fm 10 115 46½ 44½ 43 42½ Toro F2 Aw38000 75-22 GeorgiaRiver,Euphrates,Eliminante 9
26Dec87—Bumped start; crowded in stretch
13Dec87-9BM 1 1/16:453 1:093 1:412ft 50 115 914 912 911 64¼ HnsenRD8 Lnd Stfd H 81-22 NicklBnd,NoTimFlt,H'sADncngMn 10
May 2 SA 4f ft :472 h — Apr 23 SA 3f ft :364 h — Apr 18 SA 7f ft 1:304 h — Apr 7 SA 3f ft :371 h

Hawaiian Spring — Dk. b. or br. h. 6, by Spring Double—Twice Hawaiian, by Twice Worthy — **7–2**
MCCARRON C J — 116 — Br.—Kaye Mr-Mrs C F (Md) — 1988 3 0 0 0 $5,800
Own.—Gann E A — Tr.—Frankel Robert — $80,000 — 1987 9 3 2 1 $45,474
Lifetime 22 3 4 2 $62,132 — Turf 21 3 4 2 $60,932

14Apr88-8SA 1⅛:453 1:104 1:503sy 9¼ 116 614 613 511 511 DelhoussyeE2 Aw48000 65-27 KnightsLegend,PleasantVriety,Kdil 6
14Apr88—Bumped, steadied start
26Mar88-3SA 1⅛Ⓣ:4721:1211:484fm 5¼ 116 21 31½ 53 56¾ DelahoussyeE6 140000 76-12 KnightsLegnd,SuprDupont,AvitorII 7
14Jan88-8SA 1⅛Ⓣ:4711:1141:492fm 7¾ 115 86½ 51½ 42½ 44¾ Hawley S1 Aw44000 75-20 Light Sabre, Mazilier, Gorky 10
14Jan88—Wide 3/8 turn
23Dec87-8Hol 1 1/16 Ⓣ:4841:13 1:433fm 4 116 74½ 73½ 83¾ 42¾ ValenzuelPA4 Aw45000 73-24 FiveDddyFive,RufusDwes,GllntSilor 8
12Dec87-8Hol 1 Ⓣ:4611:1041:354fm 30 116 88½ 3½ 32 42 Hawley S9 Aw45000 86-14 DrkPromise,Digger'sRst,HppyInSpc 9
12Dec87—Wide backstretch
14Aug87♦6Clairefonte(Fra) a1½ 2:352yl 7½ 118 Ⓣ 3¾ LequeuxA G P d Clrfnt Ordinance,Shimbori,HawiinSpring 12
1Aug87♦3Deauville(Fra) a1 9/16 2:46 sf 13 128 Ⓣ 21 LequeuxA Px d Ssy H Bullseye,HawiinSpring,PuyVlence 16
27Jun87♦3Longchamp(Fra) a1½ 2:334yl 8 127 Ⓣ 12 LequeuxA Px Cstrs H Hardelot, Limbo Dance, Tongan 18
7Jun87♦7Chantilly(Fra) a1 5/16 2:154gd 6¼ 127 Ⓣ 1¾ LequuxA Px d Etngs H HwiinSpring,Bmwhite,SunnyHunt 12
20May87♦7Evry(Fra) a1½ 2:402yl 9 116 Ⓣ 1½ Camus E Px d St Chrn HwiinSpring,LimboDnc,HilingShip 13
Apr 29 Hol 5f ft 1:003 h — Apr 23 Hol 3f ft :363 h — Apr 3 Hol 4f ft :482 h — Mar 22 Hol 6f ft 1:14 h

***Monroe** — B. g. 5, by Mr Long—Numancia, by Melody Rock — **7–1**
SIBILLE R — 116 — Br.—Haras Villa Rosa (Chile) — 1988 6 0 0 0 $6,225
Own.—Waranch R — Tr.—Stute Warren — $80,000 — 1987 4 2 1 0 $14,732
Lifetime 21 4 4 1 $79,366 — Turf 12 3 1 1 $73,378

25Apr88-8SA 1¼Ⓣ:4641:36 2:014gd 46 112 1021 1019 1019 1020¾ OrtgLE 10 ⓇSn Jcnt H 57-24 The Medic, Trokhos, Uptothehilt 10
15Apr88-8SA 1 :462 1:111 1:362m 9 115 44½ 55½ 57½ 513¾ Velasquez J 3 Aw54000 72-21 Mark Chip, Joel, Rufjan 5
2Apr88-8SA 1¼Ⓣ:4521:3522:004fm 8½ 115 66½ 74½ 54½ 55½ SibilleR 6 ⓇSta Grts H 77-17 Fiction, Proud Cat, Five DaddyFive 9
2Apr88—Bumped start; steadied 1/4
12Mar88-8SA 1½Ⓣ:4642:0142:261fm 12 115 1112 41¾ 45½ 55¾ SibilleR 4 ⓇSn Mrno H 78-11 Putting, Fiction, Chinoiserie 11
12Mar88—Broke slowly
19Feb88-8SA 1 Ⓣ:4731:1121:36 fm 21 115 2hd 3nk 54 66½ Sibille R 4 Aw50000 88-05 Putting, Neshad, Motley 9
19Feb88—Bumped, steadied 1/8
24Jan88-3SA a6½f Ⓣ:221 :4441:151fm 31 115 77¾ 79 69½ 58 Sibille R 1 Aw45000 75-21 Mohamed Abdu,Fioravanti,Lordalik 8
15Jun87♦6ClubHipico(Chile a1½ 2:39 fm — 128 Ⓣ 1 BarrazaJ Cl Invrno(Gr2) Monroe, Platini, Felipon 5
31May87♦6ClubHipico(Chile a1⅜ 2:172sf 3-2 126 Ⓣ 22¾ Barraza J Cl Mrcrio Grosor, Monroe, Platini 5
25Apr87♦7H'podromo(Chile) a1½2:312ft 4 123 7 MnozL G P Hip Chile (Gr1) Grosor, Poalco, Gran Evento 10
2Mar87♦8ClubHipico(Chile a1⅜ 2:121fm — 123 Ⓣ 1 BarrazaJ Cl L Csino(Gr3) Monroe, Tegal, Melodico 6
May 6 Hol 4f ft :49 h — Apr 24 SA 3f m :354 h — Apr 13 SA 4f ft :504 h — Apr 8 SA 5f ft 1:023 h

BETTING CHART FOR HOLLYWOOD PARK, MAY 7, 1988

Race	Planned Bet	Actual Bet	Return	Profit on Race	Total Profit
1					
Double 1 & 2					
Kent. Derby					
3					
4					
5					
6					
7					
8					
9					

Hollywood Park Analysis

RACE ONE

Your worksheet should contain only two or possibly three horses. Coron Miss, dropping in class, has the best back time, a poor but-in-the-lead six-furlong fraction, and a swift bullet work. Hidden Past, in her second race after a layoff, has the top recent time (which does not exceed her best ever) and is dropping in class.

Unassailable, with a good six-furlong fraction and a better-than-average work, makes the worksheet but only in the saver category, since she is a distance horse and her few tries at sprints have been poor.

The others, including the favorite, have slow last races or are running at an unsuitable distance or have poor win-consistency.

RACE TWO

Dropping four pounds after a win in the best time in the last thirty days, Hijo El Toro has to be considered the horse to beat, but he is not an outstanding favorite. He ran his best time ever last time out. (He did have a higher rating at Longacres, Lga, but a race at the small track should not be considered.) Older horses should not be expected to better their best efforts in their very next race.

Classy Vigors, with a good last race, which was his first after a long layoff, seems the horse most likely to vanquish the favorite. He is dropping only slightly in claiming price but ran with much better in 1987.

Lightly raced Roll a Natural is the mystery horse. He has only nine starts in two years, which always indicates infirmities, but he finished close up in his last race and in 1986 was a far better sprinter than any of these.

Rimmou, claimed in his last race and the only clear front-runner, is a possibility.

Doubles: The top two in the first should have been bet into Classy Vigors for larger doubles and saved with the other horses named here for smaller doubles.

RACE THREE

Shigamba's last race, even though run at a mile, was actually run at the wrong distance. One-turn and two-turn mile races are as different as apples and bananas.

The majority of one-turn distance races are won by pressers and closers that catch the front-runners fatigued by dueling for the lead in the long run out of the chute. In a two-turn race, however, a quick front-runner on the inside can sprint to an early lead, with the pressers losing ground on the outside, and have plenty of vigor left to hold off the come-from-behind types.

Closers at one turn; front-runners at two. This is the preference, but it hardly ranks as a commandment. Some front-runners, especially when allowed to go unchallenged, win one-turn races with authority. Many pressers and closers overtake tiring front-runners at two turns, especially if there has been a fight for the lead.

Shigamba ran a smashing two-turn mile in his last outing, but his one-turn record has been poor. As a matter of fact, he was beaten decisively by Fanticola when they faced each other in a one-turn event.

But Fanticola, like all the other horses in the race, has some knocks against him. He would be the clear choice in the race with his best-ever time and three workouts in twelve days. However, these comparatively slow works are hardly indicative of a horse that is ready to win.

Bugarian has been working bullets, but has very poor consistency. Claramount has great consistency and a good work last out, but he has never won at this claiming price.

Scrapbook, dropping in class after a race at the wrong distance and with a bullet work prior to that, has all the markings of an upsetter, but he has never run a one-turn mile, and he has an inside post, a hindrance at this distance.

Extranix beat Scrapbook in his last race, but he has no works after being idle for four weeks.

Since all his opponents have negative factors, Shigamba is the selection, but he cannot qualify as a Best Bet.

RACE FOUR

This is another race in which we seem to have a solid favorite. Premiere is taking a big class drop after a race run in superior time. Claimed twice in the last two months, he certainly has been the choice of those in the business.

But why the big class drop? In today's race he can be claimed for less than what his connections paid for him, and all he has done for them since they put up their money is bring back a tiny sum for coming in fourth.

Claimed in his last race, which was a very strong front-running effort, and sporting the best back time, Peppy's Consul, at first, looks like the horse that can beat him. But Peppy has had no workouts in three weeks. Have his new owners claimed an ailing horse?

The main thing Urbana Cowboy has going for him is the expected pace. He is the only confirmed closer, an advantage in a seven-furlong affair. Since the others all have negative comments, he is the reluctant choice but not a Best Bet.

RACE FIVE

We do not normally consider the times of races run more than thirty days prior to be important for judging current speed. However, thirty-one days before Derby Day there was a split stakes of the same type as today's race. Since four of the horses had run in that race, you should have compared how these horses ran against each other.

This race has a favorite that should be bet with confidence. The class of the field, Bel Air Dancer, has a good dirt race last out and the best turf time by far.

The only threat to a favorite like this comes from a horse like Balote, who has never run on the turf but has sparkled on the dirt. However, his handler has not seen fit to give him a turf workout or a workout of any kind in the past three weeks. At best, Balote can be bet as a saver.

RACE SIX

Any horse that wins a maiden race in a time that is much faster than the times posted recently by his competitors is usually made the favorite in his next race. Delegant, who had surprised at 23–1 in his first race on the dirt in the United States, was made the even-money favorite in this race.

Such support is not usually justified. The rise from maiden special to allowance conditions is different from a rise in claiming price. The horses faced now are a cut above the nonwinners recently trounced, many of whom may never cross the finish line first.

Although a few super horses go swiftly through their conditions, the vast majority do not win their next race after breaking their maidens. Having failed five times in France, Delegant does not seem like a super horse.

This race, therefore, presents a superb betting opportunity. Because so much money is bet on Delegant, other horses will go off at much better odds than they should.

And so the question for this race becomes, if Delegant is not the winner, who is?

Northern Valor has the best back time (but not at Hollywood Park) and will probably improve in his second race after a layoff. However, he has been looking for his second allowance win for a long time. At 5–2, he can hardly be considered an overlay.

Look again at the types of runners we have. All are closers except for two front-runners. But Fleetspur has never gone a distance. Willie N Waylon, on the other hand, went off as the favorite in a distance race twenty-four days ago.

Willie was 3–1 on the morning line and was rated highly by the *Racing Form* selectors. How can we explain his high odds? His poor last race undoubtedly had many fans dismissing him. But that race can be thrown out because it was run in the mud. At 7–1, he seems like a great overlay.

Because he has three things going for him—a pattern of running most likely to produce victory, the best back time at a major track, and excellent odds—Willie becomes a Best Bet.

If this were an exacta race, we would bet one combination as a saver. Delegant might turn out to be a super horse. It would be worth the small cost of insurance to put him over our choice.

With no exacta possible, Willie N Waylon should also be bet to place.

RACE SEVEN

This division of the Spotlight Handicap also seems like an easy race for the favorite. Roberto's Dancer has a near record time at the distance, is a proven turf horse (three for five), and has excellent workouts to show that he's ready.

But the second choice, Exclusive Nureyev, is a very creditable threat. As the favorite, he won a division of the sprint stakes that several of these horses had run in. He failed in the late part of a mile-and-one-eighth race on the dirt, but a mile on the turf may fit him well.

His chances of upsetting look even greater when we consider how the race will be run. As the only front-runner, Exclusive Nureyev might take an easy lead, while Roberto's Dancer will have to maneuver his way through the other come-from-behind horses.

Roberto's Dancer is a very tough favorite to bet against, but the pace of the race seems stacked against him. Exclusive Nureyev gets a nervous vote.

RACE EIGHT

Very Subtle, the lady millionaire, has beaten the best of the boys in the past. Her 1988 record has not been superlative, but her two fine workouts indicate that she is ready to win.

Although their lifetime earnings cannot compare with the Breeders' Cup champ, her opponents are a solid band of sprinters going off at much higher odds than usual because of the money bet on Very Subtle in the mutuels.

Reconnoitering is a co-holder of the track record for six and one-half furlongs, and three others have times that are within a second of track records.

Two of these, Don's Irish Melody and Perfec Travel, have excellent workouts at six and seven furlongs, respectively, showing their trainers are serious about this race.

Very Subtle will have to be at her very best to win. In fact, Don's Irish Melody has to be given a good chance to best the young lady. Winner of five of six last year and the victim of bad luck in his first race after a long layoff, he would be the clear choice if Very Subtle were not in the race. At 7–1, he makes an excellent wager.

RACE NINE

One thing that should catch your eye immediately when examining the *Racing Form* is a series of long workouts.

If you look at the workout page in any edition of the *Racing Form* you will see that only a small number of horses work out at six furlongs and even fewer at seven furlongs or a mile. When a trainer puts his horse through a series of these long workouts, it usually means he is trying to give him the stamina for a particular distance race that he has spotted in the conditions book (the list of races coming up for a couple of weeks in advance).

Look at the workouts on Feraud—three good long workouts in eighteen days. Notice his claiming price—trainer John Russell has dropped him $10,000 in price to ensure his going off at low weight.

Feraud's best time ever at the infrequently run mile-and-one-quarter distance is the same as the favorite's recent winning rating. He is tied for best back time at the more common mile-and-one-eighth distance. Not only is there no question that Feraud is going to try to score in his first race back after a rest, but there is also no question that he has the ability to win.

Because of his dismal last race before his layoff, and because it is difficult to win first crack at a long distance, Feraud is completely ignored in the betting.

The money is going to Danielli, who has had two sharp races in a row, and to Narghile, with his fine turf record. These horses, along with Coasting Cougar, would normally be considered contenders, and one of them would probably get our backing.

But Feraud is our version of the "hot" horse. He is dropping in claiming price, dropping in weight, working out beautifully, and has solid back times in distance turf races. Of course, he is risky—can he go a mile and one quarter without a race under his belt?

We are at the track to take a few risks. At 22–1, far above his average odds of 5–1, Feraud is a super overlay, easily qualifying as a Best Bet.

He should be played in a saver exacta underneath the favorite and, at his very high odds, also backed to place.

Hollywood Park Results

RACE ONE

Horse	Finish	Prices		
Hidden Past	1^6	12.80	6.80	4.80
Promise Me Luck	2^1		5.40	4.40
Weather Eye Open	3^1			14.20

(No exacta wagering)

Hidden Past broke well but stayed five lengths off the pace. She began moving up after a quarter mile, and simply blew by the others in the stretch.

Coron Miss ran a disappointing race.

RACE TWO

Horse	Finish	Prices		
Roll a Natural	1^{hd}	12.40	5.80	5.00
Rimmou	2^{nk}		5.40	4.40
Hovering Presence	3^3			14.20

(No exacta wagering)
$2 Daily Double paid $75.20

Classy Vigors gave up the race after only a quarter mile. Rimmou took over the lead and almost lasted. Showing a bit of his old form, the eight-year-old Roll a Natural closed nicely to get up at the wire.

The favorite, Hijo El Toro, closed to third in the stretch, but couldn't hold on, disappointing those who had him in their show parlays.

The big surprise was Hovering Presence. This wake-up horse closed from last, took the show spot away from the favorite, and came within a few strides of winning the whole thing. Had he made it, the tote board would have blazed with a $121 mutuel, and we would have gone back to the charts in an unsuccessful effort to find something that could be said in this horse's favor. He did have a fairly good back time at Golden Gate, but his races for the past couple of months had been terrible.

Still, he did not make it, and we collected our saver double.

SIMULCAST OF THE KENTUCKY DERBY

Between the second and third races, Hollywood Park simulcast the Derby.

If you didn't have the winner in New York, you were less likely to have her in California, since the bettors sent their hometown girl off at odds of 6–5 in their mutuels pool.

She did make it, but her odds at Churchill Downs (3.4–1) and at Aqueduct (almost 4–1) made her much more of a bettable proposition in a difficult race.

Horse	Finish	Prices		
Winning Colors	1^{nk}	4.40	3.80	3.40
Forty Niner	2^3		7.60	5.60
Risen Star	$3^{1/2}$			4.80

$2 Exacta paid $52.20

RACE THREE

Horse	Finish	Prices		
Shigamba	$1^{31/2}$	6.00	3.20	2.60
Claramount	2^6		4.00	3.20
Extranix	$3^{11/4}$			4.60

$2 Exacta paid $21.20

Shigamba took the lead after a half and slowly kept extending it over Claramount, who could not keep pace with him. Although this front-runner won easily, you should still keep in mind for future handicapping that a good closer will usually beat a good front-runner at this distance.

Fanticola ran wide around the turn and did not respond when urged. This confirmed our conclusion that his slow works did not show a readiness to win.

On the other hand, Bugarian did not run to his morning workouts at all. He finished last, having trailed the field the whole way.

RACE FOUR

Horse	Finish	Prices		
A Little Speed	1^4	38.80	16.40	7.20
Urbana Cowboy	2$^{1/2}$		6.20	3.60
Premiere	3$^{3/4}$			3.00

$2 Exacta paid $308.40
$3 Triple paid $1,008.30

The difficulties of picking a winner solely on the basis of pace are well illustrated here. Fairly Omen, Cojak Man, and A Little Speed were supposed to kill each other off setting up the race for our closer.

But A Little Speed displayed a lot of speed right from the start. Allowed to increase his front-running advantage at every pole, he came out of the turn leading by an insurmountable six lengths.

Meanwhile, the jockey aboard Urbana Cowboy (Chris McCarron, one of the truly great ones) ran an unconcerned last, twelve lengths off the pace after a quarter mile. He finally closed "a ton of ground" going seven wide around the turn, but this heroic effort was only good enough for the place spot.

Note that Cojak Man couldn't get that elusive three wins in a row.

There are system players who wait for horses that drop back to the claiming price they ran at in their next-to-last race *and* were favorites in that race. They collected nicely on A Little Speed, who exhibited these two factors.

By the way, there was one horse claimed out of this race.

You undoubtedly think it was the oft-claimed Premiere.

Wrong.

The only horse claimed was A Little Speed. Did they know something around the barns?

RACE FIVE

Horse	Finish	Prices		
Bel Air Dancer	$1^{2\frac{1}{2}}$	5.60	3.00	2.60
Prospector's Gamble	$2^{3\frac{1}{2}}$		3.60	3.00
Balote	3^{nk}			4.80

$2 Exacta paid $17.40

Balote ran quite well in his first turf appearance. He moved to within a length of Bel Air Dancer at the top of the stretch but couldn't quite keep up when the favorite pulled away on the road to an easy win.

RACE SIX

Horse	Finish	Prices		
Willie N Waylon	1^3	16.20	8.60	5.20
Old Shanty Town	2^3		18.20	9.20
Wily	$3^{1\frac{1}{4}}$			5.80

(No exacta wagering)

This race ran quite closely to the way it was predicted. Fleetspur got the lead but showed he wasn't a distance horse by dropping out after a half mile. Willie N Waylon was never headed from then on and drew away from the field in the stretch. May all of your Best Bets win as easily and with such inflated odds.

What about the vaunted favorite? For the first half mile Delegant ran fourth, a couple of lengths behind the leaders. But he was tackling a field much tougher than the maidens he had casually whipped. He packed it in before the race was half over and finished a dismal seventh, twenty lengths behind the winner.

RACE SEVEN

Horse	Finish	Prices		
Exclusive Nureyev	$1^{1\frac{1}{4}}$	7.00	4.60	3.80
Prove Splendid	2^{nk}		26.20	11.60
Glad Music	$3^{3\frac{1}{4}}$			4.00

$2 Exacta paid $253.60
$2 Pick Six paid $30,434.00 (Six wins)
(Five wins paid $755.20)

Cash in Store looked like the kind of outsider who wrecks the chances of a good front-runner like Exclusive Nureyev. He had not shown the slightest speed in any of his American races, but he broke on top and led our choice for half a mile. A glance at the teletimer would have been reassuring. The time for the half was quite slow—only :47 as compared with the :45³/₅ run in the fifth race, the first division of the stakes.

Unaccustomed to front-running, even in slow time, Cash in Store gave up after a half mile and finished last.

The slow pace left Exclusive Nureyev with plenty of staying power. He needed it because once he shot to the lead he had to fight off another longshot around the entire turn before finally pulling away.

Roberto's Dancer ran last most of the way. With the rail clogged with horses trying not to let the leaders get too far in front, he had to go four wide around the turn and finished a close fourth.

Had he been able to get through horses without going wide, the result would have been much closer.

But he didn't get through. Our selection was made on the chance he might get into trouble, and this prediction proved correct.

RACE EIGHT

Horse	Finish	Prices		
Perfec Travel	$1^{1\frac{1}{4}}$	74.40	18.20	7.20
Reconnoitering	2^{hd}		11.60	6.80
Don's Irish Melody	$3^{3\frac{4}}$			6.40

$2 Exacta paid $1,019.40
$3 Triple paid $9,765.20

Very Subtle was not at her very best. She couldn't keep up with Don's Irish Melody, who blazed the half mile in :44. She gave way after this grueling effort and finished far back.

Had this been a match race, Don's Irish Melody would have looked like a champ. But after putting away the favorite he had to contend with Reconnoitering, who battled with him for almost the entire last three-eighths of a mile. It was only in the last hundred yards that Don's Irish Melody succumbed, but Reconnoitering paid the price of head-to-head combat when Perfec Travel rallied from last to first to best the exhausted leaders.

When a longshot like Perfec Travel takes the major race of the day, derisive comments about the winner and about the folly of handicapping are sure to follow. "How could anyone pick a cheap horse like that in a race like this?"

A legitimate question—and there is a legitimate answer.

First of all, Perfec Travel should not have been allowed to go off at such astronomical odds. This was a race where the weights were assigned by the track handicapper. Far from being the lightweight of the field, Perfec Travel was assigned only one pound less than the horse who went off as the 5–2 second choice.

He had not been a big 1988 money winner, but he was coming off a big victory at a longer distance, and he was the only horse with a seven-furlong workout.

He was ready to win, and the pace of the race made him a winner. In retrospect, the pace could have been predicted.

There were simply too many confirmed front-runners in the race. Very Subtle would certainly be challenged early, or else the front-runners would have no chance at all. A suicidal pace might easily have been foreseen.

Now, if a pace like that had been predicted, then an opportunistic horse with the stamina to make a good close would be the choice. What better selection than the only horse who had been competing recently at a longer distance and had worked out the distance of today's race just five days before?

The derisive comments should have been directed neither at the horse nor at the art of horse race handicapping. They should have been directed at us. We picked a front-runner in a field of good front-runners and did not save with a horse that had clearly shown it had the stamina to win if the front-runners tired.

Dummy!

RACE NINE

Horse	Finish	Prices		
Feraud	1no	47.00	15.00	8.40
Hawaiian Spring	2$^{2\frac{1}{2}}$		5.20	4.20
Coasting Cougar	3$^{\frac{1}{2}}$			4.40

$2 Exacta paid $206.80

The saver place bet on Feraud looked better and better during the eternity the photo sign was up.

Feraud had pressed Coasting Cougar all the way around the turn, had finally gotten the lead in midstretch, and then hit the wire in the same instant as the fast-closing Hawaiian Spring, piloted by Chris McCarron.

In a finish like this, there is a tendency to give the nod to the horse making the big close because he is certainly ahead after the wire. It seemed as if McCarron had made his move perfectly this time.

But then Feraud's number was posted—a sweet, sweet sensation . . . to win the last race in a photo . . . and on such a huge longshot!

If it had been your day at the track, it would have been a good day indeed.

CHAPTER XXII

Have a Good Time!

There are some psychiatrists who claim that gamblers are masochists. Unconsciously, they want to punish themselves for some unthinkable guilt that's eating at them inside. Since losing is inevitable, the gambler gets his wish.

I have no doubt there are as many, or as few, masochists among professional horseplayers as there are among doctors, politicians, and members of the clergy. Whatever their psychological kinks, gambling is a business for them, not a psychological disease. They no more want to lose than do their counterparts on Wall Street.

Sometimes, however, when I look over some of the people at the racetrack toward the end of an afternoon, I begin to wonder if the Freudians don't have a point. Some of the bettors seem to have forgotten they are supposed to be having a good time.

They must have set out to have a day of fun, but now their faces are grim, their voices are harsh and snappy, and their bodies strain with tension. What happened to the excitement, the thrills, the enjoyment they were looking for when they entered the track?

All of those things were there for the asking, but they allowed the loss of a few bets to unreasonably affect their emotions and their actions.

Because of this, a final word or two must be said on how to increase your chances for an enjoyable day at the track, whether or not it is profitable.

Let's forget money for a while and talk about the things you can do to increase the pleasure you can get from simply being at the track.

A pair of binoculars is a must for getting maximum enjoyment from watching the races themselves. At most tracks, they can be rented for a nominal fee.

Without binocs, the horses on the far side of the track are difficult to distinguish. Most people without field glasses resort to watching the numbers flash on the board giving the positions of the four leaders at different points of call. Not only is this a terribly lifeless substitute for watching the actual race, but by the time the numbers are posted the positions of the leaders have invariably changed.

Watching a TV monitor is a bit of an improvement, but the television camera focuses almost entirely on the front-runners. If your horse is a closer, you will have no idea where it is during most of the race.

With a pair of binoculars and the knowledge of the colors of your jockey's cap and silks, which are listed in the program, you can easily follow your horse during the entire race. You can see what kind of start he gets, where his jockey positions him, what kind of trouble he gets into, how wide he might be coming out of the turn, and what kind of move he is making. To fail to see these things is to give up the thrill of racing as a spectator sport.

Races that are run once around the entire track start from in front of the grandstand. When one of these is ready to go off, go down to trackside and watch the start of the race from the rail. The ringing of the bell, the shouting, the sudden surging of horses out of the gate, often knocking each other about, not only will be stirring but will also give you some idea of how dangerous horse racing is.

Another spot from which to watch a race is far up along the rail at the end of the turn. Away from the hubbub of the grandstand, you will be surprised at how quiet it can get. That quiet will be broken when the horses come charging out of the turn, hoofs thumping rhythmically into the dirt, heads and necks straining forward under the urging of their jockeys. They swoop by in a blazing flash of color, and suddenly the quiet returns.

Only from a close-up position on the rail like this can you appreciate just how fast the horses move. You need this flesh-and-bone aspect of racing to prevent your day from becoming a sterile analysis of numbers. The horse that was just a name and a couple of lines in the past-performance chart, a claiming price, or a speed rating is transformed into a magnificently muscular individual displaying, in a minute or two, its whole reason for being—to run as fast as its legs and heart will allow.

This feeling for the horses as superbly trained animals can also be achieved by a visit to the walking ring, something you should do at least once during your afternoon.

From the grandstand you can get no genuine appreciation of how big and powerful the older horses are. You can sense this as they amble only a few feet from you in the walking ring, and you can marvel at the courage their jockeys must have to even mount these huge animals, much less fly with them around the turns of a racecourse.

The walking ring is also a great place for people-watching and for picking up tidbits of conversation which may occasionally affect your selecting. Getting off a winning selection because of something you heard in the paddock might be a genuine source of depression, but it really should be only the basis of a good story. And this brings us back to handling the money aspects of your afternoon.

Whether professionals or not, most bettors who go to the track regularly are able to casually cope with the depressive aspects of a losing day. They are well aware that even the best of handicappers will have more losing than winning races. They know that on some days part or all of their betting money will go through the mutuel machines into the hands of some more fortunate others. They are solaced by the thought that there is always the next day or the next weekend to get their money back.

On the other hand, very few occasional bettors can really handle a losing day, especially one in which they lost far more than they intended.

I'm not going to pretend that taking a loss at the track is a cause for great joy. But with the right perspective and the right attitude, it need never be the cause for sorrow. You can *always* have a good time at the track.

The trick is to be prepared. Be ready for everything: selecting, betting, and even losing.

The only way to be prepared for selecting and betting is through practice. It takes a lot of shrewd analytical skills and logical decision-making to win at the races, and the time to learn is before the races, not during them.

For a day or two before you combat the pari-mutuel machines, buy a *Daily Racing Form* and chart the races just as we did in Chapter XXI.

Make a selection in each race, set a goal, and place "mind" bets to reach the goal. Carefully review the results, noting what you've done right and finding out what caused you to go wrong. It doesn't cost you a nickel in losing bets, but when the big day comes, you will be ready.

You won't be moaning during the course of an afternoon about racing being a sucker's game that requires dumb luck or inside information. From your practice you know what kind of favorites hold up, what kind of races produce longshots, and what kind of situations make for solid Best Bets. You won't have any wild dreams crushed, because your days of practice will tell you exactly what you're up against. And you will know how to bet to reach a goal that fits your personality.

Preparations will certainly include selecting horses *before* you get to the track. If this seems unnecessary, let me remind you of the importance of not having to make up your mind as the minutes tick away before post time.

For one thing, the twenty to thirty minutes between races is simply not long enough to make good selections when you also have to stand in line to collect and make bets and sometimes to enjoy a drink or a snack.

The emotional pressures also build up during the course of the afternoon. You will be far more likely to make a poor selection and a foolish bet if you have to do the job knowing that you are behind and that you must come up with a winner in order to get even.

Finally, if you haven't made your selections before you get to the track, you can't establish your goal, since your goal depends in large part on what kind of card you are trying to beat, which races call for increased bets, and so on.

In most large cities the *Daily Racing Form* is available early in the morning at many local vendors. In the relaxed atmosphere of your home, you should chart the races and make up a worksheet. From this, you should be able to get an overview of the day's races. You can decide which races contain standout horses and which seem unplayable because of the closeness of the competition. Knowing these facts, you should be able to decide on your goal and your betting method.

Horse racing is a participant sport. You are a competitor, not a mere spectator. Obviously, as in all sports, a winning attitude is a necessity. But on some days the races offered may be extremely difficult. The card may have too many races with horses untried at the distances they are running, too many races with numerous contenders, or too many races with odds-on favorites that can be neither bet nor bet against.

On days like this, you will still enter the track with a winning attitude, but it will be tempered by your understanding of the problems to be faced. And you will adjust your goal accordingly.

On other days, it may seem as if every race contains a bettable proposition. You can't wait until post time. You have good reason to enlarge your goal.

After you have set your goal, the best approach to take is to forget the possible profits. Yes, forget about money!

Think of your day at the track as a game of wits. You have prepared a strategy to win. You think so much of your strategy that you're willing to bet you're right. (If you don't think much of it, you shouldn't be betting at all.) If you *are* right, if your strategy is correct, you win. If you're wrong, you've invested some money in a strategy that didn't work, but you'll have a better one next time.

Notice that you concentrate on the strategy. This is what is being tested. The money is important only to the extent that, without it, your strategy cannot be truly tested. Anyone can make a "mind" bet. You are backing your vision with money.

But, once you add up the money needed for the *day* to carry out your strategy, you forget it. You consider it only as a figure that has already been invested. Then you can concentrate on how well you play the game.

Since it forces you to concentrate on your total strategy for the day, and not on individual races, this kind of attitude makes it far more likely for you to pass the test, to reach your goal, to show one and all that with enough thought the game is yours.

And this kind of attitude ensures an enjoyable day. You don't worry about losing money. The total amount your strategy will cost, no matter what happens, is just another number, like the price of admission. You can devote all your attention to the running of the races.

If you can acquire this attitude, if you use this book to make the proper preparations, if you make quite clear to yourself what you want from the track and how much you're willing to risk to get it, then you'll be at the cashier's window more often than you ever thought possible.

I hope to see you there!

RECOMMENDED READING

Ainslie's Complete Guide to Thoroughbred Racing by Tom Ainslie (Fireside/Simon & Schuster, 1986)

Ainslie's New Complete Guide to Harness Racing by Tom Ainslie (Fireside/Simon & Schuster, 1986)

Investing at the Racetrack by William L. Scott (Fireside/Simon & Schuster, 1986)

ABOUT THE AUTHOR

Charles S. Romanelli has been a racing fan since he was taken by his father to Saratoga at the age of twelve. Since then, in addition to putting his seven children through college, he has found time to cash winning tickets at race tracks all over the country. A graduate of the University of Chicago, Romanelli received an M.A. in English from Fordham University and teaches in a high school on Staten Island where he lives with his wife (who is also a racing enthusiast).